"WE MET IN PARIS"

"WE MET IN PARIS"

Grace Frick and Her Life with Marguerite Yourcenar

JOAN E. HOWARD

UNIVERSITY OF MISSOURI PRESS

COLUMBIA

Paperback ISBN: 9780826222107

Library of Congress Cataloging-in-Publication Data

Names: Howard, Joan E., 1951- author.
Title: "We met in Paris" : Grace Frick and her life with Marguerite Yourcenar
    / by Joan E Howard.
Description: Columbia : University of Missouri, [2018] | Includes
    bibliographical references and index. |
Identifiers: LCCN 2017050790 (print) | LCCN 2017053317 (ebook) | ISBN
    9780826274045 (e-book) | ISBN 9780826221551 (hardback)
Subjects: LCSH: Yourcenar, Marguerite--Friends and associates. | Frick,
    Grace. | Authors, French--20th century--Biography. | Women
    translators--Missouri--Biography. | Women--France--Paris--Biography. |
    BISAC: BIOGRAPHY & AUTOBIOGRAPHY / Literary.
Classification: LCC PQ2649.O8 (ebook) | LCC PQ2649.O8 Z713 2018 (print) | DDC
    848/.91209 [B] --dc23
LC record available at https://lccn.loc.gov/2017050790

Acknowledgment of permissions for this volume appears on pages 435–36

Typefaces: Grotesk and Bembo

Come, then, loose me from cruelties.

Give my tethered heart its full desire.

Fulfill, and, come, lock your shield with mine

Throughout the siege.

—Sappho, "Ode to Aphrodite"
Translated by Guy Davenport

For Jayne Marie Persson

Contents

Illustrations

Illustrations from the Petite Plaisance Archives are reproduced by permission of the Marguerite Yourcenar Trust. All rights reserved.

Abbreviations

The following abbreviations of frequently cited documents and archives will be used in reference notes throughout the present work.

DLA   Donna Levinsohn archives

FFA   Frick family archives

GFAB   Grace Frick, appointment books, 1944–75, 1977–78. Marguerite Yourcenar Collection, Additional Papers, 1842–1996, MS Fr 372.2 (853)

GFC   Grace Frick, chronology [Chronology of Marguerite Yourcenar and Grace Frick], Marguerite Yourcenar Papers, 1920–1986, MS Fr 372 (1373), Houghton Library, Harvard University

HCCHJCC   Howell Cheney Collection of Hartford Junior College Correspondence

HCWC   Hartford College for Women Collection*

HFA   Harris family archives

MFA   Minear family archives

MYC   Marguerite Yourcenar Collection, Additional Papers, 1842–1996, MS Fr 372.2, Houghton Library, Harvard University

MYP   Marguerite Yourcenar Papers, 1920–1986, MS Fr 372, Houghton Library, Harvard University

NCBC   Natalie Clifford Barney Collection, Bibliothèque Jacques Doucet, Paris, France

PPA   Petite Plaisance Archives

SLCA   Sarah Lawrence College Archives

* Audio recordings from this collection are from the project titled Toward a Working Majority: Perspectives on Educated American Women, 1930 to 1990. The Connecticut Humanities Council provided funding for this project; conclusions and recommendations expressed are not necessarily those of the council.

Abbreviations

UHASC	University of Hartford Archives and Special Collections
WCA	Wellesley College Archives
WCCC	Wellesley College *Chat Cat*
YMA	Yale Manuscripts and Archives

Frequently Cited Works by Marguerite Yourcenar

The following works by Marguerite Yourcenar are cited frequently in the text. Where two sets of titles and years are given, the latter set refers to the first edition in English translation.

For works by Yourcenar and other authors, I have quoted published translations of French texts whenever they exist; all other translations from the French are my own.

Alexis, 1929.

Blues et gospels (Blues and gospels), 1984.

"Carnets de notes de *L'Œuvre au Noir*" (Reflections on the composition of *The Abyss*), in *Œuvres romanesques*, 1991.

Les Charités d'Alcippe, 1956; *The Alms of Alcippe*, 1982.

Le Coup de grâce, 1939; *Coup de Grâce*, 1957.

"D'après Greco" (After El Greco), in *La Mort conduit l'attelage*, 1934.

Denier du rêve, 1959; *A Coin in Nine Hands*, 1982.

Électre ou la Chute des masques, *Théâtre I*, 1971; *Electra, or the Fall of the Masks*, in *Plays*, 1984.

Feux, 1936; *Fires*, 1981.

Fleuve profond, sombre rivière (Deep river, dark river), 1964.

Mémoires d'Hadrien, 1951; *Memoirs of Hadrian*, 1954.

Le Mystère d'Alceste (The mystery play of Alcestis), in *Théâtre I*, 1971.

La Nouvelle Eurydice (The new Eurydice), 1931.

Nouvelles orientales, 1938; *Oriental Tales*, 1983.

L'Œuvre au Noir, 1968; *The Abyss*, 1976.

Présentation critique de Constantin Cavafy, 1863–1933 (Critical presentation of Constantine Cavafy, 1863–1933), 1958.

Qui n'a pas son Minotaure?, in *Théâtre I*, 1971; *To Each His Minotaur*, in *Plays*, 1984.

Quoi? L'Éternité (What? Eternity), 1988.

Rendre à César, in *Théâtre I*, 1971; *Render unto Caesar*, in *Plays*, 1984.

Les Songes et les sorts, 1938; *Dreams and Destinies*, 1999.

Sous bénéfice d'inventaire, 1962; *The Dark Brain of Piranesi*, 1985.

Preface

Biography has nothing to gain by remaining indifferent.

—Edmond Jaloux

ON AUGUST 17, 1982, AFTER a brief exchange of letters, I found myself knocking at the door of Marguerite Yourcenar's home, Petite Plaisance, in Northeast Harbor, Maine. I was writing a doctoral dissertation on sacrifice in the French author's novels and plays, and she had graciously agreed to let me speak with her in person. I arrived with piles of notes, hoping to show that I had found the key to her oeuvre. But I soon realized that Madame, as she preferred to be called, would not be easy to convince. Sacrifice had a role in her works, surely, but in her view not a terribly important one. So we spoke of other things, laying the foundation of a friendship.

In June of 1983 Mme Yourcenar invited me to spend what ended up being the better part of the summer with her, a routine that repeated itself over the next two years. Sharing a house for months at a time with the subject of one's dissertation is without a doubt highly unusual, and it certainly did not contribute to the speedy completion of my own. But it was the first in a series of events that aroused my interest in Marguerite Yourcenar's life companion, Grace Frick. The second occurred on the morning of July 13, 1983, when Mme Yourcenar offered me a garment that she had removed from her living room closet. It was a floor-length, hooded wool cape in the ancient paenula style that had belonged to Frick, one of many she had owned over the previous decades. She had bought it not long before her death and worn it only a few times. Mme Yourcenar turned to me and said, "You're very tall, like Grace, who was taller than I am. Would you like to have this cape? It's quite elegant. If you do a lot of walking, it's practical." I was deeply moved, and I have felt a connection to Grace Frick ever since that day.

At about the same time, Mme Yourcenar began handing me pages she had just finished drafting of projects she was working on that summer. The first batch was the beginning of an essay collection about her recent trip to Japan.[1] Because I was "not an Orientalist," she wondered whether I would find the content accessible. "You should see these pages," I wrote in my journal at the time about her spliced revisions. Each typed page was festooned with "taped fragments of pages, as one might piece together disparate fragments of an antique statue." More drafts came my way as time went by, including some from a poignant essay that will come into play later in this volume. It was a thrill to read and comment on those pages, as I knew Grace Frick had done over the course of many years with an authority and a sharp editorial eye that I did not possess. But I did eventually work with Mme Yourcenar on a few translation projects, which gave me an idea of what daily life must have been like at Petite Plaisance before Grace died.

Ten years later, I translated into English Josyane Savigneau's *Marguerite Yourcenar: Inventing a Life*. The release of that book brought me a letter from one of Mme Yourcenar's oldest and closest American friends, Paul Minear, a retired professor of theology at Yale Divinity School and a highly regarded New Testament scholar. He and his wife, Gladys, had known Grace Frick since 1931, when they were the host and hostess of the women's graduate residence at Yale. It was they who in 1942 first brought Frick and Yourcenar to Mount Desert Island, where the two women would eventually take up permanent residence. Paul Minear saw much that was good about the Savigneau biography, and he was grateful for it. But his primary intention in writing to me was to express his distress at its "grossly unfair" depiction of Yourcenar's American companion and translator. Savigneau's biography presents Frick as a controlling figure who dominated Yourcenar, forcing her to remain in the United States after World War II ended rather than return to Europe. At the same time, paradoxically, Yourcenar's partner of more than four decades is viewed by Savigneau as a peripheral figure. Minear emphatically protests this assessment in his letter's final, passionate paragraph: "The bonds between the two friends were so strongly rooted in intellectual, psychological, societal and spiritual affinities that they created together a single life. . . . Their mutuality in living was so authentic that this book should have been a biography of Marguerite Yourcenar *and* Grace Frick, with a subtitle: *Inventing a Single Life*."[2]

Jean Hazelton, another close friend of Frick and Yourcenar, was similarly disturbed by the portrayal of Grace in the Savigneau biography. Hazelton and her husband, Roger, had met the two women in the early 1950s. They were the ones who, on Thanksgiving Day in 1951, celebrated the news with Yourcenar and Frick that Gaston Gallimard had finally surrendered his right to the manuscript of *Memoirs of Hadrian*, thus handing Yourcenar the first of many victories in her numerous battles with publishers.[3] Hazelton took notes as she was reading the Savigneau biography, most of which pertain to the negative way her friend was treated. Knowing Grace as a woman of considerable intellect, she was shocked, for example, by references to Grace's " 'wifely schemes'!" and by "deductions without foundation" in which Grace was "always the villain." She could not square her perception of Grace, the product of a decades-long friendship, with what she viewed as the biography's stress on a kind of "amorous self-interest slanting toward sensationalism" and on "Frick's mad love."[4]

On November 26, 1993, Hazelton sent her thoughts about *Marguerite Yourcenar: Inventing a Life* to Gladys Minear. Her reaction to the work was so intense that she found it hard to write coherently. "I resented the author's belittlement of Grace in almost every reference to her," she starts off by saying. "She is made to seem a silly American," Hazelton continues, offended by the use of "such words about her as maniacal, fits of passion, indignant, shocked, eccentricities, etc." Like the Minears, the Hazeltons had known Grace and Marguerite for decades. They had dined, attended plays, and taken trips with the couple in France, just as they had stayed with them on several occasions at Petite Plaisance or hosted them at their own homes in Massachusetts and Maine. They remained in touch until Grace's death in 1979 and Marguerite's eight years later. But in reading the Savigneau biography, Hazelton wrote, "at times I thought I was reading about strangers whom I had never known."[5]

Nor was it only Grace and Marguerite's old friends who found tendentiousness in Savigneau. Stephen Goode of the *Washington Times*, for example, wrote skeptically about *Marguerite Yourcenar: Inventing a Life*, "In a very French manner, the author lacerates America. Yourcenar, though born in France, chose to live most of her life on Desert Island [*sic*] in Maine with Frick. But this wasn't a happy time for her, according to the author, because Yourcenar was living in a country 'without civilization,' and which she could endure only with the greatest pain."[6] *Publishers Weekly* notes that Savigneau "simply cannot believe this practitioner *par excellence* of the French language would want to live in the U.S.—or, for that matter, with Frick. Savigneau does not present convincing evidence for the oft repeated thesis that Yourcenar, tough though she decidedly was, was bullied by Frick into staying in the U.S."[7] And L. Peat O'Neil observes in her witty *Belles Lettres* review "Invent Your Life— Lest Someone Beat You to It" that Savigneau "creates a tension between the two principals that I did not find in the supporting quotes. . . . Furthermore, the character painted so adroitly in early chapters would hardly put up with a destructive partnership or be held hostage by guilt. A woman willing to do legal battle with the powers of French publishing hardly needs 50 ways to leave her lover."[8]

So eager was Savigneau to disparage the country in which Yourcenar nonetheless spent fifty of her eighty-four years that she even managed to turn an appreciative comment that the young author made to a friend about America into a criticism. That friend was the French essayist Charles Du Bos, who knew many noted European authors and was close to André Gide. Du Bos, whose writings on Shakespeare, Shelley, and Keats helped draw attention in France to English literature, had come to the United States to give a series of lectures in New York. Yourcenar corresponded with Du Bos during the last two years of his life.[9] On April 27, 1938, she was nearing the end of her first, seven-month stay in Connecticut with Frick. By this time Yourcenar had spent all but a few weeks of the previous fourteen months with Grace either in Europe or in the United States. What she actually wrote to Du Bos was "Like you, I appreciate the calm of my American retreat more and more with each passing day." Savigneau takes only the noun phrase from this sentence and, as if speaking for the author herself, uses it to invalidate Yourcenar's first experience of America:

> At that particular time in her life, Yourcenar was above all in a state of uncertainty regarding her feelings, to which she would never admit. The only true advantage she saw in spending the winter of 1937–38 in the United States was, as she wrote to Du Bos from Canada, on the day before her departure, "the calm of my American retreat. It's curious, and quite contrary to the legend of the United States, that it should be precisely these opportunities for meditation, detachment, and peace that we have sought and found here." "Detachment"? Is this yet another pious vow?[10]

If indeed Yourcenar thought so little of her months in the United States with Frick, it is hard to imagine why, on the eve of her return to Europe, she would write that she appreciated the country she was leaving "more and more with each passing day." One almost gets the impression that she might have liked to stay.

It is not my intention to denigrate Josyane Savigneau's achievement. I admired her work when I translated it in the early 1990s, and I admire it still.

When Savigneau's biography was released by the prestigious Éditions Gallimard, Yourcenar's own chosen publisher, it was greeted in France with near universal praise.[11] It was an amazing feat to compose and publish in the short space of three years after Yourcenar's death a book as thoroughly researched and compelling as Savigneau's. It is *the* biography of Yourcenar, to which scholars and devotees of the first *académicienne* will long recur. But where Grace Frick and her relationship with Yourcenar are concerned, that is precisely the problem. Once Savigneau had laid the groundwork, subsequent biographers and commentators built on that foundation in their portrayals of Frick, some of them upping the ante.

Michèle Goslar, the Belgian author of *Yourcenar: "Qu'il eût été fade d'être heureux"* has, for example, gone so far as to call Frick a "last resort," a "consolation prize" with whom Yourcenar was forced to make do "because she could not succeed at seducing the men she desired: homosexuals."[12] George Rousseau, in his short British biography *Yourcenar,* depicts his subject as fantasizing for years about leaving her companion.[13] Michèle Sarde's *Vous, Marguerite Yourcenar: La Passion et ses masques* describes Yourcenar as having abandoned her impetus toward life and passion to enter "a phase of renunciation and transcendence of the self" at the time she and Frick came together. Indeed, Sarde calls the fifty-year period of Yourcenar's life that began when she met Frick "the apogee of her life as a writer, but the end of her life as a woman."[14] Sensuality in all its forms was central to Yourcenar throughout her life. Loving Grace did not make Marguerite any less a woman, and a statement she made at the end of Frick's life refutes this assertion almost word for word.

My understanding of Marguerite Yourcenar's life has nonetheless been enriched by all of these works. Moreover, I believe that Michèle Sarde and Josyane Savigneau, in particular, have gained respect for Frick over the years. It may simply be in the nature of the biographical beast to cast a dim light on the secondary characters in order to shine a beam all the more brightly on the biographee. As Janet Malcolm pertinently notes in her fascinating *Two Lives: Gertrude and Alice,* "the minor characters of biography, like their counterparts in fiction, are less tenderly treated than major characters." And perhaps it is true, as Malcolm goes on to say, that the biographer's single-minded focus on his subject "blinds him to the full humanity of anyone else."[15] But when two lives are as intimately entwined as those of Frick and Yourcenar, there comes a point at which the less-than-tender treatment of the one yields a distorted portrayal of the other.

I would be remiss, however, if I failed to acknowledge that Yourcenar herself is at least in part to blame for biographers' negative perceptions of Frick. Although she often spoke of her companion with admiration, tenderness, and gratitude in the years after her death, she also made a number of dismissive comments about Grace, both publicly and privately. One almost got the impression that Yourcenar was as determined not to sentimentalize her relationship with Frick as she so resolutely was to refute the notion that her life had been in any way diminished by the absence of a mother, Fernande de Crayencour having died of complications related to her only child's birth. Joan Acocella picked up on one of Yourcenar's trivializing remarks in her 2005 *New Yorker* article, writing that "when she was old, she said that her passion for Grace exhausted itself after two years."[16] But it was in an interview conducted by Shusha Guppy in the months before Yourcenar's death that the author's attempts to write Frick out of her life reached their peak. The original typewritten translation into English of Guppy's posthumously published *Paris Review* interview bears so many of the interviewee's strikeouts and changes in Flair pen that some sections of the text are almost illegible.[17] What Yourcenar did allow through her own censorial filter was the following terse synopsis:

> As for my relationship with Grace Frick, I met her when we were both women of a certain age, and it went through different stages; first passionate friendship, then the usual story of two people living and traveling together for the sake of convenience and because they have common literary interests. During the last ten years of her life she was very ill. For the last eight years she couldn't travel and that's why I stayed in Maine during those winters. I tried to help her till the end, but she was no longer the center of my existence, and perhaps had never been. The same is true reciprocally, of course.[18]

Every mention of Grace as an intimate partner is crossed out and replaced by text that is either unrelated to Frick or pertains only to her function as a translator.

"There is nothing more ambivalent than a marriage," said one longtime acquaintance years ago in the midst of a discussion of Frick and Yourcenar's relationship. Of course there were difficulties, conflicts, struggles for control. What intimate partnership lacks them? But there was also affection, harmony, joy—and, yes, passion of all kinds. If we look not at what Yourcenar sometimes would say after Grace was gone but at the kinds of things the author was saying to her friends before Frick's final illness took over their lives, we will get a more nuanced, and more accurate, view. As the distinguished English scholar and critic P. N. Furbank noted about Yourcenar and Frick in his review of the Savigneau biography, "One gets the impression that . . . they made a very desirable life together. After Frick's death, Yourcenar was inclined to speak of it dismissively as a 'marriage of convenience,' but we are not compelled to believe her."[19]

Indeed, we will see that the romance did not exhaust itself "after two years"; it was part of their everyday life. When Grace and Marguerite were home in Maine, for example, they often motored to the top of nearby Cadillac Mountain to greet the sun rising over the ocean or to gaze at the heavens on midsummer nights. In July 1956, when the two women had been together nearly twenty years, Yourcenar described such an occasion in a letter to her friend Natalie Barney in Paris. Barney had summered with her family in Bar Harbor as a girl, in a twenty-six-room mansion thirteen miles from the white clapboard cottage that Grace and Marguerite bought in 1950. "'Your' Mount Desert Island," Yourcenar wrote, "is extremely beautiful right now. Although less so perhaps than in the solitude of winter. But moonlit nights over the island archipelago, summer nights at once transparent and veiled, are incomparably sweet."[20]

Twenty-three years later, near the end of her two-decades-long battle with cancer, Grace was still mistress of Petite Plaisance. Even during the most excruciating months before her death, she would insist on getting up for part of every day to receive friends, scholars, or members of the media seeking to interview Marguerite. On May 12, 1979, the popular Parisian radio host Jacques Chancel arrived in Northeast Harbor for two days. Perhaps not realizing that Marguerite Yourcenar's personal life was off-limits for a public broadcast, Chancel dared to ask the famously private author about the woman who had graciously received him and his crew, then discreetly retired from their midst. "I promise not to go back over your ancestors," he began, "I won't discuss your family again, but I would still like to situate your present relationship. You live with a friend, a young woman, a lady . . ."

In the background one then hears a nervous stirring of tea and rattling of teacups as Marguerite Yourcenar hastens to inject, "An American, who is my translator and who has translated three of my books into English."

"Is she a writer, too?" Chancel queries.

"No, simply a translator, an excellent translator. Her spoken French is somewhat hesitant and timid, but her knowledge of languages is extraordinary."

"I would like to tell you how remarkable that woman is," Chancel re-marks, "because she welcomed us, she took care of us, but for you . . . , I think I know what she represents by your side."

"Probably fidelity," Yourcenar replied in a trembling voice; "a great desire for devotion." She then speaks of knowing Grace both in Europe and Ameri-ca in the 1930s, adding that Grace's "wish to help, to be of service at that time was extremely great. I remember that an excellent Dutch translator I had—I was in Amsterdam at the time with her—was a man who never went out, who never went anywhere, and I managed to get him to come out to dinner with us. The next day, he sent me a little note, written in a shaking hand that said, 'As for that other lady, I believe I saw in her the visage of fidelity.'"

"It's true," responded Chancel. I have seen it, too."[21]

At the very end of her own life, Marguerite Yourcenar was working on the semiautobiographical *Quoi? L'Éternité.* In the latter pages of that unfin-ished work, she recalled "unforgettable moments" from a long-ago trip to England, a country to which both she and Grace were deeply attached. "In my mind's eye," wrote Yourcenar, describing one of those moments, "I see a young woman, with a young Sibyl's features, sitting on one of the gates that separate the fields from the pastures over there; we're at the foot of Hadrian's Wall; her hair is waving in the wind from the mountaintops; she seems to embody that expanse of air and sky."[22] That young Sibyl probably did not possess the ancient prophetesses' gift to tell what lay ahead; but the aged au-thor, looking back, clearly saw what lay behind and, in one of many guises, it was love.

Prologue

O! when mine eyes did see Olivia first . . .

—William Shakespeare

"DID YOU FIRST MEET HER in Hartford?" Donald Harris queried as he chauffeured Grace Frick around Mount Desert Island on a raw November morning in 1977.

"Oh, heavens no!" Grace replied. "We met in Paris."

So begins the only known extant recording of Grace Frick's voice and the only firsthand account of Frick and Yourcenar's meeting whose source is not Marguerite Yourcenar. The composer Donald Harris had come to Northeast Harbor with his then wife, Nadine Bicher, on Thanksgiving weekend in 1977 to discuss his plan to write an operetta based on Yourcenar's play *The Little Mermaid*.[1] That same weekend a French television crew had traveled to Maine from Washington, DC, intending to film Yourcenar in some of her favorite island locations. Harris offered to drive Frick from place to place on that cold and windy Sunday, trailing the vehicle in which Yourcenar was riding with the television crew. She was filmed on Sargeant Drive, the road that winds along the beautiful arm of the sea known as Somes Sound; near Somes Brook, where Marguerite and Grace once loved to swim on a hot summer's day; and in the Brookside Cemetery, where the two women would one day be buried. Frick spoke of the past as they drove from Northeast Harbor to Somesville, stopping near the log cabin she and Yourcenar had rented during their first summers on Mount Desert Island.

Frick had gone to Paris in early 1937 at the behest of her Uncle George and Aunt Dolly LaRue. For the family that raised her, she had long been the person to turn to in a crisis. This time her twenty-five-year-old cousin Nancy Gallagher had contracted tuberculosis. An orphan taken in by the LaRues when she was six, Nancy had grown up in Kansas City with Grace, seeing her as a kind of older sister. The two girls had even shared a bedroom for a time. After graduating from Notre Dame de Sion High School in 1931, Nancy took the veil at the mother convent of that Catholic order in Paris. Henceforth, she would be Sister Marie Yann.

Grace had already been to France twice, and she was the only family member who could negotiate her way in French, though she did not feel particularly proficient in the language at the time.[2] She most likely left New York on January 27, 1937, on the SS *Deutschland*, which called at Cherbourg on February 4, dropping off two passengers.[3] By that afternoon she had reached Paris and taken a room at the Hôtel Wagram. Overlooking the Tuileries Garden from 208 rue de Rivoli, the Wagram was where Oscar Wilde and his bride, Constance, had honeymooned in June of 1884, occupying a small suite on the third floor.[4] Perhaps it was in part for its literary pedigree that Marguerite Yourcenar always stayed at the Wagram when she was in Paris during the 1930s. Grace had stayed there previously, too, when she, Uncle George, and Aunt Dolly had gone to visit Sister Yann in August of 1934. But this would be a very different trip. Grace Frick was now traveling solo, and Marguerite Yourcenar was in residence at the hotel. The lives of both women were about to be forever changed.

Grace had this to say about her first night at the Wagram forty years after the fact:

> Marguerite Yourcenar lived there in winters, and I saw her in this kind of a daze, you know. I sail very well, but I'm land-sick. I'm reeling in the dining room traffic. The dining room wasn't very full, and I noticed this young woman—she was quite a young woman—in a corner table with guests, obviously a man and wife. [. . .] She was wearing a Russian dress in which she was photographed later for a large painting. And . . . and her eyes were so striking . . . *immense* gray-blue eyes. And I said, I'll seek her out.[5]

The next morning Grace went immediately to the convent at Issy-les-Moulineaux, where her cousin was nearing death.[6] "Nancy died just three days after I got there," Grace continues, adding,

> I stayed on to settle the various problems of the estate. That hotel had a little bar, and when I learned it was cheaper, I went there, because everybody else did. Marguerite was having drinks with a French friend, and I . . . That was a small place, and I sort of heard the word "America." I recognized it. When he

left, she went up to the bar and ordered dinner. So I went up and said, "Do you speak English, Madame?" And she said, "Yes, I do."

Grace then pauses briefly before adding, to peals of laughter from her listeners, "And she now says to me, 'What if I'd said, "No, I don't"?!'"[7]

When Josyane Savigneau was writing her biography in the late 1980s, there were only two primary versions of the meeting between Grace and Marguerite, the one that Yourcenar told her young traveling companion Jerry Wilson after Grace's death and the one that Frick related to a friend back in 1937. In Wilson's account, Savigneau writes, Grace was alone in the bar of the Wagram:

> At the table next to hers, Marguerite Yourcenar was conversing with Emmanuel Boudot-Lamotte. In Yourcenar's version, they were talking in a general way about traveling, and also about their respective travel plans. It was reportedly then that Frick intervened asking Yourcenar, in order to start up a conversation, if she would like to make a trip to the United States. "The next morning," Jerry Wilson goes on to say in his journal, "the young 'chasseur' [page boy] came to Mme. Y's room saying that the American lady sent a message that some lovely birds could be seen on a roof through her window, wouldn't she come up to see. She did and they became friends," concludes Jerry Wilson euphemistically.[8]

Florence Codman, Grace Frick's former classmate at Wellesley College, told the other version of the story to Savigneau in March of 1989. It contains an interesting twist. Grace had phoned Florence in New York City immediately after returning from Europe in the late summer of 1937. Soon she would be heading back to Yale University to work on a PhD dissertation on the poet George Meredith. According to Codman, Grace "was immediately dazzled by Marguerite; it was a real case of love at first sight." As for the meeting itself, Codman recalled that "Grace was in fact alone in the bar and Marguerite was engaged in conversation with a man. They were talking about literature, about Coleridge in particular. 'They were saying things that were so inaccurate, indeed so stupid, that I intervened to tell them they had it all wrong,' Grace told me." Savigneau, for her part, "given everything we know about Frick and the peremptory way in which she would intervene without being solicited," finds Codman's version of events to be "certainly the more plausible.["9] While no one who knew Frick would likely minimize her teacherly propensities, what Grace said in 1977 about her new French acquaintance stands in stark contrast to what Codman remembered: "We got to talking that first dinner. Marguerite asked if I was working on the early poetry of George Meredith. Well, it turned out she knew more about English literature than I did!"[10]

In the mid-1980s Marguerite Yourcenar also told me about meeting Grace. Here is what I wrote in my journal on July 14, 1983:

> G.F. was staying at the same small but luxurious hotel, rue de Rivoli (Hôtel Wagram—which was pillaged during the war and no longer exists except for the words on the sidewalk), where M.Y. kept two rooms. The hotel had both a restaurant and a bar, where M.Y. would eat because it was less expensive. . . . M.Y. was in the bar one night with a journalist friend (male), and they were talking about traveling. M.Y. told him she'd like to perhaps go to America (for a short time) but was really interested in going to Persia. The man left and G.F., who had heard their conversation from her table, asked M.Y. if she wanted to go to America. M.Y. joined her and they had a drink (wine) or a sandwich together and talked.
>
> During the conversation M.Y. said something about liking birds. Next day— Mme Yourcenar smiles and is animated telling this story—she gets, through the intermediary of the hotel staff, a pretty little card from G.F. saying to come to her room and see the birds on the roof. M.Y. invited her to a nightclub, where they didn't enjoy themselves, and then invited her to Sicily and Greece.[11] They spent three months traveling thus, and then G.F. returned to the U.S.A.

There is no way to be sure exactly what happened or was said in the bar of the Hôtel Wagram that February day. But Yourcenar's 1983 account clearly echoes that of Frick in several respects, including the chronology of the episode, the mention of a possible trip to America as an initial point of contact, and the meal that the two young women shared. The conclusion of Frick's 1977 reminiscence, while omitting the tale of the birds on the roof, continues to resonate with Yourcenar's version of the story, and adds to it a detail that she may have been the only living soul to recall:

> After we met in Paris, Marguerite was going south. She'd never been in Sicily, and I had never, at that time, never been in Italy. So we . . . Since I was there and my cousin was gone, why, I stayed, and we set off to Sicily together. [. . .]

We were to take a boat at Genoa, and . . . She suffered terribly from dizziness, and there was a gangplank—the boat was like this, you know. They had to blindfold her to get her up there. "I can't take it," she said. So she left.

Reenvisioning this abortive attempt to board ship, Grace can't conceal her amusement. Whereupon she exclaims with a mischievous giggle, "So that was the beginning of our travels together!"[12]

"WE MET IN PARIS"

CHAPTER 1 ✿ The Early Years
1903–1921

My mind to me a kingdom is.

—Sir Edward Dyer

GRACE MARIAN FRICK WAS BORN on January 12, 1903, in Toledo, Ohio, the daughter of John Henry Frick and Alice May (Self) Frick.[1] Toledo, connected to the Great Lakes by the Wabash and Erie Canal and an important railroad destination, was a flourishing site of commerce and industry in the early twentieth century. The progressive reformer Samuel M. Jones had been elected mayor of the city in 1897 and, over the course of four terms, instituted a number of reforms that benefited working people and their families. An expanding economy that included furniture manufacturers, glass making, oil companies, and railroad-related businesses made Toledo the kind of place where a young family could hope to thrive.[2]

Grace had two brothers, Frederick Carleton Frick and Gage Carlin Frick, who were six and four years old, respectively, when she came along. Nine months later, on October 17, Grace's thirty-one-year-old father suffered a bout of acute appendicitis and died. John Frick had earned a decent living as a fireman for the Paragon Oil and Refining Company until 1901, then as a skilled carpenter for the Wheeling and Lake Erie Railway in Toledo; but in those days before Social Security, with life insurance policies still confined to a relative elite, his young widow had few resources to fall back on.[3] Alice May, known to family members as May, had obtained a teaching certificate from a normal school in Indiana and did some teaching before she was married.[4] But she could not support herself and three young children on a teacher's salary. Difficult choices had to be made.

Among the first was the decision to leave the modest home at 233 Fremont Street where the Fricks had lived before John Henry's death and rent

3

an apartment above a store in Toledo. May's son Gage remembered chasing sleighs down snow-packed streets with his brother in the winter after that move and catching rides on the runners. It was not long, though, before the boys were separated—not only from each other but also from their mother and baby sister.

The oldest child, Fred, had been named after his paternal grandfather, Frederick Fricke, an immigrant who, like his wife Mary, was born in the town of Salzwedel in northern Germany. The Fricke family had been inn-keepers there in the early nineteenth century. Frederick and Mary arrived in the United States during the Civil War, and one of Frederick's earliest memories of his new country was the sight of Abraham Lincoln's funeral procession.[5]

Frederick Fricke the elder, born in 1833, managed a lumber yard for the Chicago and Alton Railroad in Illinois. Mary, nine years younger, was a housewife with five children ranging in age from three months to sixteen years in 1880. John Henry's eldest brother was already working in a railroad shop then at age sixteen. John Henry followed suit when he was old enough to join the workforce. Eventually the elder Frickes acquired a farm in Bloom-ington, Illinois. After their son John Henry died, they offered to take in Frederick's youngest namesake.

Gage was also sent briefly to the Fricke farm, but in 1904 or 1905 he went to live with his maternal aunt Dolly and her husband, George A. LaRue, in Kansas City, Missouri. Dolly Frances (Self) LaRue, born in 1873, had grown up, like her older sister May, in Fort Wayne, Indiana. She was the second of seven children born to Jasper N. Self and his wife, Katharine (Crane) Self. He and Katharine owned a store in Fort Wayne.[6]

Dolly's husband, George LaRue, was raised on his family's farm in Adams County, Pennsylvania, near Gettysburg. He had eleven brothers and sisters. In 1886 George left Pennsylvania at age seventeen and traveled west to join his brother John LaRue in Kansas City.[7] Situated at the confluence of the Kansas and Missouri Rivers, Kansas City was in the midst of a building boom. From a frontier town and destination for cattle drives, the city was evolving into a commercial and cultural hub whose many boulevards would earn it the nick-name Paris of the Plains. Fittingly, French fur traders were its first permanent European settlers.[8] During the Civil War, the city's population was sharply divided between proponents of slavery and abolitionists. With the extension of the railroad from St. Louis after the war, Kansas City entered a period of rapid expansion that continued into the twentieth century.

George LaRue had worked his way through normal school in Pennsylvania grinding wheat and corn at a water-powered grist mill. In Kansas City he worked for the Richards and Conover Hardware Company for several years. With that practical experience under his belt, George became a salesman for Simmons Hardware, based in St. Louis. Working for Simmons, George did lots of traveling by train. Family lore has it that Dolly Self had been a "Harvey Girl" when she and George met—that is, she was working as a waitress in one of the Fred Harvey restaurants George frequented in his travels. This first U.S. restaurant chain had a policy of hiring attractive and intelligent young women of good character, and managers kept a close eye on them. George and Dolly married in 1902 in Paducah, Kentucky, where George's sales work was headquartered at that time. The following year, the couple returned to Kansas City, and George joined his brother Charles as a partner in the LaRue Printing Company.[9] George and Dolly had no children, and the printing business was going strong. They could afford to take in a child, and it was not long before they thought of Grace's brother Gage as their own son.

While Grace was still a toddler, May Frick stayed put in Toledo, teaching school and serving as a restaurant cashier. May's twice-widowed mother

FIGURE 1. Grace Frick at eighteen months. Petite Plaisance Archives.

Katharine (Crane) Self Pennell also lived in Toledo in the early 1900s, at a rooming house run by her sister, Anna Welch.[10] She helped care for little Grace. Katharine's adolescent son Marion C. Self, an elevator boy in 1900, was also a member of that household. Known as Bud, Marion was the only brother of the four Self girls—May, Dolly, Cora, and Georgia—who lived beyond infancy, and he was doted on by all. He did not live a long life, however. In early 1916, at the age of thirty-one, Marion died of a respiratory infection.[11] It was from this much-loved family member that Grace received her middle name.

Once Grace got beyond the toddler stage, May packed up and joined her sister Dolly, son Gage, and brother-in-law George in Kansas City. Her entire family was reunited when Fred left the Illinois farm of his paternal grandparents in time to spend his high school years with the Fricks and LaRues. May Frick had begun to work for the LaRue Printing Company, and before long she was managing the books for the business. Both May and George LaRue had had experience as teachers, and they put a high value on education. The Frick children were all encouraged to do well in school, and they took that encouragement seriously.

In the early 1900s the LaRues owned a home at 3315 Paseo Boulevard, a major turn-of-the-century thoroughfare in Kansas City that was constructed as part of the City Beautiful movement. During the second decade of that century, a series of events would change first the composition and later the location of the LaRue household. On September 14, 1913, when Grace was ten years old, her mother married George W. Bacon and moved in with him at 2330 Spruce Avenue in Kansas City.[12] Bacon was nearly seven years May's junior and had worked as a bookkeeper for the MoKan Telephone Company for a number of years. Though May and her children, particularly Grace, had always been close, none of the young Fricks—Fred was seventeen by this time and Gage fifteen—went to live with their mother and her new husband. Uncle George LaRue, known to all as Unk, was the only father figure Grace had ever known. From all accounts, he cared deeply for the young Fricks and was beloved by them all.[13] Dolly, known simply as Aunt, had a more peripheral role in their upbringing. According to Marguerite Yourcenar, Grace was also brought up by "black mammies and black gardeners."[14] And, indeed, the 1910 census of Kansas City, taken when Grace was seven years old, lists an eighteen-year-old Lillie Johnson, identified as a "mulatto" and a servant, among the members of the LaRue household.

By the fall of 1916, both of Grace's older brothers had left Kansas City. Fred spent the academic year 1916–17 at the University of Missouri in Columbia, then left the country for the battlefields of northern France. For two months beginning on July 4, 1917, he volunteered for the American Field Service (AFS), taking wounded French soldiers off the front lines. Fred was one of twenty-eight young men from his university who participated in the AFS at that time.[15] Though many of his fellow students returned to the United States in time for the fall semester at college, Fred stayed on, becoming part of the Army Ambulance Corps when the United States entered the war. He remained in France through the end of World War I, receiving two Croix de Guerre for his bravery. He was the first Kansas Citian to receive the prestigious French medal.[16] Fred thus became the first member of Grace's family to form a strong attachment to a country that would also loom large in the lives of at least two others.

Fred's brother Gage began his college career at the University of Kansas in 1915 to pursue a printing program whose advanced techniques Uncle George hoped would benefit the family business. It was during Gage's time at KU, when Grace was twelve or thirteen years old, that an incident occurred which gives a glimpse of Grace's budding sense of racial justice. Home from school on vacation, Gage told a story at the dinner table of a young black student who entered a classroom and sat down at a desk next to a white coed. The white girl instantly leapt from her chair and scurried to a seat on the far side of the room. Grace was horrified to hear of the girl's rudeness and insensitivity, and that sense of indignation where racial matters were concerned stuck with her.

As for Gage, he transferred the following year to Harvard University, where he joined the Students' Army Training Corps, forerunner of the ROTC. Gage was about to ship out with his unit in November 1918 when the armistice was signed that ended World War I.

In 1916, with the LaRue household now half as large as it had been before the departure of May, Fred, and Gage, the family moved from Paseo Boulevard to the nearby Ormond Hotel at the corner of Linwood Boulevard and Troost Avenue. The following year found George and May Bacon also moving into the Ormond, with its upscale restaurant and drugstore. Grace, who turned fourteen in early 1917, could now easily visit with her mother every day.

Exactly what the sequence of events was here is a bit vague, but Grace's mother was not well. In fact, it may have been so that Unk, Aunt, and Grace could keep an eye on her that everyone ended up moving to the Ormond Hotel. May's health did not prevent her from taking an active interest in Grace's future, however, as she had in that of her sons. She and other family members began looking into colleges for Grace early on, counseling her in particular to take more Latin than French. The family had friends in Kansas City whose daughters had gone east to college, and May did not hesitate to press them for information about the various schools. Grace also knew at least one fellow high school student who was headed for the highly regarded and progressive Wellesley College. M. Lucille Carpenter, a year ahead of Grace, attended the Barstow School in Kansas City, right around the corner from Grace's public high school. As teenagers, Grace and Lucille lived in the same neighborhood. Barstow had been founded in 1884 by two Wellesley graduates, Ada Brann and Mary Louise Barstow, at the urging of Wellesley's dynamic young second president, Alice Freeman, who realized that her college would thrive only if enough well-trained young women were up to the challenge of its rigorous curriculum. She persuaded several business and educational leaders to become involved in launching high-quality secondary schools for young women in cities such as Chicago, New York, and Philadelphia, as well as Kansas City.[17]

May Bacon's desire to settle the college question early may have had to do with her sense that she would not be around to see her daughter all the way through high school. Grace once recalled a midwinter train trip from which May returned to Kansas City's Union Station shivering and exhausted. In Grace's mind that train trip had marked the onset of her mother's ill health. With her health declining, May stopped working for the LaRue brothers. She died at the age of forty-six on October 18, 1918, of pulmonary tuberculosis. Grace was a sophomore in high school.

During the year leading up to May's death, another sister of Dolly LaRue's, Cora (Self) Gallagher, was also nearing the end of her life. Cora had married John J. Gallagher, a childhood émigré from England, in 1892.[18] After marrying in Indiana the pair moved east to New Jersey, where John's family had settled. In 1900 the young Gallaghers were living at 105 Bowery Street in Newark, in what was then known as the Down Neck section of the city.[19] John was a steel rougher.[20] Ten years later John and Cora were still at the same address and still childless, but John, in his midforties, was now keeping a saloon.[21] On August 26, 1911, Cora gave birth to a daughter. As if foretelling the role she would one day play in the life of her older cousin, that baby was named Grace Marian Gallagher. Both girls were the namesakes not only of their uncle Marion "Bud" Self but also of Marion's short-lived sister Gracie, who succumbed to "congestion of the brain" at age four.[22]

At some point along the way, Cora developed diabetes. As her health worsened, she returned to the Midwest with her daughter to stay with her mother,

Katharine Pennell, in Chicago. During the summer of 1918, with Cora unable to care for a rambunctious six-year-old, Grace Gallagher was sent to visit the LaRues in Kansas City. On October 28, 1918, ten days after Alice May's death in that city, Cora Gallagher slipped into a coma and never woke up.

According to her death certificate, Cora was a widow when she died. But the 1920 U.S. census, taken fifteen months after Cora's death, lists a fifty-four-year-old John J. Gallagher living with his brother Patrick in West Paterson, New Jersey.[23] John was now a reeler in a jute mill, Prohibition having no doubt shut down his saloon. In any case, it would have been highly unusual for a man of that age in that era to attempt to raise a little girl on his own. Grace Gallagher thus became a permanent presence in the LaRue household. To distinguish her from the fifteen-year-old Grace Marian Frick, the new arrival was referred to by family members variously as Grace G., Little Grace, or Gracie. Eventually, for reasons unknown to surviving family members, they started calling her Nancy.[24]

To accommodate this new addition to their family, George and Dolly left the Ormond Hotel in 1919 and rented a stunning three-story home at 4340 Oak Street. Located in the predominantly residential and cultural district of Kansas City known as South Hyde Park, the building is now listed on the National Register of Historic Places. Louis S. Curtiss designed the unusual stone structure, built between 1903 and 1905, as "an eclectic Prairie Style amalgam of Second Empire, Art Nouveau and Neoclassic elements." It acquired the nickname Mineral Hall after Roland E. Bruner bought it to house parts of his outstanding mineral collection. A prominent feature of the

FIGURE 2. Mineral Hall, the LaRue residence beginning in 1919. Frick family archives.

distinctive residence is its dramatic art nouveau main entrance.[25] Grace and Nancy shared a second-floor bedroom whose windows were located directly above that grand entryway.

It was around this time that Grace became active in the Church of Christ, Scientist.[26] She was sixteen years old and a junior in high school. George and Dolly LaRue were members of Kansas City's Second Presbyterian Church, so Grace was striking out on her own in this regard. She had lost both her mother and Aunt Cora within days of each other the previous year. Perhaps Grace was attracted to the Christian Science emphasis on health and self-healing. It is also highly likely she was drawn to the religion's support of civil liberties and women's rights.

Business by this time was booming at the LaRue Printing Company. In 1910 Charles and George LaRue had moved their operation into a larger building at 810 Baltimore Avenue.[27] The brothers took pride in the quality of their service. According to one historical description of the business, "experience, effort and real human interest is applied to every job going through the plant, no matter how large or small."[28]

The "real human interest" that stood George LaRue in good stead as a businessman extended also to his participation in civic and charitable activities. One newspaper article, entitled "Now Take a Man of His Type," notes that "Mr. LaRue finds time to help build a better city in which all types of people can live. . . . Mr. LaRue also is active in the work of the Council of Social Agencies. He always is pleading for support of the Red Cross and other worthy enterprises."[29]

But the LaRues were not priggish do-gooders. In the 1910s they were one of the first families in Kansas City to allow themselves the luxury of an automobile, which Grace promptly dubbed the Tally Ho. Whenever a family outing was proposed, the high-spirited youngster would exclaim, "Let's take the Tally Ho!"

Grace began attending Westport High School, on East Thirty-Ninth Street, in the fall of 1917. The Westport section of Kansas City was originally a town in its own right, built along the Santa Fe Trail.[30] During the first half of the nineteenth century, it became the launching point for pioneers heading farther west. In October of 1864 Westport was the site of a bloody Civil War encounter involving more than thirty thousand Union and Confederate troops and resulting in some three thousand casualties.[31] Missouri was a slaveholding border state with ties to both sides of the conflict, but a

FIGURE 3. George A. "Unk"
LaRue. Frick family archives.

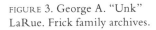

decisive Union victory put it firmly beyond the reach of Confederate aspi-
rations. Often called the Gettysburg of the West, the Battle of Westport still
reverberated in the community where Grace Frick grew up.

After a fire destroyed Westport's previous high school, the new building
welcomed its first students in the fall of 1908.[32] The school would be the
scene of violent race riots in the late 1960s and 1970s, and its academic reputation progressively declined, but for many years it was the finest school in
Kansas City. When Grace was a student there, Westport High School stood
at the edge of Hyde Park. The area to the south of the school, extending
to Mineral Hall, was an affluent neighborhood of primarily single-family
homes anchored by an extensive park system.[33]

Though Grace got off to something of a slow start at Westport High, owing perhaps to her mother's ill health, she eventually took every advantage of
the opportunities offered by the school. She joined several clubs, all of which
promoted scholastic excellence as part of their organizational ethic. Westport

High's exclusive "pioneer society," the Clionians, was devoted to literature and the cultivation of high moral standards. On December 10, 1920, Grace gave a talk on the life of Booth Tarkington as part of a Clionian program that included a sketch from that author's humorous novel of adolescent love, *Seventeen*.[34] She also joined the service-oriented Girls' High School Club, a citywide association, and Fleur de Lis, whose goal of "uniting the interests of France and the United States" Grace would one day take more seriously than she could ever have imagined in high school.[35] In her junior year Grace earned her school letter as a field hockey player. A tall girl at five foot eight, she added basketball to her activity list as a senior. Grace was also on the staff of her yearbook, the Westport *Herald*, and the school newspaper, the *Westport Crier*, in her senior year, as was her classmate Ruth Hall, who would be a friend for life.

Members of the *Crier*'s editorial staff are identified on the paper's masthead only by class affiliation, with no indication of hierarchy. One of four seniors, Grace was obviously among the most active members of the staff. She and James Britt, another senior, may have been considered the *Crier*'s coeditors, as the two of them were delegated to attend a three-day high school journalism conference at the University of Kansas in Lawrence in the fall of 1920. Sponsored by KU's Department of Journalism, the meeting gathered editors of secondary school newspapers from all over Kansas and from neighboring Kansas City, Missouri.[36] Attendees were addressed not only by KU professors and an editor from the *Kansas City Star* but also by Henry J. Allen, then governor of Kansas and himself a newspaper publisher.

Grace was obviously a serious student, but she also had a well-developed sense of fun. The *Westport Crier* of January 5, 1921, contains a satirical piece that was almost certainly written by Frick. None of the articles in the *Crier* appear with bylines, but it is often possible to identify pieces that display the style and wit she would later become known for. Grace's earlier talk on Booth Tarkington provides one clue to the author of the piece; another consists in a humorous question-and-answer in the *Crier*'s tongue-in-cheek advice column "Uncle Dudley," whose motto was "If you are pleased, tell others; if not, keep it to yourself":

Dear Uncle Dudley:

What is the most graceful way of walking down stairs?

GRACE FRICK.

Ans.: —Try roller skates.[37]

It seems that Grace took a tumble down a stairway at Westport High one day during her senior year. On January 5, 1921, that contretemps was folded into the following editorial lament, entitled "Pity the Seniors":

> It has long been a pet delusion among the demented of the school, that is the faculty and under classmen, that the Seniors occupy a lofty position, entailing much flattery and little work. Not so, O benighted ones! Most abused of all students are those in the Senior class!
>
> For years Seniors have accepted the abuses heaped upon them, have been trampled under foot, contenting themselves with the empty glory of their name. To no such depths would the proud class of '21 stoop. Many are the insults we have endured. For example, if a Senior falls down the steps, an over bold under classman remarks in a superior tone: "You resembled anything but a Senior. By this time, one would expect you to have a little self-control." "What!" shriek our teachers in amazed horror. "Fifty minutes for a test on your novel! Never! Thirty minutes is more than enough for Seniors." Or they say with cold indifference, "Your grade is too low! Certainly not. Remember that an E in Freshman work is not an E in Senior work. You must really inconvenience yourself a little to do E work in your Senior year." The most insulting and most common remarks are these: "I should think you would have learned how to do that by this time," and "My dear child, you will never again know as much as you do now!" "My dear child." As William of "Seventeen" would say, "Ye gods!" . . . Will this blind faculty—they who have taught us all of their characteristics for four long years—will they never treat us as equals, not as subordinates? Alas for the difficulty of Seniorhood!
>
> Rejoice O under classmen! This fate is not to be yours. You who lightly frolic in the halls of Westport, will no longer have to flunk to avoid Senior days! O happy, happy ones, between whom and disrespect the class of '21 stands an unyielding barrier! The power of this class shall save you from our sufferings. Long have Seniors slumbered, but now they wake. Will they endure disrespect longer? Quoth the Seniors: "Nevermore!"[38]

Only an excellent student with plenty of self-confidence could have written such a spoof of her teachers and her school, and Grace Frick filled the bill on both counts. Westport's grading system at that time consisted of E (excellent), G (good), F (fair), and P (poor). Altogether, Grace received thirty-six E's and five G's. When she graduated on June 9, 1921, she did so with the highest academic distinction, one of only five students in her class of 281 to achieve it.[39]

Grace's senior portrait, which contrasts with the more lighthearted images typical of her club or sports photographs, displays a seriousness that is also reflected in the quotation accompanying it: "My mind to me a kingdom is."

FIGURE 4. Grace Frick senior portrait, 1921 Westport *Herald*.

That Grace chose this line from the English courtier Sir Edward Dyer's most famous poem as her personal motto suggests that, already at age eighteen, she valued above all else the quest for knowledge and the life of the mind. Her choice also affords an early confirmation of something that Marguerite Yourcenar would say about Grace many years later: that her favorite literature was that of the Elizabethan era.[40]

Grace's level gaze is trained upon the distance, not the photographer, as if she were looking beyond him or her into the depths of her future. Her expression is open and quietly determined. There is no demure tilting of the head to one side in a gesture suggestive of deference as there is in the case of other female portraits on Grace's yearbook page. She has a thick, full head of dark wavy hair and deep-set, soulful eyes. The only jarring note in the photograph consists of the lacey variation on the Buster Brown collar that is tightly cinched around Grace's neck. Wide, flat collars were stylish in that era, but, to my mind at least, Grace's dainty ruffles strike an odd sartorial contrast to the gravity of her demeanor.

In 1921 George LaRue purchased a home for his family at 5200 Oak Street.[41] It was a spacious three-story structure situated on a landscaped corner lot about a mile south of Mineral Hall. Joining George, Dolly, Fred, Gage, Grace, and Cousin Nancy in the move to this new residence would be the twenty-one-year-old private servant Jim Yajanoto. Fred and Gage, having finished college and now in their early twenties, were both working with their uncle at the LaRue Printing Company. Nancy was still in elementary school. In the fall of that year, Grace left this new home for Wellesley College, but she would continue to consider 5200 Oak Street her permanent address throughout the 1920s, 1930s, and even into the early 1940s.

CHAPTER 2 ✿ Wellesley College
1921–1925

Enflamed with the study of learning, and the admiration of virtue.

—John Milton

GRACE FRICK HAD A KNACK for making friends. Shirley McGarr, her next-door neighbor in Northeast Harbor, Maine, has attributed this trait to Grace's upbringing in the Midwest, where people are reputedly less standoffish than prickly New Englanders.[1] Marguerite Yourcenar's biographers often comment on Grace's eagerness to connect with others. Michèle Goslar, for example, describes the thirty-four-year-old Grace as "a tall, thin, elegant young woman, erect in her bearing," who enjoyed unexpected encounters and "was constantly on the lookout for chances to make contact with others."[2] Male or female, she befriended them all, but her closest friends were intellectually gifted, independent women.

The one great friend we know of from Grace's Kansas City youth, Ruth Hall, came east in the fall of 1921, as Grace did, to attend a prestigious women's college. Ruth went to Vassar, then to Yale, and eventually returned to her hometown, where she became a prominent attorney. She never married. There is no other record of Grace's youthful friendships. Nor do we know of any amorous adventures in high school.[3] Her brother Gage once said that he regretted never having introduced any of his male friends to Grace.

When Grace stepped onto the campus of Wellesley College in the fall of 1921, she was entering America's citadel of higher education. The greater Boston area is home to more institutions of higher learning than any other city. Wellesley is one of the original Seven Sister colleges, along with Barnard, Bryn Mawr, Mount Holyoke, Radcliffe, Smith, and Vassar. All were founded in the mid- to late 1800s and are considered to be the rough equivalent in their level of academic excellence of the male Ivy League. Wellesley was initially unique in its commitment not only to women's education but to an all-female faculty.[4] While its faculty is now mixed, Wellesley still admits only women as students; Radcliffe, by contrast, has merged with Harvard, and Vassar became coeducational in the 1960s. The Wellesley College motto, emphasizing women's capacity to act boldly and think for themselves, is "Non ministrari sed ministrare": not to be ministered unto but to minister. That dictum would have held great appeal for someone like Frick, who intended to make her mark on the world.

We have seen the seriousness of purpose that characterized Frick's high school years. There can be no doubt that she chose Wellesley for its outstanding academic reputation and its emphasis on training intelligent young women to be leaders.[5] Grace's brother Gage may have been another factor in her choice. Gage graduated from Harvard University in the spring of 1919. The following year, when Grace was exploring college options, he became secretary of the Kansas City chapter of the Harvard Alumni. In nearby Cambridge, Massachusetts, Harvard has traditionally had a strong social connection to Wellesley. In the early decades of the twentieth century, part of Wellesley's draw for many women was the prospect of marrying a Harvard man.

Nonetheless, like its all-female counterparts in other locations, Wellesley did not escape being labeled a haven for lesbians in the late nineteenth and early twentieth centuries. "Indeed," Tirza True Latimer has noted, "in countries where colleges for women existed, euphemisms for same-sex relations between women—such as Wellesley marriage or Newnham friendship—frequently incorporated the names of women's schools."[6] Romantic friendships (whether secretly sexual or not) and mad crushes were a frequent phenomenon among the students at all-female schools. Unmarried faculty women, moreover, often set up households together on or near their campuses whether for the practical purpose of sharing expenses or for more intimate reasons.

As Michelle Gibson and Deborah T. Meem have noted, "long-term partnerships between women were seen as neither unnatural nor immoral" and were often treated with the same respect accorded heterosexual marriages.[7] As Patricia Ann Palmieri has written, "Lifelong relationships of deep significance were commonplace at Wellesley, fostering verbal and physical expressions of love." Vida Scudder, a professor of English and social activist, became the lifelong companion of her former student Florence Converse. Katharine Lee Bates, an 1880 Wellesley graduate who came back to teach English literature at her alma mater, called Katharine Coman "her partner and 'Joy-of-Life.' "[8] Margaret Pollack Sherwood and her disciple Martha Hale Shackford, an 1896 Wellesley graduate who, like Bates, returned to Wellesley to teach, attained such iconic status as a couple that Gibson and Meem chose their photograph to adorn the cover of the essay collection *Lesbian Academic Couples*. Both women were professors of English literature, which, alongside Latin, would be Grace's major. Sherwood specialized in the Romantic movement in Great Britain, and Shackford was one of the first scholars to recognize Emily Dickinson as a significant poet. Grace would take advanced courses from both women in her senior year. The rich history of woman-identified women of accomplishment that Sherwood and Shackford represented would not be lost on her.

Grace arrived at Wellesley early in what a centennial history of the college calls the Jazz Age, an era during which mores at Wellesley underwent considerable change.[9] World War I had ended three years earlier, and the Nineteenth Amendment to the U.S. Constitution had finally granted women the right to vote in August of 1920. Grace E. Hawk, who wrote one chapter of *Wellesley College, 1875–1975: A Century of Women*, notes regarding the spirit of the time that "for social activists the doctrines inculcated during the Progressive Era still formed a sound basis for protests against newly powerful enemies of the people: racism, at its worst in the Ku Klux Klan; fundamentalism, as it was exhibited in the Scopes trial; restriction of immigration; anti-intellectualism."[10] During Grace's freshman year, Vice President Calvin Coolidge denounced Wellesley as a "hotbed of radicalism," singling out one professor, Mary Calkins, for particular criticism: she was rumored to have voted for the socialist Eugene V. Debs in the 1920 presidential race! Wellesley aimed to inculcate in its students the ideals of service to others and what was called "symmetrical womanhood," which entailed, if not entirely rejecting the privatized sphere to which women had traditionally been confined, stepping onto "the public stage of community activism and careers."[11] Wellesley was clearly a school that would further shape Grace's childhood sense of justice and expose her to a community of like-minded women.

In early 1921, one of Grace's former schoolmates had given readers of the *Westport Crier* a taste of what to expect if they were headed to Wellesley. Eleanor Brown was a freshman at that school when she spoke to the *Crier*. One of the aspects of life that most strikingly impressed her was "that one has to walk miles and miles every day." All that exercise made for an exceptionally fit student body, as it were, and sports were all the rage. Freshmen often lived in Wellesley Village rather than on campus and "practically govern[ed] themselves" under the oversight of an elected student government. A dramatics club called the Barnswallows mounted plays every year so that every Wellesley student, by the time she graduated, would see "at least one Greek play, one modern play, and two Shakespearian plays." Finally, Brown pointed out, the grading scale at Wellesley at that time was so high that an E, the highest mark at Westport High, would be no more than a C at Wellesley. Even Harvard was reputed to have a more lenient grading policy than Wellesley.[12]

Thanks to a 1950 speech given by Grace's classmate Eleanor (Wallace) Allen, we have a firsthand account of what it was like the day the Wellesley class of 1925 embarked upon its freshman year. By virtue of their matriculation date, the members of this class would find their lives forever entwined with the history of their alma mater:

On a warm, hazy September day in 1921, 402 young ladies . . . arrived in Wellesley, having come from every section of the United States and eight from foreign lands. It was a memorable day for them, and, although they were oblivious of the fact, an even more significant one for the College. . . . The College had waited forty-six years for the Class of 1925 to arrive and, here at last, it actually was. Now, the College could look ahead four years and plan its fiftieth birthday and even project further into the future to its seventy-fifth, for 1925 was to stand forever firmly to mark these important occasions, the first by its graduation and the second by its twenty-fifth reunion. . . . So no wonder our first week was spent in being welcomed on all sides. Everyone was so glad to see us. As we descended from the train, smiling "Ask Me's" stepped forward to dispel our fears. . . . Then in rapid succession came our first chapel with President [Ellen Fitz] Pendleton's welcome, the C[hristian] A[association] Reception, the Barnswallows' Reception, the Sophomore Serenade, and then the Sophomore Prom—each of us being escorted by a sophomore and dancing gaily through an evening, until nine-thirty, with other sophomores. Is it any wonder that we questioned how the college had got along without us?[13]

While American women were gaining new freedoms in the wake of World War I, Wellesley College was still imposing strict rules of conduct on its students. If Eleanor Allen mentions the Sophomore Prom ending at nine-thirty, it's because that was when school policy required dances to end. Nor could Wellesley women play golf or tennis or volleyball on Sunday. Students were admonished to wear "knickers" only for sport, not to tea rooms, shops, or dinner. There were also wide-ranging curriculum requirements.

All first-year students had to take gymnastics and outdoor sports classes five hours a week, for example. At its founding, the college had been known as the Wellesley Female Seminary; in the 1920s, although the name had changed, classes in biblical history were still required of all sophomores and juniors. Members of the college met daily in the Houghton Memorial Chapel for morning prayers.

Not surprisingly, Grace—or Fricky, as she came to be known—undertook a challenging array of yearlong classes in addition to the five that were required of all freshmen. Her choices are uncannily predictive of what became enduring passions. Botany 101, Plant Studies, sought to give the Wellesley woman a "familiar and intimate acquaintance with her living environment."[14] The school's three-hundred-acre campus, with its fields, woods, hills, and lake, was an idyllic setting in which to develop that acquaintance, and Grace became a lifelong lover of nature.

French 102 included readings from notable contemporary authors, exercises in speaking, and writing from dictation. Latin 102 focused on authors whose ideas "are part of the classical heritage of modern life": imperial destiny, citizenship, humanism, and the like.[15]

Fascinated by the ancient world, Grace proceeded in her sophomore year to study Roman history and take three more courses in Latin: Horace, Tacitus and Pliny, and Latin prose composition. She also sought to hone her writing skills in English, electing to take two semesters of Advanced Expository Writing. Despite her emphasis on Latin, Grace did not abandon French, taking a yearlong course in translation, themes, and oral composition, which aimed to prepare students for more advanced work in language and literature.[16]

Not content with the hefty load of courses she had tackled during two years at Wellesley, in 1923 Grace attended summer school at the University of Colorado. David M. Hays, archivist at the University Libraries in Boulder, calls those summer sessions "marketed nationally, with prominent visiting professors, a mountain recreation program, and other perks."[17] Grace loved to hike, and counted "mild climbing" among her habitual recreational activities well into middle age.[18] The city of Boulder and the nearby Rocky Mountains were an obvious draw.

Back at Wellesley that fall, Grace turned at least some of her attention to extracurricular matters. Until the 1930s only juniors and seniors were allowed to join one of Wellesley's six private "societies," which entailed secret initiation rites and competed with one another for members. The process involved a series of "teas" held at the various houses during which members and those hoping to join could size each other up. One Wellesley student near the turn of the twentieth century complained in a letter to her mother about the undemocratic nature of these clubs: "I *never* saw such a place for snobby cliques. . . . Here a person counts for *absolutely nothing* unless she is a Society girl." All these groups involved a social component, of course, but they also had various, sometimes overlapping, fields of concentration. Phi Sigma and Zeta Alpha, for example, were literary societies. Tau Zeta Epsilon focused on art and music. The Agora Society was primarily political in nature and encouraged Wellesley women to devote themselves to making the world a better place.[19] Grace joined Alpha Kappa Chi, whose focus was the study and performance of the classics.

Alpha Kappa Chi had been founded in the spring of 1892, modeling itself on the highly regarded Shakespeare Society.[20] Founders hoped to do as fine a job of staging Greek drama as the "Shakespeare girls" were doing with their Elizabethan plays. From its humble beginnings, the society became one of the most popular ones on campus. Also joining AKX her junior year was one of Grace's closest friends at Wellesley, Elizabeth "Betsy" Teter of Chicago, Illinois. Betsy would go on to teach biology at Lake Forest College in her home state. Frances Ilg, another Midwesterner and friend of Grace's, also pledged Alpha Kappa Chi. Frances would become a medical doctor and distinguished authority on child behavior.

Among the other most important friends that Grace made during her years at Wellesley were classmates Phyllis "Phyll" Bartlett, Mary Grace "M.G." Coates, and Florence Codman. Phyllis hailed from New York City and shared Grace's love of English literature. She and Fran Ilg were both members of the Wellesley College Government Association in 1925. M.G. came from Bayville, New York, and was president of the Agora Society. M.G. went to nursing school after graduation and married a doctor. Florence, a Philadelphia native, became a writer and literary critic, publishing in prominent magazines such as the *Nation* and the *New Yorker*.

During the years of Grace's membership in the classical society, the group staged selected scenes from Sophocles's *Antigone* and Aristophanes's *Frogs*, sometimes adorning them with Greek statuary.[21] But the major annual offerings of the group were two plays by Euripides, *Iphigenia in Aulis* in 1924 and *Iphigenia in Tauride* in 1925. Several of Frick's friends played roles in these productions. Grace contented herself with chairing the costume committee.

An *in facultate* associate of the Society Alpha Kappa Chi was Katharine Canby Balderston, who at that time was still a young English instructor. Katharine had graduated from Wellesley in 1916 and gone on, after obtaining a master's at Radcliffe, to earn a doctorate at Yale, as many promising English majors at Wellesley were encouraged by their mentors to do. Her most celebrated work was a groundbreaking scholarly edition of the diary of an eighteenth-century British friend of Samuel Johnson, Hester Lynch Thrale, entitled *Thraliana*.[22] Balderston and another renowned Wellesley professor, the classicist Margaret "Peg" Taylor, would join forces after Taylor's arrival in the 1930s and eventually share a home in Wellesley village. With the publication of the *Thraliana*, Balderston was appointed to the Martha Hale Shackford Chair in English Literature in 1942, a post she held until her retirement in 1960.[23]

The development of a woman-focused academic culture was crucial to these kinds of mentor-student relationships, especially in the early years when conservative opinion held that women could not hope to match wits with men. Those connections had strong and lasting effects on teacher and student alike. Balderston and Taylor maintained ties with Grace for decades after she left Wellesley. In 1969 and 1970, forty-four and forty-five years after Frick's graduation, she and Marguerite Yourcenar made the three-hour drive to Round Pond, Maine, from Northeast Harbor to share Thanksgiving dinner with the Wellesley pair.[24]

Frick's extracurricular pursuits may have affected her scholarship in her junior year, the only time during her Wellesley career when four of Grace's ten semester grades, all in academic subjects, were C's. Those subjects were requirements, however, which—to use an expression for which Grace would later be known—were not her cup of tea. One of the two-semester courses in question was the yearlong Introduction to Philosophy. The *Wellesley College Bulletin* makes this class sound like something Grace would greatly enjoy, concentrating as it did on ethics, psychology, and the science of the moral self,[25] but Grace obviously gave it short shrift. Her performance was equally lackluster in Biblical History 202 and 204, The Life of Christ and The Apostolic Age, respectively. Grace was still a Christian Scientist when she entered Wellesley.[26] In a biographical questionnaire filled out later by members of her class, Grace made a point of noting that she left the United Church of Christ, Scientist, between her sophomore and her junior years—which is to say, between her first and second yearlong bouts with biblical history.[27] Although these courses apparently failed to engage Grace in a meaningful way, they may have caused her to view Christianity in a different light. Mme Yourcenar would later tell me that Grace had long ago rejected religion when the two of them met.[28]

Things went better for Grace in Economics 201, Principles of Economics, a study of current economic thought, and Economics 204, Economic History of the United States. Economics classes at Wellesley had historically focused more on social problems and industrial conditions than had, for example, the more theoretically oriented Harvard.[29] Grace did well in both of these courses, as she did in the yearlong Development of Thought from Classic Times through the Middle Ages.

It was also during Grace's junior year that she took her first advanced class in English literature. English was one of the strongest departments at Wellesley, if not the strongest. Grace took English Literature 204, a course in Milton, from Laura Lockwood. A Yale PhD, Lockwood was known for her unerring memory and for challenging students "to walk up the highest hill in South Natick reciting *Paradise Lost* from memory."[30] Whether or not it was because of this pedagogical tactic, her teaching of *Paradise Lost* made an indelible impression on Frick.[31]

Grace excelled in all her English courses. English Literature 309, taught by the legendary Renaissance specialist Martha Hale Shackford, entailed reading all of Shakespeare's sonnets and plays.[32] Patricia Palmieri describes Shackford's Shakespeare seminar as commanding "such respect that she became known as the female counterpart to George Kittredge of Harvard." Lockwood's Eighteenth Century Literature devoted two semesters, first to Joseph Addison, Daniel Defoe, Alexander Pope, Richard Steele, and Jonathan Swift, and then to Samuel Johnson and his circle. In English Literature 322, Grace studied the Romantic movement in England and its influence on the work of the early nineteenth-century poets with Margaret Sherwood.[33]

Classes in early Roman history and religion, European history, and Latin literature took up the rest of Grace's senior year. By the time Grace was done with her bachelor's degree, she had taken more courses in Latin and ancient Rome than she had in English literature. Those classes laid the intellectual foundation for the personal and professional partnership of her life.

Whether it was simply her Midwestern companionability or a more distinctive blend of personal qualities—intelligence, good humor, concern for the well-being of others—Grace eventually emerged as something of a leader among her band of friends. Reading the Wellesley College directories from her undergraduate years, one can follow the way those young women coalesced residentially as time went by. Grace spent her first year at 599 Washington Street in Wellesley Village with seven other students, none of whom seems to have become a lasting friend. In her sophomore year she roomed at Fiske with Betsy Teter; next door were Phyllis Bartlett and Rusty

Montgomery. Fran Ilg was a few doors down the hall. Florence Codman stayed on for a second year at Wood Cottage, the homey shingle-style residence where the future Madame Chiang Kai-Shek had lived as a sophomore at Wellesley in 1914–15. M.G. Coates and another member of the group, Alice E. K. Wood, moved from Wood to Wilder Hall on Norumbega Hill; they turned out to be the advance guard for most of the rest of the gang.

Wilder Hall, completed in 1900, represented a distinct architectural departure from the residential "cottages" of the 1880s. As described in *The Landscape and Architecture of Wellesley College*, "Wilder took the form of a neo-classical, pedimented pavilion of red brick with white trim. Its blind arcade and Palladian motif echoed other Bulfinchian work designed by Boston architects at the turn of the century."[34] By their junior year, Bartlett, Coates, Frick, Montgomery, Teter, and Wood had all moved over to or stayed on at Wilder, where they would remain until graduation. As seniors, Grace's pals joined other Wilder residents in electing their organized and energetic friend from Kansas City president of that house.

The end of Grace's senior year was punctuated by two momentous occasions, the Wellesley College anniversary pageant and commencement for the class of 1925. The observances connected with Wellesley's fiftieth anniversary began on Saturday, May 24, with Tree Day, an annual ceremony in which the freshman class would plant a tree on the green in front of College Hall. Organizers eschewed the elaborate costumed performances of recent years, preferring to revive the simplicity of the first Tree Day in 1877, two years after the college was founded. That initial event featured a handful of undergraduate marchers; forty-eight years later the participants "stretched out to such a distance that when the freshman line had turned onto the green, the seniors could still be seen on the hill by Norumbega" far away.[35] Those marchers, carrying on a sacred tradition, formed a vivid illustration of how much Wellesley College had grown in its first fifty years.

A few days later, on Thursday evening, May 28, a cast of more than two hundred students would perform *The Winged Soul* by Marie Warren Potter (class of 1907) at Alumnae Hall. Designed and directed by Dugald Stuart Walker of New York's Studio Theater, this main event of the Semi-Centennial was described in the *Wellesley College News* of April 16 as the "Most Spectacular Project Ever Launched at Wellesley."[36] Based on Plato's *Phaedrus*, the production sought to express "the beauty of the arts, knowledge, and finally brotherhood, the beauty that 'floods all other loveliness with light.'"[37]

Friday morning, May 29, brought the culmination of the Semi-Centennial, an academic procession in which Wellesley students and faculty were joined by delegates from colleges throughout the United States and around the world, including the College of Kobe, Japan; Constantinople College; Montreal's McGill University; Oxford University; the University of Paris; and Wellesley's sister college, Yenching, in China.[38] Members of the senior class, wearing their caps and gowns, "marched in double file from the hill in back of Founders Hall along the road leading to the chapel. Through those lines came the long procession of guests and delegates to the celebration."[39]

President James Rowland Angell of Yale delivered the Semi-Centennial address, "The Theory and Practice of Education in the American College," at the Houghton Memorial Chapel. Other speakers included President Abbott Lawrence Lowell of Harvard, representing Wellesley's male counterparts throughout New England; Louise Pope Johnson, president of the Wellesley Alumnae Association; and President Mary Emma Woolley of Mount Holyoke College, bearer of greetings from the other women's colleges.[40] As the *Wellesley College News* reported, "President Lowell recalled the ancient myth of Pallas springing out fully armed and endowed with all the wisdom of the time from the forehead of Zeus" (to which Barbara P. McCarthy spunkily replied in her chapter of *Wellesley College, 1875–1975*, "Zeus of course being colleges for men").[41] President Lowell discussed the rapid development of women's colleges and declared, "As the representative of the men's colleges, I am privileged to bring their congratulations, marveling, like other elder brothers, that their younger sister has grown so fair and tall.'"[42]

Wellesley president Ellen Fitz Pendleton took advantage of the fifty-year milestone to confer five honorary doctorates. The laureates were Annie Jump Cannon, the astronomer who devised the Harvard Classification of stellar spectra; Caroline Hazard and Julia Josephine Irvine, former presidents of Wellesley; Helen Barrett Montgomery, a New Testament scholar and dedicated social reformer; and the retiring Katharine Lee Bates, "for forty years the moving force in one of the strongest departments of the College, cherished in the hearts of all alumnae, scholar, poet, and author of one of the greatest of our national hymns." Indeed, when Rev. John J. Callan of Saint Andrew's Episcopal Church had pronounced his benediction, the anniversary celebration came to an end with the singing of Bates's *America the Beautiful*.[43]

That same day, as Barbara McCarthy reported, Wellesley alumnae in Paris held their own Semi-Centennial dinner at the University Women's Club in the sixth arrondissement: "Parisian pride in their *alma mater* was intensified by an anniversary gift to Wellesley College from the French Government:

two large Sèvres vases and busts by Houdon of Washington and Franklin, which had been presented on April 17 in a ceremony at the Elysée Palace."[44] With anniversary events broadcast on WBZ radio, the eyes of the world were on Wellesley College.

On Sunday morning, June 14, Hugh M. Black addressed the class of 1925 at their baccalaureate service. Black was an honorary member of that class and the father of two of its soon-to-be graduates. Seniors were attired in academic dress, and Rev. Black wore scarlet ecclesiastical robes about which he remarked that he had worn "his most gorgeous robes to honor the occasion." He urged the graduating class "to acquire and cultivate the habit of mind which looks on the world in terms of dynamics, not statics, of force, not mass."[45] Eleanor Allen thought so highly of Black's speech that she quoted him twenty-five years later when addressing her classmates gathered for their twenty-fifth reunion. "The words he spoke to us are as full of meaning today as they were then—perhaps more so—and I should like to leave them with you as we begin our next twenty-five years. 'The world is big as we are big enough to use it, beautiful as we have the capacity to see beauty, rich as we acquire richness of the mind. May you, my dears, get as much of your hearts' desire, as much true success and happiness, as I wish for you. It is all well. You are born for the love of God.' "[46] On June 16, 351 Wellesley College seniors received their degrees in the Houghton Memorial Chapel.

The members of the class of 1925 changed in appearance during their college years. As Eleanor Allen remarked to her fellow alumnae at their twenty-fifth reunion, "We arrived as freshmen in what might be called the long—ear-long hair, long skirts, long waists, and long earrings. After the spring vacation of our junior year, seventy-six girls and one faculty member returned with 'bobbed' hair—the reason given [being] that it was time-saving and hygienic, and that it was necessary to the all-around life that women were going to lead."[47] Grace was no exception; her class portrait in the Wellesley *Legenda* shows how much she had changed during her four years at Wellesley. She and her friend Betsy Teter wore almost identical "bobs," cut square around the base of the head to ear length, parted on the side, and stylishly waved.

In the *Legenda* portrait, Grace has come into her own and found a style of clothing that suits her. Gone are the rows of frilly lace that struck such a discordant note in her high school picture. In their place Grace sports the clean, geometric lines of a white blouse with the sailor's collar that was popular early

FIGURE 5. Grace Frick senior portrait, 1925 Wellesley *Legenda*. Wellesley College Archives.

in the twentieth century. That collar is handsomely draped over the lapels of a tailored, waist-length fine wool jacket. Adorning the blouse's V-shaped opening at her throat is a simple string of seed pearls. Grace's gaze rests here again—as in her Westport *Herald* portrait—not on the photographer but on a point in the distance. The enigmatic twinkle in her eye and mischievous half smile on her lips contrast with the grave demeanor of her previous class photo. Her shoulders are square and her bearing confident. One gets the sense that she knows who she is, feels proud of what she has accomplished, and is ready for whatever comes next.

CHAPTER 3 ❦ Pursuing the Academic Life 1925–1933

She also serves . . .

—*Chat Cat*, 1927, paraphrasing John Milton

IN FEBRUARY OF 1926 GRACE Frick returned to Wellesley College to work on a master's degree, moving into a colonial style residence at 18 Upland Road with her friend Phyllis Bartlett. She would be a graduate assistant in the Department of English, taking her place (albeit a lowly one) alongside professors Margaret Sherwood, Martha Shackford, and department chair Laura Lockwood. Appointed to assist Miss Lockwood, Grace assumed academic duties, such as reading student papers, and administrative functions.[1] She also coedited the first alumnae bulletin for her graduating class, called the *Chat Cat*, in 1927.[2] As that first issue of the *Cat* reported, "Our Fricky waltzed back to Wellesley and the Literature Department where she also serves who acts as Miss Lockwood's Assistant. Departmental meetings, faculty receptions and life in Horton House, things of which we commoners dimly remember as having mystic connotations, all have a new aspect for her. Meanwhile she tackles the mastery of the German tongue in three months' time but finds that she is an exception to the laws of heredity."[3]

During spring semester 1926 a highly regarded visiting professor from Great Britain was in residence at Wellesley. Helen Darbishire was a senior tutor and lecturer at Somerville College of Oxford University. Frick took two courses from Darbishire: English Poetry of the Nineteenth Century and English Romanticism. Phyllis Bartlett was also a graduate assistant that year, and she worked with the visiting Miss Darbishire. The experience would be a turning point for her. At Darbishire's urging, Bartlett applied to Somerville College as a candidate for the BLitt, or bachelor of letters, degree. In October of 1926 she enrolled there and undertook a critical study of William Wordsworth. During her two years at Oxford, Phyllis shared an address with

Helen Darbishire within easy walking distance of the lecture and examination halls she frequented.[4] Grace, meanwhile, opting not to write a thesis, completed her master's in only three semesters. A born teacher, she could not wait to lead classes of her own.

In June of 1927 Grace returned to Missouri, where she was hired as an instructor of English at Stephens College in Columbia.[5] Stephens was, like Wellesley, a private liberal arts school for women with a strong Christian—in this case, Baptist—affiliation. Established in 1833, Stephens lays claim to being the second oldest women's college in the United States.[6] The school has always taken pride in its cutting-edge programs, one of which, during World War II, was the first aviation program for women.[7] Frick enthusiastically embraced the school's outlook on the education of young women. In 1926, the year before Grace was hired, Stephens inaugurated a program in equestrian studies that may have been where Grace first developed her enthusiasm for horseback riding. The college had excellent facilities for horsewomen, and riding became for Grace a lifelong passion.

True to its innovative tradition, Stephens was looking to the future. Since 1913 it had been a two-year junior college. Coinciding with Grace's arrival in Columbia, Stephens launched a five-year experimental reorganization of its structure. In the introductory pages to the 1928 *Stephensophia*, the college yearbook, President James M. Wood envisioned a four-year curriculum covering the last two years of high school and the first two years of college. The 1928 *Sophie*, as the yearbook was affectionately known, is a virtual celebration of Stephens's progressive principles and its efforts to improve the quality of women's education. Raymond A. Kent, dean of the College of Liberal Arts at Northwestern University, called the experiments at Stephens "outstanding in their significance," adding that they were "one of the first attempts to apply scientific principles to actual procedure in the field of higher education."[8]

The innovative educational policies being put into practice at Stephens in the 1920s appear all the more remarkable against their historical backdrop. The city of Columbia in that era was a world away from the East Coast bastion of liberalism where Grace had spent most of the previous six years. Central Missouri still bore deep scars from the fighting that had pitched Missourians against one another before, during, and even after the Civil War. As the Mid-Missouri Civil War Project has noted, "guerrilla violence plagued Missouri until Appomattox and beyond." Communities were torn asunder, and "citizens killed each other in small, personal encounters."[9] This experience of a kind of strife that took place not only on traditional battlefields but also in the settings of everyday life continued to shape the culture of the region.

On April 29, 1923, only four years before Grace arrived at Stephens, a thirty-five-year-old black man was lynched in Columbia for a rape he almost certainly did not commit. James T. Scott was a janitor at the University of Missouri, right next door to Stephens College. On April 21 Regina Almstedt, the fourteen-year-old daughter of an MU German professor, identified Scott as having the same mustache and body odor as the man who had raped her the day before. Eight days later an angry mob hauled him from his jail cell. He soon found himself with a noose around his neck on the Old Stewart Road Bridge, surrounded by a thousand jeering spectators, many of them MU students and pillars of the Columbia community. Scott insisted on his innocence, evoking his own teenage daughter and alleging that one of his cellmates had confessed to raping the young white girl. He was hung from the same bridge under which Regina was assaulted. Not until November of 2010 would Scott's record be corrected.[10]

Knowing Grace Frick's youthful sensitivity to the race issue, it is easy to imagine with what horror she learned of Scott's lynching. Like many college towns, Columbia tends now toward the political left. But in Grace's time Stephens students often descended from families that sided with the Confederacy during the Civil War.[11] Frick made a point of including racial tolerance as one of the specific aims of her literature curriculum at Stephens.

Stephens was a small school with a close-knit faculty. During her three years there, Grace came particularly under the influence of her colleague Louise Dudley, who began her extended career at Stephens in 1920 at the age of thirty-five.[12] Two years later, she was acting dean of women. Dudley had grown up in Kentucky and received a bachelor's degree in English literature from Georgetown College in her hometown. In 1910, after lengthy research stints in Paris and London, she received her doctorate from Bryn Mawr College. In 1918, like Grace's brother Fred, Dudley was in France helping with the war effort—in her case as a social worker in French munitions camps under the direction of the Young Women's Christian Association.[13] She loved to travel, and France was one of her favorite destinations.

Dudley was well known at Stephens for her charm, her "taste for adventure," and her all-embracing love of the arts.[14] In 1927, the year Grace arrived, Dudley would establish and head up the Humanities Division at Stephens. John Crighton, a retired Stephens instructor, later noted that "in the late 1920s, Dr. Louise Dudley found no model in the world of education for the invaluable, integrated study of music, literature and art, so Dr. Dudley and her staff created a groundbreaking Humanities core that inspired a nation."[15] Grace Frick was a key member of that staff. As such, she learned a lot about building a well-rounded educational program for young women in a junior college environment. She also made a meaningful contribution to her mentor's conception of the humanities. In 1940 Dudley inscribed a copy of the first edition of her coauthored *The Humanities: Applied Aesthetics* to "Grace Frick, with my love and appreciation of her part in this book."[16] When the fourth edition came out twenty-seven years later, she sent Grace a copy of the book again, writing, "I shall always be grateful to Grace Frick who helped me teach my first class in The Humanities."[17]

Learning her craft at Dudley's side, Grace also followed in her mentor's footsteps as faculty sponsor of the Book Club, one of the college's most popular extracurricular organizations. Meetings were often held in Frick's apartment, and refreshments were always a prominent feature of the gathering. The 1929 *Stephensophia* described one Book Club session as follows: "Picture a cold, disagreeable afternoon, the wind moaning, the snow flakes falling, and inside a cozy apartment, an interested group absorbed in a review of the latest books. After the review has been given, tea is served with dainty sandwiches, and a spirited discussion of the book at hand begins." These meetings may have been the inspiration for a type of "edutainment" that Frick would develop and perfect over the years, apparently on the theory that the most enjoyable way to impart knowledge of other cultures is through a young person's stomach. One evening in 1929, for example, the Book Club held a reading of Russian plays that was accompanied by "true Russian refreshments";[18] the following year there was "an afternoon with Japanese poetry with tea served by dainty maidens, dressed in the native costume."[19] Louise Dudley knew that Grace made the humanities come alive for her students. A warm friendship between the two women endured throughout the rest of Dudley's long life.[20]

Another member of the Humanities faculty, Hazel Mikkelson, is almost certainly responsible for a second personal memento of Grace's years at Stephens that has made its way down to us. It is an inscribed copy of the *Autobiography* of the sixteenth-century Florentine goldsmith and sculptor Benvenuto Cellini, who seems to be at least as well known for his colorful life as for his artwork.[21] From an adolescent brawl that forced him to flee his native Florence to the murder of a rival goldsmith in Rome to an embezzlement charge that got him locked up at the Castel Sant'Angelo, Cellini was often on the wrong side of the law. While Cellini's autobiography is an embellished relation of his life, it is considered to be uniquely valuable as a passionate participant's account of the artistic, social, and political tensions that characterized the late Renaissance.[22] Grace's copy of the book is inscribed,

> To Grace,
> With love and best wishes for a happy Christmas and New Year
> From Hazel
> Columbia, Missouri,
> December 25, 1927.

Mikkelson was an instructor of violin, teaching in the Music department with Grace's housemates Nesta Williams and Honor Winer. Though Grace was particularly drawn to the literature of Elizabethan England, Cellini's account of his trials and achievements, conflicts and adventures in continental Europe during that same century would have fascinated her.

With the end of her first year at Stephens in the spring of 1928, Grace was free to spend the summer as she chose. Her friend Phyllis Bartlett was at Oxford, which gave Grace the perfect opportunity to make her maiden voyage to the country whose literary masters were the central focus of her professional life. On Wednesday, June 6, third-class ticket in hand, Grace boarded the Cunard Line's RMS *Berengaria*, bound for England, at New York City's West Fourteenth Street pier. Years later, in trying to convince her friends Paul and Gladys Minear to accept from her a financial boost as they prepared to embark upon a year abroad, Grace wrote about a windfall that she had received just before leaving for England: "The first time I went to Europe, I had an unexpected gift of a hundred dollars at the Pier on the moment of departure. The exhilaration of that moment (when I was already taken care of, and had only my own fares to think of) is something that I would like to pass on."[23]

On arriving in Southampton on June 13, Grace traveled to Oxford, where she would stay with Phyllis in Helen Darbishire's Beaumont Street townhouse. Phyllis had successfully completed her Wordsworth project and passed her viva, or oral exam, four days earlier.[24] Grace was there to watch Phyllis receive her British degree at a ceremony held on June 28.[25] Phyllis was a spunky young woman with a sense of adventure. Despite her scholarly prowess, she never took herself too seriously. Years later, she would make light of her British academic success in a manner that friends say was typical of her. Referring to the fur lining of the ceremonial hood she wore, along with an Oxford velvet beret instead of a mortar board, for occasions requiring academic regalia, Phyllis jokingly told her Queens College student Ann Birstein, "It's supposed to be ermine, but it's mangy spotted rabbit!"[26]

Grace took advantage of this first trip to England to pursue her literary and theatrical interests on their native soil. Stratford-upon-Avon was only an hour away. The Oxford Playhouse was a one-minute walk down Beaumont Street from Phyllis's lodgings, and the Oxford University Dramatics Society was staging John Galsworthy's *Escape* there that summer, as well as the English premiere of Eugene O'Neill's *Where the Cross Is Made*.[27] But Phyllis had completed her degree, and she was eager to reward herself with some less bookish recreation. Like Grace, she loved hiking and traveling. Phyllis had spent the previous summer touring London, Paris, Heidelberg, and Zurich. Now she and Grace would join up with their Wellesley friend Rusty Montgomery for a summer ramble in the north of England. As the *Chat Cat* would report, the three chums "toured the Lake Country and the hi-ways and by-ways of merrie England."[28]

En route to the lakes region, on July 2, 1928, the women stopped in York, where Grace bought herself a copy of the Haworth Edition of Elizabeth Gaskell's *Life of Charlotte Brontë*.[29] It was a story, as the many passages annotated by Grace suggest, that had resonance for her. Charlotte Brontë's mother had died when she was five years old, leaving Charlotte and five sisters and a brother behind. When her older sisters fell victim to "consumption," the eleven-year-old Charlotte became a motherly presence for her siblings and, even after the success of *Jane Eyre* years later, remained devoted to caring for her elderly father. She disagreed with her sisters Emily and Anne about what makes a compelling novelistic heroine, and the popularity of "plain, small, and unattractive" Jane proved her right. She even went so far as to consider her sisters "morally wrong" to make their heroines beautiful, an attitude appreciatively underlined in Grace's copy of Gaskell's *Life*.[30]

Another book purchased on this trip casts a literary light on the Wellesley chums' British walking tour: William Wordsworth's *Guide to the Lakes*, bought by Grace on July 5 at Read's Book Shop in the Lake District village of Grasmere. Wordsworth spent most of his life in the English lake country and describes the region in his 1802 poem "A Farewell" as "the loveliest spot that man hath ever found." On the blank pages at the back of the *Guide*,

Grace noted that she and her friends took "a series of walks about Easedale," featuring a well-known mountain lake.[31]

After this trek in the lake country, Rusty Montgomery went her own way, and Phyllis set about convincing a reluctant Grace that they should visit Paris together. Grace had been in England for less than a month, and she had spent a long time preparing for this trip. She had not yet gone to half the places that she wanted to see. But Phyllis was insistent, and Grace finally gave in. After all, their Wellesley classmate "M.G." Coates was spending the summer with her family on rue Jasmin in the sixteenth arrondissement.[32] It would be marvelous to see her. Coates had finished nursing school and would be working for the Henry Street Nursing Staff in New York City that fall. As the *Chat Cat* reported, "She spent the summer in Paris, where . . . most of Wellesley College visited her. Grace Frick and Phyllis Bartlett were two of M.G.'s visitors. Alice [E. K. Wood] visited her too but unfortunately missed both Gracie and Phil."[33]

Grace fell in love with the City of Light and, forsaking a planned return to England, decided to remain there through the end of her summer vacation. Phyllis knew Paris quite well, and for Grace's first fortnight in the city she served as her escort. Over the following month, Grace continued on her own to immerse herself in the architectural, artistic, and culinary splendor of the French capital, meandering along narrow streets or loping down wide, tree-lined boulevards, taking in shows, trying out her French, marveling at the wealth and diversity of the city's cultural treasures. She did not leave France until August 21, when she boarded the SS *California* in Le Havre. Ten days later, having had the time of her life, she was back in New York.[34]

Some twenty years after the fact, Grace reflected on that first taste of Paris in a letter to Paul and Gladys Minear, whom she wished to help choose a destination in Europe to tour briefly with their young children. Grace had been taken off guard at twenty-five by the cultural and religious differences between France, a Latin and Catholic country, and America: "I remember how strongly I felt the difference myself," she wrote,

and how ill-prepared I was for it. Forgive me if I attribute some of my own limitations to you, even when I know that some of your preparation is much better than mine was; but I do know that the first shock of the differences will be strong for you as it was for me, and you will not have the time in France, and perhaps the personal guidance, that I was lucky enough to have there even on my first visit of six weeks, long before I knew any French people there.

Surprisingly, given how central France would one day become in Grace's life, she goes on to say,

> I did not even want to go to Paris on my first visit to Europe. . . . I was sure that I knew too little of France to understand it or like it, and equally sure that a single summer in England was far too little for my desires at the time. An American friend persuaded me that I ought to go with her to Paris while she could offer me some guidance, and while a classmate of ours was in residence there. Imagine my surprise, therefore, in realizing on the first evening of my arrival that Paris is as beautiful as everyone says that it is. I changed my plans and stayed there and only there till time to sail for home. But I was a freer lance than you will be, perhaps. My mind is divided for you![35]

However free a lance she may have been that summer, Grace returned to Columbia in September to resume her instructorship at Stephens. Unearthing information about the ninety-year-old appointment of a faculty member at a college that had not yet begun to keep systematic records is no mean feat. There are no personnel files from that time, no contracts from which one might learn the terms of Frick's employment, no general information about faculty salaries; not even a photograph of Grace in any of the college yearbooks from that era.[36] Fortunately, however, one relic of the late 1920s was preserved all these years in the Stephens College Archives that, despite its uninspiring title, is nothing less than Grace Frick's paean to the value of literature. It is an 11,000-word, bound and numbered typescript, composed after Frick left Stephens, to be used by her successors as a guide to teaching English literature to students who may not have had the benefit of serious literary training. Entitled "A Survey Unit for the Study of English Literature," the text reveals not only the scope of Frick's knowledge of her field but also how deeply she had engaged with Louise Dudley's vision of the interconnectedness of the arts.

Frick's "Survey Unit" is a distillation of what one dedicated young instructor learned teaching English II, Introduction to English Literature, over the course of three years. Into each successive syllabus Grace incorporated lessons from the previous year or years, finally extracting from all of them what she deemed would be most helpful to the person who would follow in her footsteps. Her pedagogical strategy evolved over the period from a primarily lecture-based format during her first year to a mainly discussion-oriented approach with only one formal lecture during her third. She would be right at home in the classroom today.

Frick saw literature as a record of civilization and the arts more generally as "a subject which deals primarily with meaning and value in life."[37]
She sought to introduce each student to all of the great arts as a foundation
for "increasing his knowledge in these fields and thereby enriching his own
life." The text used in the course, at least in Grace's second and third years
at Stephens, was Louise Dudley's *Study of Literature*, the preface of which
emphasizes "knowledge and understanding of the great classics" and "the
ability to give an intelligent account of one's literary likes and dislikes."[38] In
addition to training young women to judge for themselves, Grace's summa
places stress on intellectual tolerance.[39] It is divided into six major topics, all
of them covered in detail, with specific recommendations regarding the most
propitious timing for the sequencing of increasingly complex course content.

Regarding the relevance of literary study to modern life, especially for
young female students, Frick presses home the point that "for the twentieth
century woman an adequate means of communication is just as essential as it
is now and always has been for men. The college girl of today expects to be
able to speak readily in public, whether it be in formal address, in the reading
of a prepared paper, or in informal discussion at a club or public meeting."
More important, she notes, literature introduces us to people and ways of life
we might not otherwise encounter: "Most of us come to college with a fairly
limited experience, necessarily limited because of our age and sometimes
limited by other conditions. We continue to learn more about life, of course,
each day of our existence but by studying the records of past experience we
can begin at once to enlarge our own experience and to prepare ourselves for
fuller and richer living."[40]

Not only does every human being have "a desire for and a capacity for
enjoying the truly beautiful things in life," a quality that we sometimes refer to as "our *aesthetic* nature," but studying the arts broadens and enno-
bles the mind. Frick makes a point of zeroing in on a specific type of mind
broadening:

Through the best literature of different periods and different races, we can gain
a sort of vicarious experience which may serve as the first step toward greater
universal sympathy.

   Too often we are not conscious of how many and how petty our individual
prejudices are until we have those prejudices challenged by the thought pro-
cesses of some artist. In a class of students composed both of northerners and
southerners a sequence of poems from an anthology of Negro poetry proved
startling because the poet had imagined for himself a black Madonna tenderly

soothing a little black Christ. No one in the class would admit that she had a race prejudice and yet each member of the class was inclined at first thought to resent the fact that a Negro poet should picture Mary and her child as members of his race rather than of the white race. The moral of this experience is obvious. We do need our sympathies "stretched," often in the place where we least suspect the need of this "stretching."[41]

Grace, who once saw from afar a Ku Klux Klan cross-burning, does not preach to her students from on high; rather, she counts herself among them, thus allowing the young women to recognize themselves without feeling that their biases should be a source of shame.[42] For Grace, the scholarly point of view is an attitude of open-mindedness and one that should extend beyond the bounds of intellectual inquiry to all of life.[43]

Of course, Grace also extols the virtues of studying French, German, Latin, and Greek, as well as history, religion, economics, psychology, philosophy, and sociology, for what they can contribute to a deeper understanding of literary works. Nor should one overlook the other arts, such as drama, dance, the visual arts, and particularly music. But most surprising, given Grace's Elizabethan bent, may be how current her recommendations were with regard to contemporary writers. In speaking of what one can learn from books about places one has never seen, Frick gives the example of a British novel, only three years old at the time she was writing, that has since become a modernist classic: "In 1927 Virginia Woolf, a prominent contemporary English novelist, published *To the Lighthouse* which has its setting in the Hebrides, and the theme of this novel is brought out as much by the wild storm winds of this remote region, as by the characters themselves." She finds "an unusual number of new currents both in poetry and prose, and particularly in drama in this post-war period." Two leaders whom she singles out for mention, representing disparate tendencies of modern poetry, had recently died: the American modernist Amy Lowell in 1925 and the more conventional Englishman Robert Bridges in 1930. Bridges did important work on prosody that "dispens[ed] with classical models entirely and return[ed] to the early English accentual system." Lowell left behind her "not only a series of volumes of poetry, but the finest scholarly biography of the poet Keats which has ever been written."[44]

The contemporary British and American authors whom Frick saw as advancing new methods in both poetry and prose were Virginia Woolf, Humbert Wolfe, E. M. Forster, and Gertrude Stein. Her "Survey" discusses the husband-and-wife team of Leonard and Virginia Woolf, whose Hogarth

Press published innovators such as T. S. Eliot; Sigmund Freud; Edith, Osbert, and Sacheverell Sitwell; and Gertrude Stein. Stein, she notes, "has created a sensation in modern literature by dispensing with the element of consecutive development of ideas in her literary work. She throws her chief emphasis upon the sounds of the words, and in her more extreme work, makes apparently no appeal to thought other than through the repetition of certain sounds and combinations." In what is surely the most ironic passage in her essay, Frick comments on one literary genre whose glory days she thought were gone: "Historical novels continue with a steady popularity although we can point to no examples in the twentieth century which give much promise of becoming classics."[45] Little did she know what a role she would play in transforming that state of affairs!

When Grace arrived at Stephens she was a healthy, energetic twenty-five-year-old. In the normal course of things, she would have been exploring her sexuality, whether with men or with women. Commentators have wondered about the nature of Grace's relationship with Phyllis Bartlett, who eventually married late in life, and with Ruth Hall, who remained single, but there is no documentary basis on which to speculate that either of these friendships was anything other than platonic.[46] Nor is there any evidence from her years at Wellesley that Grace ever dated anyone while she was there. In fact, Florence Codman, the only college chum we know of whose primary adult relationship was lesbian, told Josyane Savigneau that she was "not sure if Grace had had other women in her life before Marguerite. Or even other love affairs."[47] We do know, however, thanks to a postcard sent to Grace in 1933, that she had a special friend at Yale University. "How are you and your friend, to whom please remember me," wrote Marianne Zerner from Berne, Switzerland, where she was studying German literature and philology.[48] "Friend" was often a code word for "lover" in that era—and for many lesbians, including Yourcenar, well beyond that time.

As familiar as Frick was with contemporary British and American literature, she could hardly have failed to hear the hue and cry that greeted Radclyffe Hall's *Well of Loneliness* on both sides of the Atlantic in midsummer 1928. The book, which was released in Great Britain during Grace's first stay in Paris, quickly made its way to both France and the United States. It wasn't banned in Boston or New York, but Hall's publisher, Jonathan Cape, was brought up on charges of obscenity. The ensuing trial brought the book and the issue of "sexual inversion" to the attention of an increasingly larger public. Forster and Woolf lent their stature to the fight against suppressing

The Well, penning a joint letter to the *Nation and Atheneum* and going so far as to attend the obscenity trial. The denizens of Bloomsbury were by and large unenthused about the traditional, even antiquated, style of Hall's novel, but they were deeply disturbed by the implications that censorship of such a work would have on the creative freedom of all writers.[49] The British magistrate nonetheless ordered that the book be destroyed, finding that a literary plea to tolerate a vice as insidious as homosexuality could not possibly be anything other than obscene.

In the United States, meanwhile, *The Well* had gone through six reprintings before the British verdict was rendered that November. It faced obscenity challenges here too, but, held to a more lenient standard than in the British legal system, it was cleared of all charges in April of 1929. In its first year of U.S. publication, *The Well* sold more than one hundred thousand copies. It also prospered in France, where issues of sexuality were less apt to scandalize.

Eleven years later the fictionalized account of another lesbian life, this time an American one, was released: *Diana, a Strange Autobiography*, by the pseudonymous Diana Frederics. By the quality of its prose and the forthrightness of its narrative, it was a remarkable work for its day and remains one still. *Diana* tells the story of a brilliant and intrepid young woman who, already as an adolescent, confronts her homosexual leanings head-on. With a modicum of support from a respected sibling, and despite the many obstacles strewn along her path, Diana comes to accept who she is and forges for herself an independent life as a teacher and writer. Unlike most other such novels of the 1920s and 1930s, *Diana* ends with its protagonist's professional and sexual fulfillment. If it merits mention here, it is because *Diana*'s real-life author, Frances V. Rummell, and Grace Frick taught at Stephens College together.[50] Frances was four or five years younger than Grace, and she taught French. When Rummell started working at Stephens, Grace had just been dazzled by her discovery of Paris. She and Rummell both taught in the oh-so-interconnected humanities, more than likely in the same building. As outgoing as Grace was, and knowing what a difference a mentor can make from her experience at Wellesley, she undoubtedly welcomed young Frances into the fold, doing her best to smooth her transition from student to teacher.

Thanks to *Diana, a Strange Autobiography*, we can picture what it might have been like to be a lesbian faculty member at a women's college in the late 1920s. Like Grace, the fictional Diana had gotten her master's degree at an all-female school in Massachusetts. A few years later, having made an eye-opening tour of Europe, she returned to that college and its small town with her woman lover to teach French. Professionally, Diana was a standout. Hired to cover technical language courses, she soon was asked to give a seminar in nineteenth-century French literature. Everything seemed to be working out perfectly, until one day she was called into the office of the dean for an unspecified reason. The dean's embarrassed opening question was, said Diana, "to my horror, clue enough" as to his purpose: " 'Do you mind telling me how long your friend—I understand she is an artist—has been with you?' " Trying to find the right words, the dean adds, " 'The teachers resent your lack of sociability. . . . I believe you should know there have been innuendoes here and there about your friendship.' " The school did not want to lose Diana because of her excellent teaching and scholarship. The dean suggested that she live—alone—the following year in a campus dormitory and make an effort to befriend other faculty members. Diana's mind raced: "I was so tense my hands were stiff. Of course I had been all kinds of a fool in my wishful thinking, and now I was discovered. Dishonor and shame pressed in on me—such anguish as I have never known."[51]

Grace was never the subject of such an incident during her years at Stephens, but lesbian educators of that era lived with the fear of exposure every day. Many young women undoubtedly chose to deny, ignore, or carefully conceal any same-sex attraction they might feel for fear of losing their job or their dignity. Was Grace one of their number? Or did she cross her personal Rubicon in response to the singular allure of an extraordinary Frenchwoman? We may never have a definitive answer to these questions, but there are indications that Grace was more comfortable with her sexuality than even the supposedly notorious womanizer Marguerite Yourcenar.

While she was at Stephens, Grace became part of a vibrant academic community. She loved her work, and she was inspired by her colleagues. Her horizons were also inestimably broadened, beyond the walls of the classroom, by her trip to England and by her spontaneous discovery of the movable feast that was Paris. She did not know then what the future had in store—and it held many surprises. But she knew that she had found her calling. It was time to craft a plan that would take her, like so many other gifted graduates of Wellesley's Department of English Literature, to Yale University.

Grace left Columbia in June of 1930 to return to Kansas City. She would move back in with the LaRues until the fall of 1931. Also in the house besides Uncle George and Aunt Dolly were Grace's older brother Gage, who at thirty-one was still unmarried and working for the LaRue Printing Company, and her eighteen-year-old cousin Nancy. Nancy had transferred from Southwest High to Notre Dame de Sion in February of 1929 and was in her senior year there.[52] She was not a scholar like Grace, but she was an affectionate and caring young woman.[53] Fred, the eldest of the Frick siblings, had married by this time and left home.

Grace spent the academic year 1930–31 commuting forty miles to the University of Kansas in Lawrence, where she took two advanced courses.[54] In the spring of 1931 she was accepted by Yale's PhD program in English literature. Yale was still an all-male undergraduate school, but the administration allowed qualified women to undertake graduate degrees. Frick moved to New Haven that October, taking a room in the women's graduate residence at 158 Whitney Avenue. That stately building, with its spacious back lawn and lovely porch, occupied a choice spot next to the president's house and gardens.[55] It was there that Grace met and befriended Paul and Gladys Minear.

Paul was working on his doctorate in the New Testament at Yale. He and his wife had taken a position as the host and hostess of the women's residence in the fall of 1930. Gladys also worked in the circulation department at Yale's Sterling Memorial Library to supplement the couple's income. As she once wrote of their house-hosting experience, "Paul kept the coal furnace functioning, and the maids, who cleaned every day, were responsible to me. I think there were about twenty women in those gorgeous great rooms."[56]

Grace would later tell some younger friends about that era and the Minears,

> They had a sort of ground-floor apartment in this old inn, on Whitney Avenue
> in New Haven, in which the women were quartered as a dormitory. It was old,
> and there was this enormous furnace, which Paul's job was to fire. He'd get up
> at four in the morning, and sometimes it would go and sometimes it wouldn't.
> He'd have to get up again at five, while he was writing his doctoral dissertation.
> My room was a tiny thing over their kitchen, and there was a back stairs. . . .
> I had the liberty of going down and getting anything I wanted, particularly
> bananas, out of their larder. They were Middle Westerners by the way, people
> from a small town in Iowa who dairy farmed. Tops! I never saw any two people
> open to every opportunity that that university city had to offer.[57]

Grace would remain at 158 Whitney, raiding the Minears' stash of bananas, until June of 1933.

At the end of her first year at Yale, Frick told her former Wellesley classmates what it was like to be a woman in a predominantly male environment: "My life is that of a 'Yale Lady,' as we are not too happily designated by the less kind. No one treats us as badly as the name implies, however, and life is more than fair, I can tell you. My courses are corking and I have four splendid people, Tucker Brooke, Karl Young, [Alexander] Witherspoon and [William Clyde] DeVane. If I could just get one or two things half-way finished all would be serene."[58]

Grace was no slouch, however. According to her transcript from Yale, she satisfied three foreign language requirements—in French, German, and Latin—in one fell swoop, on October 14, 1931, not long after her arrival in New Haven. Yale granted her a year's worth of credit toward the PhD for her Wellesley master's degree and the graduate courses she had taken at the University of Kansas. She passed her oral examinations for the doctorate on January 20, 1932, after only one semester of coursework.[59]

Frick's professors at Yale were, of course, all men; indeed, the first female instructor to get tenure in the English department there was not appointed until 1957.[60] During her first year Grace took four yearlong courses ranging from Medieval Drama through the Victorian Poets. Predictably, she excelled in the subjects she loved, earning Yale's highest mark in both English Drama, 1500–1642, and Victorian Poets. She made do with passing the other two.

Frick excelled again in 1932–33 in Tucker Brooke's Shakespeare seminar. Knowing Grace's love of the Bard, Phyllis Bartlett gave her J. Dover Wilson's *Essential Shakespeare*, fresh off the presses, for Christmas that year.[61] Phyllis by this time was teaching English and working on her own PhD at the University of Wisconsin. The Shakespeare volume was both a memento of the 1928 trip they had taken to Stratford-upon-Avon and a useful addition to Grace's library. On June 6, 1933, Yale officially accepted Grace's dissertation proposal. Under the direction of DeVane, she would investigate not an Elizabethan poet or playwright but "The First Period of the Poetry of George Meredith from 1851 to 1862."[62] This was neither a topic of her choosing nor an author who interested her.[63] Nonetheless, her plan upon completing her coursework was to spend the next year writing her dissertation back home in Kansas City. That is not exactly what happened, however.

CHAPTER 4 ❦ Time Out

1933–1937

For there is no friend like a sister.

—Christina Rossetti

IN THE SPRING OF 1933 Grace Frick returned to a Kansas City that was under the control of Tom Pendergast's political machine. According to an online political exhibit of the University of Missouri, "Louisiana had Huey Long, New York had Tammany Hall, and Chicago had Daly, but for sheer gall, guts, and greed, no town could match the political machinations of Kansas City's Thomas J. "Boss Tom" Pendergast. From honest hard-working ward heelers to ruthless office seekers, Pendergast held the city's political players in the palm of his hand for nearly two decades."[1] Tom had come to Kansas City from St. Joseph, Missouri, in the late nineteenth century to join his brother James "Big Jim" Pendergast, a saloon owner and political strongman, and Tom initially enriched himself in the liquor trade by setting up gambling establishments.[2] After Big Jim's death, he was elected to his brother's former seat on the city council. Jim's political organization grew increasingly powerful, and increasingly corrupt, under Boss Tom's stewardship. Like many machine politicians, Pendergast traded jobs for favors, rigged elections, rewarded the loyal, and punished those who crossed him. Though he did not enrich himself by dipping directly into city coffers, the influence that he exercised over elections, bond issues, and city officials brought many a lucrative contract to businesses he owned. While the rest of the nation struggled under the weight of the Depression in the early 1930s, Kansas City built a new county courthouse, city hall, police headquarters, and a municipal auditorium using Pendergast materials.

Upon her return, Grace joined the National Youth Movement, an independent organization of young, college-educated citizens formed to oust the Pendergast machine.[3] For two years she served as the group's subchairman in the Eighth Ward.[4] Their effort failed in 1934, when four people were killed and several injured in polling place violence.[5] Two years later sixty thousand "ghosts" registered to vote in Kansas City, handing Pendergast another triumph.[6]

It was during the bloody election of 1934 that Grace had a personal run-in with Pendergast's minions. She had driven to the polling place, eager to vote against the slate of Boss Tom's loyalists. Always attuned to what was going on around her, Grace suddenly realized that the man ahead of her in line was attempting to pass himself off as a neighbor of the LaRues who had died the previous year. In other words, he was putting into practice the proverbial recommendation of machine politicians to "vote early and often." Grace could not keep quiet in the face of what she knew to be an act of fraud. Challenging the voter's false identity, she promptly found herself escorted from the polling place by local police. Given the unprecedented level of election-related violence that day, things could have gone a lot worse. But Grace would never forget what it felt like to realize that the very officers responsible for ensuring her safety and protecting her rights as a citizen were cogs in the Pendergast machine.[7]

Like all machines, Pendergast's eventually broke down. And women ran the campaign to destroy it. Many businessmen did not dare oppose Pendergast for fear of never getting another government contract. Women, however, could fly under the radar. They handed out cookies at the polls along with leaflets supporting reformers. They pinned little brooms to their dresses, symbolizing their desire to sweep the city clean of political corruption. (Some of the crusaders arrived at the polls with real brooms!) In April of 1940, operation "clean sweep" finally succeeded, as the *Kansas City Star* put it, in giving Pendergast and his candidates "the bum's rush."[8] Nearly three hundred election workers and Pendergast lieutenants were tried for election rigging and related charges. Not one was acquitted. Boss Tom himself went to prison for income tax evasion.[9] His hold on Kansas City had finally been broken.

Meanwhile, things had taken an unexpected turn in the LaRue household. Grace's cousin Nancy Gallagher had graduated from Notre Dame de Sion High School in Kansas City in June of 1931.[10]

The Sion order was founded in Paris by a Jewish convert to Catholicism in the mid-nineteenth century. Its distinctive early commitment was then, as it still is today, to "make no distinction between Latin and Greek, Moslem and

FIGURE 6. Nancy Gallagher senior portrait, 1931 *Sionian*.

Jew."[11] When the Sisters of Sion built their first campus on Locust Street in 1929, their establishment was considered a "school for the daughters of the area's elite families."[12] It is still flourishing today.

The LaRues were Presbyterians, and Uncle George had served for many years as a trustee of Kansas City's Second Presbyterian Church.[13] Nancy and Grace were both brought up Protestant, but Nancy's father was Catholic, and Nancy had originally been baptized in that religion.[14] The year after her high school graduation, Nancy decided to become a Catholic nun. She entered the novitiate in September of 1932 at the mother house of the Sisters of Sion at 61 rue Notre-Dame-des-Champs in Paris.[15] Frick at the time was beginning a challenging semester at Yale. Nancy's departure was frowned on by all the members of her family, but the young woman had just turned twenty-one, and there was nothing anyone could do to stop her.

Nancy made the transition from the postulancy into the novitiate on May 14, 1933. In that era, novices of Notre Dame de Sion were required to give up their given and family names and take new names to express their new identities. It was customary to choose a religious name in honor of a saint or family member, and the Sisters of Sion traditionally included Mary in their names. Nancy seems to have chosen to honor her father, John Gallagher, in calling herself Sister Marie Yann. By the time she entered the religious life in 1932, Gallagher had died.[16] Since names containing John were popular because of John the Baptist, Yann, a Breton equivalent, may have been the only available expedient.[17]

FIGURE 7. Sister Marie Yann. Frick family archives.

The family estrangement must have been hard for both Grace and Nancy after Nancy took the veil. The two girls had grown close during the summer of 1918, when their mothers, May and Cora, were dying. In mid-1934 the LaRues decided that the time had come to heal the family rift. Their younger niece had been away for nearly two years and showed no signs of abandoning her vocation, so they made a plan to visit her with Grace. Aunt Dolly LaRue left for France in July, stopping in Italy and Switzerland en route. Grace and Uncle George sailed to France together on the SS *Bremen*, leaving New York on August 4 for the six-day crossing. On arriving in Cherbourg, Grace and her uncle boarded the boat train to Paris, where they took rooms at the small but upscale Hôtel Wagram. An artifact from that time preserved now at Petite Plaisance suggests that Grace and Unk had originally planned to stay at the Hôtel Claridge, where Grace may have gone with Phyllis Bartlett in 1928. It is a postcard featuring a photograph of the Claridge overlooking Sunday strollers on a wide, pedestrian-only stretch of the Champs-Élysées. On the back Grace had jotted down the names of four other fashionable hotels. First on the list is "Hôtel Wagram, 208 Rue de Rivoli," and next to it the phonetic pronunciation "Vogram," for use by a still timid French speaker in a Parisian taxicab.[18] After a short stay in Paris, Grace and her uncle joined Dolly at Évry-Petit-Bourg in the French countryside between Paris and Fontainebleau.[19] Sister Yann was on retreat there at Sion's Grandbourg Convent with her fellow novices, who would make their first vows in the fall.[20]

With the family duly reconciled, Dolly, George, and Grace returned to Paris for another brief stay at the Hôtel Wagram before going their separate ways. George left for New York and Kansas City on August 21. Dolly took a side trip to Stratford-upon-Avon, then followed her husband back home. Grace visited Oxford again, then stayed long enough in London to do "a bit of study" at the British Museum and attend a performance of Alfred Sangster's *The Brontës* at the Piccadilly Theatre.[21] Her next stop was Cologne, Germany, a city whose nineteenth-century tensions between Roman Catholics and Prussian Protestants cast an ironic reflection on the LaRue family rupture that had just been set right. This was Grace's first visit to the country of her German ancestors, though she did not travel to Salzwedel. But she did go from Cologne down the Rhine, staying at youth hostels along the way— quite a change of pace from the likes of the Claridge or the Hôtel Wagram.

Dolly LaRue's youngest sister, Georgia—known to Grace as Aunt George—was also in Europe at this time. Then in her midfifties, Georgia was sometimes called the femme fatale of the Self family for her good looks and flirtatious nature. Grace met her in Munich in September. From there the two women traveled to Vienna, where Grace, a music lover, remained a bit longer than her aunt before returning to France. The two met up again in Paris and left for the United States together on October 10 aboard the SS *Île de France*, with its four-deck-high Grand Foyer.

No one knows how much progress Grace had made on "The Early Poetry of George Meredith" during the year off from school that she was supposed to be devoting to her dissertation. But she wanted to return to Yale that fall and put her nose to the grindstone. Instead of heading west with Aunt George, Grace stayed in New York, where Ruth Hall had an apartment. Ruth had been hired by a leading law firm in that city, Sullivan and Cromwell, and had been working there for three years. Both women were looking forward to Grace being nearby in New Haven again.

That agreeable prospect was not to be realized, however. No sooner had Grace caught her breath in New York than a telegram arrived from Kansas City announcing that George "Unk" LaRue had had a stroke and was gravely ill. There would now be no question of returning to Yale. Grace left for home on the next train.[22]

George LaRue's health only worsened over the next several months; in June of 1935 Grace wrote in her chronology, "Unk at very lowest point." The years that followed were neither productive nor pleasant for Grace. Things got so bad that on one alumni report she listed her occupation as "nursing"![23]

Grace did participate in the Kansas City Wellesley Club in the 1930s, where she worked on the scholarship and fund-raising committees. But despite her fond attachment to her alma mater, she did not attend her tenth reunion, held in June of 1935. One of her British friends, Margaret Bottrall, who had been at Yale with Frick as a Hartness Commonwealth Scholar, sent her a long, detailed letter in late 1934 about her recent marriage and exciting relocation with her professor husband to Singapore.[24] Grace, meanwhile, was treading water.

Across the ocean Cousin Nancy had taken her first vows at the mother house of Notre Dame de Sion in November of 1934. Shortly thereafter she was sent to Bayswater, England, to train as a teacher. In the fall of 1935, according to archival records, she began to develop lung problems and was sent back to France, to the Sion house at Issy-les-Moulineaux, just southwest of Paris, which was "reserved for invalids of the congregation." The Bayswater house journal recorded "with affection the departure of Sr. Yann from the community."[25]

Grace's version of what happened to her cousin is reminiscent of what she recalled about the onset of her mother's fatal illness back in Kansas City. Sister Yann, said Grace years later, "caught a terrible cold in a good drenching rain on a picnic and got TB."[26] Whether that rainy picnic was the culprit or not, Sister Yann did indeed have tuberculosis. Not until 1944, with the discovery of streptomycin, was there a reliable cure for what had long been the world's most lethal contagious disease.[27]

As an early 1937 Sionian letter from the mother house in Paris reported, when Sister Yann had arrived at Issy-les-Moulineaux in 1935 she was "already very ill but still able to share in community life, which she held to very much because she had an ardent nature, faithful to the teachings that she received in the novitiate. . . . Twice she went to the hospital, which was a real trial for her because she had one desire: to remain with her religious family."[28] By early January 1937 Sister Yann's condition was critical. Uncle George, having only partially recovered from his own grave illness, dispatched Grace to France to do whatever could be done for her cousin.

Grace arrived in Paris on February 4, 1937. The next morning she made the short trip to the Sion house at 11 rue Jules Guesde in Issy. Sister Yann's doctor also came to see his patient that day. The ailing young nun was on her deathbed but alert and able, to Grace's great relief, to communicate with her cousin. Every available treatment had been tried in vain. After Sister Yann returned from her second stay at the American Hospital, "she received Extreme Unction with great fervour, although she kept hope until the end that a cure was possible." Two days later, at the age of twenty-five, "dear little Sister Yann died. Miss Frick had just arrived and thus was present for her final moments."[29] Grace spent that day with the sisters at Issy, meeting with a Dr. Blanchart late that afternoon.

As the Sionion letter concluded about Sister Marie Yann,

> The good Lord himself gave her a great joy. On the eve of her death a cousin that she loved as a sister arrived from America just in time to embrace her. She was a witness to her happiness, while remaining perfectly religious, because her illness made her grow in the love of God. A complaint never left her lips and she had multiplied her sacrifices for the intentions of the Congregation, especially for Kansas City and the Mothers who helped her in her vocation. She was able to communicate until her last day, Sunday, 7 February, and fell asleep as a child in the arms of the Virgin of Sion.[30]

Sister Yann's corpse was laid in its coffin at dawn on February 9. At eight o'clock the same morning Grace Frick arrived at Issy-les-Moulineaux for her cousin's funeral mass, which was held in an ancillary chapel there. Mother Théotime rode with Grace in the latter's automobile to the nearby cemetery where Sister Yann would be buried. Though it had rained all night, the storm had given way to an unexpectedly beautiful morning.[31]

Over the following few days, Grace made two more trips back to Issy. On February 11 she met with a Dr. Fareil, who had been involved in Sister Yann's care. Three days later, "visit of Miss Frick" is the sole entry in the Issy house journal. On March 8 Grace attended a requiem mass in memory of Sister Yann at Issy-les-Moulineaux.[32] Back in Missouri, a similar mass for the former Grace Marian "Nancy" Gallagher was held two days later.[33]

One friend of the LaRues and their niece in Kansas City wrote a long, mournful letter to Grace shortly after Nancy's death. Emily Sophian had graduated from Notre Dame de Sion High School in 1930, a year ahead of Nancy Gallagher.[34] She had known Nancy well and was devastated by her death:

> Dearest Grace—
>
> How good you were to write me! I wanted so much to hear from you that I was almost afraid to hope. And your letter was wonderful. It told me so much I wanted—needed—to know, and although, inevitably, it hurt badly, it helped too a great deal as you must have known it would. I deeply appreciate your getting the bed jacket and flowers for her. You spent the money just as I had hoped you would and exactly as I would have myself had I been able to be there. I'm so glad too that you got the watch. It's the one thing I wanted. I feel very much in your debt and thank you for everything with all my heart.
>
> In spite of the fact that I was prepared for it, the news of Nancy's death came as a terrific shock. It left me with a sense of loss intensified rather than lessened by the fact that I felt that I was losing her for the second time. My reaction when she entered the convent was one of such extreme bitterness that I felt for a long time as though I had been robbed of a friend whom I needed and loved above all else and toward whom I never expected to feel the same again. With the gradual passing of the worst of that bitterness came naturally the return of all the friendship I had ever felt for her but it was tinged with an unreality and remoteness that her being a nun made inevitable.[35]

Sophian was incensed by the Sions' Catholic platitudes about her friend's death, and she knew Frick would share the feeling. "I can readily imagine what an ordeal this whole thing has been for you," she said, "and hope that the rest of your trip will compensate for it to some extent."[36]

On April 8, 1937, the Sisters of Sion at Issy-les-Moulineaux received a substantial check from Dolly LaRue "for the community."[37] It represented the proceeds of a life insurance policy that the LaRues had taken out on their niece. As for Emily Sophian's hope that the rest of Grace's trip to France would compensate "to some extent" for the ordeal with which it began, one is tempted to call it the understatement of the century.

CHAPTER 5 ✿ Incipit Vita Nova
1937

A thousand lovely fancies
Play upon my mind.

—Anonymous

WHEN GRACE FRICK ARRIVED AT the Hôtel Wagram on February 4, 1937, Marguerite Yourcenar was enjoying one of her usual winter stopovers there. As a writer, her star was on the rise. Having first stepped onto the Parisian literary scene with the critically acclaimed short novel *Alexis* in 1929, the thirty-three-year-old author had just published *Feux*, an extraordinary work depicting a certain "notion of love."[1] The beautiful short story "Notre-Dame-des-Hirondelles" had appeared in January, and the essay "Mozart à Salzbourg" would come out early the following month.[2] *Les Nouvelles littéraires* would publish "Le Lait de la mort" in March.[3] Two more stories and one essay would appear before the end of the year.

In Yourcenar's personal life things were not going quite as well. The critical success of her writing had not made her a best-selling author. Her literary earnings were far from enough to live on in the fashion to which she was accustomed. The precious capital salvaged at the beginning of the 1930s from the estate of her Belgian mother's family, the Cartiers de Marchienne, had shrunk over the course of a peripatetic seven years. She who had long had the means to travel freely about France, Italy, Greece, Switzerland, and Central Europe could not continue to do so indefinitely. The contract she had signed to translate into French Virginia Woolf's most recent work, *The Waves*, was an attempt to ameliorate her financial situation.[4]

Where her intimate life was concerned, the 1936 work *Feux* is widely believed to have been a means of exorcising Yourcenar's "impossible passion" for the homosexual editor and writer André Fraigneau.[5] Yourcenar had also very recently broken off what she would later call a "seven-year

51

relationship" with another man, probably André Embiricos, the communist son of a wealthy Greek shipping magnate. When asked what brought that liaison to an end, Yourcenar replied, "He was an extremely difficult man. And I was young. But I learned a great deal, and also in the trade."[6] She had spent the summer of 1935 cruising the Black Sea with Embiricos on a large commercial vessel belonging to the latter's father. Yourcenar had contracted malaria and was recovering in Athens when Embiricos convinced her that she would get better only at sea.[7]

Grace knew none of this, of course, when, still reeling from her own sea voyage, she entered the dining room of the Hôtel Wagram and saw for the first time a young Frenchwoman with luminous blue eyes dining with guests across the room. According to Yourcenar years later, Grace had heard her talking to a group in the dining room of the hotel the day before they met and had been impressed by her manner of speaking: "Grace said to herself, 'There's a young woman who knows a lot about a variety of things and who is going somewhere.'"[8]

No one has ever been able to pin down precisely on what day Grace and Marguerite met. Josyane Savigneau places their encounter sometime after Yourcenar's return from London to consult Virginia Woolf about *The Waves*.[9] That meeting, chronicled in the essay "Une Visite à Virginia Woolf," took place on February 23, 1937.[10] Michèle Goslar opts for "one day in February 1937—probably the fifteenth."[11] But the late-life testimony we now have from both Frick and Yourcenar, along with detailed records kept every day and preserved by the Sisters of Sion, suggests that the women met earlier. From the house journal of Issy-les-Moulineaux, we know that Sister Marie Yann died on February 7. From Frick's 1977 recording, we learn that Grace arrived in Paris three days before that death, on February 4, and that she first laid eyes on Marguerite in the dining room of the Wagram that same evening. Mme Yourcenar remembered in 1984 that Grace had first seen her in the hotel dining room *the day before* they met. All of which suggests that their first conversation took place on February 5.

By fortuitous coincidence, three professional photographs, taken that very afternoon, show us exactly what Yourcenar looked like when Frick first laid eyes on her.[12] The pictures were taken at the Tuileries Garden, across from the Hôtel Wagram, by the Parisian celebrity photographer Albert Harlingue. Hatless in one of the three, the young writer sports boyishly short-cropped hair and what seems to be a sealskin wrap around her shoulders. Because the photos are not in color, we can't see what struck Grace first and foremost

FIGURE 8. Yourcenar, Tuileries Garden, February 5, 1937. ©
The Image Works.

about Marguerite, her stunning blue eyes. But one can certainly see why she
would have been intrigued.

The two women had a lot in common. They were born in the same year,
1903, five months apart. Grace's birthday, January 12, was also the day on
which Marguerite's beloved father, Michel de Crayencour, had died in 1929.
Alice May Frick, Grace's mother, and Fernande de Crayencour, Marguerite's,
were both thirty-one years old when they gave birth to their only daughters.[13] Grace and Marguerite had both lost a thirty-one-year-old parent the

same year they were born. Both loved literature, art, the ancient world, and visiting museums. Both were avid travelers. Both had a deep fondness for birds and the natural world. Both were open to a same-sex romance. It's no wonder they hit it off so famously.

On the morning after they met, Grace asked a bellboy to deliver a note to Marguerite inviting her to come see "lovely birds" on the roof outside the window of her room. It is hard to imagine that, gazing on those sparrows or starlings, Marguerite gave no thought to her just-published tale in which mischievously amorous nymphs, condemned by a Christianizing monk, are transformed into joyful young swallows.[14] As Jerry Wilson put it in his journal, it was right then and there that Grace and Marguerite "became friends."[15]

Michèle Sarde comments in *Vous, Marguerite Yourcenar: La Passion et ses masques* that Wilson's "poetic" version of Yourcenar's encounter with Frick

> prophesies in a single metaphor the partnership with Grace in which you engaged for fifty years: an entirely inward relationship consisting of "looking together in the same direction." The authoritarian American, even in the heart of Paris, summons you onto her territory to contemplate from the rue de Rivoli, not the rooftop vistas and the architectural splendors of the capital, but flights of birds. A prelude to the rustic existence, amid the animal world, that you would lead together on Mount Desert Island.[16]

Years later Yourcenar did not recall being "summoned" by Frick; rather, she remembered receiving "a pretty little card" of invitation. Her own next move was to take Grace to a Parisian nightclub.[17] As one witness from the 1930s, André Fraigneau, told Josyane Savigneau, Yourcenar "liked bars, alcohol, long conversations. She was constantly seeking to seduce. . . . She was the very epitome of a woman who loves women." But Fraigneau, who knew Yourcenar long before Frick arrived on the scene, goes on to observe that the young Frenchwoman "did not enjoy herself in cities; there was something rather wild about her."[18]

Grace visited the Issy house three times in February to tend to her cousin's affairs. On February 19 Yourcenar left Paris to meet Virginia Woolf, the "prominent contemporary English novelist" about whom Frick had written admiringly in her "Survey Unit for the Study of English Literature" at Stephens College. What a thrill it must have been to know someone who was translating one of her novels!

Woolf was less enthusiastic, as her published diaries reveal, about her visit with "the translator." On Tuesday, February 23, she wrote,

> That extraordinary scribble means, I suppose, the translator coming. Madame or Mlle Youniac (?) Not her name. And I had so much to write about Julian. . . . So I've no time or room to describe the translator, save that she wore some nice gold leaves on her black dress; is a woman I suppose with a past; amorous; intellectual; lives half the year in Athens; is in with Jaloux &c, red lipped, strenuous; a working Fchwoman [sic]; friend of the Margeries; matter of fact; intellectual; we went through The Waves. What does "See here he comes?" mean & so on.[19]

This fit of pique probably had less to do with "Madame or Mlle Youniac" than with Woolf's well-known distaste for obligations that cut into her writing time. Yourcenar, in any case, was much more sympathetic toward Woolf. In "Une Visite à Virginia Woolf," first published in 1937, she wrote,

> Only a few days ago, in the sitting room dimly lit by firelight where Mrs. Woolf had been so kind as to welcome me, I watched the profile emerge in the half-light of that young Fate's face, hardly aged, but delicately etched with signs of thought and lassitude, and I said to myself that the reproach of intellectualism is often directed at the most sensitive natures, those most ardently alive, those obliged by their frailty or excess of strength to constantly resort to the arduous disciplines of the mind.[20]

While Yourcenar was crossing the English Channel to meet Virginia Woolf, Phyllis Bartlett was crossing the same body of water in the opposite direction, traveling with one Phyllis Rothschild, to join Grace at the Hôtel Wagram. Bartlett, who first introduced Frick to the splendors of Paris in 1928, had recently completed her PhD at the University of Wisconsin. She was spending the 1936–37 academic year in London on a postdoctoral traveling fellowship.[21] On March 8, 1937, Grace was back at Issy-les-Moulineaux. She would go to England for a few weeks doing literary research later that month.[22] After visiting a Kansas City friend in Biarritz, Grace returned to Paris and prepared to set off with Marguerite.

About those glorious months which Grace and Marguerite spent discovering new places and each other, Josyane Savigneau has written that Yourcenar

> played the "lovers' journey" to the hilt with Grace: from Venice to Capri by way of Corfu and Delphi. There are no traces left of those first months spent side by side, except a photograph of Grace, in profile, in an unidentifiable place, and another one of Marguerite, probably taken by Frick, on the Piazza del Duomo in Florence. They are ordinary pictures that don't reveal a thing. The photographs of Frick allow for only one observation: she was not very pretty.[23]

Savigneau's negative assessment of Frick's appearance has become almost an article of faith among Yourcenar biographers, journalists, and other commentators. Though buttressed by a number of unflattering photographs, the appraisal is not shared by all observers. One Frenchwoman who knew Yourcenar in the 1930s, the artist Charlotte Musson, had this to say years later: "Please remember me to Grace Frick, whose beautiful face I was struck by. I have spent my life painting or wanting to paint faces that, probably, escaped me. Joys and regrets."[24] Deirdre "Dee Dee" Wilson, who would be an American neighbor and close friend of Grace and Marguerite later in their lives, often speaks of Grace's beauty, emphasizing her lovely, "doelike eyes."[25] Mme Yourcenar professed throughout her life to be attracted to "a certain human type." As she remarked in 1983, "When I remember my preferences as far as dolls were concerned at the age of seven or eight, I see in them my present sexuality."[26] The tall, dark-haired André Fraigneau and André Embiricos, two male objects of Yourcenar's desire in the 1930s, fit her type to a T. So too, with her luxuriously thick dark hair, did the tall, slim Grace Frick. She may not have been a stunning beauty like Yourcenar's Greek "friend" Lucy Kyriakos, but Grace had physical appeal—let there be no doubt about it.

Marguerite Yourcenar's passport from 1937, issued on May 19, helps us track the two travelers' itinerary.[27] Judging from the stamps it is possible to decipher, and from some later correspondence, the women set off from Paris in a leisurely fashion toward Lausanne, Switzerland. En route they stopped in Dijon, the historical capital of Burgundy, which Phyllis Bartlett had urged Grace to visit when she was in Paris the previous February. Grace wrote of Dijon and nearby Beaune to Paul and Gladys Minear in 1949, when they were trying to choose a French city to tour with their children. She and Marguerite had spent a Sunday afternoon poring over maps on the Minears' behalf:

> If you can afford, say three days in Dijon and its surroundings and five days in Paris as a bare minimum (a week is far better) you would have some idea of a very typical provincial region as well as of France's capital city. Also you would see in Dijon a great center of medieval culture, especially in the arts, and the capital of a sovereign state which endured independent of France, and making a unit with Flanders, until the Renaissance.[28]

After Dijon they spent some time in Geneva, where Yourcenar had once audited one or two classes.

Yourcenar's passport awaited her at the French Consulate in Lausanne, a city that was something of a home base for the young woman. Michel de Crayencour had died in a clinic there eight years earlier. Christine Brown-Hovelt de Crayencour, his third wife, still maintained an apartment on Lausanne's avenue de Florimont, and Marguerite often stopped to see her amid her European comings and goings. On May 21 she visited Lausanne's Banque Cantonale Vaudoise to withdraw funds for her trip. By May 24 she and Grace were crossing the border by rail into Italy. The long Mediterranean leg of their journey was about to begin.

  The travelers' first maritime destination, for which they would embark from the Italian port of Genoa, was to be Sicily, where neither Grace nor Marguerite had ever been. Although a swaying gangplank almost brought their journey to an end shortly after it began, Marguerite eventually managed to board ship, and the pair set sail for Palermo. The highlight of their stay in that city was, without a doubt, the rowdy performances of Sicily's "sublime" marionettes.[29] As Yourcenar wrote in a short essay the following year, these oversized puppets, maneuvered not by strings but by steel rods, bring the warlike fury of Japanese samurai and the fervor of medieval mystery plays to an ingenious series of heroic plots. Sicilians had gathered the twelfth-century chansons de geste that in France were now of interest only to scholars and infused them with riotous life. There was valiant Roland and beautiful Aude, along with traitorous Ganelon and plenty of infidels on whom to heap riotous scorn. For Yourcenar, who throughout her life joyfully remembered the colorful, costumed celebrations of saints and village rituals of her pastoral childhood, these folk art shows with their magnificently outfitted puppets were the stuff of myth and legend brought to life. For Grace, who loved children, youth, and every kind of theater, they were a revelation. The clamoring children of even the poorest sections of Palermo all somehow managed to scrounge up twenty centimes to buy a ticket to the marionettes: "A hundred children and young men, ranging in age from four to eighteen years, shout, laugh, cry, clap their hands, jostle one another in the bleachers or in boxes built into the wall, jeering at latecomers who, refused entry, try to force their way in through the theater's single small window." A "marvelous menagerie," including horses decked out for battle, a snake, and a lion, along with one sad and one happy strain of hurdy-gurdy music, round out the elements of the three-week series of performances that recounts a whole "history of France."[30] What Marguerite Yourcenar finds most beautiful about the spectacle are the angels who swing down from on high at the end of a string, tremulous in their élan, to coax from the dead soldiers their souls. She no doubt remembered them when writing her first U.S. play, *The Young Siren*.

The couple's first excursion in Sicily was to Segesta, an ancient Elymian city about seventy-five kilometers southwest of Palermo.[31] Segesta boasts a superbly preserved fifth-century BCE Doric temple and a classical amphitheater.[32] There being no tourist shuttle to the site, Grace, the avid equestrian, convinced Marguerite that they should make the three-kilometer trip from Calatafimi on horses. Yourcenar later spoke of that ride as one of her fondest memories, recalling, among other experiences from that summer with Grace, "a morning arrival in Segesta, on horseback, via trails that in those days were deserted and rocky and smelled of thyme."[33]

In the opposite direction from Palermo, Grace and Marguerite set a course for another ancient city, Taormina, on the northeast coast of the island, stopping wherever fancy struck them along the way. Here again they were on the trail of a remarkably preserved *teatro greco*, this one Corinthian in style.[34] Taormina was originally occupied by an early Sicilian tribe and later taken over in successive waves by Romans, Arabs, and Normans. From the mountainside theater, the two voyagers enjoyed an unimpeded view of Mount Etna and the Ionian Sea.

Crossing over to Villa San Giovanni on the mainland, the women eventually proceeded by train to Naples. Yourcenar had heard Adolf Hitler speak in that ancient maritime city with her father in 1922 and later made it the setting of the short story "D'après Greco."[35] Having first explored Naples with Michel, Yourcenar was eager to return there with her new friend. Grace quickly came to share Marguerite's love of the southwestern coast of Italy. From Naples they took their time heading northward, making long stops in Rome and Florence, and shorter stops in smaller towns. In Florence, re- nowned for its artistic and architectural treasures, she and Grace took in everything from the Boboli Gardens to Michelangelo's unfinished Pietà. Of particular interest to them were the fifteenth-century paintings and frescos of Fra Angelico, inspired by the life of Christ, at the church and onetime friary of San Marco.

The two travelers likely spent all of June in Italy, either on the west coast or touring other sites on the peninsula; no departures are recorded in Yource- nar's passport until July 16, when they embarked at Venice on a cruise of the Dalmatian Coast. The next day their ship, the RMS *Adriatic*, made its first stop at the Yugoslavian port of Dubrovnik. From that city, known in Latin as Ragusa, Grace sent a postcard to Ruth Hall in New York City that featured long-skirted peasant women wearing headscarves at an outdoor clothing, fruit, and produce market. She was enthralled by the medieval aspects of Ragusa and the beautiful, richly colored native costumes with their heavy embroidery. "Our boat stopped for seven hours," she wrote, "and as it was a festival day we saw a great deal both in the streets and from the city walls. We have a boat almost to ourselves and feel like kings."[36]

On July 19 Grace and Marguerite landed on the Greek island of Corfu. Over the course of the next three weeks they would make Athens their base of operations, taking excursions by train or by car from there to various destina- tions: Thebes, a powerful ancient Greek city renowned for its association with Oedipus the King and Dionysus; Delphi, the sacred site of the female Earth deity Gaea during the Mycenaean period and later home to the temple and oracle of Apollo; Eleusis, seat of the Eleusinian Mysteries, which so fascinated the emperor Hadrian that he and his lover Antinoüs were initiated into them; and Cape Sounion, a promontory at the southeastern tip of the Attic Peninsula from which, according to legend, King Aegeus leapt into the sea to his death. All of these places were sites of spectacular beauty. Yourcenar would cherish the memory of these experiences throughout her life, including them among those she would like to see pass before her eyes at the moment of her death: "Cape Sounion at sunset," she told Matthieu Galey, "Olympia at noon. Peasants on a road in Delphi, offering to give their mule's bells to a stranger."[37] That strang- er was Grace Frick, who received the bells from a peasant woman who had stopped to let her donkey drink from a spring.[38]

Shortly before leaving Greece, Grace and Marguerite attended another Mediterranean folk art performance, this one of the Turkish shadow theater, in a garden on the outskirts of Athens. Yourcenar was inspired to write about these plays, known by the name of their main character, Karagöz, as she had Sicily's marionettes. Thanks to her essay, we can imagine what it must have been like that August night in 1937. For the outdoor show, a sheet is hung in the manner of a movie screen, and a small orchestra of flutes, guitars, and drums plays ancient popular music. The stage is thus set for the arrival of Karagöz, illiterate but wily, and his rival, the learned rich man. Old regulars and little boys make up the bulk of the audience. "Among children who are crunching on pistachios and connoisseurs savoring a Turkish coffee," Yourcenar writes, "it is as if we are witnessing rites as old as the human imagination."[39]

Accompanying Marguerite and Grace to this all-night show was a Greek acquaintance, Zoé N. Dragoumis. The fifty-five-year-old Zoé belonged to an important political family. Her father, Stephanos N. Dragoumis, had served as Greece's prime minister and held other high posts. Shortly after attending the shadow play performance, Zoé gave an inscribed copy of Giulio Caïmi's *Karaghiozi, ou La Comédie grecque dans l'âme du théâtre d'ombres* to her fellow theatergoers: "In memory of our delicious initiation to the rites of Karagöz in the night of August 5 to 6, 1937, Athens, August 7, 1937, Z.D."[40] That same day Grace and Marguerite departed the port of Piraeus for Naples. On August 9 they made a quick trip to Capri so that Marguerite could reserve the small villa, La Casarella, on the Via Matermania for the summer of 1938.

Three days later Grace boarded the SS *Conte di Savoia*, bound for home, at the maritime terminal in Naples. So too, despite her susceptibility to vertigo and distaste for gangplanks, did Marguerite Yourcenar.[41] Could she not bear the thought of the two of them parting after all those weeks spent so intensely together? Or was it simply a matter of wanting to bid Grace goodbye in the privacy of her cabin? Whatever the case may be, she did not want their tête-à-tête to end. Marguerite immediately set about making arrangements to follow Grace to America. On September 18, from Le Havre, she too would board a ship bound for New York.

Ciro Sandomenico's *Il "viaggio di nozze" di Marguerite Yourcenar a Capri* calls those spring and summer months which Grace and Marguerite spent touring southern Europe in 1937 a "honeymoon."[42] Though no recorded testimony or love letter exists to bear out Sandomenico's implication, one precious memento from that lengthy excursion has been overlooked. At some point during their long, unhurried wanderings through Italy, almost certainly in early July, Grace and Marguerite purchased two identical gold rings.

FIGURE 9. Italian gold rings. Petite Plaisance Archives.

In the art nouveau style popular at the turn of the twentieth century, those simple bands, with their sensuous floral swirls, now reside in the safe deposit box of the Yourcenar estate in Northeast Harbor, Maine. According to their hallmarks, the rings were fashioned of eighteen-karat gold in the Tuscan province of Arezzo, by Uno a Erre in the city of the same name.[43]

Marguerite may have taken Grace to Arezzo, located some fifty miles southeast of Florence and ten miles off the direct route from Rome, because it was the birthplace of the great Renaissance humanist Petrarch. Yourcenar had read Petrarch's love sonnets in her youth and would later make that figure one of the historical models for the adventurer-poet Henri-Maximilien Ligre in *The Abyss*. Where better to make a pledge of love?

Whether the couple's gold rings stood in fact for an intimate vow cannot of course be stated with certainty; but the ex libris designed at Marguerite's request twenty-eight years later, now found in most of the volumes on the bookshelves of Petite Plaisance, features two thin bands, one atop the other, encircling the binding of an open book on whose otherwise blank pages appear the names Marguerite Yourcenar and Grace Frick.[44] Laid across those fluttering leaves, as if to still them in a light breeze, is each woman's right hand.[45] Directly beneath the bound book, perhaps suggestive of the floral swirls on the gold rings themselves, is a simple garland of flowers.

FIGURE 10. Ex libris of Marguerite Yourcenar and Grace Frick. Petite Plaisance Archives.

CHAPTER 6 ✂ Passage to America
1937–1938

> Ah! let me make no claim
> On life's incognizable sea
> To too exact a steering of our way.
> Let us not fret and fear to miss our aim
> If some fair coast has lur'd us to make stay,
> Or some friend hail'd us to keep company.
>
> —Matthew Arnold

GRACE COULD HARDLY WAIT TO tell her friends about Marguerite. No sooner had she settled herself aboard ship than she dashed off a letter to her British friend Margaret "Daisy" Symons of Wormelow, Herefordshire. Grace had visited with Daisy, whose wealthy family bred racehorses in that English village, before returning to France to tour Italy and Greece with Marguerite. In 2012, the ninety-seven-year-old Herefordshire resident Cecil Miller remembered Symons, who died in 1949, as "a very masculine looking woman very keen on her horses."[1] Given Grace's love of riding, one can easily imagine how the two became friends.

Frick's letter to Symons has not survived, but Symons answered it on September 6, 1937, from Penllyn Castle in the Welsh village of Cowbridge.[2] She and Grace had visited another Norman fortress together, Chepstow Castle, in southeast Wales during Grace's spring trip to England. "Your letter written on board the Conte di Savoie interested me most deeply," Symons writes. "In spite of uncomfortable Italian boats I envied you your tour and wished I was with you. . . . Please tell your friend Marguerite I would love to make her acquaintance either in Paris or Capri. I know for certain any real friend of yours would fill my soul."

Back in the United States, Grace spent a few days with Ruth Hall in New York, where she wasted no time in calling her Wellesley classmate Florence

Codman. Florence came away with the impression that Grace had fallen head over heels in love.[3] Codman called Frick "a very brilliant student" and later, on meeting Marguerite, immediately grasped the allure of the Frenchwoman's intelligence and bearing.

Yourcenar's financial situation was somewhat at odds with her aristocratic manner, however. Yourcenar had been battling since 1928 to recover what was left of her maternal inheritance, which her half brother, Michel de Crayencour, had invested unwisely. To read the extensive correspondence between Yourcenar and her Parisian lawyer, Joseph Massabuau, you would think that she had spent the 1930s on the verge of financial catastrophe. Her letters grow increasingly anxious over that period, evoking everything from her stepmother's medical expenses and cruelly inadequate income to her own fragile health and indebtedness. She nonetheless continued throughout the decade to patronize some of Europe's most fashionable hotels, traveling routinely from Paris to Athens to Vienna in high style and throwing caution to the wind for several months while escorting Grace about the Mediterranean.

Nor was there any attempt to curtail expenses when she followed Grace to America in the fall of 1937. Sailing on the luxurious SS *Paris*, with its art deco and art nouveau decor, Yourcenar arrived in New York on September 25.[4] She and Frick spent a week together in that city, at the elegant Barbizon Plaza Hotel on Central Park South, before proceeding to New Haven. Yourcenar was not charmed by New York City, finding that it lacked "French grace."[5] But the Barbizon Plaza, with its emphasis on the arts and artists, must have gone a good way toward smoothing the rough edges, at the same time it cushioned the transition between Mediterranean shores left so recently behind and the small Connecticut city of New Haven.

By this time Grace had rented a furnished apartment in a five-story brick building at 516 Orange Street, a five-minute walk from her former residence on Whitney Avenue and less than a mile from Yale University. She would remain there until September of 1939. Just in case some of Frick's friends had not heard the big news, on October 9 the *New York Times* society column for New York and Connecticut announced that "Miss Grace Frick of New Haven is entertaining Miss Marguerite Yourcenar, French author."[6]

Indeed, entertainment may have taken precedence, where Grace was concerned, over any sustained attention to her dissertation on George Meredith's poems. And entertainment, first and foremost for her and Marguerite, meant travel, though it also apparently included attendance at a Yale football game. As Yourcenar wrote about America to Emmanuel "Nel" Boudot-Lamotte in Paris, "'Indian summer' is remarkable; the landscape in autumn sports the livery of the Redskin, the copper-tinged epidermis of Atala. And it is also football season now, which, in this country, partakes of carnival, the circus, and Bastille Day."[7] New England's most colorful and poignant season also provided the decor for several trips to nearby Massachusetts. Of course, Grace took Marguerite to Wellesley, where they visited the bucolic campus of her alma mater as well as Grace's several friends who were still teaching there. They also went to Lexington and nearby Concord, site of the first military battle of the American Revolution. Of more interest to Grace in Concord would have been Walden Pond, where the transcendentalist philosopher and antislavery activist Henry David Thoreau spent two years in the mid-nineteenth century communing with nature. The importance that Thoreau placed on frugality, living simply, racial justice, and the natural world resonated strongly with Grace. As Bérengère Deprez has shown, Thoreau became one of Yourcenar's "main American inspirations."[8] The women also visited the culturally vibrant town of Northampton, home to Smith College, where Grace's friends Charles and Ruth Hill had been teaching since 1932.[9] One place they pointedly did not go together—whether then or at any other time—was to Kansas City to visit Frick's family.

Grace eagerly introduced Marguerite to her Yale friends. Alice Parker shared Grace's love of Shakespeare and her sense of social justice; several years before the civil rights movement began, Parker would give a series of talks in England promoting the importance of racial fairness.[10] Yourcenar later called Alice "one of my first American friends" and spoke of "her generous optimism regarding human nature and at the same time her courageous lack of prejudices. . . . Through her one could touch the great America of old, which does not mean that she was not thoroughly and admirably concerned with contemporary problems."[11]

Another friend, Mary Hatch Marshall, wrote a remembrance of Yourcenar in 1937. To Marshall's mind, Grace was not hosting her French friend in high style: "All I remember of first meeting Marguerite, in that shabby little Orange Street apartment in New Haven, was the image of an attractive dark-browed young French woman, with a light accent, which she never lost—and an immediate impression of charm, intelligence, and very blue eyes." Marshall went on to call Marguerite "vivid, lively, energetic, and beautifully dressed." Grace, for her part, was "the kindest and most generous of women, with a slightly offbeat intelligence—a bit eccentric, more than a bit compulsive. She loved literature, was interested in problems of style, and willing, as Marguerite Yourcenar wrote, to discuss matters of phrasing again and again, with total concentration. She had great physical energy, and was a strong swimmer, swimming recklessly far out to sea, I remember."[12]

Two more friends from that era mentioned by Marshall "taught at Hunter College and were both of distinguished mind and sensibility—Katherine Gatch and Marion Witt. Like Grace Frick, Katherine Gatch was a Wellesley graduate. . . . These friends had a car, and from time to time would drive Marguerite Yourcenar and Grace Frick on jaunts into the country. I well remember hearing how entranced Marguerite was by a field of wild flowers."[13]

The relative inelegance of Grace Frick's apartment may have intensified Yourcenar's sense of penury. By midwinter her attempts to recover funds from her mother's estate had shown no sure signs of success. On February 5, 1938, she reported in the exaggerated fashion characteristic of her letters to attorney Massabuau that she had so strictly reined in her expenses that her life in New Haven resembled "that of a cleaning woman and a librarian."[14] Yourcenar had been reduced to borrowing not only from a Swiss bank but also from the "American friends"—a masculine noun in her original French—with whom she was staying. Though she was of course neither cleaning houses nor manning a circulation desk, her distress was undoubtedly genuine. Writing to her lawyer from her stepmother's apartment in Lausanne in January of 1935, Yourcenar had already described herself as "*extremely tormented*" by her financial predicament.[15] Three years later she announced that if she didn't receive at least part of the sum she was owed within two months, she would have to sell some of her stocks![16] While this was not a pleasant prospect during the recession of 1937–38, it should not go unnoted that she nonetheless had stocks to sell.

What Frick's financial circumstances were at the time is hard to say. She was obviously able to help Yourcenar out, but Marshall's description of the Orange Street apartment certainly suggests that she wasn't living in luxury. She was a graduate student, after all, and she likely still received support from the LaRues in Kansas City. Unlike Marguerite, whose father had gambled away an inherited fortune, Grace had been raised in a family whose wealth, while substantial, was the fruit of its own industry. She was known throughout her life for her generosity, but Grace knew how important it was to manage her money with care. Every penny saved on daily living was a penny she could put toward the passion for travel that she and her friend shared.

Fortunately, one of Grace and Marguerite's activities during those months in New Haven did not cost a cent: patronizing Yale's outstanding libraries. Frick, of course, was working on a doctoral dissertation. Yourcenar, for her part, was discovering how much more accessible U.S. libraries were than those she frequented in Europe. In one interview conducted long after her financial troubles had been solved, she acknowledged their importance. American libraries, she said, "serve the public so much better [than French ones]. At Harvard and at Yale, for example, there are a great number of books available to a writer without a great deal of expenditure of his time. In France, it would have taken much effort to do the research I did while writing Hadrian."[17] In fact, Yourcenar did some of the reading for that crucial book as early as 1937 in the extensive collections available at Yale.[18]

Yourcenar was also engaged in another project, one she hoped would supplement her literary and investment income. It was a translation into French of Willa Cather's 1927 novel *Death Comes for the Archbishop*, which many consider to be that author's finest work. The book may have held particular interest for Yourcenar, as it was based on the lives of the first French missionaries to enter New Mexico, a former Spanish territory. According to a letter that Cather wrote to the American critic Alexander Woollcott in 1931, Woollcott helped her see that "the underlying theme" in *Death Comes for the Archbishop* and another of her novels was "a certain moral [gravity] in the French people."[19] But the project did not go smoothly, though Yourcenar did meet with Cather in New York to talk it over. By mid-March 1938 she began requesting a series of extensions of the deadline for completing the French text.[20]

In late April a Monsieur Delamain from Éditions Stock tried with considerable insistence to establish a firm completion date of August 1 for the manuscript, even offering to pay Yourcenar for incremental submissions in the interim. On May 4 the situation grew more urgent. "Excuse me for bombarding you on the subject of *Death Comes for the Archbishop*," Delamain wrote again.

> Rightly or wrongly, it turns out that the author is very worried about the translation and has had her dander up a bit in that regard since the meeting you had with her. We have in hand a long letter in which she protests quite vigorously against your refusal to use Spanish terms to describe things that cannot otherwise be rendered understandable and your intention to "paraphrase" those descriptions though you have not "the slightest knowledge" of the American region in question. . . . What it boils down to is that Mrs. Willa Cather wants to review a copy of the translation prior to any publication. Furthermore, the powers that be are proving to be absolutely intransigent with regard to the deadline of October 30 at the latest.[21]

In view of that deadline, the principals at Stock asked Yourcenar to send them as much of the manuscript as she had completed. They would then hire a speedy translator to finish it. To sweeten the offer, they promised her the contract for Frederic Prokosch's novel *The Asiatics*, which Yourcenar had brought to their attention. It was merely a question of reaching an agreement with the English publisher.

Yourcenar submitted 253 of the novel's 303 pages to Delamain. Cather rejected them outright. As for *The Asiatics*, Stock subsequently wrote to say that they had gotten mixed reviews of the novel and were hesitant to publish it. In the end, not surprisingly, they didn't.

Cather later criticized Yourcenar's translation in a letter to the director of Houghton Mifflin from, of all places, the Asticou Inn in Northeast Harbor, Maine. To Ferris Greenslet Cather wrote,

> In my bookcase at home, I have translations of Death Comes for the Archbish-op in nine different languages, and of the nine translations the one in Italian is much the best. One might think that the French translation would be very good, but I had to send back to the French publishers the first translation be-cause it sounded like a school girl's exercise in French and, above all, because the footnotes explaining Western terminology were incorrect and absurd. "Trappers," for instance, in the footnote appeared as "a religious order." I sup-pose the eventual French translation is better, but I have never had the heart to examine it very closely.[22]

Yourcenar was always noted for translations that, while beautiful, were not scrupulously faithful to the original texts. Constantine Dimaras, for example, often struggled with her over Constantine Cavafy's poems: "Marguerite Yourcenar, as I think everyone today is aware, was rather authoritarian. And stubborn. I, for my part, had some very specific ideas about what a translation should be. She did not share these ideas. My view of translation is not at all lenient. I don't like the idea of 'euphonious inaccuracies.' Marguerite, for her part, was solely concerned with what she thought sounded good in French."[23] Echoing Dimaras, Françoise Pellen, in "Translating Virginia Woolf into French," calls Yourcenar's rendition of Virginia Woolf's *The Waves* "beautiful and a pleasure to read," adding that as a translation it is "deeply, almost insidiously, unfaithful to the original."[24] Yourcenar's deviations from Woolf's original text were eventually considered significant enough to inspire Cecile Wajsbrot to undertake a new, more faithful translation in the early 1990s. Nevertheless, when an important new collection of Woolf's fiction was published in France in 1993, Marguerite Yourcenar's translation was chosen over Wajsbrot's.[25]

Given the widespread perception of the beauty of Yourcenar's translations, to say nothing of the highly sophisticated, stylistically polished prose she was composing in her own name during the mid- to late 1930s, it is hard to imagine that there was anything schoolgirlish about the language of *L'Archevêque va mourir.*[26] But one can speculate about what might have rubbed Cather the wrong way. Yourcenar was a boyish-looking thirty-four-year-old with short-cropped hair when she met Willa Cather in the spring of 1938. Her often-noted air of self-assurance could sometimes be interpreted as Gallic hauteur. Cather, who would soon turn sixty-five, was already entering what Andrew Jewell has called the "misanthropic years" late in life when she became increasingly obsessed with protecting her image. With Edith Lewis's assistance, as Jewell goes on to say, Cather is widely known to have "systematically collected and destroyed all the letters she could find in order to prevent undignified exposure to the rotting world."[27] Her most flagrantly "undignified" years were likely those when, with the audacity of youth, she identified herself as William Cather, favored suits and ties over more feminine attire, and wore her hair in a brush cut. Yourcenar may simply have been much too vivid a reminder of a persona whose traces the aging Cather was trying to erase. *Death Comes for the Archbishop* did not come out in French, translated by M. C. Carel, until 1940.[28]

Neither the Cather debacle nor Yourcenar's financial distress prevented her and Frick from setting off on a tour of the U.S. Southeast. In March of 1938 the two women traveled to Georgia and South Carolina, where Yourcenar first became interested in Negro spirituals, the original music of America's African slaves. Twenty-six years later, as racial tensions reached a fever pitch in the United States, she would publish *Fleuve profond, sombre rivière*, containing an important essay on the history and condition of American blacks, along with her translations into French of a wide variety of Negro spirituals.

En route home from the Deep South, Frick and Yourcenar made their first trip to Virginia, visiting Charlottesville, Richmond, Jamestown, and York.[29] Marguerite would be returning to Europe in late April, and Grace did not want her friend to leave America without seeing the home of one of its founding dissenters, Thomas Jefferson. Writing about the experience years later, Yourcenar spoke of "the great president imbued with the spirit of the Age of Enlightenment" who had traveled to Italy and France and whose neoclassical residence outside Charlottesville resembled an Italian villa.[30] As she noted in the documentary *Saturday Blues*,[31] it was at Monticello that Yourcenar had one of several memorable encounters with American blacks. While walking up the hill toward Jefferson's historic home on a rustic, tree-lined lane, she encountered an old black man in ragged clothes. Standing there motionless, he was listening to the trilling of a bird with an expression of rapture on his lined face. Yourcenar asked him what kind of bird it was.

"Why, honey, it's a mockingbird," the man replied.

It was the first time she had ever observed such a "capacity to enjoy life through every sense, as if through every pore. . . . Andersen's Emperor of China took no more pleasure from his nightingale than did this probably jobless black man from his mockingbird."[32] Yourcenar saw in him a way of experiencing the world that was fundamentally different from her own European sensibility, and she never forgot it.

Finally, in early April, the welcome news arrived that 300,000 of the 500,000 Belgian francs that Yourcenar was owed from her mother's estate had been deposited into her account.[33] She had already purchased her return passage to Europe, where her latest book, *Les Songes et les sorts*, was about to be released; but the receipt of these funds meant that she could pay back the American "friends" who had kept her financially afloat and take one more trip before departing. Yvon Bernier provides a detailed description of that trip in his contribution to *Les Voyages de Marguerite Yourcenar*.[34]

On the evening of April 25 Grace and Marguerite dined at the New Haven home of Frederic Prokosch, whom Grace first met in the English department at Yale in 1931–32. After dinner, they boarded a train bound for Montreal. It was a particularly warm and verdant spring in Connecticut, where early wildflowers were blooming and the trees were lush with new foliage. The two women had taken several leisurely drives through the awakening countryside. In Canada, by contrast, it was bitterly cold. Crossing the dreary plain between Montreal and Quebec City, as Yourcenar wrote in an unpublished notebook, she and Frick found "trees without buds, plants with not a single leaf," a landscape that was "hard and sad." Upon arriving in Quebec, they took a room at the historic Hotel Clarendon within the walls of the Old City. From there they visited Sainte-Anne-de-Beaupré, an important pilgrimage site. Yourcenar was particularly struck by an atmosphere of oppressive Catholicism, which held no appeal for either her or Frick. She found Quebec's churches—fifty-seven of them—"ugly and overwhelming." The next day, after a taxi ride around Quebec, the couple took the last train out of the city.[35]

Their spirits rose once they were on a train heading home. At lunch on the Canadian Pacific, they had a "sweet, lighthearted conversation about everything." But Yourcenar regretted "having squandered in too hasty a jaunt three days we could have spent peacefully in some New England inn among the spring flowers and foliage."[36] Her state of mind may also be reflected in the repeated occurrences of the word "sad" in the few lines from Yourcenar's notes about this trip that are cited in Bernier's article: everything from Quebec's landscape to its silver foxes to the Citadel's glacis is seen through the same gloomy lens. One begins to wonder if her imminent departure was casting a pall over Marguerite's last few days with Grace.

Yourcenar would leave on April 30, 1938, returning not to France but to Naples on the same *Conte di Savoia* that Grace had taken back to New York the previous August. Before sailing, she bestowed a unique gift on her American friend, a copy of her latest book dedicated to Grace and adorned throughout with her own hand-drawn illustrations. *Nouvelles orientales* had come out in Paris in mid-February 1938. It was a collection of short stories based on Balkan and Asian myths and legends. Sue Lonoff de Cuevas has interpreted the drawings that Yourcenar created for Frick in her fascinating *Marguerite Yourcenar: Croquis et griffonnis*. In the original edition of *Nouvelles orientales*, the story "Kâli Décapitée" came first. As Lonoff notes, the placement of "Kâli" at the opening of *Nouvelles orientales* "in itself is suggestive: all of Marguerite Yourcenar's books from that period—*Alexis, Feux, Le Coup de grâce*, even parts of *Denier du rêve*—investigate a troubling sensuality. She herself suffered from an unrequited love yet also indulged in erotic adventures, including one with a married woman, at least until she made a more permanent commitment. In the dedication she added to this copy, she celebrates her new liaison . . . and perhaps she also playfully alludes to it" in the image drawn for Grace on the title page of "Kâli Décapitée."[37]

In Yourcenar's tale, based on Hindu myth, the once perfect and beautiful goddess Kali has been set upon by jealous gods who cut off her head and attach it to the body of a prostitute. Kali is now intellect and flesh, saintly and profane. She roams the earth, as Lonoff recounts, "condemned to copulate with all who desire her."[38] Yourcenar's text describes Kali's shoulders as "round like the rising autumn moon; her breasts are [pointed] like buds about to burst. . . . Her mouth is as warm as life. . . . But her lips have never smiled; . . . and upon her face, paler than the rest of her body, her large eyes are pure and sad."[39] But, as Lonoff observes, Marguerite's drawing of Kali is often at odds with her textual description:

Kali's kohl-rimmed eyes gaze directly at the viewer, and her rudimentary mouth reveals no sign of anguish. The small head is out of proportion to the arms, which angle out to offset the torso's roundness. The hands that flutter

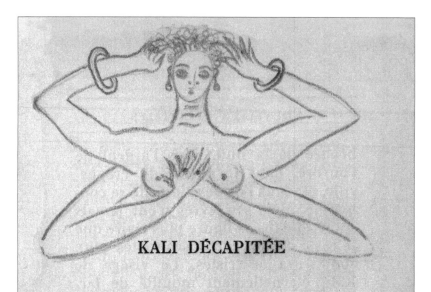

KALI DÉCAPITÉE

Kâli, la déesse amoureuse, rôde à travers l'Inde.

On la rencontre partout. Les femmes tremblent en la voyant passer, et les jeunes hommes, dilatant les narines, s'avancent sur le seuil des portes. Kâli est belle. Les poètes qui la chantent la comparent au jeune bananier. Elle a des épaules rondes comme le lever de la lune d'automne, des seins pointus comme de longues fleurs, des hanches larges, et la taille si mince que les dix doigts d'un amant se rejoignent quand ils l'enserrent. Sa bouche est chaude comme la vie; sa joue est douce comme la mort. Elle se mire tour à tour dans le

— 9 —

FIGURE 11. Kali drawing for Grace Frick by Marguerite Yourcenar, 1938. Document preserved at Houghton Library of Harvard University and reproduced by permission of the Marguerite Yourcenar Trust. All rights reserved.

in the wiry hair are prominent and active. The lower arms are perhaps more intriguing than the upper, in that the right one comes from behind, as if it could belong to another figure, and the meeting of the left one with the body is ambiguous. Whether Kali is modestly crossing her chest or playing with a nipple is also ambiguous, although the more visible hand is plainly active, its two rings echoing the dots of the nipples as well as the nostrils above. While the eyes are appropriately large, they hardly appear "pure and sad," and if poor drafting prevents the shoulders from appearing "round like the rising autumn moon," the breasts are drawn as semicircles, rather than "[pointed] like buds about to burst." They are also high and small, and so more in accord with Western than with Hindu tradition. If to these discrepancies is added the fact that the hair is uncharacteristically curly, this Kali seems less based on an Indian model than on one that was closer to hand. Photographs of Grace Frick from this period show her as a curly-haired young woman who gazes at the camera forthrightly. In all of them her eyebrows are clearly marked and the nostrils are conspicuous.[40]

If indeed the sketches drawn for Grace in April of 1938 "display an unexpected erotic playfulness," as Lonoff notes,[41] then one might also propose that the two prominent rings on the ambiguously intertwined hands may recall the gold bands the two women purchased in Arezzo as a sign of their new love.

In Marguerite Yourcenar's bedroom at Petite Plaisance, where books from the twentieth century reside, Gertrude Stein's sparsely punctuated *Paris France* sits on a shelf next to T. S. Eliot's *Poems Written in Early Youth*. In that slim volume, the expatriate American Stein comments on various aspects of her adopted homeland. Yourcenar, her French counterpart living in America, found one observation to be of special interest. She marked the second sentence in this passage from Stein with an *X*: "Everything is private and personal in France. . . . As my old servant Hélène once said, no Madame it is not a secret but one does not tell it."[42] Sometimes truths that can't be told find an alternate mode of expression.

CHAPTER 7 ⁂ Separation
1938–1939

> So, go break off this last lamenting kiss,
> Which sucks two souls and vapours both away.
>
> —John Donne

FOR THE FIRST TIME IN more than a year Grace found herself alone, not knowing when—or if—Marguerite would return. Though Yale University's Committee on the Degree of Doctor of Philosophy had approved a June 1938 receipt of her degree, absent a completed dissertation that date would be postponed for one year.[1]

About the months spent in New Haven, Connecticut, with Frick, Yourcenar "never consented to speak," wrote Josyane Savigneau, though it "must have been the most intense moment of her passion with Grace."[2] Not until 2037 are we likely to learn more about that time. For at the age of seventy-six Yourcenar decided to create, alongside Harvard University's primary collection of materials related to her life and work, a sealed archive to be withheld from public view for fifty years after her death. It would contain her most intimate papers. The aging Willa Cather, who destroyed her letters or forbade their publication, comes to mind, although Yourcenar professed that she was sealing certain documents, particularly from her younger years, to protect the privacy of people mentioned in them who could outlive her. One suspects that there were also other motives. Most painfully inaccessible for my purposes are "fifty-odd pages of a personal diary covering the years 1935 to 1945" and the many letters that Marguerite wrote Grace in 1938–39 (sent from Capri and Sorrento, Italy; Geneva, Lausanne, and Sierre, Switzerland; Athens and Chalkis, Greece; and Beaune, Paris, and Bordeaux, France).[3]

We do, however, have one short letter from Frick that Yourcenar carefully saved. It bears no date, but its content suggests that it was written in the summer of 1938, after Yourcenar's *Les Songes et les sorts* was released in late

June. Except for the first line, the text is entirely in Grace's fluent—if on rare occasion ever so slightly offbeat—French:

> *So*—I love you, believe it or not. I had dinner with Alice last night in a great storm. She received her copy of *Les Songes* and I love you because you didn't forget it. Why are you so nice?
>
> Yesterday, I worked too late into the night and I went to bed, not thinking that I was very tired, but I must have been because I wondered why I seemed to be making an effort to call for you. You weren't there during the entire evening. But this morning, the moment I'm awake there you are, with no effort, and I'm ready for you.
>
> And you can tear this up if you wish, right away, without fail.
>
> Beloved.
>
> Grace[4]

Grace makes no attempt to hide her desire, though she is playfully mindful that it is forbidden. And Marguerite did not tear her letter up. Later she would place it in an album of photographs and mementos from her early years with Grace that is preserved at Petite Plaisance.

Les Songes et les sorts was a collection of short texts relating a series of dreams that Yourcenar had between her "twenty-eighth and thirty-third year." At the end of her preface to the book, Yourcenar calls its twenty-two narratives "memoirs of my dream life." As such, they come at an important juncture in her emotional life. The volume chronicles a series of dreams, the last of which likely occurred very near the time that Marguerite Yourcenar left André Embiricos at the mouth of a Paris Metro station and Grace Frick unexpectedly entered her world. With its several mentions of "the man I love" or "loved," who caused her so much suffering;[5] of her late father, whom she adored; and of the kinds of ambiguously sexual triangular relationships in which Yourcenar was frequently entangled in the 1930s, *Les Songes et les sorts* is at once a summing up and, after *Feux*, a second step toward surmounting the losses of the past several years.[6] Although the biographical chronology composed for the Pléiade edition of her fictional works disavows "psychological theories in vogue," *Les Songes et les sorts* was undoubtedly influenced, like *Feux*, by her relationship with the psychoanalyst André Embiricos.[7]

Also carefully preserved at Petite Plaisance is another handwritten artifact, one that almost certainly dates from the period immediately following Yourcenar's departure from New Haven. It is a four-by-six-inch sheet of paper inscribed on both sides in the same black ink that Grace used for her "So—I love you" letter, and it contains the partial or complete transcription of six love poems by the British lyrical poet John Donne. As a physical specimen, these transcribed verses are in noticeably worse shape than Grace's letter. Not only is the ink apparently tear-stained here and there, but the paper itself has been subjected to considerable wear and tear. Someone obviously folded the small sheet—lengthwise, widthwise, then lengthwise again—into a rectangle measuring one and one-half by two inches, which, judging from the discoloration of the two exposed surfaces, was then carried around in a wallet or card case—almost certainly, given the autobiographical nature of the album in which it is preserved, Marguerite's.

Though there is no indication of which side of the paper is recto or verso, it is possible to discern a thematic progression in the poems cited or excerpted, from the dawning of love to separation or death. The first fragment in that series, from "The Good Morrow," is:

> I wonder, by my troth, what thou and I
> Did, till we loved?[8]

Harold Bloom has interpreted this poem as evoking "the awakening of sexual awareness," while the expression "by my troth" suggests the speaker's desire for "true love rather than mere sexual dalliance."[9] The phrase may also have brought to Grace's mind the pledge signified by the Italian gold bands from the birthplace of Petrarch—all the more so, inasmuch as the poems she chooses to transcribe are from Donne's most Petrarchan book of poems, *Songs and Sonnets*. It is hard to imagine that the relationship between Grace and Marguerite was ever a "mere sexual dalliance," but the pleasures of the flesh were very much a part of it.

The ironically comical "Song" calls the possibility of fidelity into question. One might just as easily catch a falling star, the poet suggests, or impregnate a mandrake root as find a beautiful woman who is capable of fidelity. "Love's Deity," too, evokes the specter of inconstancy in love.

The lines Grace quotes from "A Fever" reveal the intensity of her attachment to Marguerite. Donne's "Expiration," partially cited in this chapter's epigraph, construes the pain of separation from one's lover as a kind of death. It is the only poem that Grace transcribes in full. The pertinence of its fifth line—"We ask none leave to love"—for the kind of couple she formed with Marguerite did not escape her notice. "Sonnet X," Frick's

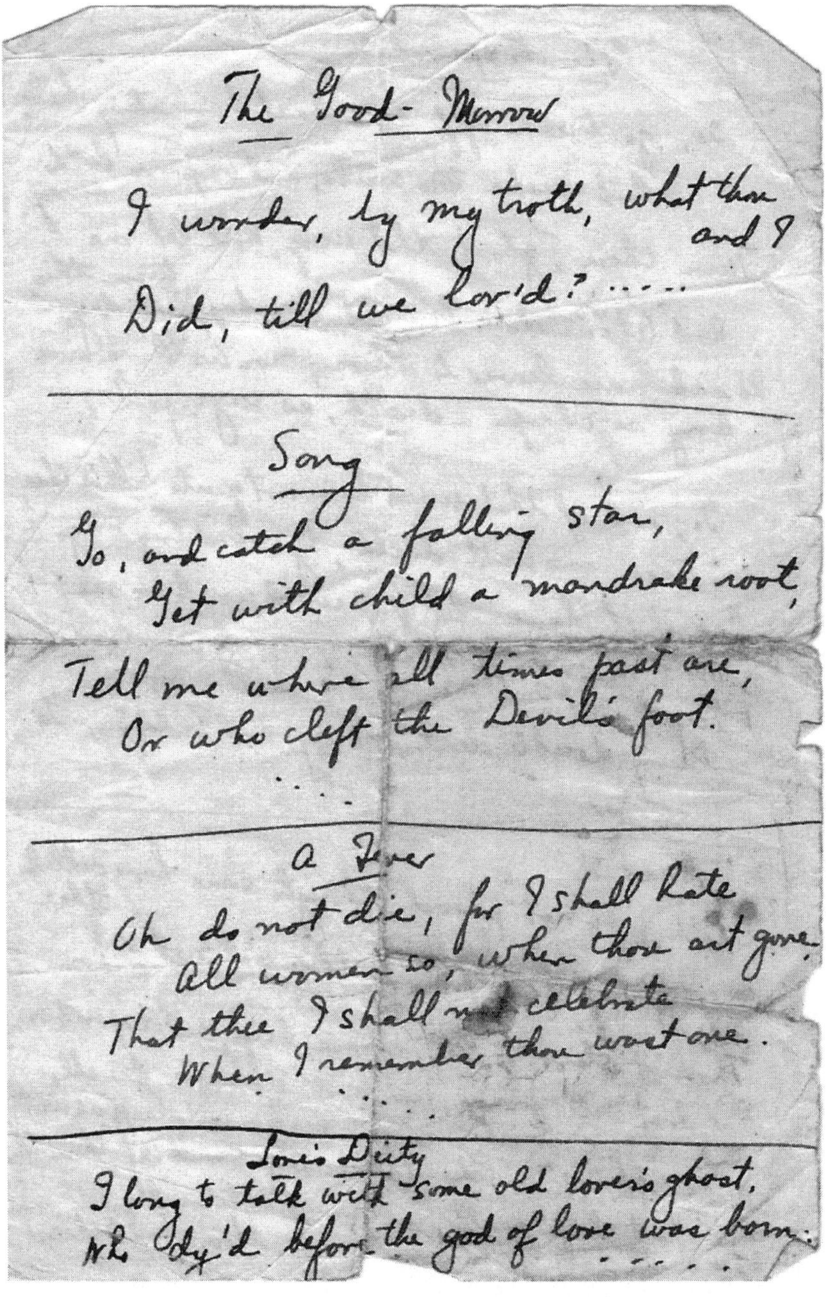

The Good-Morrow

I wonder, by my troth, what thou
and I
Did, till we lov'd? .....

Song

Go, and catch a falling star,
    Get with child a mandrake root,
Tell me where all times past are,
Or who cleft the Devil's foot.
        . . . .

A Fever

Oh do not die, for I shall hate
    All women so, when thou art gone,
That thee I shall not celebrate
    When I remember, thou wast one.
        . . . .

Love's Deity
I long to talk with some old lover's ghost,
Who dy'd before the god of love was born.
        . . . .

FIGURE 12. John Donne poems, transcribed by Grace Frick. Petite Plaisance Archives.

final offering, refuses to accept the finality of death and, by extension, that of separation:

> "One short sleep past, we wake eternally;
> And death shall be no more, death, thou shalt die."

Though the last two lines of this poem seem Christian in their inspiration, it is for an earthly reawakening that Grace yearns. When would she see Marguerite again?

Yourcenar, for her part, entered Italy by sea on May 7, 1938. The Europe to which Yourcenar returned was not the same place she and Frick had toured so lightheartedly the previous year. Tens of thousands of supporters of the republican cause in Spain had been massacred in November of 1937. Adolf Hitler had outlined his intention to acquire *Lebensraum*, or living room, for his fellow countrymen and had taken direct control of the German armed forces. In March of 1938 those forces had occupied Austria prior to the latter's annexation. Darkness was descending on the European continent, and it would be reflected in the novel that Yourcenar was on the verge of writing.

After taking possession, as planned, of La Casarella, an apartment overlooking the sea on Capri, Yourcenar traveled to Lausanne to check in with Christine de Crayencour.[10] It was during this short stay in Switzerland that Yourcenar heard the shocking true story that would form the basis of *Le Coup de grâce*.[11] As stated in the Pléiade chronology, "this short novel was inspired by an authentic episode from the years 1918–1919 that had been related to her a few days earlier, in Switzerland, by a friend of the principal character."[12] Michèle Goslar has identified that friend as Conrad de Vietinghoff, the homosexual musician whose wife, Jeanne, had been Fernande de Crayencour's closest friend in boarding school.[13] It may also have been Jacques de Saussure, son of the Swiss linguist Ferdinand de Saussure, whom Yourcenar met through the literary critic Edmond Jaloux. The Saussures knew a German couple who were connected, probably by blood, to the mercenary soldier on whom Yourcenar modeled her protagonist.[14] Jacques's daughter Alix de Weck told Josyane Savigneau that her father had also given Yourcenar information about the Baltic wars of 1918–19, which would serve as the setting of her novel.

Jeanne de Vietinghoff's beauty had stunned Michel de Crayencour when he saw her for the first time on the day he married Fernande. After Fernande died, the two had an on-again, off-again but passionate affair that ended in Jeanne's refusal to leave her husband, despite his sexual proclivities. It was a loss that Yourcenar's father never got over. The Vietinghoffs, individually and as a couple, held such fascination for Yourcenar that three of her novels from the years between the wars—*Alexis, La Nouvelle Eurydice*, and *Le Coup de grâce*—along with the posthumous *Quoi? L'Éternité*, owe much of their content to them. Young Marguerite so admired Jeanne, in particular, that she became a lifelong ideal of womanhood and motherhood for her.

Le Coup de grâce, which Yourcenar started to write immediately upon returning to Capri, shares with both *Alexis* and *La Nouvelle Eurydice* the implied or explicit presence of a love triangle involving at least one primarily homosexual male. But it diverges dramatically from the earlier novels in the violence of its setting and its implacable narrative. *Le Coup de grâce* is the tragic tale, told twenty years after the fact, of Erick von Lhomond, a half-Balt, half-Prussian mercenary who returns to the estate, Kratovitsy, of the beloved companion of his adolescence, Conrad (!), after World War I to fight the Bolsheviks in war-torn Lithuania. There is no overt sexual activity between the two characters, but we are left with no doubt that a strong eroticism underlies Erick's attachment to his more delicate comrade-in-arms. Conrad's boyish but highly feminine sister Sophie loves Erick with a passion as violent as the conflict going on around the embattled château they inhabit, but Erick's response to her ardor devolves over time from indifference to physical brutality. It's not just that Sophie is not the one for him; it is simply that she is a woman, a species representing for Erick the fearful prospect of a smothering entanglement.

Finally, a proud and indignant young Sophie, as disgusted by Erick's preference for Conrad as by his cruelty toward her, leaves her ancestral home to take up arms with the Reds. How better to cast off the disdainful Erick than to consort with the enemy forces he has come to Kratovitsy to rout? A few weeks later, she and Erick meet again in a small village where a ragtag contingent of enemy fighters "were still holding out in the hayloft of a barn."[15] Among them are Sophie and her "young blond giant" of a lover. Taking prisoners is out of the question, so Erick, having already shot and killed the wounded Russian, grants Sophie the one favor she requests—to die at his hand. As Erick recounts,

> Her lips did not move: hardly aware of what she was doing she had begun to unbutton the upper half of her jacket, as if I were about to press the revolver against her very heart. I must admit that the few thoughts I had at the moment went out to that body, so alive and warm, which the intimacy of our life

together had made almost as familiar to me as the body of any soldier friend; and I felt pangs of something like regret, absurdly enough, for the children that this woman might have borne, who would have inherited her courage, and her eyes. . . .

. . . I fired, turning my head away like a frightened child setting off a torpedo on Christmas Eve. The first shot did no more than tear open the face, so that I shall never know (and it haunts me still) what expression Sophie would have had in death. On the second shot everything was over.[16]

Le Coup de grâce, with its horrifying denouement, has been widely viewed as Yourcenar's most autobiographical novel, one that enacts a final and definitive exorcism of her unrequited passion for André Fraigneau.[17] Fraigneau himself, whose reactionary politics certainly qualify him for the part, claimed years later that he and Emmanuel Boudot-Lamotte had served as the models for Erick and Conrad.[18] Yourcenar scholars have pointed out how indeterminate the meaning of the title of this book is.[19] Was Erick's botched execution a merciful gesture or a vengeful one? We can say with confidence, however, that in Yourcenar's personal trajectory, *Le Coup de grâce* dealt a death blow to a passion that had caused the young writer nothing but misery—and that no such blow could have been struck without Grace Frick, whose first name Yourcenar often spelled with the French circumflex over the *a*. When Marguerite inscribed a brown leather-bound copy of this novel for Grace in May of 1939, she wrote, "To my very dear Grace. The dedication of every copy of this book should bear her name. In any case her first name is there."[20] She then went on, revealingly, to quote from her novel what Erick says about his youthful intimacy with Conrad: " 'I always astound them in saying that I have known happiness, the real thing, the inalterable gold piece . . . such happiness leaves one proof against vague philosophizing; it helps to simplify life, and life's opposite, as well.' "

In a letter to Charles Du Bos written three months after leaving New Haven, Yourcenar touches on a fundamental change of outlook that she had undergone:

Yes, it did in fact take me years to cease being blind to the virtues of hope, which I confused with the vilest illusions, and I fully believe that your commentary on Goethe's five Orphic poems is one of the things that contributed the most to making me open my eyes. And there may also be a *second* hope, infinitely less fragile and more belated than the first, which is born upon the ruins of the latter on the day we finally realize that events, endowed with all possible power to cause suffering, do not for all that have the power to break us.[21]

Hope—*Elpis*—was one of the five "Primal Words" around which Goethe organized his Orphic poems. As Du Bos commented in his essay, when Goethe wrote those poems in 1817, "he was not yet aware that . . . *Elpis* would assume for him a human face."[22] In Yourcenar's case, that face belonged to Grace Frick.

Matthieu Galey once asked the mature Marguerite Yourcenar what the difference was for her between passion and love. "Most people see no difference," she replied,

> viewing passion as love pitched one degree higher. But it would be more accurate to say that the two emotions are close to being opposites. In passion there is a desire to satisfy oneself, to slake one's thirst, in some cases coupled with a desire to control, to dominate another person. By contrast, in love there is abnegation. When I wrote *Fires* I combined the two, sometimes describing love-as-abnegation, sometimes love-as-passion. Ultimately, though, passion has more to do with aggression than with abnegation.[23]

With Frick, love came much closer to what Yourcenar said about the fictional character she felt closest to in her own oeuvre, the Flemish alchemist-philosopher-physician Zeno: "He prefers someone who resembles him, whom he can approach as it were on a footing of equality, a lover who is also a traveling companion and a comrade in time of danger."[24] Like Sophie's young Russian, Grace had shown Marguerite that it was possible to love and be loved in return.

In August of 1938 Frick returned to Kansas City to visit her family. A letter was waiting for her there from Elisabeth Frick, probably a cousin, who had come to America from her native Berlin and then gone back to that city. Marguerite had been in touch with her: "Your friend was kind enough to send me such a nice 'cadeau,'" Elisabeth reported. "Would you be kind enough to give me her address?"[25] Whether this "cadeau" was a copy of *Les Songes et les sorts*, which Yourcenar had sent to Alice Parker, one can't be sure, but it is clear from the few documents we have from 1938 that, even back in Europe, Yourcenar was making a point of connecting with people connected to Grace. She also had in mind the possibility of returning to the United States, as another letter from that summer suggests. On July 14 Yourcenar wrote to Charles Du Bos from Paris saying that she hoped to see him again "on one side of the Atlantic or the other."[26] However long it might take, Grace stood ready to receive her with arms open wide.

CHAPTER 8 ✱ Interlude
1939–1940

> If equal affection cannot be,
> Let the more loving one be me.
>
> —W. H. Auden

WHILE GRACE FRICK WAS BURNING the midnight oil in New Haven, Connecticut, Marguerite Yourcenar resumed her nomadic ways back in Europe. After a summer spent writing *Le Coup de grâce*, she left Italy on September 9, 1938, and headed to Sierre, one of her usual stopovers. Yourcenar's fondness for that southeastern Swiss city was almost certainly occasioned by her love of the poet Rainer Maria Rilke, whose last home, Château de Muzot, a thirteenth-century stone farmhouse surrounded by beautiful orchards, was located there.[1] She was still in Sierre in late September when the Munich Pact was signed, allowing the Third Reich to annex the strategic Sudetenland in Czechoslovakia.[2]

Yourcenar returned to Paris in October, where she had several literary irons in the fire. She was translating *What Maisie Knew* by Henry James into French; *Le Coup de grâce* was being considered for serial prepublication in the *Revue de Paris*; and she was trying to convince Gallimard to let her translate Frederic Prokosch's *Asiatics*, which had been rejected by Stock. On December 10, 1938, Yourcenar was in Brussels to celebrate the election of the Paris-born Peruvian author Ventura Garcia Calderon to the Belgian Royal Academy of French Language and Literature.[3] Returning to Paris after Calderon's induction, she then crossed into Germany by train at Strasbourg on December 16 en route to the Austrian village of Kitzbühel.

By contrast with Paris, the irons that Yourcenar had in the fire at Kitzbühel had little to do with literature. One of the photographs she saved from that New Year's holiday rendezvous shows her and the dark-haired Lucy Kyriakos standing side by side on a snowy ski slope. Looking at this picture, Josyane Savigneau has observed, "it is impossible to be mistaken about the relations between the two women. They are clearly a couple, in which, just as clearly, Marguerite is the dominant figure."[4] Michèle Sarde likens Lucy's beauty to that of Jeanne de Vietinghoff; Lucy also shared with the object of Michel de Crayencour's passionate affection the fact of being married to a homosexual.[5] Seducing Lucy held all the mimetic attraction for Yourcenar of inhabiting the place her father had occupied with respect to his most ardently desired mistress; of possessing the woman who, in adolescence, had awakened her young mother Fernande's capacity for passion at the Sisters of Sacred Heart convent in Brussels; of physically consummating a lifelong love that, while primarily like that of a daughter, also had a transgressively carnal component; and of being, for once, the amorous victor in the kind of love triangle that had dealt her such pain in the 1930s.[6] Lucy was in André Embiricos's wealthy circle of friends. Her husband, furthermore, was a cousin of Constantine Dimaras, the Athenian bookstore owner who translated Constantine Cavafy's poems into French with Yourcenar.

Not much is known about Yourcenar's relationship with Kyriakos, who was approximately two years younger than the author.[7] The two women were friends before Yourcenar met Frick, however. This much we learn from a letter that Dimaras wrote to his cotranslator in November of 1937, by which time Marguerite was in New Haven with Grace. Dimaras had heard that the family of "the American young lady who is your friend" was involved in publishing and hoped to interest the LaRues in commissioning from him a manual of neo-Greek literature. About his and Yourcenar's mutual acquaintances in Greece, Dimaras writes—a bit mysteriously—at the end of his letter, "There is nothing to tell you about Athens. I have mentioned Calamaris to you twice, and I plan to get your address from André Embiricos.[8] So, you see, everything takes its course, Lucy is vanishing beneath a sky too fair for her. I think that by coming back to settle in Athens, you will be sure to find at least some real friends."[9] Whether Yourcenar had mentioned the possibility of settling in Athens one day or Dimaras, as in the rest of his letter, was trying to convince her to do so, we can only guess. But what Dimaras says about Lucy Kyriakos may refer to the young woman's overindulgence in alcohol.[10]

One thing we do know about Lucy is that she was not, like most of Yourcenar's acquaintances, an artist or a writer.[11] Lucy also had a young son, though it is probably safe to assume that he was not a major focus of his mother's ski vacation in Kitzbühel.

In July of 1983 Mme Yourcenar showed me her personal photograph albums, providing brief descriptions of the important people in them. As I wrote in my journal at the time, when we reached the photograph of "M.Y. in slacks smoking a cigarette with the three dark-haired Greek women with whom she shared for four months the house of 'un ami' in Greece," she leaned over to single out Lucy, saying, "She's the one who was my friend."[12] Asked how they got along, she replied, "Oh, *very* well," laughing heartily.

Because Kyriakos was an excellent skier, which Yourcenar was not, it was more than likely she who invited her French friend to spend the winter holidays vacationing in Kitzbühel.[13] They may both have stayed with a certain Baron Gutsmansthal in that Tyrolean village. As Yourcenar wrote to "Nel" Boudot-Lamotte on January 6, 1939, "In the event that the proofs of *Coup de grâce* are ready before 1 February, could you have them sent to me?" She would be staying, "until 18 January, c/o Baronin Gutsmansthal in Kitzbühl; afterward, and until 30 January, at a Viennese boardinghouse."[14]

Contrary to this expressed intention, and to her own memory of staying in Austria until March, Yourcenar left Vienna on January 26.[15] Two days earlier she had gone to the Consulate General of Greece and obtained a visa for a one-year stay in that country. From Vienna's Hungarian Consulate on the same day, she received permission to pass once through Hungary until March 24. On January 25 Yugoslavia's General Consulate stamped her passport with a visa for transit through that kingdom, valid for one month. She left Vienna by train the next day and crossed the border into Hungary. January 27 found her traversing Yugoslavia and entering Greece at Idomeni. This was the beginning of the four-month stay that she mentioned to me in 1983.

One of the photographs from this period shows Lucy Kyriakos posing on the rocks at the edge of the sea, wrapped only in a towel.[16] Yourcenar spoke of this holiday in a letter to Boudot-Lamotte:

> I spent Easter week on Eubeoa, far from any road and more than half an hour's boat ride to the nearest village. The worries of the world arrived there muffled, but they arrived nonetheless. The landscape was so beautiful there is nothing one can say about it: sunbathing on the rocks in perfect solitude, the sound of a magical little bell in haunted woods, Easter's roast lambs, midnight mass on Holy Saturday in a mountain monastery among drunken monks, dirty and solemn, reciting prayers like incantations.[17]

Several other photographs were taken on the property of Athanase Christomanos, also on Euboea, where Yourcenar was staying with Lucy, Lucy's cousin

FIGURE 13. Lucy
Kyriakos, Euboea,
1939. Petite Plaisance
Archives.

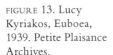

Nelly Liambey, and Lucy's sister Kharis. One of them shows Marguerite, smoking a cigarette, arm in arm with Lucy in Christomanos's courtyard.

As correspondence from that era now confirms, Yourcenar spent much of those four months in Athens, where she was translating with Constantine Dimaras.[18] On May 18, 1939, after what was probably the longest stretch of time she ever spent in Greece, Yourcenar left Piraeus on a freighter, headed for France.[19] Five days later her passport was stamped for a transit stop at Genoa, Italy, and on May 25, she went ashore at Marseilles.

There is little doubt that Kyriakos was one of Yourcenar's feminine conquests. Though she and Frick had forged an amorous liaison that stayed very much alive in the letters they wrote to each other, it is not entirely surprising that Yourcenar would revert to her womanizing ways once she was back in Europe on her own. She had never been involved in a long-term relationship with another woman, and her father had certainly not been a model of fidelity. She may even have been troubled by Lucy's drinking problem, which could have become more pronounced—or more obvious—over the course of Yourcenar's long stay in Greece. It was still a painful memory more than forty years later when she spoke of it in regard to the alcoholism of another friend. Kyriakos was the only other person in her life who had struggled with that particular affliction.[20]

Contrary to much that has been written about this period, some of it by Yourcenar herself, a return to the United States was already in the works before she even left Greece. It was not a last-ditch plan that cropped up in August of 1939, as the political situation in Europe grew ever more ominous. As Yourcenar states in an unfinished "Self-Commentary": "In Greece, I was working on a translation of Constantine Cavafy; I had booked passage on the *Nieuw Amsterdam*, whose maiden voyage was to take place in September, planning to spend several months visiting an American friend."[21] By early June 1939 she was in Belgium, almost certainly for reasons related to her American voyage: in the passenger manifest of the ship on which she eventually sailed—the SS *Manhattan*, and not, as has been reported, the SS *California*—she is identified, for the first and only time in her life, as being Belgian.[22] In fact, Yourcenar's listing for this crossing displays several anomalies. Her first name is listed as "Margarete"; in the "Married or Single" column next to her name appears the letter D, for "divorced"; her nationality is listed as "Belguin," her birthplace as "Belgum," and the city of her birth as "Brussel"!

From Brussels she returned to France on June 11 via Flines-les-Mortagnes en route to Paris and the Hôtel Wagram.[23] By July 19 she had already been to the American Consulate in Geneva trying to procure her U.S. visa, as she had done in 1937. This time, however, since she had no fixed address, and since international travel was now more closely monitored, someone would have to attest to her habitual residence in Paris. She told Boudot-Lamotte at Gallimard that the United States wanted "to be sure it could get rid of me at the end of one year."[24] She needed Gallimard to say—as quickly as possible— that she was working on translations of American authors and would have to return to France in that connection in 1940. On August 16, 1939, she was "seen for the journey to the United States" by Heyward G. Hill at the American Consulate in Geneva. Her visa was issued that same day.

On September 3 Great Britain and France declared war on Germany, throwing Yourcenar's plans into disarray. When she got back to Paris later that month, she learned that the *Nieuw Amsterdam* would not sail after all, and ships to the United States were scarce. She thought briefly of returning to

Greece as an envoy of the French Ministry of Information, but no appropriate opening was available for her to fill.[25] About her short stay in Paris during the uneasy weeks of the Phony War, Yourcenar remembered a conversation at the Hôtel Ritz bar with Jean Cocteau, who was "as always more concerned with charming and bedazzling than with the things that were happening, which had not yet affected him." Another acquaintance, the French singer Marianne Oswald, dreamed of "starting up a nightclub in New York, exclusively for women." The surrealist writer Julien Gracq was "glimpsed in an English friend's salon, . . . where I heard a woman sing a song one evening in Gaelic whose name I don't remember but whose rhythm later found its way into *La Petite Sirène*."[26]

Yourcenar had crossed into France from Switzerland on September 28. Six days later, having heard that a ship would be sailing to New York from Bordeaux, she obtained a time-limited visa to leave France from that port for the United States from the Passport Office of the Paris Préfecture de Police. On October 15, 1939, she finally was able to sail.

The contrast at this juncture between Marguerite Yourcenar's experiences in Europe and Grace Frick's back in New Haven could hardly be sharper. By July of 1939, having received yet another extension, Grace had made what she considered to be respectable progress on her dissertation.[27] While Yourcenar was desperately trying to find a way out of France, Frick was pursuing a variety of pleasurable hobbies: hiking, music, reading, and theater.[28] She had just been hired to teach English composition at Barnard College for the 1939–40 academic year. After spending August and most of September with her family in Kansas City, Frick moved into a faculty apartment owned by Columbia University at 448 Riverside Drive in Upper Manhattan. Yourcenar would join her there on October 22, 1939. The crossing from Bordeaux to New York was extremely nerve-racking because the ship had to make several detours to avoid German submarines.[29] She arrived in New York just in time for a pro-Nazi parade organized in Manhattan by the German-American Bund;[30] for someone fleeing Hitler's aggression in Europe, it was not a welcome spectacle.

At Barnard Grace was working yet again, as she had at Wellesley and Stephens, for an ardent promoter of women's education. Virginia Gildersleeve taught English and was dean of Barnard College for more than thirty years.[31] Coincidentally, she had been one of the speakers at the celebration that took place the year Frick graduated from Wellesley College.[32]

While Grace fulfilled her duties at Barnard, Yourcenar tried her hand at commercial translation and worked with some of Frick's Yale friends to plan a Midwestern lecture tour.[33] Paris fell to the Germans in June of 1940, and the world that Yourcenar knew seemed to be coming to an end. But as the French scholar Mireille Blanchet-Douspis has observed, another world was opening its doors. Blanchet-Douspis describes how expansive Marguerite Yourcenar's experiences in America would be:

> Through her contact with the intellectual milieus that Grace Frick opened up to her, she was introduced to problems to which her personal sensitivities rendered her receptive but which French culture had not yet begun to address: ecology and minority rights; and she began to familiarize herself with cultures that, viewed from Europe and submitted to the decadent judgment expressed in "European Diagnosis," did not appear worthy of the same consideration as European civilization. The intellectual universe of Marguerite Yourcenar was enriched by unknown, perhaps even unimagined novelties; she acquired maturity and a broader, certainly keener comprehension of living beings considered as a whole. What could be described as "more modern" aspects insinuated themselves into her makeup, but without separating her from her native language and culture.[34]

Yourcenar's interest in American blacks was piqued, as we have seen, during her trip down south in the spring of 1938. The apartment that she and Frick shared on Riverside Drive was not far from Harlem, Manhattan's noted African American neighborhood. In the 1920s and 1930s that quarter was home to the explosion of music and art known as the Harlem Renaissance. The aging Yourcenar spoke often of her early contact with certain members of Harlem's black community. As she told Matthieu Galey, she and Frick had met "Father Divine, a sort of prophet, who was well known at the time," during the year they spent living in New York:

> My American friend and I sometimes ventured up to Harlem to hear him. Or rather to watch him, because he didn't talk, he ate. He used to sit at a very large table, but the meal he ate was quite modest, consisting of chicken necks and feet, potatoes, and various other low-cost items, served by magnificent black women dressed in white synthetic satin. Each dish was set before Father Divine, who stared at the food with a vacant look while continuing to eat. The people, the blacks, who were there, quite a large crowd, pressed up against the table and said, "Bless us, Father, touch us, Father." It was quite moving. I made

use of this scene in my attempt to portray the prophets' banquet at Münster in *The Abyss*. I tried to capture the almost sensual enthusiasm of the crowd at Father Divine's dinners.

When we returned home to our tiny apartment on Riverside Drive, which was not then the dangerous neighborhood that people tell me it has since become, the [black] doorman came up to us with a worried look and said, "What! You mean to say you went to Father Divine's? That wasn't very smart, he's probably cast a spell over you."[35]

The black doorkeepers at 448 Riverside Drive were indeed leery of "sorcerers" like Father Divine, but they loved gospel music and the blues. And they weren't above breaking the rules to "covertly let street singers into the courtyard of the building."[36] As Marguerite would later write,

One of them, whose tenor voice could almost reach the highest notes of a soprano, had become friendly with Grace Frick. . . . We would invite him to have supper with us.

One evening she said, "Jim, the range of your voice goes up very high."

"High?" he exclaimed. "I'll say. All the way up to the third floor!"[37]

As soon as they were able, Frick and Yourcenar were traveling south again. Barnard's winter vacation in December 1939–January 1940 found them back in Charlottesville, Virginia. Over spring break they returned to South Carolina.[38] A postcard from the latter trip, preserved in one of Yourcenar's personal photograph albums, suggests the kind of pleasure the two of them took in their visits to the South. It is an artistic image from Charleston's Cypress Gardens in which lush subtropical foliage fills the scene.

Prominent in the foreground is a weathered wooden bench overlooking still water beside a walking path. On the back of the card, Yourcenar transcribed in French two verses from the seventeenth-century poem "The Two Lovers' Promenade":

These waves, tired of moving
Across this gravel,
Are reposing in this pond
Where long ago Narcissus died.

The shadows of this crimson flower
And of those bending reeds

Seem in the depths to be
The dreams of the sleeping water.[39]

FIGURE 14. Cypress Gardens, Charleston, South Carolina. Petite Plaisance Archives.

On Easter Day 1940 Yourcenar wrote another postcard—in English—to
Lucy Kyriakos. It bore Elizabeth O'Neill Verner's well-known drawing of
Charleston's Marshall Gate. The spelling, punctuation, and other style ele-
ments are all her own:

> Dearest Lucy — Do you remember St. Georges? (my greetings to all) Only a
> year ago — I am for a few days in this lovely little town, in the middle of mag-
> nolias gardens. I had your letter and will answer — but I worked hard and had
> no time yet. When will we see each other again? Times *are* bad — But life all
> the same has pretty moments.
>   Love from Marguerite[40]

In one of those temporal disjunctions so typical of Yourcenar, the postcard
bears a notation appended to it by the author stating, almost as if this were a
reason for not mailing it: "Never sent. She died during the bombardment of
Ioannina during Easter week in 1941."

The only mention of Lucy—or rather of "L.K."—in the Pléiade chronology appears in a description of two poems that Yourcenar wrote during the
first six months of 1942.[41] "Greek Flag" recounts in seven quatrains the true
story of a Greek evzone who, charged with removing the national flag flying
over the Acropolis when enemy troops entered Athens, wrapped himself in
the banner and leapt to his death. The poem about Lucy, "Epitaph, Wartime," is a short but loving rhyme that eerily echoes Constantine Dimaras's
1937 comment about her disappearing beneath a sky too fair for her:

> The iron sky crashed down onto
> That tender statue.[42]

When speaking of Lucy in the 1980s, Marguerite Yourcenar said that at
the end of her life, the Greek woman plunged deeper and deeper into alcoholism, drifting from bar to bar.[43] Our only hope of learning more about
what really happened between the two of them may reside in the sealed file
at Houghton Library—but it's a long way to 2037. What Grace thought of all
of this we may never know.

It is hard to imagine that the Fricks and LaRues of Kansas City ever got wind
of Yourcenar's European affairs. They did not think much of Grace taking
up with an exiled Frenchwoman about whom they knew almost nothing,
however. Yourcenar told one friend, Deirdre "Dee Dee" Wilson, that she
had never been welcome to visit Kansas City with Grace.[44] To another she
stated that the family had tried to separate the two of them—and almost
succeeded—by hiring a lawyer to deprive Grace of her inheritance.[45] Yet another friend once wrote that Grace's "Kansas City family did not approve of
her teaming up with MY, feeling that she was only wanting to be financially
supported while she pursued her career."[46]

Much has been made of Yourcenar's poverty upon arriving in the United
States, but she was not penniless. Grace in fact asked her brother Gage if
he would be willing to oversee Marguerite's investments. He declined. The
Fricks and the LaRues, conservative Midwesterners, simply did not want
Grace to partner up with a woman. Nor, in their eyes, was there any good
reason for her to hitch her wagon to a dim French star.

CHAPTER 9 ✂ Dean Frick
1940–1941

She was always attending rummage sales to buy things for the girls.

—Early Hartford Junior College trustee

GRACE FRICK'S PROFESSIONAL AMBITIONS HINGED on her finishing "The Early Poetry of George Meredith." As an ABD—shorthand for one who has completed *all* the requirements for the doctorate *but* the *dissertation*)—she could go only so far in her field. But ABDs who take temporary teaching jobs are often plagued by a catch-22: they who need nothing more than time and energy to devote to their research and writing have class loads that are almost always heavier than those of their tenured or tenure-track colleagues. For Frick, the pressure was about to be ratcheted up a few notches. In the spring of 1940 the position of academic dean opened up at Connecticut's fledgling Hartford Junior College, about 125 miles from New York City. Helen Randall, on leave from Smith College, had served as the school's administrator during its first year, but she was returning to Smith. Frick eagerly applied for the job. She was also being courted at the time by Hunter College in New York. Coincidentally, the appointment secretary at Wellesley had recommended both her and Phyllis Bartlett for the Hartford position.[1] Bartlett, who by now was an assistant professor at Rockford College in Illinois, wrote a letter to the search committee recommending her friend.[2]

Hartford Junior College was first launched during the Great Depression as Mount Holyoke in Hartford with the intention of providing "the first two years of an academically challenging curriculum to young women who could not afford to attend a four year residential college."[3] In the beginning there were no campus buildings, and classes were held at the YWCA. Professors from Mount Holyoke gave courses in ancient history, Latin, German, French, mathematics, hygiene, and physical education. According to a history of the college, this "noble experiment" lasted until 1938, when Mount Holyoke chose to discontinue the program.[4] Howell Cheney, a Hartford businessman, was determined to take over where Mount Holyoke left off and establish an independent two-year school. In the fall of 1939, having acquired a house at 47 Highland Street, Hartford Junior College opened its doors with thirty-five students.

Letters recommending Frick for the deanship poured in from all quarters. Charles Hill, Grace's fellow student at Yale University, was now teaching at Smith; he wrote calling Frick

a woman of wide culture, with keen interest in art, music, and the theatre and a contagious enthusiasm for all she cares about. Of her qualification for an administrative office I should again venture to speak with assurance. Her judgment is excellent, and her ability to get on with all kinds of people is unusual. She is certain to give unstintingly of her own time and energy, and to be zealous for the standards and the prestige of her institution. In fact, the best thing in the picture as I see it is that Miss Frick is the type of person to inspire quickly, and to keep, the respect and loyal cooperation of colleagues, students, parents, and alumnae in the interests of the college.[5]

The chairman of the English department at Barnard College, Minor W. Latham, wrote of Frick's "high ideals and scholarly attainments."[6] Tucker Brooke of Yale University called her "a person of marked dignity." Along with the appointment secretary at Wellesley, he felt it important to mention that various family emergencies had more than once interrupted Grace's progress toward her PhD. Lauding her "determination in sticking to her profession," Brooke was confident that she would "bring tact and energy, as well as intelligence, to the duties of a dean."[7] Even the former dean of Stephens College, who had not seen Grace for ten years, chimed in to recall her good character, high scholarship, stability, and poise.[8]

But the most meaningful letters of support came from the two Wellesley professors who knew Grace best, Laura Lockwood and Martha Hale Shackford. Lockwood found her former graduate assistant "excellent in every way," adding that Frick had

good executive ability, high ideals of scholarship and conduct, imagination and quick sympathy, much ingenuity, and a keen sense of humor. She is the kind of person I should like any young friend of mine to know and admire.

If she comes to you, may I hope you will allow her time to give one course in English literature, as she is an excellent teacher.[9]

Shackford took the time to compose a handwritten letter of praise:

In response to your inquiry about Miss Grace Frick's suitability to be dean of liberal arts, I am happy to say at once that she seems to me an ideal candidate for such a position. I have known Miss Frick for many years, first when she was a student in my course in Shakespeare, then later as she was pursuing graduate work. Besides being a very well-equipped and trained scholar she has the essential tact and insight needed in dealing with girls of college age. Her sense of humor is evident, though never at all boisterous or unseemly. She has charming manners, is attractive personally, has no physical defects of speech or any other drawback. There is a certain very pleasing quietness and reserve about her which shows her self-command. Students will like and respect her; they will find her a kindly, interested, companionable friend. Probably I sound rather lavish in my praise of Miss Frick, but I assure you I am perfectly sincere. She is admirably fitted for a deanship. Miss Margaret Sherwood, Professor Emeritus, agrees with me in these opinions of Miss Frick. I certainly hope that you will make this appointment.
    Very truly yours,
    Martha Hale Shackford[10]

The only letter of recommendation to strike any note of discord in its appraisal of Grace was written by Yale's William C. DeVane, her dissertation adviser:

I feel that Miss Frick will make an admirable administrator. She is clear-headed, decisive, and fair. She would get business done in a pleasant and efficient way. She is a mature person for her years, and I think is very able to see things objectively. I should expect her to be at her best in the matter of personal problems. I think she has an air of authority in spite of her youth. I recommend her heartily, with only the possible reservation that she may occasionally be a little sharp in her speaking, but I have always found her a reasonable and fair-minded person.[11]

During her year teaching at Barnard, Frick had acquired the experience of working with an urban student body very different from that of the residential campus where she had spent three years in Missouri. She was thoroughly committed to the cause of educating young women. Her recommendations were glowing, and, even without a PhD, Grace got the job. She could indeed teach English literature, but finances were tight and Howell Cheney would rule them with a firm hand. As he wrote just before Frick was hired, "I trust we made it clear to you that the administration of this position will involve the exercise of the most rigid economy while we are in the process of demonstrating the success of this undertaking."[12] Even Frick's letter of appointment as dean alluded to the college's tenuous financial situation, assuring her that "the Trustees desire to make your service here yield you the maximum of return and to stand by you in every way possible within their means."[13] Her salary for the academic year would be $3,000.

During the summer of 1940 Grace and Marguerite found a ground-floor apartment at 549 Prospect Avenue in West Hartford, less than half a mile from the college. Frick moved in there alone in early September. Alice Parker was staying with the couple in New York that August, and when she left she took Marguerite with her. This was the beginning of Yourcenar's Midwestern lecture tour. Over the course of a few weeks, she gave three talks in Missouri: one at Lindenwood College in St. Charles, where Parker taught English; one at Stephens College in Columbia, where Frick had learned the ropes; and another in Jefferson City, Alice Parker's hometown. She then moved on to Rockford, Illinois, where Phyllis Bartlett was teaching; Louisville, Kentucky; and Cleveland, Ohio.[14]

Frick, meanwhile, threw herself into her new job with every ounce of the remarkable energy for which she would be known throughout her life. As head of the small college, Frick was responsible, on the tiniest of annual budgets, for everything from buying dish towels and tablecloths to recruiting members of the faculty and expanding the college's course offerings. One early trustee of the school, Beatrice Kneeland, later remembered that "there were no utensils for even getting lunch. I remember someone saw Grace Frick at a rummage sale, and they wanted to know what in the world she was doing. And I said, 'Well, I know what she was doing—she was trying to get a few pots and pans and cups and saucers and things for lunch for those girls!' "[15] Increasing student enrollment was another one of Frick's major tasks. One day, not owning a car, she walked the eighteen miles from West Hartford to Middletown, Connecticut, to meet a prospective student's family.[16]

One of Frick's most challenging endeavors—her own idea—would be to create a new biology lab for the school. Frick believed an on-site facility would be a source of "economy, publicity, and good standing with the major colleges."[17] It would pave the way for a course designed to prepare girls for jobs as

FIGURE 15. Grace Frick, dean of
Hartford Junior College. Frick
family archives.

assistants to physicians or go on to further study at a four-year school. As early
as mid-July, before she had even moved to Hartford, Frick was measuring the
garage and the basement of the college building to assess their suitability for
that purpose.[18] Consulting her Wellesley roommate Betsy Lunn, now a biology
professor at Northwestern University, she learned what one would need to
equip a biology classroom. From the New York Biological Supply Company
she obtained a price list for the basic equipment, including frogs, microscopes,
and lab tables: $922.00 altogether. To save every possible penny, the microscopes
could be secondhand. Frick's laboratory was promptly installed in the basement
at 47 Highland Street, where biology or zoology classes would meet for many
years. The ceiling was so low, it would later be noted, that "Dr. Copeland and
his successors learned to duck their heads in certain places to avoid bumping
against water pipes and other obstacles."[19] When school opened on September
23, Frick had added four new courses to the curriculum: biology, government,
psychology, and speech. There were thirty-nine students, including the fifteen
who were continuing from the previous year.

In addition to the new lab, the Highland Street location boasted a kitch-
en, a cafeteria, an indoor student recreational space, a living room, a library,
and a classroom, all of which needed to be furnished before the fall semester

began. One housekeeper later remembered Frick "banging on walls to hang pictures at midnight."[20] The *Hartford Times* was soon on hand to document what she was hanging. The artworks, often focused on women, were chosen to adorn and instruct. Many of them will sound familiar to readers of Marguerite Yourcenar:

> Among the interesting new features of special educational value is a series of prints and photographs taken from various masterpieces of art, including some original engravings from Piranesi, 18th century Italian artist, whose rare folios are now on special exhibition at the New York Public Library. . . . All represent the Rome of his time, the Forum, the gardens of Hadrian's Villa at Tivoli, and two interiors of churches famous for their architectural beauty, and all are overcast by the romantic melancholy characteristic of the poetry of ruins. Such a collection is of value to the student of literature as well as of art because it is typical of that conception of classical Italy which was to be celebrated a generation later by the great poets of English romanticism.

Along a hallway and stairwell were photographs of portraits of women obtained from European and American collections. Chronologically arranged, they gave "almost a history of womankind, and of costume, from the Egyptian Queen Nefertiti to the 20th century writer Katherine Mansfield."[21]

From her experience at Stephens College, Frick had learned well the importance of a richly varied offering of curricular and extracurricular activities in the education of young women. Her little school already had a choir, led by Muriel Crewe Ainley, who worked with Frick to coordinate the group's musical offerings with the literature courses being taught.[22] Frick engaged the modern dance pioneer, teacher, and choreographer Truda Kaschmann to conduct a six-week dance program for her "girls" that would meet twice a week. Soon Marguerite Yourcenar would be teaching French and art history as a gift to the cash-strapped but burgeoning college. There was a French club, a German club, a press club, and a field hockey team. In October of 1940 the Armenian pianist Juan Nazarian, who had studied in Paris with Nadia Boulanger and left France to live in Hartford, gave a concert of French music for the French club. As one of the local newspapers reported, Marguerite Yourcenar and Miss Elizabeth Williams, a Hartford Junior College trustee, poured at the tea that followed the performance.[23]

Frick had played field hockey in high school, and she took an active interest in her school's new team. She was proud of their performance in one early game, even though the Hartford Junior College girls got clobbered. "Last Saturday," she wrote to Howell Cheney,

> we mustered enough of a hockey team to play against St. Joseph's College at their field, and we were roundly whipped by the largest, brawniest, "Irishest" team that it has ever been my lot to behold. Our girls looked liked sylphs beside them. But we played a good game, nevertheless, for entrants who are new to the field, and our defense gained steadily through the successive quarters. So we learned a great deal even if the score does sound appalling, 14–0. My opinion of our group rose as I watched them, and I felt that we had reached a high point in morale when I found Millicent Bolling, chief player on the team, typing away in the basement, twenty minutes after the game, "Hartford Junior College's plucky eleven met St. Joseph's hockey team" etc., for the *Hartford Times*, without delay![24]

Of course, for young women at an all-female school one also had to allow for social activities involving the opposite sex. The most convenient source of the latter was nearby Trinity College, with which Hartford Junior College sometimes shared instructors. To arrange for such encounters there existed a Date Bureau, which Frick described with some humor to board chairman Cheney that fall. Her letter is a masterpiece of subtle persuasion, designed to get the outcome she wanted for her "young ladies" by preemptively meeting Cheney's potential objections:

> A few of the more ambitious (socially ambitious) members of the Freshman Class stirred up an appeal for Trinity men, offered to negotiate with the "Date Bureau" at Trinity, and finally persuaded a majority of the class to sanction such negotiations. The "Date Bureau" is a student enterprise at Trinity which arranges dates at a cost of fifty cents a man, I am told. Our girls bargained over the telephone for a wholesale lot at ten cents per man, a total of thirty-five men. I hope it won't seem to you a scandal. I write it in all its baldness.
>
> . . . I certainly preferred to have them make the effort for each other rather than ask Dr. Copeland and Dr. Buell to "get them men" as the young ladies had at first suggested. An occasional dance they must have, there is little doubt about that, and if they were in residence at a small college elsewhere the administration would probably invite boys from the neighboring colleges to meet them.[25]

In the fall of 1940 Frick launched a lecture series to bring women of accomplishment to campus to talk about their lives: the internationally known newspaperwoman Betty Ross, a Hartford native, described what it was like to live in England during World War I; Mrs. Michael Corovilles, a member of the Greek Refugee Committee, spoke of that group's effort, bringing with her "modern linen and lace hand work, finely wrought peasant costumes," and Greek vases; Mrs. Albert Goodwin of the University of Birmingham, England, one of several British mothers and children who were guests of Yale University during the war, lectured on insect life and social organization.[26] Frick wished to give young women of modest means learning experiences that would allow them to develop their talents and participate fully in a more equitable society. As she wrote to the board of trustees that first year, "The college belongs to the community in its efforts to offer to girls of ability an opportunity equivalent to that offered boys for preparation for leadership in their several fields. Such training is more than a privilege; it is a necessity if our local women are to play a part which their abilities are opening to them more and more in our democratic community."[27]

At the same time that Frick was setting up the college, she and Marguerite were also moving into their new home. Judging from comments made by Hartford Junior College alumnae, it was one that students often visited and in which they felt comfortable. A founding trustee of the school, Dorothy Pietrallo, had this to say about a visit she made to the apartment at 549 Prospect Avenue:

> I remember going to dinner at Miss Frick's house one night. This has nothing to do with education, but the first moment I came into the house she says, "Look what we've just done! We've taken off the cupboard doors, so we've got color all through the kitchen, because all the packages that we have on the shelf are so colorful." She said, "Don't you like that touch?" That is typical, I think, of her in some respects. She had bits of a flair, let's say, for the unusual, the different. And she contributed much to make the college lively.[28]

Carolyn Taylor lived across the hall from Frick and Yourcenar in the 1940s and recalled sharing many meals with them. The writer Jordon Pecile met with Taylor, still occupying the same apartment in the early 1980s, after Yourcenar's election to the Académie française. His "When France's Immortal Lived among Us" reports on Taylor's recollections: "Marguerite she remembers as a heavy-set handsome young woman with a lot of energy. She was always on the go and of course, being a busy teacher, didn't usually have much time to talk. Taylor liked her because she was witty and had good common sense. On the occasions when Marguerite gave a dinner party, the sensible conversation was as important as the French provincial dishes she served." Frick, she said, "had a love of pageantry and a flair for it, and she often entertained the students from the college by giving sumptuous English breakfast buffets that covered several tables with the splendor of a medieval banquet. Marguerite, on the other hand, liked to give small parties on winter evenings when, right in the living room, she cooked up delicious and filling omelettes over the hearth and kept the kettle bubbling in the fireplace the whole time."[29]

Further details regarding the decor of the women's apartment appear in an unusual note that Yourcenar wrote after she and Frick had been living in Hartford awhile. Frick's aunt Dolly contributed significantly to outfitting her niece's places in both New York City and Hartford. Marguerite sent Dolly a Christmas card one year in which she lightheartedly enumerates, in English, "the pieces of furniture you gave Grace as a permanent Xmas present, and what they are doing now." The list is interspersed with Grace's comments (indicated here in italics), which give the text the flavor of a three-way conversation. Although it is in some ways a typical bread-and-butter letter, the fact that it was addressed to one of Frick's closest relatives suggests that Yourcenar, who was known to be resistant to family relations, wrote it at least in part to please her partner. It also shows that she and Frick did not shy away from depicting themselves to family members as a consolidated unit. (They did not go so far as to mention that they shared a bedroom, however.) It is worth noting as well that Grace was entitled to the only desk in the house, while Marguerite had to content herself with writing on the dining room table.

1) The sofa is old, for so many people have sat on it, but happy, and dressed up with a newly dyed slipcover.
2) The lamp is in the big bedroom.
    (And believe it or not we still have some of the
    sheets you bought us in New York. Laundering
    at home does help to keep things.)
3) The armchair with a newly washed slipcover is near the fireplace.
4) The silver is much in use.
5) The slipcover is elegant and I call it "blacky."
    (She means the black and purple comfort
    you gave me years ago.)

6) The potato-peeler gadget is in the kitchen drawer, much in use.
   It is, in fact, M.Y.'s favorite. Not mine!

7) The small cast-iron frying-pan is nice and shining.
   We argue over this. She says you gave it to
   us. I don't remember.

8) The tea table has now wheels on it and is used every day. It is called "Aunt-Georges-on-wheels," but being a formal Frenchwoman I do not know if that is respectful or not.
   (We had wheels put on to roll it around.
   It is pretty.)

9) Grace's desk is full of papers and newspaper. It functions very much.

10) The drop-leaf table is in use all the time near the window. I write this on it. It is an old friend.
    We eat all our meals on it here, as in New
    York. How do you like our inventory?
    Hasn't it held up well?

Grace is well but has had a bad cold. So have I. We have a lot of snow now, but we like it very much. I do hope that your health will be better this next year. . . .

All my best wishes for a happy and peaceful year.

Greetings,

Marguerite Yourcenar[30]

"Aunt George" was Grace's mother's youngest sister, Georgia. Grace, as we know, had a lively sense of humor. She and Marguerite may have called their tea table "Aunt-Georges-on-wheels" because Grace's aunt was such an avid traveler, always in motion. Or the table may have originally belonged to Aunt George. One hesitates to suggest, from the pen of "a formal Frenchwoman," that the expression might hark back to the traveling bordellos and saloons known as "Hell on Wheels."

The testimony of a student from Grace's first year directing Hartford Junior College provides another glimpse inside Frick and Yourcenar's home. Millicent Bolling (later Smith), a young black woman in her second year at the college, took an English class from Frick. She remembered her as taking a special interest in her writing ability, honing her skills, and having an important influence on her intellectual development. As usual, Grace was still trying to reach her students' minds by way of their stomachs: "Oh, we would have a May Day breakfast with strawberries," Bolling Smith remarked. "Or

sometimes some of us would go over when Marguerite Yourcenar was there.
I remember snowshoeing over to Prospect Street, where her apartment
was. . . . And over the years, sometimes we would sit around and have tea
and talk about literature. At that time we did do plays in French. I remember
one play was *Tartuffe*, which I was in."[31] Those times of sitting around talking
about literature were actually part of a series of discussion groups that Frick,
or both she and Yourcenar, would hold regularly in their living room.

Millicent Bolling may never have known about another service rendered
her by Grace Frick. In January of 1941 Frick traveled to Hartford Junior
College's progenitor, Mount Holyoke College, to speak with the admissions
director there, Miss Harriet Newhall. Bolling's application to continue her education at Mount Holyoke had been rejected. On returning to Hartford, Frick
wrote to Howell Cheney about her case. Miss Newhall had insisted that Millicent hadn't been rejected because she was black, but her conversation with
Frick "turned on the question of race, 'the large number of Negro and Jewish
applicants this year,' so frequently that I must feel that the decision was on basis
of race alone." Frick worried about other students in possible difficulty:

> Paula Later, one of our honor students, has been notified that she is on the wait-
> ing list at Connecticut College for Women, where she prefers to go, although
> she has already been accepted at Simmons College. As she is Jewish I am not
> sure that she will be welcomed and therefore I may go down to New London
> on Monday morning to call on the new Registrar there, Dr. Leib's successor,
> and see which way the wind lies. I have stayed away previously because I did
> not wish to appear to push the matter. Paula is a pretty and charming girl and
> will make a good reputation for us if they admit her.
>
> The applicant to Barnard, Ethel Lutwack, also Jewish, has not yet received a
> reply. She is our first ranking student.[32]

Whether on account of Frick's machinations or not, Paula Later was indeed
accepted by Connecticut College for Women, from which she graduated in
1943; Ethel Lutwack graduated cum laude from Barnard the same year.[33]
Millicent Bolling did not go to Mount Holyoke, however, but to Colby College in Maine. It is probably not a coincidence that Frick's friend Mary Hatch
Marshall from Yale was on the faculty there at the time.

Marguerite Yourcenar began teaching French at Hartford Junior College in
the spring semester of 1941.[34] In May of that year she traveled to Canada
to renew her American visa. Usually Grace would accompany her on such

missions, but she was gearing up for the first commencement of the newly chartered Hartford Junior College. Marguerite would have to go alone. As Yvon Bernier recounts, she went by train to the American consulate in Montreal. Things did not go smoothly: "The age of suspicion that would reach its zenith with the sinister Senator [Joseph] McCarthy had already begun." Informed that renewing her visa would not be a speedy process, Yourcenar grew anxious. According to Bernier, "A cynical secretary who scoffed at her alarm, heedlessly saying 'it could very well take six months,' wrung from Marguerite Yourcenar a fit of sobbing so violent that she was immediately received by the vice-consul." That official managed to calm her down, but despondency set in again when she learned that she would have to wait another eight or ten more days. In an attempt to find lodging less expensive than the Windsor Hotel—"Host to Royalty"—Yourcenar left Montreal for the village of Rawdon, about forty-five miles north of the city. There she took long walks in nature and "buried herself in an English edition of the *Complete Works of Plutarch*."[35]

This description of carefree hours spent relaxing in the countryside leaves out an aspect of her stay in Canada that Yourcenar related to Jerry Wilson. En route to Miami in March of 1980, the two were discussing Halloween traditions over dinner. As Wilson wrote in his journal that night, "I told about JWW [Jerry's brother] getting to go to jail for throwing eggs and she about her night in jail in Canada during the war for some paper trouble—hearing a man being beaten next door—and the jailer bringing food cooked by his mother and finally letting her go having made a little money on the food."[36] Wilson's account is a bit flat—and leaves us wondering *why* Yourcenar was locked up—but it must not have been easy for a woman who had already lost her homeland to face the possibility of a second, involuntary exile. Though she eventually succeeded at getting her visa and returning to the safety of Hartford, both Marguerite and Grace were traumatized by the incident.

Fifteen years later, the two of them would compile a curious list of what they called "affaires historiques," using the word "affaires" as it was used, for example, in regard to the Dreyfus Affair—that is, for episodes involving fierce controversy. Those pertaining only to Grace were identified with the letter *G*, and Marguerite's, far more numerous, were assigned the letter *M*. The first entry on the *M* list is "1941 American Consul in Canada."[37]

Wednesday, June 18, 1941, was commencement day. It began with what would become an annual tradition at Hartford Junior College, the Shakespeare Breakfast. A scrapbook from that year contains a snippet from a newspaper article about the breakfast, which occurred at the home of Dean Frick. It "was served according to the style of the banquet described by Shakespeare in his story of Anthony and Cleopatra, with the menu similar to that of the time."[38] Beatrice Kneeland spoke in the early 1980s of Frick and the tradition she initiated:

> She was a scholarly person. I think she was considered a little erratic at times, the way she did things, but I felt that she had much to offer in the way of the head of a small college. And one thing she did that I thought was so nice was her Shakespearean breakfast at her home, at her apartment, that she gave the girls. And they dressed in Shakespearean costumes as much as they could, and they had the typical Shakespearean food and all. It was a lovely thing. She was quite the start of that, to set that tone for the college.[39]

The commencement ceremony itself began with an invocation by the Reverend Quincy Blakely. The freshman choir then sang a choral arrangement of the Twenty-Third Psalm to the tune of "Brother James's Air." Mary Woolley, president emeritus of Mount Holyoke College, was the speaker. Mount Holyoke in Hartford had been Woolley's original idea. Judging from the description of her address in a Hartford newspaper the next day, one strongly suspects that Grace Frick had a hand in her choice of topic, the still unrealized promise of democracy: "Among the weaknesses of democracy, Dr. Woolley said, are its failure to provide economic security and the prevalence of an anti-alien and anti-racial spirit. . . . Anti-alien activities are as dangerous as fifth column activities, Dr. Woolley said, as they strike at the very foundations on which democracy is built."[40] Dean Frick presented the fifteen candidates for the associate of arts degree to Howell Cheney, chairman of the board of trustees, who conferred on each young woman her diploma. It was a major achievement for all concerned.

CHAPTER 10 ✿ Echoes of the War
1941–1942

> For all we have and are,
> For all our children's sake,
> Stand up and take the war.
> The Hun is at the gate!
>
> —Rudyard Kipling

THE TRUSTEES OF HARTFORD JUNIOR College were pleased enough with Grace Frick's performance as dean that they raised her salary by 20 percent for the 1941–42 academic year. Finances at the school had not improved, however, and student enrollment had fallen from thirty-nine to twenty-seven. Events on the world stage weren't helping. Though the United States had not entered World War II, Hartford was a weapons manufacturing center; "a superfluity of good jobs at very high wages" confronted all of the city's educational institutions.[1] Frick scrambled throughout the summer and early fall of 1941 to find qualified young women to fill openings in the freshman class. The city's two primary newspapers did everything they could to support the struggling school. In the fall of 1940, following Frick's push to furnish the new Highland Street building, the *Hartford Courant* ran a series of large photographs in its Sunday magazine depicting daily life at the small college. It showed the library, with its four thousand volumes (and more on the way), the social room, the refectory, the reference room, the biology lab, and a sociology classroom.[2] The pictures fairly teemed with young women looking happily studious in ankle socks, saddle shoes, jumpers, or round-necked cashmere sweaters.

The local papers rarely failed to publicize events at the college. One such was the addition of another new course to the curriculum, History of Art. It was a gift to the school from Marguerite Yourcenar in response to a recent fund-raising campaign. She would cover art from prehistory to the present,

taking students to museums in Hartford and New York. Though both papers ran articles about the new course, they used sharply contrasting images
to illustrate them. The *Hartford Times* featured an artwork in its own right,
Charlotte Musson's pastel portrait from 1934 or 1935 of Yourcenar in lip-
stick and earrings.[3] The *Hartford Courant* used a more recent, much more

FIGURE 16. Pastel portrait of Marguerite Yourcenar by
Charlotte Musson, 1934–35. © Musée Elise Rieuf, Massiac,
France, www.musee-elise-rieuf.org.

boyish-looking photograph of Yourcenar, which suggests a shift in her persona over the course of the 1930s.[4]

The war years, which coincided with the strengthening of Grace and Marguerite's couple, were a life-changing time for Marguerite Yourcenar. Biographers have depicted these years as a personal and literary nadir from which
Yourcenar would emerge triumphant in 1951 with the publication of *Mémoires*

FIGURE 17. Marguerite Yourcenar, late 1930s. Petite Plaisance Archives.

d'Hadrien. Josyane Savigneau calls those early years in the United States "the dark years," contending that "the mixture of Puritanism and megalomania that typified this people without a civilization"—that is, Americans—held no appeal for the Frenchwoman.[5] Michèle Sarde dubs Yourcenar's nearly five decades in the United States "the American Night."[6] Michèle Goslar titles her chapter on Yourcenar's experience in the 1940s "Dying as Little as Possible."[7]

The phrase itself comes from a 1943 journal entry penned by Yourcenar. It evokes a context that is both personal and communal, the blackout drills that occurred periodically during the war along America's vulnerable Atlantic coastline: "*1943*. Lights out: the lights on steamships and in streetlamps, nightlights at the bedsides of the sick and candles in churches. The rare lamps that are still burning tremble with fear on the horizon. In this complete darkness where for us it is a matter of dying as little as possible, our task will be to rediscover, humbly groping our way, the eternal shape of things."[8]

There can be no doubt that the collapse of European civilization as Yourcenar had known it was a source of real suffering for her. Nor that the material tribulations of living in an unfamiliar culture amid wartime privations took their toll on a person whose background and privileged lifestyle had accustomed her to luxury. In one particularly gloomy assessment from early 1942 Yourcenar wrote that she had "no news from France, no news from Greece" and that her discouragement was nearing "the width and the depth of the Atlantic Ocean."[9] Bérengère Deprez has spoken aptly of the "fracturing" effect of Yourcenar's American exile, one manifest on both the personal and literary levels.[10] But she was not, for all that, paralyzed. In fact, the early 1940s were a time of active political engagement on Yourcenar's part that has not been sufficiently acknowledged. She had already published, in 1934, a novel about fascism in Italy, *Denier du rêve*, that she later described as

> one of the first French novels of its day (perhaps the first) to see the hollow reality hidden behind fascism's bloated façade for what it really was, at a time when so many writers touring the Italian peninsula were still content to be enchanted yet again by Italy's traditional picturesqueness or to congratulate themselves because the trains were arriving on time (in theory at least), without thinking to ask toward what terminal those trains were headed.[11]

When Yourcenar visited Virginia Woolf in 1937, Woolf was working on the antifascist essay *Three Guineas*. Americans in the late 1930s were far from united in opposing European fascism, as the pro-Nazi parade that greeted Yourcenar's arrival in New York made shockingly obvious. *Three Guineas* sold widely here.[12] Grace Frick, who had followed Woolf's career with such interest when she was teaching at Stephens College in the late 1920s, would have read every new title by Woolf.[13] Yourcenar's personal connection to Woolf would only have heightened her interest in the unique British novelist and polemicist.

In 1940, not long after she arrived in the United States, Yourcenar wrote her own essay denouncing fascism. "Forces du passé et forces de l'avenir" was a powerful rebuttal of Anne Morrow Lindbergh's *Wave of the Future*.[14] Translated into English, and heartily endorsed, by the fiercely justice-minded Frick, the essay was published in an official bulletin of the French Consulate in New York City.[15] Lindbergh's book, which Yourcenar calls a "work of Nazi propaganda" in the Pléiade chronology,[16] views fascism as a regrettable but irresistible phenomenon. Yourcenar sees things differently.

While acknowledging Lindbergh's important contribution to American contemporary literature and placing the author "among the legendary figures of our time," Yourcenar takes Lindbergh to task for linking Adolf Hitler to the future and his adversaries to the past. Not surprisingly, and well before anyone knew the full extent of Nazi atrocities, she takes the long view:

Is Hitler's Germany the representative of the future? None of the formulas of Hitlerian dictatorship is new: War, exasperated nationalism, the extermination of so-called inferior races, terrorism, secret police, power concentrated in the hands of a military faction, revolutions and massacres within the organization, religious intolerance, forced labor, the fanatic cult of the chief, nothing of all this is new under the somber sun of history. Not only is Poland thrown into the state in which she was before the famous Partition, but even into the frightful chaos which followed the great Tartar invasions, and France, beaten and humiliated, is re-living the disastrous times of the Hundred Years War. Not only are those countries in which civil liberty developed it's [*sic*] most glorious fruits, Holland, Belgium and the Scandinavian States, now battered down to their ancient status of vassal provinces, but victorious Germany herself, renouncing her 18th century and a large part of her 19th, no longer holds any more positive ideal than that of resembling a pre-Christian Germany as best she can. If this is the direction the Forces of the Future, symbolized by the tanks of the three dictators, are taking today, only a few more turns of the wheel and mankind will find itself in the full flower of the Stone Age.[17]

"Forces of the Past" may not display the fine craftsmanship of later Yourcenar essays, but it rejects Lindbergh's call for submission to Hitlerism with great vigor. In opposing fascism more firmly than Yourcenar's 1934 *Denier du rêve* had done, the text may be seen as marking an evolution in its author's political consciousness.[18] Its comparison of the Nazi scourge to the Barbarian invasions of previous centuries calls to mind Constantine Cavafy's 1904 poem "Waiting for the Barbarians," which takes an ironic look at political leaders who cultivate fear of an outside enemy to achieve their own, not necessarily benevolent, ends. The barbarian metaphor, moreover, was topical in the years leading up to the war. It was also used by the German exile Erika Mann in her *School for Barbarians*, a 1938 book about the Nazi educational system that was widely read in the United States.[19]

Grace Frick, in her turn, translated Yourcenar's French version of Cavafy's poem into English.[20] Although the typed text, preserved at the Houghton Library, bears no date, it was undoubtedly composed, like "Forces of the Past," in the early 1940s. These were Frick's earliest translations of Yourcenar's writings. The British-born W. H. Auden also saw the relevance of Cavafy's poem to the prevailing situation in the early years of World War II: he composed his own translation based on Yourcenar's, though without collaborating with the Frenchwoman. Grace Frick would never have laid claim to Auden's poetic genius, but her composition thoroughly captures Cavafy's essence and simple elegance.

Another early antifascist effort on Yourcenar's part may have been inspired by the man with whom she did collaborate on the Cavafy poems, Constantine Dimaras. On November 25, 1940, before Greece was overrun by the Axis powers, Dimaras wrote to Yourcenar from Athens. He spoke of the "magnificent war" that his countrymen were waging "to liberate humanity from the barbarity that threatened it," urging her to do what she could to help Greece out: "You have friends over there; talk to them about us; tell them that all of us here are proud and happy to be fighting this war. But also tell them how much we need to know that they are with us, near us, how much their moral and material support would be precious to us."[21]

A *Hartford Times* article by Marian Murray suggests that Yourcenar took Dimaras's plea to heart. Entitled "French Author and Teacher Pleads for Greeks, Cites Heroic Struggle of Hellenic People" and published on February 12, 1941, it details Yourcenar's commitment to supporting Greece in its fight against Italian forces and to furthering the Greek relief effort that was going on in Hartford at that time. The lengthy article features a stunning photograph of Yourcenar wearing a black shirt with a man-tailored collar and a classically knotted white tie.

Its description of the then thirty-seven-year-old writer, to anyone who knows her only as the literary eminence she later became, is worth its weight in gold. She is "serious, attractive and piquante, with straight, short dark hair and peculiarly lucid grey-blue eyes that light with an inner flame as she talks rapidly in fluent English, with a beguiling accent." Already she was known as Mme—not Miss—Yourcenar.[22]

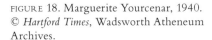

FIGURE 18. Marguerite Yourcenar, 1940. © *Hartford Times*, Wadsworth Atheneum Archives.

"Of the Greeks, she speaks with the understanding of a scholar and the sympathy of a novelist," writes Murray. In describing her work on Cavafy, Yourcenar calls the poet "a sort of Greek Browning," but one "with a great civic spirit. Many of his poems were created to show to others great examples of Greek courage and vitality through the centuries. He insisted on the value of making a stand, even if defeated. There's one about Thermopylae, which glorifies those who stand and try to defend what is good and worthwhile, even if they know they must perish in the end." Yourcenar goes on to discuss her great fondness for the Greek people, adding, "I lived in Athens, Corfu, Euboeia and Mytillene, and everywhere I went I was struck by the nobility and inner dignity of the peasants and the existence of a certain elegance from the old civilization which persists even in the humblest village."[23]

No one has ever been able to establish with certainty when Yourcenar traveled to Greece for the first time. The Pléiade chronology calls 1934–38 "years largely centered on Greece."[24] Murray's *Hartford Times* article, by contrast, quotes Yourcenar as saying that she spent the years between 1931 and 1939 in Greece, writing.[25] Echoing some passages from "Forces of the Past," Murray states, "Mme. Yourcenar would have us remember that the Greeks not only gave us a great ancient civilization, but that they helped that civilization to continue in Alexandria, and in the Middle Ages fought and survived against Asia. They kept the tradition of civilization vital until Europe was ready to accept it again."[26]

"I believe," says Yourcenar at the end of the article, "that we not only can't afford to let the Greek cause lose, but can't afford to lose the Greeks."[27] Whether she reported her activities in favor of Greece to her friend back in Athens we don't know. The earliest extant letter from Yourcenar to Dimaras dates from July 1951, by which time she had spent more than a decade in America and had written a book concentrating on an entirely different era of Greek—and Roman—history.[28] That book, in depicting a leader who was in crucial ways the antithesis of Hitler, would offer Yourcenar's ultimate response to the tragedy of World War II.

In early November of 1941, halfway through the first semester of her art history class, Yourcenar left Hartford for a busy week of lecturing in Ohio that Frick had arranged with the assistance of academic friends. To the State Congress of Teachers of French in Columbus, Yourcenar spoke of "Energy and Will in the French Novel"; at Ohio State University the topic was "French Paintings in American Galleries." In Cleveland she stayed with Virginia Corwin, Frick's schoolmate from both Wellesley and Yale and a pioneer in the study of world religions. With a view to what she hoped would happen when the war in Europe ended, Yourcenar's subject at Mather College was "French Civilizations throughout the Ages, Successive Survivals."[29]

Frick, meanwhile, had organized another series of cultural events for her second year as dean that were intended, as always, to expose her young charges to the wider world. On November 25, 1941, the renowned anthropologist Bronislaw Malinowski delivered a lecture entitled "The Democratic Principle in Human Evolution." Malinowski was highly sought after as a speaker, having been proclaimed "one of the four greatest minds in the world today" in news reports on his speech at the Tercentenary Symposium of Harvard University in 1936.[30] Prior to his evening address, Dr. Malinowski and his wife dined with Frick and Yourcenar at their home on Prospect Avenue. "War is by no means a biological, inherent and instinctive part of human nature," Malinowski told his audience, adding that the "present dilemma" has "imposed upon humanity the greatest catastrophe in history."[31]

On the program in early December was Frick's friend Mary Hatch Marshall, professor of English at Colby College. Dr. Marshall's specialty was medieval drama, and her talk was entitled "Origins of Medieval Religious Drama." A week later James Soby, author of a recent book on the artist Giorgio de Chirico, lectured on modern painting.[32] Next on the agenda was a concert of French ballads and folk songs ranging from the Middle Ages to the present.[33] Students and friends of the college were invited to join in the singing and folk dancing, and to attend an informal *goûter* (snack) after the performance. Frick and Yourcenar would, of course, be hosting a holiday open house in their apartment for their students before the Christmas break. As America was gearing up for war, the little college running on a shoestring, led by a woman on a mission, bravely soldiered on.

CHAPTER 11 ✿ Extracurricular Activities
1942

Cool waters tumble, singing as they go
Through appled boughs. Softly the leaves are dancing.
Down streams a slumber on the drowsy flow,
My soul entrancing.

—Sappho

THERE WAS MORE TO LIFE than work. It did not take long for Grace Frick and Marguerite Yourcenar to discover a cultural institution that would play a major role in their life during the Hartford years, the Wadsworth Atheneum. Its director, the dynamic and innovative art impresario A. Everett Austin Jr., became an immediate friend.[1] Known as Chick, Austin was Harvard educated, fluent in four languages, and comfortable with his bisexuality in an era of strict conformity. He loved European art. How could Grace and Marguerite not have befriended him?

The Atheneum had chosen the then twenty-six-year-old Austin as director in 1927. He had an eye for rising artists and made many purchases for the museum's collection that became the envy of much larger and better-endowed institutions: a Mondrian in 1935, Salvador Dalí's *Apparition of Face and Fruit Dish on a Beach* in 1939, and Max Ernst's *Europe after the Rain* in 1942, to name a few. At the oldest public art museum in the United States, Austin was responsible for many American "firsts": the first Picasso retrospective, the first opera with an all-black cast, the first Balanchine ballet—all of them in the single year 1934. He was also a magician, a classical dancer, and an amateur actor.

But his talents were not always cherished by the Wadsworth's conservative trustees. In their eyes Austin took too many risks and spent money altogether too lavishly. In a 1982 interview, Yourcenar remembered her friend: "There is a line of Shakespeare. It's Cleopatra who says it in Shakespeare:

'I am air and fire.' Well, Chick Austin was air and fire. [He had] great enthusiasm, a great facility to respond to the moment, the excitation of the moment. . . . He was of course a prince."[2]

Yourcenar's biographers have had little good to say about Hartford. Josyane Savigneau calls it "a rather uninteresting city"; Michèle Goslar, "a city plagued by laborers and rats."[3] Yourcenar herself once described it as "reactionary, chauvinist, and Protestant."[4] But Chick Austin was a one-man cultural revolution. In 1935, no less a figure than the French architect Le Corbusier enthused that Austin and his museum had turned the small provincial capital of Connecticut into "a spiritual center of America, a place where the lamp of the spirit burns."[5]

In 1942 Grace and Marguerite got involved in an exciting creative venture there. Chick Austin was inspired that spring to bring prominent European artists in exile to Hartford for a special show.[6] *Painters in Attendance*, so dubbed in the hope that the artists themselves would appear at the opening, would last only a week, May 22–29. It would feature the work of such luminaries as André Breton, Marc Chagall, Max Ernst, and Joan Miró. Coinciding with the first two days of this exhibit, Austin conceived a program of theater, music, and ballet called *The Elements of Magic*. Each of its parts would evoke one of the four elements: earth, water, fire, and air. For water, Yourcenar wrote a "free transcription" of a tale by Hans Christian Andersen that had been "the delight of [her] childhood."[7] Grace Frick translated the play into English under the title *The Young Siren*.[8] This was the first work of the imagination that Yourcenar had penned since her arrival in the United States, and she told her friend Jacques Kayaloff what a pleasure it was to be writing again.[9]

A few days before *The Elements of Magic* was to open, the *Hartford Times* published an article about Yourcenar's play that included an interview with the author. "I read the story long ago," Yourcenar explains,

> in one of those little books they used to sell at the stations in Paris. It has always fascinated me, and I've thought often that I'd like to do something with it.
>
> I don't know where the Danish writer got it. It may be an old folk story, but it can be treated as popular mythology, like the Greek tales or the Scandinavian. So I have taken the basic elements, and used them in my own way.
>
> The original fairy tale is extremely sweet, seen through 19th century Romanticism, but I have approached it from a more modern point of view.

Judging from the comments she made to the *Hartford Times* reporter, Yource-nar was pleased with all aspects of Chick Austin's production:

> I am very grateful to Mr. Austin for the opportunity to write this little play. It is hard to write novels now. We are too near things, in the middle of the turmoil. But I am happy still to write poetry.
>
> I am also delighted with the way Truda Kaschmann has created and directed the gestures for "The Young Siren." In the first scene the mermaid speaks, but in the second and third, you see when she has lost her voice she must express herself through another medium, and I feel that the motions Mrs. Kaschmann has devised are extraordinarily beautiful and well suited to the meaning.
>
> I have lived in the islands of Greece, but I have never met a real mermaid. However, I am sure this is what she would be like.[10]

Truda Kaschmann, who taught modern dance at Hartford Junior College, remained a friend of Grace and Marguerite's for life. She also created and per-formed in an expressionistic ballet for the element fire, inspiring Yourcenar to describe her years later as "a dancer from Berlin who left Germany in time to escape the fires of the crematoria."[11]

After Frick's death, Truda Kaschmann made a contribution to what had by then become the Hartford College for Women in memory of her friend. In thanking her, Yourcenar wrote, "All good wishes after our long silence, and all my thanks to have made a contribution to The Library Fund for Hartford College for Women in memory of Grace Frick. I still remember you so well in that décor, working with Grace."[12]

Chick Austin, for his part, would soon find himself ousted as director of the Wadsworth Atheneum, and Yourcenar considered herself at least partly responsible for his demise.[13] Austin was a forward-thinking member of the artistic avant-garde. Hartford, for the most part, was anything but. The Ath-eneum's trustees constantly tried to rein Austin in, particularly with regard to his theatrical ventures, each one in their eyes more outrageous than the last. In 1943 Yourcenar suggested that he mount the Jacobean tragedy *'Tis Pity She's a Whore*. She even lent him her copy of the text, helped him compose the script, and worked with him on staging.[14]

Like Yourcenar's 1934 short story "D'après Greco," John Ford's 1633 play concerns an incestuous brother and sister who defy the societal forces aligned against them, a fact that Ford fails to condemn. The audience for the pre-miere was stacked with friends of Chick's who came up from New York City to show their support for his daring venture. They spent the night camping out in a lounge at the Atheneum, where Marguerite and Grace joined them in a lively postperformance discussion of the symbolism and merits of incest.[15] But for the Hartford theatergoing public, any favorable treatment of this topic was beyond the pale. As Eugene Gaddis notes in *Magician of the Modern*, "more letters were addressed to the editors of the local press [about this play] than for any other program or exhibition Chick undertook, continuing for days after the production closed. They fairly shrieked about what they considered a diseased excuse for a play. Some saw it as an attack on the Roman Catholic Church and thus a slap in the face of the Irish and Italian communities in Hartford."[16] The Atheneum's trustees were not amused. Chick was urged to take a one-year sabbatical from his post. When that year was over, with Austin showing no signs of toeing a conservative line, he was quietly let go.

Incest was a topic that held special interest for Yourcenar. Her novella *Anna, Soror . . .* tells the story of forbidden passion, fought but eventually consummated, between a brother and sister in late-sixteenth-century Naples. Indeed, Yourcenar's depiction of Anna's incestuous coupling with her brother Miguel recalls the scene in Ford's play: it occurs, between two young people imbued with Christian piety, on Good Friday.

Three months before the premiere of Austin's *Elements of Magic* another theatrical event occurred in Hartford that, though relatively minor in its own right, would have the notable result of inspiring Yourcenar's next creative effort. On Valentine's Day 1942, Dean Frick hosted a meeting of the Hartford Wellesley Club at Hartford Junior College. As the *Hartford Times* reported, Frick would be speaking to the group about the various activities of her students. She would then introduce Truda Kaschmann's dance class in a performance, accompanied by the college choral group, of an abridged version of Euripides's *Alcestis*.[17] Frick's undergraduate sorority had staged the same play in May of 1923.[18] Just as Yourcenar worked closely with Kaschmann on *The Elements of Magic*, she took an active part in this production, too. She not only adapted and translated Euripides for the Hartford girls' choral performance, she directed it as well. She did not, however, attend the performance. Instead she spent that day at Hunter College in New York City at the organizational meeting of the Groupe des Hautes Études Françaises, described by the *Hartford Courant* as "a division of the New York School for Social Research and a part of its program for the University in Exile."[19] Yourcenar obviously took her responsibilities as an educator, and a French intellectual, seriously. Her formal ties to France were not immutable, however. It was also in February of 1942 that Yourcenar first filed her application for American citizenship.[20]

Having sustained a breakneck pace at Hartford Junior College for two years without respite, Grace Frick must have been ready to drop. Board chairman Howell Cheney and even the college housekeeper were urging her to take some time off.[21] But when she finally agreed to take a short vacation in the summer of 1942, she found it hard to tear herself away. While she and Marguerite were on their way to Maine for two weeks with Paul and Gladys Minear, Grace insisted on stopping en route to check out Hartford's competition in the form of Westbrook Junior College.[22]

The Minears had discovered the splendors of Mount Desert Island several years earlier, staying in Seal Harbor as guests of a colleague from the Yale Divinity School.[23] They returned to that small village in the summer of 1942, renting an apartment above the general store. It was to that apartment, fatefully, that they invited Grace and Marguerite.

Seal Harbor is one of several villages that make up the Town of Mount Desert. It is located on the southern tip of the island's easterly landmass between Northeast Harbor to the west and Otter Creek to the east. John D. Rockefeller's ninety-one-room "cottage," The Eyrie, was nestled in the woods there in the 1940s—it has since been torn down—and many other wealthy families had been drawn to the area by its rugged beauty and many outdoor recreational opportunities. Not only was Seal Harbor a prime destination for sailing adventures, it was also on the edge of Acadia National Park, where one could hike through the wilderness, horseback ride on Mr. Rockefeller's carriage trails, and swim, boat, or fish in several freshwater ponds and lakes. For Grace and Marguerite it was "an epiphany."[24]

Much has been written about the *coup de foudre* that discovering modern-day Greece was for Yourcenar in the early 1930s. A decade later, on another continent forty-five hundred miles away, a similarly life-changing event lay waiting for her, appropriately enough, on an island named by the French explorer Samuel de Champlain in 1604. Paul and Gladys Minear have testified to what a revelation Mount Desert Island was for both Yourcenar and Frick, neither of whom knew that such a place existed in America when they first went there in 1942. That the Minears used the word "epiphany" to describe the couple's reaction to this wild new place suggests how profound their immediate feeling for it was. Grace was already an ardent horsewoman, and Acadia's carriage roads drew her like a magnet; she would spend entire days in the saddle. Marguerite had long been a lover of islands, which, as she would often say, are both a kind of universe in miniature and an outpost at the edge of an unknowable beyond.[25] This island in particular, with its smattering of small villages, its dark forests of fir, and its low, rounded mountains, can hardly have failed to awaken in the Frenchwoman joyful memories of childhood summers spent in the similar landscape of Mont-Noir in northern France.

In July of 1973 Yourcenar would pen a nostalgic remembrance of her summer stays at Seal Harbor in a personal journal. She and Frick, both by that time seventy years old, had taken their Kansas City visitor Ruth Hall to the Abby Aldrich Rockefeller Garden high on a hill in the village of that family's former vacation home. Yourcenar had climbed a slight slope to a spot where one could see a Chinese bodhisattva statue and from which one could view a small lake in the distance below, "with its fringe of reeds and green foam. This was the lake," she goes on to say,

> where I often went swimming during my first stays here, over two or three
> blazing summers; I have often gone around it on foot and once or twice, un-
> forgettably, on horseback on a beautiful autumn day with a chill already in the
> air; and I remember the exact spot where, beneath a cluster of trees, I came
> across a fox, the spirit of that solitude. One of the most profoundly lived parts
> of my life is here.[26]

The two were so entranced by the island that at the end of their stay with the Minears, they set about finding a rental for themselves in another location. They chose one in the picturesque village of Somesville, the oldest permanent settlement on Mount Desert Island. Tucked away from the main road was a little log house known as Hysom's Cabin overlooking Somes Brook and located just outside the gates of a scenic old cemetery. Inside the bungalow hung a framed copy of a poem written by a previous renter, Walter C. Guthrie, entitled "The Brook (at Hysom's Cabin)." The poem—which more than seven decades later still hung where the couple first found it—suggests what appealed to Grace and Marguerite about the cabin's secluded brookside location:

> Far from the city's hectic throng
> I listen to your endless song,
> Alone with you at early morn,
> What myriad thoughts in me are born!

Rushing, eager, on your way
From the tarn where naiads play,
Caressing rocks with cooling quaff
While at would-be barriers laugh,
As I watch you wend your way,
Chanting ceaseless, vibrant lay,
Is your path from Whiting's deep
But a memory that I keep?
Or does your onward, labored course
To the Sound from natal source
Tell me, — since the world began, —
This is life to every man?[27]

Guthrie's naiads would almost certainly have called to mind for Marguerite and Grace the amorous nymphs of Yourcenar's Greek stories "The Man Who Loved the Nereids" and "Our-Lady-of-the-Swallows" from the 1938 collection *Oriental Tales*. Not only did Somes Brook wend its way from the naiads' playground to the sea, it also paused en route to form a basin deep and wide enough to swim in just a few yards from Hysom's Cabin. The

FIGURE 19. Grace Frick cavorting in Somes Brook. Petite Plaisance Archives.

vacationers wasted no time diving in, and one near neighbor, Elaine Higgins Reddish, later remembered their habit of skinny-dipping there on a hot summer's night.[28]

Grace and Marguerite liked this rustic cottage so much that they immediately reserved it for the following summer. Eventually they would try to buy both the cabin and the surrounding land. In the process of researching that possibility, they discovered that the rights to the brook were owned by four feuding families. As Grace told Donald Harris and his wife in 1977, "we ran into a terrible tangle with the deeds. We spent much of a hot summer in a courthouse in Ellsworth, and so we know much more about the families of these people than they do." This conversation took place near Somes Brook, where Yourcenar was being filmed by a French television crew. When Harris and his wife returned to the car where Frick had remained to keep warm on that November day, they reported that Yourcenar had mentioned their attempt to purchase Hysom's Cabin, adding that *she* had cleaned out the "torrent" with her own hands. Whereupon Frick replied: "Yes, we ... She says *I* but ..." When the three of them stopped laughing, Grace added, "Comes naturally in French, she tells me."[29] In the end, the two of them gave up on buying the little log house primarily because the plot of land on which it stood was so small.

FIGURE 20. Hysom's Cabin and swimming hole. Petite Plaisance Archives.

While providing both Grace and Marguerite with much-needed rest and recreation, this first visit to Mount Desert Island in 1942 also afforded Yourcenar the leisure to write *Le Mystère d'Alceste*, an offshoot of the work she had done a few months earlier with Grace Frick's students for Truda Kaschmann's modern dance production. In fact, Yourcenar hints at the Kaschmann connection in her introduction to the published version of the play when she calls one particular sequence a "tragi-comic ballet."[30]

Euripides's *Alcestis* is based on the mythical character who selflessly offers up her life in exchange for that of her husband, Admetus. Yourcenar turns this myth of wifely devotion and voluntary sacrifice on its head. In her version of the story, Alcestis repudiates the poet-husband from whose world she has largely been excluded, seeing death as a means of escape. When brawny Hercules comes along to save her, so different from the writerly, starry-eyed Admetus, it is not so much his legendary strength that brings Alcestis back to life as it is her desire for him. Hercules embodies elemental forces. He likes to eat and drink, and he indulges with gusto in all the pleasures of the flesh. Yourcenar's Alcestis returns to the world of the living in the hope of exchanging her irresolute husband for the powerful, sensual Hercules.

Yourcenar would one day see herself reflected in her voiceless young siren of 1942. A similar parallel exists between her and the character Alcestis. Yourcenar's evolution as a writer and a person in many ways so different from who she had been before the war was mediated to a significant degree by her relationship to the natural world of Mount Desert Island. As she said years later, it was because of her own contact with elemental forces that the focus of her thought slowly shifted "from archeology to geology, from a meditation on man to a meditation on the earth."[31] The predictable unfolding of Yourcenar's career as a writer had come to an abrupt halt when World War II began. In America, where her physical safety was assured but her literary lifeline was largely cut off, she underwent over the course of several years a profound philosophical metamorphosis. Like her character Alcestis, Yourcenar experienced a process akin to that of dying and being reborn. In *Le Mystère d'Alceste*, ironically, the female figure of Death describes herself to Hercules not as a killer but as "a midwife veiled in black" who gives birth to souls.[32] Though transformation did not occur over the course of one summer, Mount Desert Island was the midwife of Yourcenar's rebirth.

CHAPTER 12 ✼ Locking Horns
1942–1943

Incensed with indignation, Satan stood
Unterrified . . .

—John Milton

ON SEPTEMBER 5, 1942, THE society pages of the Hartford newspapers announced Grace Frick and Marguerite Yourcenar's return from the island. They had quite a year ahead of them. Yourcenar, for her part, would start teaching part-time at Sarah Lawrence College in Bronxville, New York. Asked years later how she came to teaching, the author explained amusingly that during the war American universities opened their arms to any number of "vague European intellectuals" without the slightest qualification to teach, she being one of them.[1] Judging from the testimony of some of her students, there was nothing vague about her, however!

Frick was faced yet again with running Hartford Junior College on a shoestring. When faculty members were reappointed for the 1942–43 academic year, they were warned that their continued employment was dependent on the success of fund-raising efforts then under way. Many agreed to a 25 percent reduction in their salaries, including Frick. By June of 1942 a $10,000 fund-raising campaign, despite support from many quarters, had yielded a grand total of $3,609.50. It was not an easy time to raise money, with urgent efforts being launched for the Greek War Relief Association, Russian War Relief, United China Relief, and so on. Hartford Junior College nonetheless continued to be held in high esteem by the senior colleges—Barnard, Colby, Mount Holyoke, Vassar, Wheaton—to which graduating students often transferred.[2]

Perhaps because of their small number and a sense that they were all in the trenches together, those students enjoyed a close relationship with their professors and a great spirit of camaraderie among themselves. The class history

123

for that year's freshmen provides a humorous students'-eye view of life at Hartford Junior College:

> On opening day we listened attentively to a lecture given by Mr. Cheney on how to use our minds for the next two years, at least. By the end of the first week we had met all our profs, including Madame Yourcenar, our most dynamic teacher, and our own dear Dr. Neumann. By the time of midyears we all knew the idiosyncrasies of our teachers, such as Miss Frick's continual reference to the D.N.B [no doubt the British *Dictionary of National Biography*] and unrelenting insistence on card notes; Dr. Neumann's calisthenics while lecturing; Dr. Arnold's lavender sports jacket; Madame Yourcenar's Russian leather boots; Dr. Buell's determination to fall off his horse; and Dr. Copeland's demonstration of throwing his hip out of joint and talking like a duck.[3]

But for Dean Frick and the college trustees, 1942–43 would be a tension-filled year.

The chairman of those trustees, Howell Cheney, was Dean Frick's almost exclusive interlocutor at the school. Born into a wealthy silk-manufacturing family and a graduate of Yale University, Cheney was a prominent businessman. He had spent some fifty years either working in or running his family's textile mills. In 1915 he had founded a trades school in his hometown of Manchester, Connecticut, today known as Howell Cheney Technical High School. Cheney's interest in education tended to be technical, vocational, and scientific. In a speech he delivered in 1910, Cheney called academic schools "hidebound by tradition," urging more emphasis on vocational and technical subjects.[4]

I have already mentioned the economic language that Chairman Cheney used to express support for Hartford Junior College's new dean in the spring of 1940, writing that "the Trustees desire to make your service here yield you the maximum of return and to stand by you in every way possible within their means."[5] As the new academic year began, those means were growing ever slimmer. But finances were not the only source of difficulty. Frick first obliquely referred to the way in which her educational philosophy differed from Cheney's in a letter dated February 17 (1941).[6] Speaking of herself and Yourcenar, Frick wrote in a typewritten letter to the board chairman,

> Saturday my friend and I were invited to a delightful tea (given for us, apparently) at Miss Fannie Johnson's. I would give a great deal to have some of our fledglings see a house like hers and meet people at all like her and her sister. My

friend and I came away feeling a little mournful in the realization that none of the students of the generation now in college will ever grow into such women as those two are. *You* feel that these present day students have gained so much in modern science. I wish I could feel half so sure.[7]

Though Miss Johnson is not further identified, it is easy to imagine her and her sister presiding over tea in one of Connecticut's colonial-era homes surrounded by books, heirloom furniture, and artworks. The "richness of background" that lent the scene its distinctive charm calls to mind the lushly integrated literary, artistic, and cultural program that for Frick constituted the essence of an education in the humanities. Which, as the energy she devoted to establishing a biology laboratory when she first took up her duties as dean clearly shows, was in no way to give short shrift to science. While she was not above bemoaning her students' lack of initiative, Frick wanted them to feel "joy in the possibilities of learning," as she went on to say. Never once does Cheney display the warmth, good nature, or enthusiasm about their joint enterprise that Frick's early letters to him in particular exhibit. At the end of Frick's first year as dean, for example, with commencement just behind them, Cheney wrote, without a word of thanks or praise,

> Since you have asked me to do so, I list below the suggestions that occur to me in connection with the last Commencement exercises:
> 1. That the invocation should be limited to not exceed three minutes
> 2. That if a distinguished speaker is invited to speak, that the address should not exceed thirty minutes in length
> 3. That a marshall [*sic*] should be appointed for the academic procession
> 4. That if good music is available, more music be introduced into the occasion
> 5. That at some future meeting of the Board of Trustees the matter of the award of honors for excellence in academic standards at Commencement be definitively ruled upon and settled.[8]

One gets the impression from Cheney's instrumental directives that he views Frick as the academic equivalent of a silk-factory foreman—a useful commodity, perhaps, but not an equal. Frick's attempts to engage him fell on deaf ears.

On March 23, 1942, someone arrived on the scene who would disrupt the status quo: Mrs. Thomas D. Macmillan, née Eva Adams, was a 1915 Smith College graduate. Having worked at the Peking Women's Medical College in China, she was hired as an executive secretary for Hartford Junior College and to assist the trustees with public relations.[9] Frick had been hoping for someone to take over three of her own many functions, as registrar, admissions officer, and fund-raiser. She was pleased with Macmillan's fund-raising abilities, as she wrote to Cheney on May 5, but she did not recommend that Macmillan be hired to fill the other two functions.[10] By June 16 she was more direct: "Please take her away."[11] The precise nature of Frick's dissatisfaction is unclear, but in the end Macmillan was indeed taken away.

Finally, the prospect was again raised of shutting the school down. Frick pleaded with Cheney not to let that happen: "Three years is not such a very long struggle in the history of institutions. Is it not worth a fourth attempt? Don't say no, please."[12]

On top of everything else, Yourcenar and Frick were giving extra help to two Hartford Junior College students—Norah Tapley, whose leg had been amputated above the knee, and Mary Lou Tucker, who walked with leg braces. "Much that was very real in terms of generosity and cooperation was given to the college in those years," states an unpublished account of Frick's tenure as dean.[13] In a letter written sometime in 1942 or 1943, Yourcenar spoke of her own involvement with the school:

> The French course was a personal contribution to Hartford Junior College toward the instruction of two very interesting students who had suffered serious handicaps in health. As for the History of Art last year, I should like to consider it as a gift to the college, for it is probably the most significant volunteer work I can do on education in these times, when the sympathetic understanding of different civilizations and cultures is of such vital importance.[14]

Needless to say, this was a conviction that she and Frick shared.

Another bone of contention between the board chairman and the dean involved the foreign film series Frick had launched at the college in the spring of 1942. Inspired perhaps by Chick Austin and his European artworks at the Wadsworth Atheneum, Frick brought Jean Cocteau's 1930 avant-garde film *Blood of a Poet*, among other foreign titles, to Hartford Junior College. Yourcenar, of course, was personally acquainted with Cocteau and an admirer of his poetry. As one Hartford newspaper noted, " 'The Blood of a Poet' is an allegorical presentation of the life of a poet. The film is famous chiefly for its attempt to translate the techniques of modern poetry and painting into the medium of motion pictures."[15] Given Dean Frick's interest in modernism, it's easy to see why she would be intrigued by this experimental work. But one suspects that Chairman Cheney and his board were not delighted by the prospect of exposing their coeds to a film containing possible anti-Christian elements, an opium smoker, and a hermaphrodite.

By early 1943 Howell Cheney was becoming exasperated with his dean. On January 22 he sought advice from Clement C. Hyde, who handled money matters for the college and often contributed funds of his own to keep it afloat. Cheney had spoken for an hour that morning with Miss Frick, "but frankly," as he wrote to Clement Hyde, "I felt I had failed to make my points clear to her as she was so voluminous and expansive in her discussion of every point."[16]

Three days later Cheney sent the following letter to Dean Frick:

My conversation of this morning left me with a conviction that I had failed to make any points clear to you.

They are as follows:

There are grave doubts whether the College can continue for another year. Since these doubts cannot be resolved before next June we recognize that you may now reasonably protect your opportunities to obtain an assured position for next year.

You advised me of your intention to take funds from the textbook account to pay for the expenses for the films representing the Art and the Life of Foreign Nations, and, if this was not sufficient, to pay for them yourself. You should do neither of these two things. No one has any authority to transfer means from one fund to another, without the approval of the Board of Trustees, or the Comptroller. I feel quite sure that the Board would object to your obligating yourself for these expenses or to your undertaking the project without its approval.

No new projects should be undertaken, and no allocations of funds made without the approval of the Trustees or the Comptroller, and this should be presented to them with the approval of the proper committee.

It is my feeling, which is shared by other members of the Board of Trustees, that you undertake to do too many things. Some of these do not properly come within your duty. In doing so you unnecessarily exhaust your energies and your more essential work suffers.

In your extreme anxiety to give of your utmost to the students, faculty, and the employees, you are so anxious to accomplish your objective that you overlook their interests, with a resulting injury to their relations to you and the College.

I have suggested to Mr. Hyde that he also give you a memorandum of certain matters which he feels are not being handled in a proper or business-like way.

Having said the above I would emphasize again our deep appreciation of the sincerity of your work and of your efforts to give of yourself unsparingly.[17]

Over the next two days, Frick wrote what Cheney would no doubt call a "voluminous" response—two and a half single-spaced typewritten pages— and put it in a drawer. A few weeks later, ironically, an article in *Wellesley* magazine saluted Frick's accomplishments in Hartford. It offers a distinctly more positive assessment of her and her work than Howell Cheney's: "Since 1940, Grace M. Frick, '25, has been doing distinguished pioneer work in Connecticut as Dean of Faculty (and acting head) of [Hartford Junior College]." The article goes on to quote several Wellesley alumnae praising Frick, among them Katherine Haynes Gatch: "Grace Frick's zeal and imagination, together with her concern for the individual student, have done much in the organization and initial stages of the college. The venture is itself a significant one in the field of education and Miss Frick has brought great ingenuity and insight to her task." Most notable is the assessment of Hartford Junior College trustee Mary Bulkley:

Miss Frick has great strength of purpose and a vital interest in the educational welfare of the students. She has a fine quality of self-forgetfulness, as well as a high sense of academic standards, so that the college has grown in value to the community under her administration. She has shown much resourcefulness with few resources, has gathered together a distinguished faculty, and has made many contacts for the students by using imagination and persistence. I hope that I am expressing something of the appreciation of the Board of Trustees for Miss Frick's fine work.[18]

One is almost tempted to ask, Will the real Grace Frick please stand up?

While all this was going on back East, Grace's seventy-four-year-old uncle George LaRue in Kansas City was once again in precarious health. Though he had eventually recovered from the crisis that kept Grace from returning to Yale in 1933, Unk had never regained his former strength. He had suffered several strokes over the past five years, each of which left him progressively weaker.[19] Frick and her uncle had always been close. Still, between her family's unenthusiastic reaction to her French friend and her professional obligations, she had not been home for almost four years. LaRue had more than once expressed his wish to see her. Ever the dutiful daughter when it came to her family, Grace would normally have dropped whatever she was doing to fly to Unk's bedside. This time she did not. Her center of gravity had shifted.

On April 2, 1943, Howell Cheney called Frick to his office and fired her. She had not mailed her long letter of January 27, fearing it was overly expressive of her indignation. On the day she was let go, she reread Cheney's letter of January 25 and sat down to type another two-page missive. Not until April 13 did she communicate both to the board chairman.

Incensed by the idea that she might have mishandled funds, Frick starts off on April 2 by noting that "one glance at the books would settle any misconceptions" in that regard and asking Cheney to clear up those misconceptions before the Board of Trustees. Frick then writes,

> I see now that I was wrong not to have sent my reply, however indignant, at once. It was naturally a matter of some shock to me that you could write a letter on finances in such an accusing tone without once mentioning the essential fact that for nearly three years now I have kept within a budget which most college administrators would find laughable. Academic and household expenses have been kept down not only to the figures set, but below some of the figures agreed upon, in order to help in payment of unforeseen expenses voted by the Board itself. I have tried not to trouble you with complaints about economies, and did not care to do so as long as the quality of the institution continued to improve. It is significant to me that your letter does not once mention the high academic status of the institution, nor the approval with which its individual instructors, whom you seem to respect, regard it.
>
> This is, I believe, the first time that I have ever addressed you on the subject of the finances of the College, but I have often wondered just how you thought those extraordinary balances were achieved, how rugs could wear out and be replaced, how cleaning and repairs could be made without expenditure, how entertainment could be given without disbursement from the budget, how cleaning could be paid for in summer, how instruction could improve in number of courses and in personnel, and how the students could be protected from burdensome extra charges which prevail in most private schools. You declare yourself dissatisfied with an administration which you have been unable to finance.
>
> You tell me that the Board is dissatisfied with my relations to the parents and to the high schools. He would be a daring teacher who would claim to be loved by students and parents alike, but I will readily challenge you to a showing of hands on that subject. I happen to care enough about the students and their

parents, too, to see that they get something really good, and if the students do
not recognize the fact at first most of them do by the end of the year. Work
such as we do cannot be carried on in an atmosphere of mutual disrespect and
dislike. Geraldine O'Connell's mother told me last summer that Geraldine was
most unhappy at the College. She is, honestly, the only case of the kind which I
have to report. Her high school principal had a similar report from the mother
when the girl was in East Hartford High School. As to the schools, I have tried
to visit them when we had no one else to send, and have not always done so
under the best conditions, therefore, but the visits proved enjoyable for me and
have produced some lasting friendships, so that I am somewhat bewildered as
to the basis of your charge.

You will be impatient of these details but I have not written without first
taking some time and some quiet to think. I am one of the few people in the
teaching profession who can afford to protest against what seems to me a most
extraordinary method of dealing with an official who has too often been left
to her own devices in a position of some responsibility. Is there any reason on
earth why you could not have said to me outright, in January or before, that
you thought that I was not fulfilling this post satisfactorily? I suspect that you
could not do so because the Board itself has not been able to take full responsibility for the College.

It is a matter of real regret to me that you have never really seen the College for what it is, and that it has always seemed to you a rather shabby little
institution which someday might outgrow its present humility. The thing *is*
good, and if only you had faith in what it now stands for you would not be so
apologetic about it in talking to others. Some of the Trustees are suggesting that
we are giving a luxury product to relatively poor girls (a curious conception of
education in a democratic country), but someone must reply that a good education is never a luxury for anyone who is able to comprehend it. Is it not a basic
distrust of the value of liberal arts which makes for so many rationalizations
about practical courses? And for these two contradictory views of the College
as unsuccessful, and at the same time extravagant because non-vocational?[20]

If Howell Cheney had expected Frick to jump ship when he told her in
January that Hartford Junior College might close, he obviously didn't know
who he was dealing with. "I realize that the doubts concerning continuation
of the College 'cannot be resolved before next June,'" Frick wrote on January
27, "but it seems to me the more necessary to strive for its continuance at
this time, therefore, and the less desirable to divert my energies to the very

absorbing matter of seeking a position elsewhere."[21] About her supposed misappropriation of funds in connection with the foreign film series, Frick was adamant, calling Cheney's remarks "serious charges upon me that are not in accordance with the facts. . . . No existing fund has been touched in any way or transferred, nor have I power to do such a thing if I wished so to do, as you must certainly know." Proud of her and her colleagues' accomplishments, she continued,

> It is quite true that more than one of us on the staff is undertaking to do too many things on behalf of the College, a condition true of many pioneer ventures. We are offering an exceptionally fine curriculum and an extraordinary social experience to some thirty girls a year on a very small budget, and that means work for all of us, and many kinds of work. Until the College can afford extension of the staff in both directions, that is to say, until it can afford both a president and a janitor, such pioneering problems can hardly be resolved, and it is mere pretending to say that they can be avoided.

To his credit, Cheney replied, "These letters fill me with deep regret."[22] A week went by between his receipt of Frick's two letters and the day he responded. During that time members of the board of trustees may have tried to impress on him the value of what Frick had accomplished. Accounting questions were not paramount in the decision to terminate Frick's employment, Cheney explained:

> I shall always retain the memory of your unselfish services and your outgoing determination to give of your utmost even beyond your strength to the life of the College. I am sure that the Board of Trustees also share this feeling toward you. This has made it much more difficult for all of us to approach the decision which probably should have been made last year, but which out of recognition of your valuable contributions was postponed. It is with deepest regret to all that it could not be postponed any longer.

This letter is dated April 20, 1943. The next day in Kansas City, George LaRue had a massive stroke and died.[23] Grace took only as much time away from her duties as she needed to travel to Missouri for her uncle's funeral. Knowing that Marguerite—surprisingly, given her renowned independence during the prewar years—did not like to be alone, Grace arranged for their friend Erika Vollger, who lived in New York, to come stay with her while she was away. Alone, exhausted, and rejected by an institution to which she had indeed given more than her utmost, Grace can only have been wondering what the point of it all was.

Marguerite Yourcenar had her own challenges to deal with during this, her initial year of teaching at Sarah Lawrence College. She had to rise before dawn on Monday mornings and, laden with whatever she would need for the week, begin the trip by bus and train that would eventually deliver her to the village of Bronxville in New York's Hudson Valley. Thursday afternoons she would make the same three-hour trip in reverse, returning to Hartford for the weekend. Sometimes Grace would rise "heroically" at four in the morning and drive her to Bronxville in a rental car.[24] One winter there was such a bad snowstorm that Yourcenar got lost in the drifts walking home on Prospect Avenue and had to be rescued by firemen![25]

Years later, shortly after her election to the Académie française, officials at the University of Hartford, into which the former Hartford Junior College had long since been folded, attempted to bestow on Yourcenar an honorary doctorate. Stephen Trachtenberg, president of the institution, wrote to her or her assistant about the matter several times.[26] So eager was Trachtenberg to bring Yourcenar to Hartford that he offered to fly her there and back on commencement day in a private plane. Yourcenar declined the award, as she would decline another honor offered by the same institution in 1987.[27] As she wrote to Beatrice Kneeland (a onetime Hartford Junior College trustee), at the time her connection to that school had to do only with helping Grace Frick: "It is to her memory that retrospective honors should come, if any."[28] Apparently unbeknownst to anyone at the University of Hartford, Yourcenar would never have accepted a tribute from a college that had fired her companion.

Not only had Howell Cheney given Frick the sack, he had enjoined her not to tell anyone about her dismissal. In early May Cheney expressed his wish to make a public announcement of Frick's departure, as if the choice to leave had been hers. Frick would have none of it:

> I do not authorize you to issue any statement about my resignation or withdrawal, since that is not the case. You may, if you like, say exactly what you said to me on April 2, for that is what I must say when people ask me, as they will, why I am leaving. Or you may say outright that you are replacing me by someone else.

A year ago, and again last fall, I offered to resign if Mrs. Macmillan were to be retained on the staff. At neither time, nor at any other time, did you give me the slightest intimation that the Board was considering my removal. The Trustees have not made an effort to understand fully how the College operates under present conditions and, with the exception of Mr. Hyde, have not helped in the problems of administration; yet without a word to me in advance, or inquiry by Committee, the Board met on April first, as I understand it, to vote on my removal. I see no excuse for this method of procedure and do not wish to be a party to any concealment whatsoever in the matter of public announcement.[29]

As far as the board's explicit reasons for removing Frick from her position are concerned, they are stated in three sentences of the otherwise highly laudatory letter that Howell Cheney composed for inclusion in Frick's Wellesley placement file. Cheney first acknowledges the challenges with which Frick had always to grapple. He then goes on to say, "At the end of her three years, even allowing for the difficulties, we feel that she has not proven herself a natural administrator. It is very difficult for her to delegate work to others and to refrain from having a part in every enterprise. Confronted with more things than one person could possibly do, Miss Frick tried to do them all, rather than to select the most important demands."[30]

One member of the board of trustees, Dorothy Pietrallo, was later willing to comment on what happened between Cheney and Frick:

I think that Mr. Cheney felt that this new baby, this new college was his child, and he wanted so much to steer it that he steered it instead of helping to steer it. He was overanxious. He was so totally dedicated and committed to this institution that it just had to run right. And he had to know of day-to-day operations of it. I doubt if you would call him a good one to delegate authority. I think he, perhaps unconsciously, felt the need to share rather than to delegate. But he was totally committed to every facet of the college. I think he would deeply have resented it if you'd called him a meddler.[31]

There may simply have been too many chiefs and almost no Indians. Other factors may also have entered into Cheney's and the trustees' assessment of Frick's suitability as dean, however. We have seen what happened to Chick Austin when he staged a play at the Wadsworth Atheneum that scandalized reactionary Hartford. Austin had also left his wife, Helen, a member of the Hartford elite, to move in with a male lover.[32] It may not be purely by chance that when Cheney chose to pick a bone with Frick about her supposed misappropriation of funds earmarked for textbooks, it involved her decision to screen avant-garde films like Cocteau's *Blood of a Poet*. Frick and Yourcenar's closeness to Chick Austin at a time when he was not in good odor among Hartford's leading citizens may have played a role, too; not to mention the fact that Frick herself was living with a woman and appeared to have no interest in changing that state of affairs.

There is no precise indication in the Hartford College Archives as to when a public announcement was made of Frick's departure or what that announcement consisted of. She was still manning the dean's office on June 8 when a long letter came from Cheney. Without Frick's knowledge, the board chairman had taken it upon himself, shortly after she was fired, to inform the then president of Wellesley College, Mildred McAfee, that "the present Dean is retiring at the end of this year to finish her work for a Ph.D. degree."[33] Frick, of course, did not appreciate this misrepresentation of the facts and prevailed on Cheney to set things straight with the officials at her alma mater. For Frick, the prospect of being perceived by her many friends and mentors at Wellesley as someone who would give up on a pioneering educational institution for young women just because the going got tough was far more objectionable than being seen as an incompetent administrator.

Meanwhile, word of Frick's dismissal got out. On June 14 a beautifully handwritten letter individually signed by the students of Hartford Junior College was sent to Howell Cheney:

> We, the students of Hartford Junior College, would like to have you know before we leave the college for the summer, or permanently, that your impression that we did not like Miss Frick is false.
>
> To us, Miss Frick *is* Hartford Junior College. The college, as we know it, is alive with her personality and her desire that every girl get the most from its limited facilities. Without money, the college must have ideals on which to function. These ideals have become a large part of Miss Frick's life and it is her devotion alone which has seen them fulfilled.
>
> The combination of devoted friend and cultured dean was found to such an unusual degree in Miss Frick that we wonder how anyone can take her place.[34]

Frick's dedication to Hartford Junior College can obviously be judged by the extraordinary energy we have seen her devote to that struggling institution since the day she stepped into the deanship. But her greatest joy was teaching, of which the text she used to teach *Hamlet* in the spring of 1943 provides a poignant glimpse. Frick had received a review copy of the 1939 edition of *The Tragedy of Hamlet Prince of Denmark by William Shakespeare*, edited by George Lyman Kittredge. At the top of page 2, she wrote, "Delight of taking a new text and marking it a) for the new year and its experiences (1943), b) in relation to what one has just been reading, *Dr. Faustus*, and perhaps c) a new editor, if very good."[35] The new year and its experiences did not turn out to be very pleasant ones. But what Howell Cheney and the board of trustees may never have known is that when they lost Grace Frick—and, with her, Marguerite Yourcenar—they also lost what would have been a big boost to the long-term financial well-being of their institution. So devoted was Frick to the mission of Hartford Junior College that she had initially made it one of the two ultimate beneficiaries of her estate.[36] The establishment that Frick endowed instead would make out very well indeed.

CHAPTER 13 ❦ Best-Laid Plans

1943

Money is the sinews of love, and of war.

—George Farquhar

WHEN GRACE FRICK'S FRIEND MARY Marshall learned of her dismissal in June of 1943, she called it "stupid and cruel and irresponsible—and I think so highly of you that it enraged me." Having heard about Frick and Yourcenar's island in Maine, Marshall added, "It sounds like a most beautiful spot, and my heart yearneth toward it and you."[1] The women would soon be enjoying that haven from the storm for the whole summer. But recent events had brought home to them the strength and importance of their bond. Before they left Hartford, there were pressing matters to tend to.

First and foremost it was time for Frick to revise her will. Not only did she wish to remove Hartford Junior College as a beneficiary, but her financial situation had changed quite dramatically when George "Unk" LaRue died. Unk had set down the terms of his own last will and testament on March 4, 1937, while his niece was in Paris settling the affairs of her cousin, Sister Marie Yann. According to the probate documents associated with LaRue's will, the estate was valued at just under $177,000 (almost $2.5 million in 2018).[2] LaRue made only two specific bequests: the first, in the amount of fifteen thousand dollars, to Grace Frick, and the second, in the amount of ten thousand dollars, to his brother John in Los Angeles. Uncle George thought of Grace as a daughter, and this was his way of providing for her. Fred and Gage were both actively involved in the LaRue Printing Company; their inheritance was joint ownership, along with George's wife, Dolly, of the ongoing business.

Straightaway Frick set up a trust to provide for Yourcenar in the event of her death. On May 10, 1943, Yourcenar asked her New York lawyer, Margaret Smith, to draw up a will making Frick her own sole beneficiary. Yourcenar's previous will, deposited at Lausanne, Switzerland, had assigned her estate to Christine Brown-Hovelt de Crayencour. By this time her stepmother was seventy-two years old, in poor health, and living in the southwestern French city of Pau. Marguerite knew that Grace would "do everything in her power to help Mme de Crayencour in case of my decease, if help from this country can again reach her."[3]

Yourcenar's letter provides significant information, in the author's original English, about her personal assets. It clearly shows that the young French-woman was not destitute when she came to the United States, a claim always associated with the implication—if not the outright assertion—that she formed a couple with Grace Frick only because she had nowhere else to turn. Item *a* on Yourcenar's list relates to the same real property for which she finally received a partial settlement after a ten-year legal battle—not in 1939, as she remembers, but in April of 1938:

> a) a mortgage on a property (hotel and grounds) at Knocke-Zoute (on the Dutch-Belgian border, though I think that the grounds are all situated in Belgium). The mortgage (of which half was repaid to me in 1939) is now worth 350,000 Belgian francs. The deeds and papers are in possession of Mr. Rene Peyralbe, notaire, at Bruxelles, Belgium, rue du Gouvernement Provisoire, 48. Naturally, the original deed is in the office of the Recorder of deeds in Zoute, Belgium (called in French "Registre des Hypothèques").
>
> b) The royalties on 9 books (list attached) published in Paris by two publishers 1) Mr. Bernard Grasset, 61 rue des Sts-Pères, Paris, VI. 2) Mr. Gallimard, Les Editions de la Nouvelle Revue Française, 43 rue de Beaune, Paris, VI. My two best friends on the staff of these two publishing companies were Mr. André Fraigneau, at Bernard Grasset, and Mr. Emmanuel Boudot-Lamotte at Gallimard's.[4]

She chose the quinquagenarian Edmond Jaloux of the Académie française to execute her literary estate, to be helped—or replaced, if necessary—by Constantine Dimaras and her Swiss friend Jacques de Saussure. With overseas communication cut off on account of the war, she was doing her best to foresee all possible eventualities. Yourcenar's letter continues:

> c) My step-mother, Mme Christine de Crayencour . . . left me by will made in 1938 her estate in England. . . . Mme de Crayencour confirmed that will by many of her letters addressed to me in 1942 from France, letters now in my

possession. These letters mention also that some of her personal possessions, furs, jewelry, pictures, silver, and so forth, have been left at Hotel Meurice, Lausanne, under the care of Mr. Hepp, the landlord, and are to come to me after her death.

d) I have myself left some of my silver, papers, household goods, and 6 or 7 trunks of books, packed in trunks and baskets and ready for shipping, with Mr. Hepp, in the store-room of the Hotel Meurice, Lausanne. Some of the most valuable baskets of books have perhaps now been removed to the cellars of a friend's house, Miss Berthe Vuillemin, who offered to take care of them, so as to divide the risk in case of fire, or other war eventualities. . . .

e) I have left in Paris, in the cellars of the Hotel Wagram, 206 [sic] rue de Rivoli, Paris, II, 4 trunks and about ten pieces of furniture, under the care of the night porter. This was done hastily in the last moments of my leaving Paris in 1939, after the beginning of the war, and I have no papers of any sort proving ownership in case of changed management. The hotel has been transformed into a French, and after that, to a German war office, and therefore there is, I am afraid, little hope that these things have been respected. The three trunks contain rare books, lace, and family papers.

f) On this continent, my bonds are deposited at the Bank of Montreal, 117 St.-James Street, Montreal, whence my dividends are sent, not only the dividends from the bonds deposited in their bank, but also of those left in the Westminster Bank, England, for which they act as agents. I also own some shares in General Electric, General Edison, General Motors, Shell Union, the certificates of which are with me in Hartford, the total value of which does not exceed $2000 and 750 pounds in British War Loan, likewise with me here in Hartford and which I intend next winter to place in a safe in New-York.

I have a savings account at New-York City Bank, 111th and Broadway, containing at this date $450.

Except Mme de Crayencour, my step mother, I have no other "next of kin" than a half-brother, Mr. Michel de Crayencour, ... Bruxelles, Belgium. Mr. M. de C. is married to a Belgian woman and is now a Belgian citizen. We are not on good terms, and have not written to each other for nearly ten years. . . .

[*Handwritten:*] I should add that I am a French citizen, but that I have now my first American papers, received in February, 1942.[5]

In early July Margaret Smith addressed to Yourcenar, by then on Mount Desert Island, a draft copy of the latter's new will. From Smith's cover letter we learn that the author had chosen to leave the bulk of her estate to the

Museum of Modern Art if Grace Frick should predecease her.[6] Even at this early stage of her American odyssey, Yourcenar felt strongly enough about the country in which she had found refuge to wish to benefit one of its premier art museums. It is also worth noting that she chose *not* to endow an institution to which she had closer ties but that had just suspended its creatively daring director: the Wadsworth Atheneum.

Frick and Yourcenar's friendship with Chick Austin was still going strong, and one of his disciples wrote to Yourcenar in Maine. Thomas "Tommy" Hughes was a sergeant in the Guard and in training at Camp Hood in central Texas. He had heard about the furor over *'Tis Pity She's a Whore* at the Wadsworth: "I hated to miss but I know it was every bit as wonderful as you say."[7] A year later, Hughes was in Normandy taking part in the Allied liberation of France.[8]

The war brought with it all kinds of changes on the home front, one of which was the rationing of everyday items such as sugar, coffee, and gasoline. Another, for the Fricks and LaRues, was the fact that Grace's older brother Gage, unmarried and childless, had been drafted. He shipped off to England in the spring of 1943.[9] Not only was Gage a principal in the LaRue Printing Company; he was also in control of the family trust. And therein lies a tale.

The LaRue Printing Company was a thriving concern that had made George LaRue a rich man. When his health began to fail, steps were taken to protect as much as possible of his fortune from what Grace's friend and legal adviser Ruth Hall called in early May 1943 "a system of taxing personal property which would be ruinous if it were literally applied."[10] Hall had left New York and was working now at Warrick, Koontz and Hazard back in Kansas City. As she went on to explain,

> All taxpayers that I have known who have substantial assets take some steps to minimize these taxes. Some people call it tax avoidance, some people call it evasion but each and every person that I have ever known that has anything of any substantial value does something to cut down the tax that would otherwise be due. The system that Gage described in the letters which I refer to in my memorandum is one such possible system.[11]

In accordance with that system, and over the course of several years, George LaRue had placed significant shares of his wealth in securities and bonds in the names of his wife, his nephews, and his niece. Grace had transferred the assets she received to the First National Bank of Kansas City as trustee.

But the ground was now shifting under Frick's feet: Gage had been sent overseas, she had been fired, and Unk had died, all in the space of a few weeks. Grace needed help, and she naturally turned to her trusted childhood friend. Where did things stand with respect to the LaRue funds in Grace's possession? Could she rely on them if need be? Attorney Hall's response to these questions explains the crux of the matter: "The purpose of putting property in the names of your Aunt, Gage, Fred and yourself was to minimize death taxes. A completed gift is not taxed at the time of the giver's death but if the giver retains substantial control over the gift up to the time of his death then the law treats the transfer as one subject to death taxes. It is sometimes hard to draw the line between complete and incomplete gifts."[12]

Hall then proceeded to detail several factors that make the gifts look complete. Casting possible doubt on "the unconditional and final character of the gifts" made to the four recipients would primarily be "the so-called gentlemen's agreement," according to which the recipients would not treat the securities as their own as long as George or Dolly LaRue should be living. Further:

> If you should take the position at this time that you are the unqualified owner of the securities and are entitled to use interest and principal in any way that you see fit, your Aunt might be very much upset and resentful. Her attorneys would advise her, in my opinion, that trying to enforce the gentlemen's agreement would only lead to tax complications. Your Aunt has so much to lose by opening up any such question that I feel sure that she would be reluctant to follow that route.[13]

In Hall's view, Frick should come to Missouri so that all the parties involved, along with their attorneys, could discuss the matter in person. She would leave for Kansas City in October of 1943. As usual, Grace arranged for someone to stay with Marguerite in the apartment while she was away. This time it was Bronislaw Malinowski's wife Valetta. Yourcenar had a room at Sarah Lawrence College, where she would begin her second year of teaching, but it was no place to spend three-day weekends. When her teaching day was done, as Antoinette Hoffherr writes in an unpublished essay,

> Mme Yourcenar retired into the privacy of a basement corner that the college had put at her disposal. There she kept her books, references, dictionaries, there she slept one or two nights a week rather than commuting back and forth from Hartford, Connecticut. The only other occupant from these nether regions, a

coloured man, came morning and night to attend to the furnace, and prophecy [*sic*] the weather outside. The basement room was not light, airy or cheerful but Mme Yourcenar liked its convenience and was grateful for it.[14]

Over the course of the upcoming months, with LaRue's will wending its way through probate and Gage overseas, everything went along smoothly. Frick spent the Christmas and New Year holidays touring Mexico with Aunt Dolly before returning to Hartford in January of 1944. She was even appointed to control the family trust in Gage's absence.[15]

It was not until mid-June 1945 that the topic of that trust once again took center stage. With Gage Frick now home after eighteen months in England as a member of the Army Air Corps, Grace received a flurry of letters or phone calls from her brother regarding the funds being held in her name. Predictably, each contact from Gage precipitated an immediate letter from Grace to Ruth Hall in Kansas City.[16] We don't have those letters, or Hall's responses to them. We do know, however, that the securities parceled out to Frick in the years before George LaRue's death never did find their way back to the family trust. Grace, for once, put herself first. At forty years of age, she had lost what she thought would be her life's work. She had not completed her doctorate. Even in the best of circumstances, she would never have the earning power in academia that her businessman brothers enjoyed. And there was Marguerite's welfare to consider. Yourcenar's official status in this country was still not secure, and she was definitely not getting rich as a part-time instructor at Sarah Lawrence College.[17] What's more, the couple were developing a life plan that would require an adequate, reliable income. Holding on to those investments meant financial independence.

The family was very likely shocked by Grace's noncompliance with the LaRues' estate strategy. Indeed, they may have gone so far as to take legal action against her. Marguerite Yourcenar later remembered this episode as an attempt on the part of Frick's family to split the two of them up. They had engaged an attorney, she recounted, "trying to divest [Grace] of her share in the inheritance. But she too got an attorney, and she won."[18] That may not have been exactly how things happened, but Yourcenar believed herself, or the couple she had formed with Frick, to be the root of the family's displeasure.

No one seems to have held a lasting grudge, however. In the summer of 1947 Dolly traveled to Mount Desert Island and spent almost a month being entertained by Grace and Marguerite. Gage and his children came later for shorter stays. Grace continued to visit her aunt in Kansas City well into the

1960s, by which time Dolly's mental and physical health was in sharp decline. Communication flowed freely as well between Grace and her two brothers throughout the rest of their lives. Gage, for his part, continued to handle the LaRue family investments and eventually became a partner in the Kansas City stock brokerage firm H. O. Peet and Company. In Aunt Dolly's last will and testament, drawn up on May 20, 1959, the first bequest, in the amount of twenty thousand dollars, was to her niece, Grace M. Frick.[19]

Dolly died on July 25, 1968, at the age of ninety-five. In addition to a few other bequests, only one of them equal to Grace's, her will left the remainder of her estate to Gage C. Frick "for the purpose of establishing a charitable trust." That entity, the George A. and Dolly F. LaRue Trust, came into being in March of 1971 with Gage as trustee. Its purposes were broadly defined as "religious, charitable, scientific, literary or educational," but its primary focus was on helping children and young people in need.[20] Before the turn of the twenty-first century, sums ranging from $40,000 to $150,000 a year were given to the Healthy Steps Fund for Young Children, the Johnson County (Kansas) Community College Metropolitan Performing Arts Series, and the Greater Kansas City Community Foundation, which the LaRue Trust helped establish.[21] In December of 2015, the George A. and Dolly F. LaRue Trust held assets amounting to just under $5 million. Still today, that trust bears living witness to the generosity of spirit that Unk and Aunt displayed when they opened their arms to four nieces and nephews in the early years of the twentieth century.[22]

CHAPTER 14 ❧ A Gift from Jacques Kayaloff
1944

She wrote *Electra* here . . . and did all the cooking for a *slew* of guests!

—Grace Frick

THOSE WHO HAVE FOLLOWED MARGUERITE Yourcenar's creative trajectory may already be familiar with the contribution made to twentieth-century literary history by the New York businessman Jacques Kayaloff.[1] It was through his good offices that a forgotten fragment of *Mémoires d'Hadrien* made its way from a basement in Lausanne to 549 Prospect Avenue in Hartford, Connecticut, in early 1949.[2] Kayaloff also did a much less well-known favor for Yourcenar admirers when for Christmas in 1943 he gave Grace Frick an annual appointment calendar for the new year about to begin. That first daybook was published by the French Relief Fund, created to aid France's combatants, children, and civilians who were suffering on account of the war.[3] For more than four decades, agendas like that one would be kept primarily, though not exclusively, by Frick. They provided a place both for keeping track of social, professional, and medical appointments and for recording the events of daily life. For a biographer, they are an embarrassment of riches. The list of household items the couple brought with them to Hysom Cottage that year—with its comforters, facecloths, aprons, table runners, doilies, kitchen silver, and nutcrackers, all carefully counted—is a cultural artifact in its own right.

It was Marguerite who christened that first daybook because Grace was still traveling with her aunt when the new year began. Over the first three weeks of January, Marguerite carefully tracked her partner's progress toward home: on January 2 Grace returned to Kansas City from Mexico; on the seventeenth she left Missouri bound for Illinois; on the nineteenth she saw Betsy Lunn in Chicago; and on the twentieth at 10:30 a.m. her train pulled into the station in New York. When she finally arrived after three months away, Marguerite met her in the city. They had decided to treat themselves to a few days in Manhattan to celebrate Grace's return. Staying at the Biltmore, they attended the Broadway musical *Carmen Jones* on the evening of Grace's arrival. The play was an updated version of the opera *Carmen* with an entirely African American cast, which appealed to both women. The following night they dined with Phyllis Bartlett and her new husband, John Pollard, at the Acropolis Restaurant on West Fifty-Eighth Street. Phyllis was now teaching English at Queens College.

Over the next few days they got together with Jacques and Anya Kayaloff; Kayaloff's sister, the painter Ina Garsoïan; and Grace's Wellesley friend Katherine "Katy" Gatch and her companion Marion Witt. On January 24 they saw the black American singer and actor Paul Robeson's acclaimed performance in the lead role of *Othello*. This production of Shakespeare's popular play was staged by the British-American producer and director Margaret Webster, whose work Grace and Marguerite followed with great interest. They had attended Webster's production of Anton Chekhov's *Cherry Orchard* the previous March; they would even bring one of Yourcenar's Sarah Lawrence students with them to her celebrated version of *The Tempest* in early February 1945, which featured the black actor and civil rights champion Canada Lee; and in November of 1946 they were wowed by Eva Le Gallienne's performance in *Henry VIII*.[4] Webster worked often with Le Gallienne, her former lover.[5]

On January 25 Marguerite took the train to Sarah Lawrence, and Grace headed for home. Passing through New Haven, Frick stopped off at Yale University to see the chairman of dissertation candidates and update her placement file. The only other mention of Yale in the 1944 daybook is the interrogatory "Register for Yale? Or pay Library Fee?" on March 1. In the thirty-six years' worth of Frick daybooks, one finds only three brief mentions of George Meredith, subject of her apparently forsaken attempt to complete her PhD.

Back in Hartford, Frick had many calls or visits from friends and associates at Hartford Junior College. Former students came to tea. Norah Tapley, who went on to become a physician, even spent a weekend with Frick and Yourcenar at 549 Prospect Avenue. Frick continued to receive invitations to events at the college, which she most often declined. She was not wallowing in self-pity, however. Daybook comments in the early months of 1944 are full of good humor: on March 6, for example, after "Fatal Oysters!" eaten with friends the night before, "M.Y. ill from oysters mais belle journée!" Later the two women would have lunch alfresco near the fountain at the Plaza Hotel in

Manhattan, where they had gone shopping for clothes. The days they spent together were always full of theatergoing, ballet performances, galleries and museums, movies at Hartford's Avery Theatre or New York's Museum of Modern Art (Robert Stevenson's *Jane Eyre* and Jean Renoir's *Grand Illusion*), baking bread and sharing it with neighbors, or walking the mile and a half to Hartford's Elizabeth Park. Grace also had time for horseback riding now, a pleasure she pursued with Jean McKay in Wethersfield or Ada Loewith in West Hartford. The 1944 daybook suggests that other pleasures were often indulged in, strewn as it is with those stars and crosses which biographers identify with "moments of joy, happiness in love, or sensual pleasure."[6] One often finds them in evening quadrants of the days when Marguerite came home from Bronxville.

Yourcenar had initially been hired as a part-time instructor at Sarah Lawrence College to teach French and Italian. In contrast to the experience of many women's colleges, enrollment went up at Sarah Lawrence just as faculty members were leaving to join the war effort or take better-paying war-related jobs. Thus, positions opened up for European exiles. Located fifteen miles north of New York City, the school describes itself as having been, along with Bennington College, "the first college to incorporate into its curriculum the ideas and ideals of progressive education." Harold Taylor, who was president of Sarah Lawrence during most of Yourcenar's tenure there, said this about the school: "The task of the College is to teach liberalism—not the philosophy of an ethnocentric, middle-class, nationalist, Western, white man's ethic, but liberalism conceived as a classless philosophy, which draws individual human beings closer together, teaches a concern for the welfare of all social groups and all countries, and judges the value of acts and societies by the effect they have upon enrichment of individual human lives."[7] At a time when these ideals were under siege in the culture, Sarah Lawrence was a place where differences were not merely tolerated but valued.

Although Yourcenar had little teaching experience, she was hardly unqualified as an educator. She had wide-ranging experience as a lecturer and enthusiastic recommendations from the likes of Horatio S. Krans, director of the American University Union in Europe, located in Paris; Professor Florence White of Vassar College; and Professor Frederick Hoffherr of Barnard College, among others.[8] André Morize, who had come to teach young men like Grace Frick's brother Gage how to use a machine gun at Harvard University during World War I and then became a professor of romance languages there, called Yourcenar "one of the most remarkable women I have met."[9] The only discordant voice was that of a young Sarah Lawrence instructor, Louis Barillet, who became perhaps the only person ever living to call Yourcenar's French "not as fluent as expected in a French person"! He also found her English, less surprisingly, to be "not so good." Something about Yourcenar obviously bothered Barillet: "I am not sure about her personality with students or how good she would be with them. There is a large unknown factor about this woman as regards personality, ability, communication with students."[10] She got the job anyway.

During one of Yourcenar's years at the school, 1947–48, the novelist Mary McCarthy taught English there for a semester. According to her biographer, Carol Gelderman, McCarthy did not like working at Sarah Lawrence "because 'the students were so poor' "—academically, that is.[11] She was not asked back. The fictional Jocelyn College of McCarthy's *The Groves of Academe* is believed to be largely based on Sarah Lawrence. She and Yourcenar shared similar sentiments. No matter what the time of day, wrote McCarthy, "the Jocelyn students were always sleepy, yawning, and rather gummy-eyed, as though it were seven in the morning and they unwillingly on the street."[12]

It's little wonder that Yourcenar found her American students for the most part ill prepared and intellectually uninspired. The reading lists for her courses were extremely demanding. Here are the assignments for one four-week period, as handwritten by Yourcenar, in late September–early October, during which classes were held twice a week:

Proust Un amour de Swann
André Gide La porte étroite, L'Immoraliste, L'école des femmes
Balzac Le lys dans la vallée
Rousseau Julie (1re et 2e parties)
Flaubert Mme Bovary
Prévost Manon Lescaut
La Fayette La princesse de Clèves
Chateaubriand Atalee [sic]
Montherlant Les jeunes filles
Paper due October 15.[13]

Yourcenar often assigned translation exercises from English into French. Once she asked her French II class to translate two pages of each student's choice from Gertrude Stein's *Paris France*. When Yourcenar taught comparative literature, she liked to organize her course around a theme. For the all too current theme of war, for example, she would have her students read *The Iliad, The Song of Roland, War and Peace,* Victor Hugo's famous depiction of the Battle of Waterloo in *Les Misérables*, and so on.[14] As in Hartford, she brought her advanced literature students into New York to see artworks related to their reading.[15]

Yourcenar almost never had much good to say about the nearly ten years she spent teaching at Sarah Lawrence. When the Parisian journalist Matthieu Galey asked her what she had learned from her students, she replied with considerable disillusionment, "How few are prepared for study, how many people never escape the status quo, and how brief the period of awakening is."[16] Another French journalist, Jacques Chancel, asked if she had taken up teaching as "a pastime." "No," she replied, "were it a pastime, I could no doubt have found a more enjoyable one. But it was after the war, and purely a way of making money."[17]

Probably the most positive comment that Yourcenar ever made about Sarah Lawrence was to the Quebecois television host Françoise Faucher in January of 1975:

It was a very fruitful period. It caused me to undergo certain experiences: that of earning my living, which is excessively important in our time: without it, one doesn't know what is going on for people who have had to do it continually and all the time—I did it myself, let's say, for six or seven years; also the experience of a world that was not the literary world—a world launched on the paths of novelty in art, in literature, in everything—in which I had lived in Europe, and that put me for the first time in contact if you will with the anonymous crowd, which was terribly important.[18]

But there was nothing anonymous about Yourcenar's students, and many of them vividly recall their unusual teacher. Phyllis Rothschild Farley remembers her always wearing a large-brimmed hat, possibly made of felt, while teaching: "She would stalk around the campus dressed in this exotic fashion, completely herself, like nobody else." Farley remembered classes of no more than three or four students, all of them European or French speaking. They had to be, because Yourcenar expected them to write French grammatically! Returning from summers in Maine, she would say how much she enjoyed the *solitude* there, pronouncing the word the French way.[19]

Jane Bond, a retired professor of French history at Baruch College in New York, also remembers Yourcenar wearing a hat around campus, a Napoleonic two-cornered affair. A black student, Bond had transferred to Sarah Lawrence from Spelman College in Atlanta. Her father had been sent to Haiti by President Roosevelt to head up what was then called Point Four, the equivalent of today's USAID. So Jane was one of the fluent French speakers that Phyllis Farley mentioned, one whose background differed from that of her fellow students. She does not remember most of her peers as having a deep interest in the life of the mind. Although Bond took only one class from Yourcenar, in 1949–50, its instructor made a strong impression. What Bond remembers most clearly is that Marguerite Yourcenar "was the only teacher at Sarah Lawrence College who was absolutely devoid of racism."[20]

Bond did not know that her instructor had a lover back in Hartford, but an incident occurred one day at school that made her aware of Yourcenar's sexuality. Bond was in her teacher's office, whose small Persian rugs scattered on the floor and artworks adorning the walls made the room feel more like a salon than a work space. Yourcenar was at her desk, and her student, a sensitive young person of only sixteen at the time, was seated several feet away. Remembering the moment and trying to put it into words, Bond takes pains to emphasize that her instructor's manner was never anything other than impeccable. Yourcenar's code of conduct was such that she would never behave inappropriately toward a student. But suddenly there was something indescribable in the air, "quelque chose qui a surgi," said Bond. A mysterious current had passed through the room, and then it was gone. When Bond returned to her residence, Robinson House, she related the experience to "some of the girls" gathered there. They smiled and said simply, "Well, you know, she *is* a lesbian."[21] And that was that.

Marguerite Yourcenar was noted throughout her life for having a seductive way about her. The French television personality Maurice Dumay remarked on it in his interview with her aboard the SS *Mermoz* right after she was elected to the Académie française.[22] Charlotte Pomerantz Marzani, who took Yourcenar's French civilization course at Sarah Lawrence in 1948, made a similar comment to Josyane Savigneau: "I have to admit, though I have never been attracted to women, that she was seductive like a man."[23] Those powers of seduction seem to have unwittingly exercised themselves on another Sarah Lawrence student, Marianne Mosevius, whose background, like Jane Bond's, differed markedly from that of her schoolmates. Mosevius was a Jewish refugee from Nazi Germany.[24]

Born in Berlin in 1923, Mosevius left there at the age of fifteen as part of the first Kindertransport to England. She would eventually lose two grandparents, seven uncles and aunts, and two first cousins in the Holocaust. Mosevius

FIGURE 21. Marianne Mosevius, 1940s. Donna Levinsohn archives.

came to the United States to join her parents in 1943, and by spring semester 1944 she was taking Yourcenar's course in the French novel as a scholarship student.[25] In the fall of the same year, she was in Yourcenar's civilization class. Just as Jane Bond was one of ten black students at Sarah Lawrence during her time there, Marianne Mosevius was one of ten Jews.

Mosevius was an especially gifted student, and Yourcenar took particular care in her periodic evaluations to shape her way of relating to literature. In a March 3, 1944, performance report Yourcenar credited Mosevius with "great ability in French conversation," "very good" participation in class discussions, and "a certain maturity in her views, even if they are somewhat too set." Yourcenar then went on to say that "full maturity should imply more suppleness and more sensibility for nuances, more careful weighing of evidence, and more capacity for adjustment to the views of others. She needs to widen her basis for her approach to the whole subject of literature, for she tends to consider a work of art too strictly as subject matter for ethical or political discussion, and not as a complex unit for dispassionate, though vigorous, appraisal."[26] The next report, dated April 25, suggests that Mosevius had taken her previous evaluation seriously. Her work was "excellent," her class participation "always most valuable," and her use of French "perfect." Mosevius's papers on André Gide and André Malraux showed "rare maturity, judgment, and power of concentration."[27]

By late October 1944, in a course that Yourcenar entitled French Civilization through Literature and the Arts, she had risen even higher in her teacher's esteem: "M. Mosevius may legitimately be classed as a truly advanced student. She uses her intellect with ardor, and is gifted with a remarkable capacity for work and organization." But as in the case of previous assessments, Yourcenar believed that Mosevius could still improve. Her remarks have as much to say about the Frenchwoman's own evolving manner of appropriating a literary text as they do about that of her student:

> Her inclination is toward the social and the historical, and she has yet to develop more fully her literary taste and her capacity for disinterested enjoyment of literature and the other arts. Her actual abilities [Mosevius's underlining] and her various maturing experiences, while all excellent factors, tend to make her rather rigid in her views [Mosevius's underlining], and to support her in a fixed picture of her personality; whereas she should be employing her unusual capacity for learning, as applied to the materials of literature, more to correct, transform, or even check her opinions by comparison with other points of view. She has developed already a very distinct personality and does not need to throw her effort into an intensification of it, but rather to an extension of it, imaginatively and emotionally [Yourcenar's underlining]. She needs, especially, that valuable method of study which asks of a student not only to admit the reasoning of a character in a work (especially the reasoning of a character who is unsympathetic to her) but, for the time, to be that person in order fully to evaluate his position or his temperament. (She needs, in other words, the specific exercise of the imagination which Shelley describes in his essay on poetry, when he discusses the moral use of the imagination.)[28]

Not only has Mosevius underlined the phrases indicated above, placing question marks next to them, she has also virtually filled the margins of the page with handwritten responses to Yourcenar's remarks. Namely, "Y. does not practice what she preaches" and "*Shelley*: the great secret of morals is a going out of our own nature, and an identification of ourselves with the beautiful which exists in thought, action or person not our own. A man, *to be greatly good*, must imagine intensely and comprehensively. He must put himself in the place of another and of many others. The pains and pleasures of his species must become his own. The great instrument of moral good is the imagination." Next to the preceding, Mosevius writes, "What about *kindness*? That must be included in 'to be greatly good.' *Practice what you preach*!!"

Judging from another—extraordinary—handwritten document, Mosevius still was not at peace with her instructor a year later, even though she was no longer in her class. She obviously had maintained contact; in fact, it was Mosevius who accompanied Yourcenar and Frick to Margaret Webster's production of *The Tempest* on Broadway in early 1945. Years later Mosevius's daughter Donna Levinsohn deciphered and translated what her mother had written—in her native German—on the back of an October 1945 faculty report. Some of the original text had been partially erased. What Levinsohn could make out, she put in brackets; where there were gaps in the text, they are indicated. Words with an asterisk were originally in English:

[Dear Marianne,]

Now be very calm, pull yourself together, and try to see matters concerning Y. clearly. Above all be honest. You do know very exactly in what manner and [how much you loved her . . .]. You have [. . .] seen for yourself that she [?was pleased with this?] and that she [definitely didn't? . . .] makes her uncomfortable and she is more angered than anything else. Therefore you must do whatever you can [to stop loving her.] She says that a [. . . *relationship*★] can only be very *slight*★, and that anything else is *false*. In the sense of not genuine. You know that this is *not* true. But you can see that your [*relationship*★] to her is definitely [?not genuine?], precisely because she treats it as such. So for God's sake pull yourself together and [*like*★ . . . That, too, is a part of life.]

[*Marianne*][29]

Clearly, Marianne Mosevius was infatuated with "Y.," and "Y." had done what she could to discourage her. A connection had nonetheless been forged that would last beyond Mosevius's departure from Sarah Lawrence. When she married in late 1948, Yourcenar sent the newlyweds "two different (but combinable) products of the American earth": hand-ground buckwheat flour from the South and maple syrup from the North.[30] As the future will prove, Yourcenar discussed personal topics with Mosevius that she would speak of to almost no one but Grace Frick.

From the fall of 1942, when Yourcenar started working at Sarah Lawrence, through the spring of 1950, when she took a two-year break from teaching, the life she shared with Frick followed the rhythm of the academic calendar, with school years spent in Hartford or Bronxville and long, restorative summers on Mount Desert Island. Time at Hysom Cottage meant swimming in Somes Pond before breakfast, in the nearby fjord later in the day, and occasionally at locations farther away. On August 23, 1944, for example, when the couple walked to a popular swimming spot southwest of Somesville, Grace noted in the daybook that Marguerite swam "nobly in Long Pond in her halter and black bloomers."[31] There would also be hikes in the woods; sunbathing; strawberry, blueberry, and raspberry picking; boating parties to Great Cranberry Island or the Porcupines; tea and popovers at Jordan Pond House; lobster suppers; moonlit walks along the shore; and, for Grace, horseback riding.

For Yourcenar those summers always meant time for creative as well as recreative pursuits. After composing *Le Mystère d'Alceste* on the island in 1942, she wrote *Électre ou la Chute des masques* in 1943.[32] The following summer, as more information was revealed about wartime atrocities, Yourcenar began revising *Ariane et l'aventurier*, a sketch from the 1930s, which became *Qui n'a pas son Minotaure?*. These plays are not usually considered to be Yourcenar's best work, but they are intimately tied to her most important themes and concerns: sacrifice, the love triangle, man's inhumanity to man, the always avoidable but rarely avoided resort to violence. And, of course, they are all based on ancient Greek myths.

The summer of 1944 was a particularly hot one during which Frick and Yourcenar were deluged with guests—so many, in fact, that they sometimes had to lock their doors and pretend not to be home to steal a moment of privacy. In response to one particular "onslaught," Marguerite retreated "in rage" to the Hysom Cottage pantry, then stole away for a cool swim; on returning, she summarily dispatched "the throng."[33] Guests had been overabundant the previous summer as well, but this year they seem to have prevented the completion of *Qui n'a pas son Minotaure?*, which did not finally see the light of day until 1963. The summer of 1945 would bring "Three Greek Myths in Palladian Perspective," a joint writing and translation project; that two-part essay would be published the following year in the distinguished "little magazine" *Chimera: A Literary Quarterly*.[34] Throughout these island holidays Yourcenar worked, too, on her French translations of Negro spirituals and gospel songs.

It was also during the summer of 1944 that the two women tried to purchase the log house in which they were staying for the third and, as it turned out, final time. Nearing the end of their last stay at what Grace once called "a heavenly place," Grace and Marguerite spent the early morning gathering wood for their fireplace. It was an extremely hot and humid day, and they decided to walk the two miles or so south to Echo Lake, progressing at a very slow pace because of the heat. When they arrived, they could barely make out Beech Cliff covered in gray mist across the water. Walking along Route 102 on the way back, Marguerite complained of pain climbing up a steep hill and had to take a taxi the rest of the way home. She continued to experience fatigue during the week of packing and traveling that followed.[35]

Yourcenar was well enough to return to Sarah Lawrence on September 8, though, and the weekly student newspaper published a humorous report on her summer vacation: "Mme. Yourcenar was busy finishing her book on the Greek drama, *Dramatis Personae*, and leading a country life. Cows to be milked, fish to be caught, mountains to be scaled, such were the challenges she faced. Her essay on the Greek drama was recently published in *Les Lettres Français* [*sic*], Argentine-printed French literary organ."[36]

On September 17 Yourcenar fell ill again on Fifth Avenue after dining at New York's Covent Garden Restaurant. A Dr. Bernat prescribed a week of bed rest. Another episode followed on October 11, causing Yourcenar to become "hysterical" at Sarah Lawrence. In the midst of all this, Mary Marshall wrote to offer Frick a one-year position teaching English at Colby College. She declined. Frick was on the lookout for a job, though, which may be why she tried to find an apartment in Upper Manhattan that fall. But both women were comfortable at 549 Prospect Avenue. They loved their fellow tenants—Miss Taylor, of the Taylor Lumber family, across the hall on the first floor; "the Emmas," Trebbe and Evans; and elderly Mrs. Mathewson. Their apartment also had a lovely fireplace, in which, according to the daybooks, many a "nice fire" blazed and in front of which many a "good time" was had. In the spring semester of 1945 Frick took a post at Connecticut College for Women in New London, to which she could take the train from Hartford in roughly half the time it took Yourcenar to reach Bronxville.

Not until early November did Yourcenar's health allow her to resume a normal teaching schedule. The rest of the school year went smoothly, with Yourcenar adapting Antoine de St. Exupéry's *Petit Prince* for her French students to perform as a Christmas play. On Christmas Day itself, Grace and Marguerite invited some of their neighbors and friends for eggnog, a holiday concoction around which they would create a New Year's tradition. To old Mrs. Mathewson upstairs in their building they delivered a serving of their dinner. After a "foggy evening walk in St. John's churchyard" around the corner from their apartment, they read Alice Parker's book of Christmas poems together.

Nineteen forty-four ended, as it had begun, with Yourcenar tending the daybook—though not, this time, because Frick was away. Two days after

Christmas she joyfully noted, "squirrels come to breakfast, begging nuts from us through the window panes! Much play." On December 31, despite the disappointments and alarming health problems of the previous months, Marguerite's last word, in English, was an expression of gratitude to her companion: "End of a very happy year—thank you."

CHAPTER 15 ✿ The Life Their Wishes Never Led
1945

A child is a hostage. Life has you.

—Marguerite Yourcenar

THERE WAS MORE TO GRACE Frick and Marguerite Yourcenar's eagerness to find a house on Mount Desert Island than meets the eye. And certainly more than the popular intimation to the effect that buying a house in the United States was a ploy on Frick's part to prevent her partner from moving back to Europe after the war. Yourcenar had initiated the long process of obtaining U.S. citizenship in early 1942. When she was naturalized on December 12, 1947, she relinquished her French nationality.[1] Yourcenar had roots in America now, and they were growing deeper. For the future she and Frick had in mind, the couple wanted a home of their own. Though they loved Hysom's Cabin, as soon as they knew they couldn't buy it, they started looking elsewhere.[2] West Hartford was convenient for now, with Frick teaching in New London and Yourcenar commuting to Bronxville, but Maine was their spiritual home.

In the mid- to late 1940s, they tried to wrest a cottage on the Shore Path in Bar Harbor from a stubborn realtor. Frick later wrote to the legendary Natalie Clifford Barney in Paris about the experience. Barney's wealthy family had owned a spectacular mansion, Ban-y-Bryn, overlooking the water in Bar Harbor, where young Natalie had spent her early summers swimming and riding and traipsing nymph-like through the woods with her friend Eva Palmer.[3] "The site is beautiful," Frick wrote, "and we tried for five years steadily to get hold of the small white cottage of the McClean gardener." But there were a dozen "outhouses" on the property, including a monkey cage and a bowling alley, and the realtor was determined to sell everything at once. The couple finally gave up on the place only to see it sold a year later to a local man "who ruined the tract by converting the doll's house into a *Ladies Home Journal* bungalow, and building a duplicate model on the tennis court, where we had hoped to have a garden!'"[4]

A major impetus for their house hunting, much of it done by Frick on horseback, was the couple's desire to adopt a child together.[5] Grace had always had a soft spot for children and young people. During her and Marguerite's first full summer in Somesville she inaugurated the custom of mounting plays with local children, in which she would engage off and on throughout her life, often with help from her companion. That first production, based on the biblical story of Moses in the bulrushes and staged alongside Somes Brook, is documented by a series of numbered photographs preserved at Petite Plaisance. The late Elaine Higgins Reddish of Somesville took part in this performance. In a 2002 interview she remembered Baby Moses, a child's doll, being floated down Somes Brook just across from Hysom Cottage in a basket.[6] As Jerry Wilson later wrote, having heard about the play from Yourcenar, "One boy reported that the order had been given in the 'Post Office' to kill all Jewish babies and when they got all of their towels cum costumes back, Mme Y got morphions [*sic*] and had to have her head shaved to treat them—telltale signs of village cleanliness."[7] Fortunately, short hair was her style and it was hot.

Five years later Yourcenar was willing to take her chances again when she helped Frick stage another production of the same play on the beach in Seal Harbor, where they were staying that summer.[8] The two of them would still be mounting plays with children, and taking part in them, thirty years later, when Frick, in the year before her death, played the spirit of a tree in the yard behind their home. This particular performance was adapted from a Japanese legend in which a handsome young man falls in love with and marries a beautiful girl he encounters in the forest. She turns out to be the spirit of a willow tree, and when the tree is felled, she falls to earth and dies.[9] Because there was no willow in their garden, Frick and Yourcenar pressed one of their favorite tree species into service for the occasion, a white birch.

The couple may have been inspired to think about adopting because so many European children had been orphaned by the war. Grace Frick knew from personal experience what an important role an adoptive family could play in the life of a child. And she consigned to the title page of the 1946 daybook the telephone number of New York's Child Adoption Committee.[10] But Yourcenar may have made the first contact related to the adoption project when she had "luncheon" in Bronxville with Mme Andrée Royon on February 10 and 24, 1944. Royon, a forty-eight-year-old child psychologist, was both a delegate of the Save the Children International Union based in Geneva, Switzerland, and on the staff of New York's Save the Children Federation.[11] She was also a French-speaking native of Ghent, Belgium, with a recent PhD in psychology from the University of Geneva, where Marguerite Yourcenar once studied.[12] Like Yourcenar, she had become a part-time instructor at Sarah Lawrence College in the fall of 1942.

On May 10, 1944, Frick and Yourcenar met Royon for lunch together in New York City, inviting her to visit them that summer in Maine.[13] She ended up coming to Somesville for nine days in mid-August, during the second half of Alice Parker's three-week stay. Although one can't be entirely sure what happened, the 1944 daybook bears strong suggestions that Mme Royon succumbed to Yourcenar's renowned powers of seduction during that island holiday.

Parker's visit ended on August 17, and Royon left the next day for New York. A telegram soon arrived from Royon. It was followed on August 29 by "conflicting letters" from Royon and Parker. Two days later, Frick noted in the daybook, "M.Y. writes Royon firmly."[14]

Not firmly enough it seems, however. On September 26, with Yourcenar unwell and trying to rest at Jacques and Anya Kayaloff's apartment in Manhattan, "Royon showers yellow roses on M.Y., and flees." Frick and Royon met at Schraft's three days later "for the last time." According to the daybooks, neither she nor Yourcenar ever saw Mme Royon again.[15]

Nineteen forty-five began for Frick and Yourcenar with an unusual winter trip. On January 5 the couple made a nearly seventeen-hour journey by rail and by bus to the seaside village of Camden, Maine. Florence Codman had a place on Bay View Street there called Stone Chimney, where she and her companion, Margot Hill, had spent the holidays that year. It was 1:00 a.m. when the travelers finally arrived. The next day Frick went walking in the village and climbed partway up Mount Battie. The daybook for January 7 records a spirited difference of opinion between its two contributors. Yourcenar writes, "Glass below zero outside fisherman's hut. Grace has a long walk from Camden to Rockport and back and comes back nearly frozen."

"No!" counters Frick. "Lovely walk, beautiful houses, woods in snow, little boy. *Not* frozen at all!!"[16]

On January 8, another frigid day, the two women went back to Portland, where they caught separate trains. Yourcenar headed to Bronxville for a meeting, while Frick began a two-day marathon. Over the course of forty-eight hours, she cleaned out the unheated Hysom's Cabin, spent twenty-four hours with Mary Marshall in Waterville, visited with the Minears in Newton Centre, Massachusetts, and called on Laura Lockwood at Wellesley—traveling from one place to another by train, bus, taxi, and on foot. Yourcenar was manning the daybook that evening: "Marguerite comes back from Sarah Lawrence. Grace meets her at station. Good time in front of the fire."[17] Even after only brief separations, reunions were sweet. When Grace went away for longer periods, usually to travel with Aunt Dolly or Aunt George, Marguerite often made notes in the daybook such as "Joy: Grace phones," filling up the page with her drawing of a sunrise on the days Grace would come home. These were the years when Grace started calling her companion Greta, Grete, or Gretie.

We have noted the strengthening of Frick and Yourcenar's couple that occurred when the women changed their wills in 1943. In November of 1946 Yourcenar took a step further when she added a codicil to her will making Frick both her literary executor and the sole beneficiary of her literary estate. This was an expression of confidence in her American companion's professional judgment whose importance cannot be exaggerated. In the event of a simultaneous death, or if Frick should die after Yourcenar without leaving instructions regarding a successor, Yourcenar appointed her Parisian friends Jenny de Margerie and Emmanuel Boudot-Lamotte to step in. Gone were Edmond Jaloux and "best friend" André Fraigneau, both of whom had proven too sympathetic to the Nazi regime during the war. Yourcenar also took this opportunity to switch from her previous attorney to Frick's trusted childhood friend Ruth Hall. To complete her legal business, Yourcenar stated her wish to be buried, should she die in America, "in the little cemetery of Somesville (Mount Desert Island, Maine) and in the cemetery of Chamblandes on Mount Pèlerin in the canton of Vaud, Switzerland, should I die in Europe."[18] This "little cemetery of Somesville" is, of course, the one right next to Hysom Cottage. Mount Pèlerin, overlooking Lake Geneva, is located just outside Lausanne, where Yourcenar lived while her father was treated for cancer. Jeanne de Vietinghoff is buried a few kilometers away in the cemetery of Jouxtens-Mézery.

The matter of adopting a child does not arise again in the documents at our disposal until early February 1949, when Yourcenar wrote a long letter to Marianne (Mosevius) Levinsohn, now living with her new husband in the Bronx. Levinsohn and her husband had decided against starting a family right away. Yourcenar's response to that decision illustrates in part the ability to put herself in someone else's shoes that she had tried to inculcate in her student with regard to literary texts: "I believe that it is very wise of you to put off having a child until later. Every period of life tends to be transformed or modified so quickly that it is essential to enjoy and experience it completely while one is going through it. And happiness for three (whether greater or lesser, that is not the issue) will never be exactly the same thing as happiness for two."[19]

On the topic of children, Yourcenar then goes on to say,

> As far as Grace Frick and I are concerned, our plan to adopt a child is still on, but for me the S.L.C. experience will have to be over, and we will have to have solved the problem of a more or less permanent home. What I would especially hope to do is to return to Europe for a year or two and adopt a European child over there. But immediately the great problem of knowing how, and in what tradition, to raise the child would arise: I have a prejudice against American education as it is presently conceived that grows stronger every day, but I cannot say that European education, in view of today's universal chaos, has given very good results, either.[20]

Less than two weeks after this letter was written, Yourcenar and Frick would be vacationing together in New Mexico during interim week at Sarah Lawrence. On January 24, 1949, the famous trunk containing old fragments of the *Hadrian* manuscript had arrived at 549 Prospect Avenue, where Yourcenar, atypically, was holding down the fort all by herself. Frick was caring for her maternal aunt Georgia Horner, who was undergoing cancer surgery in California. On February 10, from their opposite ends of the country, Marguerite and Grace made their way to New Mexico, reuniting in Santa Fe. Yourcenar wrote nonstop on the train as if the floodgates had opened, unleashing a narrative torrent. From this day forth for the next two years the daybook would give a detailed account of daily progress on a book that for twenty-five years had been dreamed of and attempted, despaired of and abandoned, over and over again.

Hadrian swept both Marguerite and Grace into its vortex. Frick chronicled its development with meticulous daily precision, noting along the way that they discussed the book while picking berries in Seal Harbor or read the latest pages aloud together over tea and popovers at Jordan Pond House. Grace usually read and commented on the manuscript in five- to ten-page batches, which were often the output of a day's work.

She did research, alone or with Yourcenar, in every substantial library from New York City to Bangor, Maine: "Grace is marvellous [*sic*]," wrote Yourcenar in March of 1949.[21] Frick helped her partner revise and tighten

FIGURE 22. Grace Frick in
Seal Harbor during the
writing of *Hadrian*, 1949.
Petite Plaisance Archives.

whole sections of the book upon their completion. On August 26, 1949, for
example, after a day for which the agenda bears four joyful crosses in the
evening quadrant, "M.Y. and Grace finish reading of main text of *Terra Sta-
bilita* together (through *Achievements*) by spending entire morning alone in
M.Y.'s bedroom."[22] There were almost always guests, and the couple sometimes worried about what they would think. On August 28, with Miriam
Tompkins visiting them in Seal Harbor, Grace wrote,

> M.Y. continued revision of *Terra Stabilitata* [*sic*], the tail-ends of such revision.
> Both of us conscious that we were talking much aloud of what must sound like
> too mechanical a process of revision, but both determined to use the time for

what could be done in a period not conducive to creative work on M.Y.'s part. Actually, we managed to have a very enjoyable afternoon, G. slowly sweeping living room, meanwhile, discussing the actual cause of lack of clarity in a few sentences, the reason being, as nearly always in cases of obscurity in the statement, a lack of certainty about one or more facts on which the statement should have been based. Once having rectified the number, for example, of "philosophes" who would rightly be termed "errants," the sentence fell almost as if automatically for her into its present, and correct, form.[23]

Eventually, of course, as the book advanced toward publication, there would be galleys and page proofs for the women to pore over and correct.

Yourcenar paid homage to her partner's help in "Reflections on the Composition of *Memoirs of Hadrian*," published in post-1951 editions of the novel. While her encomium is beautiful and heartfelt, it exemplifies the author's tendency, evident also in what she wrote to Marianne Levinsohn about her and Frick's adoption plan, to dispense as quickly as possible with the strictly personal and couch her remarks in more generalized terms:

This book bears no dedication. It ought to have been dedicated to G.F. . . . , and would have been, were there not a kind of impropriety in putting a personal inscription at the opening of a work where, precisely, I was trying to efface the personal. But even the longest dedication is too short and too commonplace to honor a friendship so uncommon. When I try to define this asset which has been mine now for years, I tell myself that such a privilege, however rare it may be, is surely not unique; that in the whole adventure of bringing a book successfully to its conclusion, or even in the entire life of some fortunate writers, there must have been sometimes, in the background, perhaps, someone who will not let pass the weak or inaccurate sentence which we ourselves would retain, out of fatigue; someone who would re-read with us for the twentieth time, if need be, a questionable page; someone who takes down for us from the library shelves the heavy tomes in which we may find a helpful suggestion, and who persists in continuing to peruse them long after weariness has made us give up; someone who bolsters our courage and approves, or sometimes disputes, our ideas; who shares with us, and with equal fervor, the joys of art and of living, the endless work which both require, never easy but never dull; someone who is neither our shadow nor our reflection, nor even our complement, but simply himself; someone who leaves us ideally free, but who nevertheless obliges us to be fully what we are. *Hospes Comesque.*[24]

Michèle Sarde has called *Hadrian* the couple's child, noting Frick's extraordinary role in the book's gestation.[25] Perhaps not knowing it would
be their only one, the women went steadily about fulfilling the conditions
that Yourcenar laid out in her letter to Levinsohn. In the fall of 1950 they
bought a farmhouse on a quiet lane in Northeast Harbor. By March of 1952,
having been in Europe for ten months, they had made a good dent in the
year or two that Yourcenar had hoped to spend seeking out a child abroad.
With *Mémoires d'Hadrien* finally published in France to overwhelming acclaim, the women were more secure financially than they had ever been.
Leaving France, they began a two-month stay in Rome. Not only were they
returning to the Mediterranean land of their first passion, they would be
exploring in reality the hub of an empire they had occupied in fiction for
two blazing years of their life.[26] But they may also have been looking for a
child in the country where they once sealed a lovers' pact with a pair of gold
rings. Consigned to their daybook that spring was the address of Save the
Children in Rome.[27]

Why then did the adoption project fall through? Certainly these women
who walked the streets of Northeast Harbor arm in arm in the repressive
1950s would not have been cowed by the prospect of social disapproval. As
Charlotte Pomerantz Marzani noted about Yourcenar at Sarah Lawrence, "I
think she knew about the rumor circulating that she lived with a woman.
Basically, she couldn't have cared less about people knowing this and saying
that she was a lesbian."[28]

What Yourcenar told Marianne Levinsohn in approving her decision to
put off having children may have gained additional meaning as she and Frick
learned more and more about the atrocities of World War II; "I seem to be
preaching egoism," wrote Yourcenar in 1949, "but in the highly threatening
world we live in, *thoughtful* egoism often ends up seeming to me the only
wisdom, and the only prudent form of kindness."[29]

Of course, Frick and Yourcenar were not getting any younger—they
would both turn fifty in 1953. In later years, as biographers have emphatically noted, Yourcenar showed little fondness for children in general. Josyane
Savigneau went so far as to speak, and not without reason, of a "repulsion for
procreation," noting Yourcenar's membership in the Association for Voluntary Sterilization.[30] One day in August of 1983 Yourcenar did not shy from
saying "I don't much care for children."[31] They could be so terribly conventional, even mean. Asked whether she herself had ever been tempted to have
a child, she said pensively, "For two weeks . . ."[32]

Grace, by contrast, never lost interest in children, and living as she did in a small island community, she had many opportunities for close contact with them. Whether it was parties arranged to teach young ladies (or gentlemen!) the finer points of serving tea, or group readings on the veranda of the latest local author's children's book, or celebrating an exotic foreign holiday with local youth (to say nothing of the boys who always helped out around the house), Frick filled the couple's life with children. She and Yourcenar even taught some of their young helpers, boys of nine or ten, to make French bread for household consumption!

One boy in particular, David Peckham, whom the couple had met when they were renting 5 Harborside Road in Northeast Harbor, became almost a member of the family in the 1950s. When Frick and Yourcenar's adult friends would come to the island for a few days, David was right there with them for boat rides, seaside adventures, and special treats. As Frick wrote in September of 1955, for example, when the Minear family was visiting,

FIGURE 23. David Peckham, age nine. Peckham family archives.

"Children went climbing in Cove by Rock End Dock, David Peckham delightedly joining the party and particularly enjoying the company of Anita, who is about a year older than he is. . . . 4^{00} All to Jordan Pond, including David Peckham."[33] David was a tutelary spirit, as Frick wrote to her six-year-old niece Pamela Frick, with his "big dark eyes and nice smooth olive brown skin; very handsome he is, and a pleasure to have around."[34]

In early 1956 Grace would write that David and another local boy were "here to work. After they brought wood they popped corn and helped mix popovers for tea. Very pretty, David's face, growing thoughtful over the Swedish candle which I had him light."[35]

David used the money he earned working at Petite Plaisance to buy his first bicycle. He came to speak with me about Grace in July 2008 at Petite Plaisance, by which time he was director of maintenance at New Jersey's Fort Dix. He launched the conversation by saying that Frick had had an important influence on his life, particularly with regard to his desire to broaden his horizons. His mother had been a reader, too, so he was used to living amid books, but Grace brought a new dimension to his inclination to learn. He could not recall any of the episodes involving him that Frick had noted in the daybook, but he remembered precisely how she had taught him to build a fire and bake bread. Peckham described his childhood self as having "a sort of Downeast, blue-collar association," which makes him a fairly typical observer of what for many year-round villagers was a highly unusual household. In his young eyes, "what these two were doing here was really weird. And they'd have you do things. . . . Like, Grace would have you put coffee grounds in the soil and I forget what other kinds of stuff, but it all seemed weird at the time. They didn't do things the way that normal people did. What I called normal at that time."[36]

Another thing that struck Peckham very vividly was the sense of disorder at Petite Plaisance. Pointing to the mantelpiece, with its elaborate Directory clock amid fireplace matches and postcards set there many years earlier, he confided, "For me it was chaos. . . . There were books everywhere, papers everywhere, notebooks everywhere, things everywhere."[37]

Peckham then shared some thoughts about Frick that he had written down in preparation for our meeting:

> I found her very forgiving, very patient. She would explain things and then explain them again if you needed her to. She wouldn't worry about you making a mistake as long as you were *doing* it—that was the important thing. Try, even

though you might make a mistake. Another note I made was, she was always teaching. There was never a thing that we did that she didn't explain thoroughly why we were doing something, what the basis was, and what would happen if we did it correctly. Her teaching came through every time. But the biggest thing that I remember is working around the grounds. With her. With her instructing me about this flower and that flower and this bush and that bush, all kinds of strange things—at least I thought they were strange at the time. She would point me in the right direction and tell me to do this and this and this, and I'd go off and do it.[38]

Grace Frick's desire to involve herself with children never waned. Two color photographs saved and probably taken by Marguerite Yourcenar, tiny in size but enormous in their poignancy, show Grace in a far corner of the back lawn at Petite Plaisance, attired in a high-collared, flowing white dress. In the first, she is surrounded by a clutch of little girls and boys who listen with rapt attention to instructions that Grace seems to be giving them. A young female teacher surveys the scene, holding one child's hand, from the rear of the group. In the second snapshot, the children jubilantly dash across the lawn toward a smiling Grace who clasps in front of her body a long, straight stick that seems to be the object of their joyful chase. On the back of

FIGURE 24. Grace Frick revels with the village children, 1979. Petite Plaisance Archives.

both these pictures, Marguerite wrote, "The last photograph of Grace with the nursery school children in the garden at Petite Plaisance, late August 1979. She died on November 18."

CHAPTER 16 ❧ The Saga of Emily Hall
1948–1950

Faithful are the wounds of a friend.

—Proverbs 6

AS *MÉMOIRES D'HADRIEN* WAS COMING to life, one of Grace Frick's favorite people from the past was dying. Emily Hall became head of the Rare Book Room at Yale University in 1931, the year Grace enrolled as a PhD candidate there. She retired from that post in November of 1947.[1]

It was almost a year later, in October of 1948, that Emily's name started cropping up regularly in Frick's daybooks. One day Grace and Emily drove to Wellesley together, stopping for "luncheon" in Sturbridge, Massachusetts, on the way. On another occasion, in early November 1948, both Frick and Yourcenar went for a drive with Hall to a reservoir surrounded by woods and fields, where they sipped tea from a thermos while enjoying the view. In late February 1949 Hall came to Hartford to examine the old books that Yourcenar had gotten from Switzerland the previous month. But mostly it was a matter of phone calls back and forth between Frick in Hartford and Hall, now living in her childhood home of Wallingford, Connecticut.

On November 9, 1949, Hall phoned to say she would be entering New Haven Hospital for "prolonged examinations." Frick, of course, could always be relied on to marshal her energies whenever someone close to her was ill. On November 10 she was in the hospital at Emily's side helping her place orders for personal items from local stores. Yourcenar had gone with her on the train to New Haven, and she spent the long hours of Frick's hospital visit doing research related to *Hadrian* at the Yale Library. It was midnight by the time the pair got home.

Over the next few days Frick kept tabs on Hall by telephone. When she called on November 14, a Monday, to say she would see her in New Haven on Thursday, Hall became so upset that Grace changed her plans and went to see her the next day. Emily had cancer. From then until the end of November, Grace was almost constantly by her side, waiting in the next room as she had X-ray treatment. On November 22 Hall learned that her illness was incurable. Frick spent most of the next week, a week that included Thanksgiving, at her friend's bedside.

All this was going on during a time of particular intensity with regard to *Mémoires d'Hadrien*. On Monday, November 29, Frick and Yourcenar took the train as far as New Haven together, reading manuscript pages of that work the whole way. Yourcenar then continued on to Bronxville, while Grace stayed all day at the hospital with Emily, "correcting proof." At six o'clock that evening Frick would send those corrected pages off by registered mail to John D. Barrett of the Bollingen Foundation in hopes of receiving a grant to support further research and the eventual translation of the book into English.[2] Yourcenar had requested a year of absence from Sarah Lawrence the previous month.[3] A Bollingen fellowship would be a welcome boost to the couple's finances during that unpaid sabbatical as well as a distinguished institutional acknowledgment of Yourcenar's achievement.

By early January 1950 Hall had been discharged from the hospital, and Grace and Marguerite went to see her in Wallingford. Frick wrote at length about Hall's illness to Gladys Minear. Having herself been a Yale librarian in the 1930s, Gladys knew Emily well. When Emily learned that her own case was inoperable, she was open, as Frick wrote, to "every help except consolatory remarks!" Grace admired Emily's no-nonsense acceptance of her plight:

> The effect has been something of a revelation to us all, this calling of a spade a spade, without hesitation, and nary a word of wailing as to "Why this one thing should happen to me?"
>
> People have rallied round her from far and near, until the case begins to take on the aspect of a pilgrimage, if one may use the term in all respect for its serious connotation. She is just a simple and very lovable person who has done a thousand kindnesses in her life to innumerable people now scattered far and wide, and everyone seems hungry to have some contact with her.[4]

Hall's former colleague Gilbert Troxell and his wife came up with the idea of making a purchase for the Rare Book Room in Emily's name—not in memoriam, but while she was still living. They spread the word among Emily's Yale friends. "It was a daring idea," wrote Grace,

> but they knew their woman; within four days of the doctor's announcement that the case was hopeless I, and others, received the Troxell suggestion in the form of a mimeographed letter. Within two weeks a thousand dollars had come in, simply as a result of a chain relay from friend to friend (limited to Yale connections alone), and by December 15 they could take a Sarum Missal and a Trollope Manuscript to show her before she left New Haven Hospital for her home in Wallingford. Gifts are still coming, and other purchases have been made, all under Mr. Tinker's direction, and presented by him to her for her inspection.[5] She is really quite ill, but she is as delighted as a child by Mr. Tinker's happiness.[6]

As Emily was losing her eyesight, Grace volunteered to read her mail aloud and answer it at her dictation. Many of Hall's friends were in English departments around the country, so Grace knew a good number of them. She enjoyed spending time with Emily. "But most of all," she wrote, "Marguerite and I have been struck by the fact that she has done what she has so joyously in life, and with a humility, too (for she pretends to no scholarship or high attainments), which has actually resulted in giving her a kind of special 'first place.' And she is meeting suffering and death with the same humility, and simplicity, and perhaps not altogether without joy."[7]

Yourcenar, clearly, was not uninvolved in the dealings with Emily Hall. In fact, when Hall returned to the hospital in late May 1950, Grace and Marguerite called on her together again, as Frick wrote, "all three of us thinking it might be a last visit." That was on May 24.[8]

Five days later Yourcenar sent an important letter to Ruth Hall in Kansas City modifying her will. As she noted in closing, "I am writing this long English letter completely without help, and I am in fact rather proud of it. But please excuse the many awkwardnesses and mistakes."[9] In addition to serving as her American attorney, Hall would now be granted the same full power of attorney over Yourcenar's affairs that Grace had. With Sarah Lawrence behind her for at least a year and the first chapters of *Hadrian* in the hands of a literary editor in Paris, Yourcenar wanted her legal business taken care of before leaving Hartford for Mount Desert Island.

This year for the first time, after summers spent in Somesville (two and a half), Southwest Harbor (two), and Seal Harbor (three), the couple would be renting in Northeast. Preparing for summer stays in Maine was always time-consuming and disruptive. This was the first summer with no prede-termined end point, and they had a longer list of items to take with them than usual. Cardboard boxes were scattered throughout the Prospect Avenue apartment, some packed and ready to go, some half full, and some labeled but empty. In the midst of all this Grace "dropped everything," as Mme Yource-nar remembered almost thirty-five years later, "to go off and take care of" a Yale friend. That friend "had been part of one of the happiest periods of her life. Besides," continued Yourcenar, "she felt that she and I were going to be separated, that my future would have its own trajectory which somehow wouldn't include her, and that this was for her."[10] For Yourcenar the incident was doubly prophetic, because she did have her own future, and Grace's battle with Emily's cancer foreshadowed her own.

Tellingly, this revelation about Grace Frick in 1984 occurred during a conversation about fidelity between lovers—a conversation, moreover, in which Mme Yourcenar laid claim to three or four "affairs" over the course of her forty years with Grace. In other words, the attention Frick had lavished on her friend felt like an act of infidelity. Did Yourcenar suspect—or even know—that Grace and Emily had been intimate once? Was Emily the special "friend" that Marianne Zerner asked Grace about in a 1933 postcard from Switzerland? It is hard to imagine that anyone other than a onetime lover could have caused a wound so deep that Marguerite still felt its sting decades later.

Perhaps it seemed especially incongruous that Frick was abandoning her duties on the home front while Yourcenar was giving her ever more power over her personal and literary estate. And as they may or may not have sus-pected at the time, that estate was on the verge of a precipitous increase in value. Éditions Bernard Grasset, one of Yourcenar's publishers during the 1930s, had recently put 3,320 francs on her account at the Comptoir National d'Escompte in Paris.[11] Christine Hovelt de Crayencour had died in Pau on April 24, 1950, leaving everything to her stepdaughter—including a family business near London that had supplied Mme de Crayencour with an income of four hundred pounds a year. It was extremely important to Yourcenar that Frick inherit the English concern so that she would be able to provide a small income to Crayencour's niece, Eulalie de Hovelt, who was in difficult finan-cial straits.[12] She also wished to reconfirm Grace as her sole literary executor should she herself not be able to oversee her most important project to date, the publication of *Mémoires d'Hadrien*.

Making matters more mysterious, there is an unusual two-week gap in Frick's chronicling of daily events in the appointment book that spring—this from a woman who meticulously tracked not only her own life but the travels far and wide of friends and family members whom she hadn't seen for years. She and Marguerite had gone to see Emily together at the hospital in New Haven on May 24, and Grace had recorded their visit the same day. But from May 25 through June 10, the daybook contains only a reminder written in advance of an Antiquarian and Landmarks Society open house that no one seems to have attended and a few inconsequential lines in Yourcenar's handwriting. Granted, the women were busy preparing to leave for North-east Harbor and tending to important legal matters. But on May 24 Emily had sent some blankets back to Hartford with her friends to be dry-cleaned. There can be no doubt that Grace returned those items faithfully to her friend, probably leaving Marguerite to fend for herself in an apartment full of packing boxes while she was away. Whether Yourcenar finally told Frick, possibly in no uncertain terms, how she felt about her companion's prolonged stint of extracurricular care giving is anybody's guess. What can be said with certainty, however, is that there is not a single additional mention of Emily Hall in Frick's daybooks after the joint visit of May 24—including the date of October 9, 1950, when Emily died.

CHAPTER 17 ❦ Brooks Cottage
1950

They were like summer people who stayed all year round.

—Jay McGarr

AFTER THREE STRAIGHT SUMMERS AT Anna Fletcher's cottage near the water in Seal Harbor, Maine, Grace Frick and Marguerite Yourcenar rented a house in 1950 just north of Main Street in Northeast Harbor. Compared with Somesville and Seal Harbor, both small villages with few amenities, Northeast was a thriving community. It boasted two gas stations, three year-round grocery stores, a bakery, a fish market, restaurants catering to all manner of clientele, taverns where one could drink and dance until one in the morning, a first-run movie theater called the Pastime, a department store, a bookshop, a drugstore, and a high school.[1] It was the kind of place where good walkers like Grace and Marguerite could easily get by without a car.

The couple's search for a home of their own had picked up speed in 1948. During that one summer, they examined more than two dozen properties located as far north as the Down East village of Sorrento and as far south as West Bath. They considered places furnished or unfurnished, contemporary or historic, on small islands, large islands, or the mainland. They had several prospects professionally inspected, but none turned out to be quite right. Not until September of 1950 did they finally find "*the* house" they had sought for so long.[2] Yourcenar described the experience to the Parisian radio host Jacques Chancel in 1979: "For a long time, I searched for a cabin. My friend Grace came with me on long walks. We were impatient. One evening, it was almost nightfall, an old wooden house caught our eye, called out to us. It was Petite Plaisance. The dwelling bore no resemblance to a château, or even a suburban home. But it was what we had been waiting for: a place of tranquility, of possible abandon."[3] Coincidentally, the

FIGURE 25. Early photograph of Petite Plaisance. Petite Plaisance Archives.

second payment from the Belgian real estate investment that had replenished Yourcenar's coffers back in April of 1938 was finally about to be disbursed.[4] Between those incoming funds, Frick's personal trust, and the promising outlook for *Mémoires d'Hadrien*, the couple was well placed to invest in a "more or less permanent home."

Once they had spotted what was then called Brooks Cottage, things happened fast.[5] Their first and only appointment to examine the white clapboard farmhouse came on Saturday, September 23, and they bought the property six days later. Located on South Shore Road, the house belonged to one of Northeast Harbor's oldest families, the Kimballs.[6] It was one of twelve tourist cottages that were associated with the eighty-seven-room Kimball House up the street. That hotel had been built in 1886 to accommodate seasonal "rusticators," who came, according to one historian, "for peace and rest and to seek inspiration from the natural beauty of the sea and hills."[7] Brooks Cottage had most recently served as a dormitory for summer employees of the Kimball House, and it was full of beds! Frick and Yourcenar bought the place lock, stock, and barrel.[8]

For a pair of travel lovers and history buffs, the house had a fascinating past. It was built by the thirty-three-year-old Daniel "Squire" Kimball for his fifteen-year-old bride-to-be, Emma Gilpatrick. The couple married on October 26, 1835, and research indicates that the home was constructed right around that time.[9] Squire Kimball is reputed to have felled the great trees for his new house on Brown Mountain, located on the eastern flank of Somes Sound.[10] He then floated the enormous trunks up the sound to Somesville, where they were cut into lumber. Many of the building's structural beams are still clad in the tree bark they wore on the mountainside.

The original site of the home that Daniel Kimball built was not where Frick and Yourcenar found it in 1950 but, rather, several hundred yards up South Shore Road to the east. In the early 1880s, to make way for a dramatically turreted hotel, Kimball rolled his house down the street, drawn by oxen, to its present—one hopes, permanent—location.

The couple christened their new home Petite Plaisance "for the pleasure of a French name, and in honor of Samuel de Champlain," Yourcenar told her assistant, Jean Lunt, in the 1980s.[11] One of the islands just southwest of Mount Desert, now called Little Gott, had been dubbed Petite Plaisance by Champlain in 1604.[12] The term *plaisance* also had particular resonance in the early seventeenth century, when King Henry IV dispatched Champlain to map New France. For the French explorers of that era, a *plaisance* might be a safe place to weigh anchor and replenish their supply of fresh water or pick some wild berries before continuing on their way. For Frick and Yourcenar, Petite Plaisance would be such a sheltered cove.

The house was not particularly ready for habitation, however, nor was it particularly tranquil. Between the date the two women moved in and the end of the year, they installed a gas-powered stove and refrigerator, a kitchen sink, a new tub in the upstairs bath, central heating, interior plumbing for the so-called summer bath, and new marble lavatories in the bathrooms. To crown the nearly constant disruption, on December 3 the house was raised off its moorings so that digging could begin on a full basement. "Buddy" Brown, the current owner of Northeast Harbor's hardware store, still remembers crawling around on his hands and knees in the original dirt cellar to install the new furnace. Surrounded by this cacophony, Yourcenar was finishing *Mémoires d'Hadrien*, the last page of which she wrote on the day after Christmas 1950.

Since arriving in Northeast in early June, Yourcenar had received what the daybook describes as a "very enthusiastic" response to pages 1–124 of the *Hadrian* manuscript from the highly respected Georges Poupet of Librairie Plon. From the Bollingen Foundation, by contrast, on July 11 she got a "routine refusal of aid, on grounds that no further funds were available for the year!"[13] To add insult to injury, that letter of rejection came not from the director, John Barrett, but from an assistant, Vaun Gillmor. Gillmor's letter offered only the hope that Bollingen might one day be able to provide publishing support if the book was accepted by a university press.[14] "We wrote a hot answer," Frick noted on July 11. Signed, of course, by Yourcenar, it bears a date of July 13, 1950: "May I ask you to send a copy of your letter of July 10th to me directly to Mr. Barrett in Europe, together with this note of inquiry from me, because I am puzzled both by the tone of it and by the one specific suggestion which it makes. The letter takes no note of previous conversations or exchanges of letters, for a period of more than a year, and is written as if the manuscript had but recently been received by you." Noting that her novel was not the usual fare for an academic press and that the possi- bility of a translation grant had in fact originated with John Barrett, Yource- nar concluded by informing Gillmor that she would "prefer to hear directly from Mr. Barrett himself before directing you as to the disposition of the manuscript."[15] Yourcenar had never been one to content herself with dealing with an underling. She was also more than able to stand up for herself where her writing was concerned, an observation that *Hadrian*'s route to publication in Paris would resoundingly illustrate.

There was much to be done throughout Frick and Yourcenar's new home. Over time local carpenters custom-built bookcases, shelving units, tables of various kinds, sets of drawers, and even swinging wall lamps from simple pine stock or plywood to serve carefully thought-out purposes. One of those carpenters, Charlie Smith, was particularly memorable. After celebrating his eightieth birthday one weekend, he was back at work framing drawers in the couple's shared office. Yourcenar later laughingly described him to the French journalist Pierrette Pompon-Bailhache as alternately singing hymns and swearing while he worked.[16] One day Grace stopped in to supervise his efforts. Sitting on Marguerite's side of their joint worktable, Grace noted, "Charlie is singing, in a good baritone, 'Cleanse me sinner, vile and mean, Wash me in the blood of Calvary.' Interspersing the melody from time to time with 'God damn, where's my plane?'"[17] Petite Plaisance was rarely a place of high solemnity.

January 1, 1951, marks the first use of the name Petite Plaisance in the daybooks. Villagers were more apt to speak of "Miss Frick's house," though, a tradition that persists in certain quarters well into the twenty-first century. Grace and Marguerite also gave their first Northeast Harbor eggnog party on New Year's Day, a tradition inaugurated at least as far back as 1945, when the guests were Hartford firemen!

"Miss Frick's eggnog"—heavily laced—is well remembered as a festive beverage around town even today. The landscape architect Patrick Chasse, for example, recalls New Year's as one of two days a year when the doors of Petite Plaisance were thrown wide open—Halloween, for the pleasure of the children in their costumes, being the other.[18] Chasse still owns a copy of the holiday eggnog recipe written in Yourcenar's hand; a sixteen-egg batch of the concoction contains one and a half pints of rum. Grace and Marguerite's longtime neighbor Shirley McGarr recalls having to approach Frick's eggnog with extreme caution. "I can remember, Miss Frick made the most—well, Mme Yourcenar I think did too—the most potent eggnog I ever had in my life! Just to *smell* it would send you into a spin!"[19]

Attending that first New Year's party at Petite Plaisance, among others, were Dr. Ernest Coffin, who would be one of Frick and Yourcenar's physicians, and his wife, Kitty; Hannah Kimball, Squire Kimball's granddaughter who had come into this world in the home now owned by Grace and Marguerite; and George Korkmadjian, a cigar-smoking Oriental rug repairman, and his wife, Mary. Korkmadjian had emigrated to the United States from Armenia in 1917; his family was then wiped out by the Turks.[20]

On Tuesday, January 2, 1951, Marguerite began the new year by mailing the completed final sections of *Mémoires d'Hadrien* to Georges Poupet in Paris. She had recopied the short concluding chapter between Christmas and New Year's. The first few days of January, which were exceptionally cold and icy, brought a visit from the couple's Francophile friend Jean Low of Manchester, Connecticut. On January 5, in a rented car, Frick, Yourcenar, and their guest drove the six-mile length of Sargeant Drive along Somes Sound behind the sand truck, marveling at the beautiful frozen cascades on the glacial rock faces beside the narrow roadway.

On March 5 word arrived from Paris that Georges Poupet admired Yourcenar's book with unreserved enthusiasm. It had been accepted by the "small committee" of readers and awaited only the imprimatur of the entire board. Poupet had even written to the Bollingen Foundation on Yourcenar's behalf. Ironically, one of the first readers at Plon was André Fraigneau. His support of the book was less effusive than Poupet's. "We know Marguerite Yourcenar's strengths," Fraigneau wrote, "a perfect style that is supple and mobile, in the service of an immense learnedness and a disabused, decorative philosophy. We also know her weakness: the absence of dramatic pitch, of fictional progression, the absence of effects."[21] Happily, millions of readers around the world would be willing to overlook those supposed flaws.

Soon after hearing the good news from Plon, Yourcenar received from the Bollingen Foundation, without so much as a note, the first chapter and pages 190–208 of the *Hadrian* manuscript. On March 15 what Frick calls a "suave" letter came from John Barrett, once again refusing Yourcenar's request for aid.[22] That would be the end of their two-year correspondence until Yourcenar, no doubt victoriously, mailed Barrett a copy of her novel in early 1952.

On a sunny Easter morning, March 25, Grace and Marguerite celebrated their first breakfast outdoors. The next day Yourcenar finished *Hadrian's* extensive bibliography, a text preceded, as Frick notes, by a two-page "note of explanation of use of sources, in the exact manner of Racine."[23] Grace would proofread it, making various corrections, over the next few days. No sooner was the push to finish *Hadrian* behind them than Marguerite fell ill. She was too weak to leave the house for ten days, most of them spent translating Greek poetry in bed. Yourcenar had been subject to recurrent fevers, sniffles, sore throats, and other ailments ever since early signs of her heart trouble surfaced in the fall of 1944. She was often unwell over the course of the 1940s, particularly when classes were in session at Sarah Lawrence. On January 17, 1945, for example, the daybook reports, "M.Y. telephones home to tell world she has a cold." The only entry in the daybook the next day is the intriguing "M.Y. returns [to Hartford] with bad cold. Goes to bed for a week. Not too ill for us both to have a very good time"![24]

During the years of concentrated work on the *Hadrian* project, she managed to stave off the recurring "grippes," colds, and "germs." But when they finally caught up with her, they did so with a vengeance. Only after two strong shots of penicillin did Yourcenar begin to recover. Then it was Frick's turn to be ill. Unlike her partner, Grace was constitutionally incapable of staying in bed for very long, and she pushed herself so hard that she was "clutching at chairs" to keep herself upright one day.

Yourcenar had received her first American passport on March 22, 1950. It would soon be put to use. But before leaving for Europe, she and Frick had to vacate the apartment in which they had lived for ten years. On April 12 the couple left Northeast Harbor for Hartford, traveling as usual by taxi, bus, and train. Still weak from their bouts with what turned out to be a virulent strain of influenza that had spared almost no one in their village, they put in a full day checking sources at the Boston Public Library en route. The next day was devoted to the Boston Athenaeum, where Yourcenar had never been. After eight or nine hours spent reading Greek historians and descriptions of the Villa Adriana, they made it to South Station in the nick of time to catch the evening train to Hartford.

On April 16, as word of their return to Prospect Avenue started getting around, they received the first of more than one hundred visits and phone calls from friends, neighbors, and colleagues anxious to hear about their long stay in Maine and their European travel plans. Books, dishes, glasses, and silver were carefully packed, and a moving van was hired to transport furniture directly to Petite Plaisance. Borrowing Paul Minear's car, they spent a day at the Yale library. Finally, at midnight on April 29, the couple left Hartford in the Minears' automobile for the final move to Maine. Even as worn out as they must have been, Frick could not resist the chance to stop at Wellesley College en route home the next day to see Laura Lockwood and Katharine Balderston. Freed by their borrowed car to meander at will, the women decided to spend the night near the historic coastal town of Wiscasset, Maine. They stayed at a tourist house on Route 1 there, taking eager advantage of the working fireplace in their room and gratefully slipping between outing flannel sheets for a much-needed sleep.

On May 10 the pair left Northeast Harbor to make their first transatlantic crossing together. They would sail, cabin class, from New York on May 18. That gave Frick a week in which to travel to Kansas City to see family and old friends, leaving Marguerite with the Minears in Massachusetts. From Aunt Dolly, brothers Fred and Gage, and a number of cousins to Alice Parker and Ruth Hall, everyone wanted to see Grace before she left for her fourth and longest trip to France. Gage had married Eleanor Emma Martin in Florida just before his release from the army in 1945. They now had two children, four-year-old Kathie and two-year-old Pamela. Fred and his second wife, Thelma Wilhelmy, had wed in Rio de Janeiro the previous spring.[25]

There were more friends to see on May 17, when Frick and Yourcenar arrived in New York City by train from west and east to spend the night before their departure at the Hotel Barclay. For lunch the next day they were joined by Ina Garsoïan, an artist trained in prerevolutionary Russia, and her daughter Nina, a professor of Byzantine civilization at Columbia University.[26] In 1953 Ina would paint a stunning portrait of Yourcenar.[27]

In anticipation of their trip Yourcenar had written to Ruth Hall, who was on her way to France, too: "Except for saying that Grace and I are thrilled that our time in Paris coincides with yours, and that we hope to see much of you, your mother and sister, this letter will be strictly about hotels, in order to go in today's mail." Yourcenar and Frick were not yet aware that the hotel where they had met in 1937, to which they wished to return, was no longer operating, and Yourcenar urged Hall to stay there. It was as luxurious, said she, as the Ritz but much more sympathetic. The Hôtel Wagram also had access to "very easy transportation of all sort. The elevators were good, and so, (10 years ago) the plumbing, and the place has charm; the front rooms have lovely views on the Tuileries gardens."[28]

Before the war Yourcenar's work had been published by several different houses in Paris. *Alexis* came out in 1929 at Éditions Au Sans Pareil under the benevolent direction of René Hilsum, who had issued the early work of surrealists André Breton and Louis Aragon. *La Nouvelle Eurydice* (1931), *Pindare* (1932), *La Mort conduit l'attelage* (1934), *Feux* (1936), and *Les Songes et les sorts* (1938) were brought out by Éditions Grasset. *Nouvelles orientales* (1938) and *Le Coup de grâce* (1939), the author's last prewar writings, had appeared at Éditions Gallimard. Georges Poupet of Éditions Plon had arranged to have the first three parts of *Hadrian* prepublished in a literary magazine called *La Table ronde* during the summer of 1951. When Grasset and Gallimard got wind of what both knew would be a very big book, they were reminded that Yourcenar had signed contracts with each of them during the 1930s containing first-option clauses on her next book. Gaston Gallimard, in particular, set about planning to assert his claim on this one with all the clout of France's most prestigious house. Thus began a battle that Frick and Yourcenar would come to call the *Hadrian* affair.

CHAPTER 18 ☙ Paris, France
1951

After all everybody, that is, everybody who writes is interested in living inside themselves in order to tell what is inside themselves. That is why writers have to have two countries, the one where they belong and the one in which they really live.

—Gertrude Stein

BY 1951 GRACE FRICK WAS reporting to the Yale Alumni Office that she was a self-employed "Literary Research Assistant."[1] Sometimes she just called herself a literary translator. Either way, she had made the transition from college professor to independent agent. She had also given up on George Meredith's early poetry. Soon she would be translating one of the great books of the twentieth century. Marguerite Yourcenar, for her part, had been brought back to literary life in France a few years before returning there by the publication of her French translation of Henry James's *What Maisie Knew* in 1947. Like so much else, it had been delayed by the war.

The daybook page for the couple's first week in Paris, in May of 1951, is so full it overflows, and entries are in French no matter who was writing. Settling initially into the luxurious Hôtel Lotti near the tea shops on the rue du Mont Thabor, the women threw themselves into a dizzying spate of cultural activity. They visited museums (the Cluny, the Louvre, the Guimet) and churches (Notre-Dame, Saint-Julien-le-Pauvre, Sainte-Chapelle). They saw Shakespeare's *Winter's Tale* performed in French and Gide's *Les Caves du Vatican* at the Comédie-Française. But more than anything else for this pair, Paris was a musical feast. They heard the great French pianist Robert Casadesus at the Théâtre des Champs-Élysées, revolutionary and imperial works in the illuminated courtyard of the Louvre, an evening of selections from Gluck's *Orphée* at the Palais de Chaillot. Ancient and sacred music was especially favored: they went three times to hear the a capella Chanterie de Sainte-Anne; sacred fare was again the draw at an illuminated Chapelle Royale; at Saint-Sulpice, it was Marcel Dupré performing ancient compositions on the great organ.

While Yourcenar met with old friends Jenny de Margerie, "Nel" Boudot-Lamotte, and Joseph Breitbach, among others, Grace often set off by herself on long walks, as she had done when she was discovering Paris for the first time in 1928. One day she took a three-mile round-trip trek across the Seine through Saint-Germain to take in an exhibit of old books and bindings. She loved exploring the Faubourg Saint-Honoré, alone and with Marguerite. Pleasure walks were almost always part of their day, and the Tuileries Garden was a favorite spot. One July night in 1951, the women stayed in the garden so late that they got locked in there. Whether they managed to get out or spent the night on a park bench, the daybook doesn't say![2]

Yourcenar was scheduled to sign the contract for *Mémoires d'Hadrien* in the offices of Éditions Plon on Thursday, June 7, a date that until 1960 was mistakenly believed to be her birthday.[3] Owing to a slight indisposition, she ended up signing the document on her actual birthday, June 8, a coincidence suggesting a kind of rebirth. It also serves to highlight the close personal connection between Yourcenar and this book, which she once told a friend "matters a lot more to me than the others."[4] That evening she and Frick dined with Nel Boudot-Lamotte. The next day the couple packed up and moved to the Hôtel St. James et d'Albany at 202 rue de Rivoli, where their suite contained a bedroom, a bath, and a small sitting room. They were now as close as they could get to the old Hôtel Wagram, the former occupant of number 208.

On June 9 Nel and his sister Madeleine took Yourcenar to meet the sixty-seven-year-old artist Marie Laurencin at her workshop on the rue Vaneau. She and Frick went there together on June 21. By early December both were sitting for their portraits. Laurencin is known for the feminine lines of her softly shaded works in pastel. Marguerite would later say that she became "in the last years of her life a very dear friend for Grace and me."[5] It was at Laurencin's house, momentously, that they would meet someone else who became a dear friend, the expatriate American lesbian Natalie Clifford Barney.[6]

Like Grace Frick, Barney was born in Ohio. She also shared Frick's love of horseback riding, to the extent of being nicknamed the Amazon. She had shocked proper Bar Harborites in the late nineteenth century by galloping through town astride her mount rather than in ladylike sidesaddle. Reminiscing one day about her youthful days on Mount Desert Island, Barney recalled that she often "rode forth of an evening to visit some fair lady and threw pebbles up at the window of Maisie Sturgis (after Mrs. Edgar Scott) or the Lurman sisters to whom I wrote sonnets."[7] Barney's ancestry was also, like Frick's, partly German. As their letters reveal, a quick intimacy developed between Grace and Natalie. Frick considered Barney to be such a close friend that she composed a lengthy handwritten chronology of her life like the ones she drew up for herself and Yourcenar. Barney's indignation in the face of injustice was just as sharp at a young age as Frick's: her "first memory of Europe," sometime between the ages of eight and fourteen, was "fury at the sight of women pulling carts in Belgium."[8] Both women had a playful sense of humor and a love of social contact. As the future would prove, Barney also shared with Frick a strong devotion to Marguerite Yourcenar's career.

Five days after meeting Barney, the couple attended a reception at the Amazon's sixteenth-century pavilion at 20 rue Jacob. Among the people present whose names Frick noted in the daybook on that date were Germaine Beaumont, who translated Virginia Woolf's *A Writer's Journal* into French; Yanette Delétang-Tardif, biographer of the literary critic Edmond Jaloux, whose notice of Yourcenar's *Alexis* in 1929 helped establish the young woman as a serious writer; and Anne Green, a novelist and translator who, like her brother Julien, spent most of her life in France.[9] Diana Souhami has spoken of Barney's place in the European lesbian firmament in *Wild Girls: Paris, Sappho, and Art*. She helps us imagine the scene:

> From October 1909, each Friday when Natalie was in Paris she held an afternoon salon at rue Jacob from four to eight. It was at heart a lesbian arts club, where writers, painters, and poets felt at ease. Freud, Kraft-Ebing and Havelock Ellis had pathologised homosexuality, writers like Compton Mackenzie mocked it, lawmakers criminalized it and the Bloomsbury Group euphemised it. Radclyffe Hall apologised glumly about being a "congenital invert," Gertrude Stein described herself as a husband with Alice B. Toklas as her wife, Vita Sackville-West praised marriage but pursued same-sex affairs. . . . Natalie revised attitudes. She extolled the kiss of the fictional Bilitis. "I am a lesbian," she said. "One need not hide it, nor boast of it, though being other than normal is a perilous advantage." With Sappho as her guide she lived the advantages and made light of the perils.[10]

Men were by no means banned from these occasions, however, and some of the most famous callers were F. Scott Fitzgerald, André Gide, James Joyce, and Rainer Maria Rilke.

As the passage from Souhami's *Wild Girls* illustrates, Natalie Barney was extremely straightforward about her sexuality—far more so, for example, than Marguerite Yourcenar generally was. Although we have less evidence to go on with regard to Grace Frick, there is reason to believe that her own attitude toward lesbianism was more matter-of-fact than her companion's. We may learn more when Yourcenar's sealed papers are released at Harvard in 2037, but we have already glimpsed Grace's lighthearted openness regarding sensual matters.

During Frick and Yourcenar's 1951–52 stay in Europe, Natalie Barney lent the couple what she called a "curious book about a feminine trio" that she thought would interest them.[11] It was the first published version of Gertrude Stein's *Q.E.D.* The novel was written in 1903 but did not appear, entitled *Things as They Are*, until after Stein's death, in a print run of just over five hundred copies.[12] According to Leon Katz's introduction to *Fernhurst, Q.E.D., and Other Early Writings*, it is the thinly veiled autobiographical story of a lesbian love triangle involving Stein, her friend May Bookstaver, and Mabel Haynes. Although its content is intimate and lesbian in nature—"possibly the earliest coming out story," states Karren LaLonde Alenier, among others—it does not give the lie to what Barney herself had to say about Stein's style in the foreword she reluctantly composed for *As Fine as Melanctha* in 1954: "Being a writer of pensées, I like to find a thought as in a nut or sea-shell, and while I make for a point, Gertrude seems to proceed by avoiding it . . . getting at a subject by going not for but around it, in snowball fashion, gathering up everything she meets on her rounds."[13] It was Frick who wrote to thank Barney for lending them the book, perhaps in part because Yourcenar would not have had much good to say about it:

> Dear Friend,
>
> Thank you so much for letting me take the *Things as They Are* home again. Because of its handsome format it had been put carefully away for you previously, for prompt return. I am glad to have read it at leisure, for it not only serves better to explain why Gertrude Stein developed her later style of writing, for which we chiefly know her, but also gives clues, I suspect, to much of her essential content. How close to Henry James, after all.[14]

Here Frick likely speaks at once of James's unacknowledged "inversion" and of the book he wrote about another love triangle, *The Bostonians*. Olive Chancellor's *ménage-à-deux* with the younger Verena Tarrant, whom she had heard speak at a feminist rally, is believed to be the first use of the term

"Boston marriage." Although there is no overt lesbian content in the book, both Chancellor and Ransom vie for Tarrant with what in James's decorous fictional universe amounts to steamy passion.

Grace then went on to comment appreciatively on what Stein was trying to do in *Things as They Are*, though in her view she did not go far enough:

> Labored as this effort is, I nevertheless find it admirable in many ways, and most of all for its honest attempt to set forth the situation in all its undressed dullness. That must have taken courage on the part of the writer; or am I mistaken, and was she so obsessed with the question of principles (as she understood them) that she failed to see the absurdities of her result, just as she seems to have failed in sounding the experience to its depths, in this case at least.[15]

Natalie would soon give Grace and Marguerite another volume, meant perhaps to show how thoroughly those depths could be sounded.

In her early correspondence with Barney, Yourcenar was sometimes open to a playful Sapphic allusion. In one letter from the summer of 1952, for example, she wrote Natalie's first name in Greek. Barney responded,

> "To thine own self be true" remains in fact the only livable morality. . . . You're right to write my name in Greek, for I have never had any complexes of that kind. As proof of which I submit this lived novel, written in verse, a long time ago, which has only now been published, "under cover," and which may nonetheless still strike you as too blatant? And above all from a Sappho "fastening wholly on her prey"?[16]

Barney quotes here from one of the most famous French plays of all time, Racine's *Phaedra*: "It's no longer an ardor hidden in my veins: / It's Venus fastening wholly on her prey."[17] The book she refers to is *Nos Secrètes Amours*, which had been written near the turn of the century by her lover Lucie Delarue-Mardrus. According to Suzanne Rodriguez's *Wild Heart: Natalie Clifford Barney's Journey from Victorian America to Belle Époque Paris*, Barney had that book privately printed in 1951 without naming its author. Rodriguez calls it a collection of "extremely passionate love poems," and she's not kidding.[18] The deluxe edition on Madagascar vellum at Petite Plaisance attests, by way of X's and other marks, to the fact that it was appreciatively read from cover to cover.[19]

Barney, who once traveled with a lover to Sappho's Mytillene in hopes of establishing a colony of women poets there, tried to get Yourcenar to

translate the ancient poetess of Lesbos.[20] In an August 1952 letter addressed as
her letters often were to "My Dears," Barney wrote, "That you, Marguerite
Yourcenar, have also the gift for verse makes me hope that you will reveal
to us the recent fragments of Sappho. Why wouldn't they be an appropriate suite to your fragment by Anacreon?"[21] Yourcenar answered her later
that month, sending a postcard of birch trees along a foggy wooded path on
Mount Desert Island. "Sappho, yes," she said, "but her fluidity, her limpidity
(a flame in crystal) discourage me; I prefer Theocritus's dense flesh."[22] Not
until 1979, after Barney's death, would Yourcenar translate Sappho, along
with many other ancient Greek poets, in *La Couronne et la lyre*. At least one
commentator, the Sappho scholar Joan DeJean, finds that Yourcenar's free
translations "convey more successfully than any others in French the sparse
evocative economy of Sappho's verse."[23] Natalie would have been pleased.

After many get-togethers with old and new friends, including several days
spent seeing sights with Ruth Hall and her family, Frick and Yourcenar left
Paris for Switzerland. Jacques and Marguerite de Saussure had invited them
to stay at their family home, the Château de Vufflens-sur-Morges. They were
met by the Saussures at the train station in Lausanne on July 22, with their
twelve bags. Grace and Marguerite awoke the next morning to the "sound
of hundreds of cowbells passing far below under our window on the second
floor."[24] The château, surrounded by vineyards and orchards, sat on a hillside
above the town of Morges. Mont Blanc could be seen in the distance. A few
days later Grace sent a postcard of the inner courtyard of Vufflens to Gladys
Minear, along with a description of the place. As always, Grace was game for
an adventure:

> How would you like to keep house here? Believe it or not, this is where we are
> staying for two weeks with old friends of Marguerite's. Am I thrilled! From
> cottage to palace, so to speak. I have already climbed the donjon tower which
> dates from the twelfth century, and have been over every inch of the "modern"
> part (1410) where we live. We are high on a hill above Lake Geneva (Leman)
> and vineyards cover the hills below us. If the vintage is good the owners will
> paper their own bedrooms this fall! Italian builders constructed this part for a
> Savoian [*sic*] counselor to one of the Popes at Avignon. Same family still lives
> here, so the library is magnificent.[25]

Also staying with the Saussures at that time was a German couple, Herr
and Frau Finch. When they left Vufflens on August 5, Jacques revealed

to Yourcenar, as Frick cryptically notes, their "connection with *Coup de grâce*."[26]

Meanwhile, back in Paris, Gaston Gallimard wanted *Mémoires d'Hadrien*, and, no less than Racine's Phaedra, he was wholly fastened on his prey. On September 4 Yourcenar and Frick, still in Switzerland, sent the first section of the second set of corrected proofs to Plon, requesting a third.[27] The next day Gallimard wrote to Yourcenar laying out his plan: she would convey to him the *Hadrian* manuscript and he would publish it immediately. Although the contract she had signed for *Le Coup de grâce* did indeed require her to give Gallimard first option on her next book, Yourcenar felt she had fulfilled that obligation by offering *Dramatis personae* to that house in 1947. She had high hopes for those plays written during the war. At Gallimard, *Dramatis personae* was read and rejected by Albert Camus, and Yourcenar was stung by this refusal. Nor was she pleased upon returning to Paris with Gallimard's handling of her titles from the 1930s, which had long gone out of print. Though she was willing to reach an arrangement with Gallimard for future works, she had no intention of changing horses in midstream where *Hadrian* was concerned.[28] On September 18 the final batch of corrected proof was mailed to Plon.

Six days later, at Gallimard's initiative, "a formal injunction against pursuing the publication" of *Mémoires d'Hadrien* was served at Éditions Plon.[29] In early October officials from Plon and Gallimard met with the president of the writers' union to air their respective grievances. Over the next few weeks, offers and counteroffers flew back and forth between the two houses. Not until October 14 did Frick and Yourcenar leave Switzerland for Paris, where the couple engaged the legal services of Jean Mirat with the intention of obtaining a nullification of Yourcenar's prewar contract. None of this prevented them from attending a concert of medieval music at the Church of Saint-Gervais or Bach's *Passion of Saint John* at the Protestant Temple de l'Oratoire du Louvre.[30]

Nor did it stop them from making new friends recommended by Gladys Minear. Jean and Roger Hazelton were renting a house that fall in the village of Lamorlaye outside Paris with their three young children. Roger, who taught at Andover Newton Theological School near Boston with Paul Minear, had a Fulbright Scholarship to study the manuscripts of Blaise Pascal at the Bibliothèque Nationale. Grace, as usual, took the initiative to arrange a get-together. Jean Hazelton still remembered at the age of ninety-nine the first lines of the note Frick sent her that October: "Dear Friends," she began, having never laid eyes on the Hazeltons, "it would be worth your while to come into Paris to see us just to see the view from our balcony in the hotel." Jean heard all about the lawsuit in which Yourcenar was embroiled during the very first luncheon she had with Marguerite and Grace, a lawsuit she described as "making life miserable for them." The two couples liked each other immediately and were soon going to concerts, plays, and museums together. Jean and Roger would often stop by their friends' room at the Saint-James for cocktails and hors d'oeuvres, after which the foursome would dine out at restaurants chosen almost always by Marguerite. It was a habit that made of them eyewitnesses to literary history.[31]

"One night we were up there having a drink and the telephone rang," Jean Hazelton recalled. "It was Gallimard calling to say that he was withdrawing the lawsuit! Then someone came to the door with a *huge* bunch of flowers, a bouquet of roses, and that was from the Gallimards, too. I remember thinking that was so French. And so it turned out that it would have been our Thanksgiving Day back in the U.S. So we went out on the balcony and toasted Thanksgiving and the fact that the lawsuit had been withdrawn." In the daybook Grace enthused, "Hadrien!!! Thanksgiving—and how!"[32] Yourcenar had triumphed in a months-long battle with the head of France's top publishing house. There was indeed reason to give thanks.

A few days before this momentous event, on November 17, Frick had made a personal pilgrimage in memory of the cousin whose untimely death had brought her into Yourcenar's world. She laid flowers on the grave of Sister Marie Yann at the congregation's communal cemetery and brought another bouquet to the nuns who had cared for Sister Yann so lovingly. On December 2 Grace and Marguerite visited the Sion house together, probably for the first and only time. Were they thinking of the long and improbable road they had traveled since their paths had crossed nearly fifteen years earlier? With Yourcenar soon to be a world-renowned author, that visit to Issy-les-Moulineaux would have been a fitting juncture for such musings. But no one knew yet what the future held in store. In the daybook Frick said only that they bought Christmas cards at the convent to mail to her nieces in Missouri.

Mémoires d'Hadrien finally went on sale on December 5, 1951. Frick and Yourcenar spotted it that day in two bookstores near their hotel, the Librairie Galignani and the Vendôme. Although the "*Hadrian* affair" caused this novel of a lifetime to miss the deadline for the major prizes, it suffered few if any ill effects from the loss of that favorable publicity. The book was an immediate best-seller. Reviews were universally admiring, and some of the novel's most enthusiastic readers were themselves distinguished European authors: the French writer Roger Martin du Gard, winner of the 1937 Nobel Prize for literature; the great German novelist Thomas Mann, another Nobel laureate; and Jean Cocteau, the French playwright, poet, and filmmaker whose career would soon be crowned by his election to the Académie française, were all moved to write directly to Yourcenar about her astonishing novel.

So was her old friend Emmanuel Boudot-Lamotte, who specifically addressed the death of Hadrian's adolescent favorite, paraphrasing that popular line from Racine:

> I threw myself on the bereavement of Antinoüs as on a prey. It engulfed me. At the same time, the good that's done by tears is ignoble—the unilateral character of that child is more revolting than the weakness tears express. Now there's a strange literary criticism, perhaps no more worthy of me than it is of you. But there you have it. It is justified by the one for whom the tears are shed. That is why I am abasing myself to admit them to you in a double homage. You have received and will receive more considerable testimonies. I will find, I have already found, in *Memoirs of Hadrian* a hundred other things, and even *a summa*. Today, I have nothing better to offer for your immense graces than this wordless homage. I guarantee, at least, that it was lived.[33]

Praise came as well from Yourcenar's Greek friend and cotranslator Constantine "Didy" Dimaras. Having read only the three sections published in *La Table ronde*, Dimaras wrote,

> You can imagine what a joy it was for me finally to read something of yours again in French. My first impression, still somewhat cursory, is that French readers have suffered no loss for having had to wait so long: the qualities that people infinitely more qualified than I associate with you—a masterful style, an effortless development, knowledge of the human soul, courage in seeking the truth—all of these are here again now, with more power and—how to put it?—more confidence, more calm. I have also had the pleasure, personally, of noting that one finds nowhere in this work any trace of the anguish discernable in some of your previous books; and since I am as attached to you as I am to the quality of your prose, you can well imagine how much that counts for me.[34]

Dimaras's perceptive comments touch on the transformation undergone by Marguerite Yourcenar over the years spent in America with Grace. Joan DeJean has cast a uniquely penetrating glance at Yourcenar's evolution as a writer in her *Fictions of Sappho, 1546–1937*. It should come as no surprise that Yourcenar would claim a place for herself in what DeJean calls the "unbroken

chain of fictions, from the early seventeenth century to the 1940s" that make
France a site of "uninterrupted dialogue with Sappho."[35] Yourcenar's "Sappho ou le suicide" is the final text in her 1936 collection of prose poems,
Feux. It depicts an aging Sappho who, from lyric poet, has been transformed
into a trapeze artist in a modern-day circus.

In Yourcenar's post–World War II writing, DeJean detects a change in
both her style and her subject matter: "At the same time as she developed her
new style, the petrified, sparse (more Sapphic) neoclassicism of her master-
pieces, she replaced Sappho, no longer in vogue (hers is, in fact, the last major
French Sapphic fiction) with other figures from antiquity, notably that de-
vout practitioner of the cult of Winckelmannian beauty and erotic *pederastia*,
the emperor Hadrian."[36] As we have seen, even Natalie Barney couldn't coax
her back to Sappho again.

While "petrified" is not a word I would use for Yourcenar's postwar style,
DeJean puts her finger squarely on what is at stake in *Mémoires d'Hadrien*.
Noting that the young author's initial work on the novel went back to the
interwar, "Sapphic" years and that Yourcenar finally completed it in America
after the war, DeJean goes on to say that "both her presence here and the
novel that would eventually grow out of the research and writing done in
the Yale library in 1937 are the most forceful indications of a reaction, on the
part of a member of the French Sapphic tradition, to the role reserved for the
doctrine of *pederastia* in the nationalistic German ideology that fueled World
War II."[37] As I have tried to show elsewhere, Yourcenar was already headed
down this path in her depiction of Erick von Lhomond in *Le Coup de grâce*.[38]
By 1949, when she began the definitive *Hadrian*, much more was known
about where that ideology would lead. Yourcenar, explains DeJean,

> uses the eulogy of *pederastia* to subvert the ideology of conquering nationalism
> and violent militarism that it had previously been made to serve. She portrays
> the founder of the cult of Antinoüs as a spokesman for peace: the *Mémoires
> d'Hadrien* is a profoundly antimilitaristic novel, a monument—completed after
> "what seemed the definitive end of a world"—to the need to preserve civiliza-
> tion, Yourcenar's homage to the emperor who tries to break the bond between
> nationalism and xenophobia, between the empire and the narrow definition
> of its civilizing mission as the automatic impulse to replace Other (barbarian)
> with Same (Neo-Greek or Roman).[39]

In a lamentable instance of historical irony, the country to which Yourcenar
had, however nominally, shifted her allegiance in 1947 was itself embarked

on a decade-long campaign of demonizing the Other based on the same kinds of lies, fear mongering, and false accusations that were propagated by the Nazis. Yourcenar and Frick would themselves fall under its dark shadow.

CHAPTER 19 ❦ In Collaboration with the Author
1952–1954

Art is long, and Time is fleeting.

—Henry Wadsworth Longfellow

THE WEEKS AFTER *MÉMOIRES D'HADRIEN* came out brought a whirlwind of book signings, media interviews, luncheons, dinners, and parties—one of them a Christmas Eve eggnog gathering at the Hôtel Saint-James that lasted until midnight. Marguerite Yourcenar's success and her sudden celebrity surpassed all expectations. Old friends and new, attracted by the book, came pouring in. Among the former were Grace Frick's Wellesley classmate Florence Codman, who came to Paris shortly after *Hadrian* was released and helped Yourcenar connect with the American publisher Farrar, Straus and Young;[1] Jean Cocteau, with whom the couple dined between Christmas and New Year's; Yourcenar's first publisher, René Hilsum; and the French author Roger Caillois, whose chair at the Académie française Marguerite Yourcenar would one day occupy. Among the most notable new friends were the Argentine writer and publisher Victoria Ocampo and the Chilean-born marquis and ballet impresario George de Cuevas. Ocampo's literary magazine *Sur* counted Jorge Luis Borges and José Ortega y Gasset among the members of its editorial committee and published numerous renowned French authors on its pages. A staunch antifascist during the war, Ocampo was imprisoned in the 1950s by the dictatorship of Juan Perón. Marguerite Yourcenar would join Albert Camus, François Mauriac, Ernest Hemingway, and other writers in speaking out against her detention. The Marquis de Cuevas, as Grace noted in the daybook, invited Yourcenar to dine with him on January 19, 1952, "without knowing her, but adoring the *Hadrien*."[2] Marguerite and Grace would see a lot of the marquis in the weeks to follow.

With Yourcenar a sought-after commodity, social life was very much the order of the day. The British writer and socialite Nancy Mitford provides a glimpse of those hectic weeks from an unusual angle. Angel Gurria-Quintana calls Mitford "a Francophile who never quite took to the French literary establishment," viewing it as not entirely reputable.[3] As if to exemplify its shadiness, Gurria-Quintana quotes from a letter Mitford wrote on February 1, 1952: "I went to a terrible dinner to meet Mlle Yourcenar. All but me were drugged to the eyes & clearly orgies were about to take place—prim & English, I fled."[4] Yourcenar and Frick dined with de Cuevas on January 30, along with Princess Bibesco and her attaché. It's hard to imagine them "drugged to the eyes," though the wine no doubt flowed freely at the marquis's table. If there was an orgy, it goes unmentioned in the daybook, as does Mitford.

The pace of life slowed down somewhat after Frick and Yourcenar left Paris, heading for Rome, on February 10. En route they stopped in Pau, to settle Christine de Crayencour's estate, and then on the French Riviera. In Cannes they discovered the pleasures of traveling by horse-drawn carriage, a mode of transportation that would figure prominently over the upcoming weeks. Yourcenar once told a friend that these leisurely rides were a "particular delight" for Grace, the equestrian, though they surely held appeal for Marguerite, whose bedroom at Petite Plaisance is exclusively decorated with artistic images of horses.[5] The couple's first *carrozza* trip took them to de Cuevas's villa, Les Délices, on the avenue d'Antibes. They would have luncheon at Les Délices several times over the course of their week in Cannes. *Mémoires d'Hadrien* had inspired the marquis to conceive a ballet about Antinoüs.

In Italy the couple spent two months following in the footsteps of their younger selves. They reached Rome in late February, staying at La Residenza, where they had been new lovers in 1937.[6] On Sunday, March 2, just as they had done upon arriving in Sicily in 1937, the women attended a performance of marionettes.

Hadrian's success had prompted the reissue of Yourcenar's previous works, the first one of which was *Alexis*. Both Frick and Yourcenar, each with her own copy of the text, pored over the original edition, carefully checking and correcting it. When *Alexis* was reissued in the spring of 1952, Yourcenar would inscribe a copy "to Grace, with gratitude and tenderness," adding in Greek, "You have made me forget my cares."[7]

Before departing for Spain in late April, the two women made several trips to the Villa Adriana. Spain had been off-limits to Yourcenar and Frick in 1937 because of the civil war. This time they had their sights set on Seville. Departing from Genoa, they stopped in Gibraltar, Algeciras, and Cadiz, one of Europe's oldest continuously occupied cities. Seville was near the ancient site of Italica, Trajan and Hadrian's birthplace, and its museums brimmed with artifacts from that era. It was in Seville that mention is first made in the daybook of Frick translating *Hadrian*. After visiting the Museo de Bellas Artes and a carriage ride back to the bottega for lunch, Grace wrote, "Translated the rest of afternoon and till eleven at night, when we went by taxi to Cabaret (Bar Citroën) to hear Spanish singing."[8] Three days later, with Yourcenar keeping the daybook, they translated all day long.

In "Andalusia, or the Hesperides" Yourcenar would later speak of how intimately linked for her and Frick were the human and the historical dimensions of their travels in Spain:

> Let us list its delights for us: Granada was beautiful, but that nightingale who sang every night, its dark throat swollen with song, taught us as much about Arab poetry as the inscriptions in the Ahlambra. Beside the ocean at Cádiz, among buried stones which may be those of the temple of Hercules of Gades, that young boy with his brown legs, standing up to his thighs in water which was as pale blue as his washed-out rags, concentrating only on the rewards and disappointments of his fishing, moved us as much as the ancient statue we found at the water's edge. That aged, half-blind nun who showed us the paintings in the Hospital de la Caridad without seeing them herself takes her place in our memory beside the painted figures.[9]

On May 17 a telegram arrived announcing that *Mémoires d'Hadrien* had won the Prix Femina-Vacaresco. Yourcenar was expected for the June 4 ceremony. Back in Paris, she and Frick went with Natalie Barney on May 30 to the opening of Virgil Thomson's opera based on Gertrude Stein's *Four Saints in Three Acts*. The couple were delighted to run into their old friend Chick Austin there and would see him several times before returning to America in August.

Yourcenar, who never liked command performances, was informed in a letter from the perpetual secretary of the Femina committee that she was not invited to the luncheon at the Ritz which the "Femina ladies" would attend before handing over the prize.[10] Frick's opinion of that arrangement can be deduced from her comment in that day's agenda: "Prix Femina Committee to give Vacaresco Award, at the Ritz. M.Y. to come at 2:15, like a sheep."

Yourcenar herself was often of two minds regarding literary prizes, though she knew that they performed a crucial role in bringing attention, and new readers, to her work. Moreover, June was not without its finer moments. On June 7, supposedly Marguerite's birthday, the couple took a dinner cruise on the Seine, viewing an illuminated Paris beneath a "very beautiful" full moon. On June 19 George de Cuevas took Yourcenar to meet Colette at the Palais Royal, not far from the Hôtel Saint-James. We have only one fragment of conversation from that meeting, which Yourcenar herself reported to the Belgian Royal Academy in 1971. Colette, a writer so different from herself, was one of several "invisible presences" whom Yourcenar conjured, along with her mother, Fernande, and Jean Cocteau, to join the academy audience that day: "I saw Colette only once, twenty years ago. Already sickly and re-clining on her chaise longue, she bestowed on me the general's embrace of a modest lieutenant and paid me the most succinct of tributes (at least I hope I can label it a tribute): 'Memoirs of Hadrian? Goddamn!' "[11]

With the date of the couple's departure from France, August 6, looming larg-er on the horizon, it is easy to imagine a certain amount of tension in the air. There was still a crush of people eager to spend time with Yourcenar. She was not looking forward to returning to Sarah Lawrence College. She had prom-ised one more academic year to the school, where she would be teaching the French novel and a course entitled Humanism in Literature. Frick, on the other hand, was eager to return to Petite Plaisance, where painters had been working during the couple's absence and where much remained to be done. It would also be easier for her to work on the Hadrian translation back home.

On July 7, 1952, Frick tersely noted in the daybook, "M.Y. firmly declares hatred of Grace." And, yes, tear stains are clearly visible on the page. Both Josyane Savigneau and Michèle Sarde view this incident as the beginning of Frick's campaign—and I use the word advisedly—to prevent her companion from spending time in Europe, where she was lionized. Savigneau empha-sizes the seriousness of the conflict by noting that "in English as in French, 'declare' is the word that is used in reference to starting a war."[12] According to Sarde, that war would "continue until Grace's death in 1979."[13]

Both biographers also see the disappearance of the pet name Grete from the engagement calendars as a sign of disaffection. Marguerite's nickname was never used in the daybooks before 1946—its first and only appearance that year being one "Gretie Gusto" on April 20. Only in 1948 and 1949 is it used with any frequency—ten and four times, respectively. So if one wants to use the diminutives Grete or Greta as a barometer of conjugal harmony, then one would do better to conclude that things went downhill well before

July 1952. It is more likely that these pet names gave way to "M.Y." because the latter is more dignified. After *Memoirs of Hadrian*, Frick knew she was writing for posterity.

Nor was Yourcenar's July 7 declaration of hatred a totally exceptional event. Several daybook entries from the 1951–52 stay in Europe mention moments of anger or disagreement between the two women. As early as June 10, 1951, when they had only been in Paris for a couple of weeks, Frick noted in the daybook, "Dispute au sujet de la robe Russe grise à Grete, que Grace trouve charmante pour un simple après-midi de Dimanche." Which is to say, the two of them argued over Marguerite's gray Russian dress, which Grace found charming for a simple Sunday afternoon and which her companion obviously didn't.

On April 1 in Rome, amid a painful siege of dental work for Yourcenar, Frick made another dark notation in the daybook: "M.Y. wishes very audibly that Grace were dead." When two people of strong character join forces, conflicts are bound to arise. It is difficult even for traditional couples from similar backgrounds to make it "till death do us part." Imagine how much more of a challenge it must have been for two women raised in vastly different family settings and cultures who, twenty-four hours a day, shared not only a home or a hotel room but a work schedule that almost never let up. A reporter once asked the wife of the widely revered American evangelist Billy Graham if she had ever considered divorcing her husband, who often left her alone to care for their five children while he was off on countrywide crusades. Her humorous but revealing response was "Divorce? Never! But murder . . ." If Grace Frick and Marguerite Yourcenar stayed together for more than forty years, it is because they found a way to negotiate their differences.

In early 1965 Grace Frick reached out to share her experience as part of a "mixed marriage" with her young neighbor Nancy Kimball Ho. Nancy lived just a few houses up the street on South Shore Road. Nancy had recently married an Asian man, Robert Ho, despite the adamant objections of her gravely ill father. Grace knew the Kimballs, and she knew Northeast Harbor. She believed she could help the young bride:

> I understand from your good friends, the Coffins, that it has been hard for your father to adjust to your decision about this marriage, but I have not talked to your parents about it, knowing how upset the winter has been for them. I only wanted some word to go to you from this town over the holidays (perhaps you have already heard from friends here?), *with a Northeast Harbor postmark*, that said plainly that the writer did not view with alarm a marriage with a foreigner!

I know nothing, of course, of the circumstances in which you married, but if New England is to keep its tradition of strength and resourcefulness it will have to receive new blood from time to time, as it did in the days of its seafaring captains and shipbuilders.

. . . This particular Maine coast was settled by relatively recent immigrants, of *highly mixed origins,* however good the stock proved to be, as [the historian] Sam Morison is fond of pointing out. And our civilization, if one can call it that in this whole country, is fairly young compared with that of the Orient. It is high time that we learn to combine what is good in our various cultures, and stop trying to perpetuate the mere differences.

New England, and particularly Mt. Desert, both summer and winter, has much to learn on this score, and perhaps you and Robert can make a real contribution in that direction. Every such marriage is made for highly individual reasons, but the first reactions to it, on the part of others, are apt to be wearisomely the same, so I wanted you to know that if *you* think that you have made a wise choice *we* hope that you will not be deterred by mere prejudice, and that you will be able to prove by your two lives that no such prejudice should ever have existed.

One does not break down thought habits, and non-thinking habits, of a lifetime very easily, and doubtless you will encounter points of view in yourself which you have never clearly recognized as partial, prejudiced, or provincial. (I write, you see, as one who has long had the good fortune to see myself, my country, and my Anglo-Saxon origin through Gallic eyes, and to find that even after thirty years, I am still unable to account for certain tastes and opinions when asked point blank *why* I think I am justified in holding them!) You will come to know and judge your own land better for having help from the outside, like light from another planet! The process is sometimes painful, as you may already have discovered; but the main point is to learn to evaluate correctly what is substance and what is merely external (a vestige of something real enough in the past perhaps, but no longer pertinent or true).

Good wishes to you both,
Grace Frick[14]

This handwritten letter resonates profoundly with the challenges that Frick herself faced in becoming involved with Yourcenar, from its reference to the wearisomely same first reactions of others to the idea of living as a couple in such a way as to show that "no such prejudice should ever have existed." It also acknowledges the challenges inherent to nontraditional or intercultural pairings as well as the salutary effort of self-examination to which they inevitably give rise. Even thirty years into her own "marriage," Grace still saw that effort as a stroke of good fortune.

Yourcenar's 1952 declaration of hatred was not the beginning of a twenty-six-year war punctuated by sporadic cease-fires. One insightful member of Frick's family believed that Grace had had a taming influence on her companion. Despite never knowing her father and the dislocations of her early childhood, Frick grew up in a stable, loving home. Yourcenar, by contrast, had no mother, a caring but distant father, and she hated her domineering Grandmother Noémi. Grace had learned what it meant to be there for her family. She was thus well equipped to enact that kind of caring for her partner.[15]

Another intimate, Jean Hazelton, discovered something quite by accident about Frick and Yourcenar's couple. While living in Newton Centre, Massachusetts, in the 1950s and 1960s, Hazelton belonged to a women's book club. One year she decided to compose and read a paper to "the ladies" about Yourcenar. Once it was written, she sent a copy of the text to her friend to read over and correct if necessary. "The one comment that came back," she told me in 2006,

> was that Marguerite did not like the fact that I said that Grace at times had a rather motherly attitude toward Marguerite. And Marguerite objected to that. Well, it wasn't really a motherly attitude, and I hope I made it clearer. I don't know how to describe it exactly . . . but it really wasn't motherly, but I had to use that word, I think, because I didn't know how—how exactly to talk about it.
>
> Now, afterward, when the biography came out, neither the Minears nor we had ever thought that they were lesbians. It wouldn't have mattered! . . . But maybe that's the reason she objected to me saying Grace was "motherly."[16]

Jean Hazelton never really did zero in on the sentiment she wanted to convey with the word "motherly." But it seems safe to say that she was trying to describe a particular quality of caring, warmth, and possibly protectiveness that Grace displayed toward her companion. As Jean went on to say, "Marguerite didn't want even those few little women in Newton to think that she was being mothered!"[17]

Willa Cather made a pertinent comment about being in a family in an essay on Katherine Mansfield:

> Even in harmonious families there is this double life: the group life, which is the one we can observe in our neighbour's household, and, underneath,

another—secret and passionate and intense—which is the real life that stamps the faces and gives character to the voices of our friends. Always in his mind each member of these social units is escaping, running away, trying to break the net which circumstances and his own affections have woven about him.[18]

This may be all the more true for a Gemini like Yourcenar, but once *Hadrian* came out, there was nothing to stop her from striking out on her own if she had so desired.[19] She would never have chosen to remain in a war zone.

Once Frick and Yourcenar were back in the United States, along with their eighteen pieces of luggage, there was very little time to enjoy Petite Plaisance before they had to leave for Sarah Lawrence. They quickly rented a small sublet in Scarsdale, New York, six miles north of the college in Bronxville. Two days later, on September 19, 1952, they took a night train back to Maine for a long weekend. Marguerite arranged their books for what they hoped would be the final time on the freshly painted bookshelves next to the living room fireplace. Grace took advantage of the beautiful early fall weather to stack firewood in the yard. Yourcenar then left for Scarsdale alone.

The two women would remain apart for almost a month. It was their longest separation since Frick's trip to Kansas City and California in late 1949. The telephone had not yet been connected in Scarsdale, so it was hard to keep in touch. But Marguerite did manage to call one day from Bronxville, on September 30. She was upset because the college wanted to take away the basement room in Gilbert Hall where she had always slept and worked during school weeks since she now had secured an apartment nearby. According to the daybook, "Grace insisted that she protest to President Taylor against this action, and keep the room as necessary for her health and safety." Maybe Grace was a bit motherly after all.

Frick obviously did not hold the July declaration of hatred against her partner. Indeed, she could not wait to have her home again. On the morning of October 11, Marguerite having taken an overnight train from New York to Ellsworth, Grace got up at 3:30 a.m., with the planets of love and good fortune shining brightly in the dark sky, to meet her train. Ellsworth is twenty-one miles from Northeast Harbor, but Grace thought nothing of setting off on foot and hoping for the best. She rode from Northeast to Somesville in the *Bangor News* truck, then walked from Somesville to Town Hill, where a hunter from Bar Harbor drove her a short way with his dog Smoky. After another good stint walking toward the mainland, a woman from Somesville drove her the rest of the way.[20] Presumably, she and Marguerite found another way home.

On October 19 Frick relocated to Scarsdale, where much needed to be done to make their temporary lodging livable. By October 26 she had completed the first chapter of *Hadrian*. It was mailed to the distinguished British publisher Secker and Warburg four days later.

Translating progress was slow, not surprisingly given the difficulty inherent to the text's dense and historically specific language. Josyane Savigneau has spoken of Frick's "intellectual slowness and uncertainty" in this connection, as well as what she calls the "hemming and hawing pushed nearly to the point of incapacity that seized Grace in the face of her translation work," characteristics that Yourcenar is said to have "loathed."[21] Of course, Yourcenar was eager, no doubt even impatient, for Grace to finish her translation. But she knew better than anyone that there was nothing slow or uncertain about Grace Frick's intellect. She spoke, rather, of her companion's "admirable but slow" progress and of her "infinite scruples."[22] As she wrote to Natalie Barney in June of 1953, Frick's editor at Secker and Warburg, Roger Senhouse, also kept throwing a monkey wrench into the works: "the translation of *Hadrian* advances slowly, partly because of Grace, who is very scrupulous and cannot work quickly, partly (and especially for the last few months) because of the very bad influence exerted by the English publisher's reader . . . who involves himself in very obscure corrections of the fragments we send him."[23] The problem was based in part on the differences between American and British English, but, as Natalie Barney wrote in her reply, she too had had unpleasant experience with Senhouse's editorial "biases."[24] Happily, Senhouse made "a startling reversal" in the late winter of 1953, which Frick was pleased to report to Mary Lou Aswell of Farrar, Straus and Cudahy "But alas, the first pages are not yet 'magnificent,'" wrote Grace to Aswell. "I think of them still, but leave them firmly closed, and am happy to report that now whole pages go without undue difficulty."[25] Grace was not one to toot her own horn.

Several years later Frick wrote about the experience of translating her companion's works to Roberta Todd, who was compiling the 1960 issue of the Wellesley College *Chat Cat* for the class of 1925. Frick's letter not only gives an idea of how intertwined her work life was with Yourcenar's but illustrates once again Grace's reluctance to take credit for her accomplishments:

Work of the winter, translation of another novel by Marguerite Yourcenar, but it gets interrupted by constant work with her on new text of hers, or proofs, in hand. We even out in the long run, however, since I cannot translate without her constant help, and therefore take hours of her time on what is primarily my work. That is why I refuse to sign the translations alone. It is a rather unusual situation in that she is a professional translator herself, as well as an original writer, so she knows the problems, and the fascination, of trying to express the nuances of one language in terms of another. But we frequently tear our hair, both our own and each others! One page argued over for two days by any two people of different countries, race, religion, and temperament can bring out every possible difference between them, no matter what page it is![26]

Yourcenar echoed Frick's description of the couple's literary pas de deux in 1971. They were once again correcting page proofs: "Grace Frick has . . . been a great help to me, checking the corrections one by one after the fact (a job that takes hours), and most often writing them herself in the margins, as she has finer penmanship than mine. At those moments when my head was literally spinning, her acuity and attention took over where my own left off. But naturally I always have qualms about time stolen this way (and many other ways) from her translation work."[27] Although translating was clearly the highest priority, Yourcenar does not sound here like someone who loathes her partner's intellectual slowness and uncertainty. She never had anything but high praise for Frick's talent as both a translator and an editor.

So too did the reviewers of *Memoirs of Hadrian* when the book came out in the United States in late 1954. Gerald Sykes wrote a long, highly laudatory article for the *New York Times*. Though without mentioning the translation specifically, he credits Yourcenar's book with "a cool, white marble beauty not unlike that of Maillol's sculpture."[28] Geoffrey Bruun wrote most favorably in the *New Republic*: "The noble prose of Mme. Yourcenar's *Mémoires d'Hadrien* earned her work a prize from the French Academy in 1952 and the prospect of translation into half a dozen languages. But it seems safe to predict that none of these translations will excel this superb English rendering which Grace Frick has prepared in collaboration with the author."[29] Robert Parris was even more admiring in the *Nation*:

> It is most difficult to bear in mind while reading this book that its original language was French, so precise and polished is the translation. Certainly it has been stylistically recomposed; the most expert attempt to preserve the flavor of the original could not arrive at such elegant English usage; strong flavors cancel each other. This is to the great credit of Grace Frick, who collaborated with the author in the Englishing of the book.[30]

Even more than fifty years later, when the British Museum mounted the spectacular three-month show *Hadrian: Empire and Conflict* in 2008, one journalist wrote about "the noble and vigorous" English translation of *Memoirs of Hadrian* by Grace Frick.[31]

The only negative notes that were struck in the press, not surprisingly perhaps in an America in the throes of McCarthyism, were moralizing ones. Dorothy Sinclair in the *Library Journal* called *Hadrian* "a distinguished novel for a somewhat limited audience," contending that the book moves the reader "to antipathy and admiration—which is stronger will depend on the reader's temperament. Homosexuality is accepted and the emotional climax is the suicide of the Emperor's boy-favorite."[32] Even Geoffrey Bruun, so complimentary toward Frick's work in the *New Republic*, felt compelled to speak in the *New York Herald Tribune* of Hadrian's "abnormality" and his "admiration for beautiful boys into which his starved emotions tricked him."[33] These reactions were distressing. But they did not prevent *Hadrian* from taking its place on the *New York Times* best-seller list, where it remained for twenty straight weeks.[34]

With Frick and Yourcenar traveling in Europe when the American *Hadrian* came out, Grace did not even have a chance to bask in the glory of the praises that were sung on her behalf. Perhaps she granted herself some small measure of the credit when in 1955 *Memoirs of Hadrian* won the prestigious Newspaper Guild of New York Page One Award.

CHAPTER 20 ❦ On the Road Again
1953–1954

> To move, to breathe, to fly, to float,
> To gain all while you give,
> To roam the roads of lands remote:
> To travel is to live.

> —Hans Christian Andersen

MARGUERITE YOURCENAR'S FINAL SEMESTER OF teaching at Sarah Lawrence ended in the spring of 1953. For the next two years she and Grace Frick were in constant motion. They moved out of the sublet in Scarsdale on April 30, and Yourcenar rented a room in Bronxville for the remaining few weeks of the academic year. She was also posing for Ina Garsoïan's portrait at the time.

As the couple would soon leave again for Europe, Grace went to Kansas City for a week. On May 20 Marguerite double-underlined "Grace coming back" in the daybook and took the train into New York to meet her at the station. As they often did on the occasion of such reunions, they spent a few days in the city seeing friends, dining out, and taking long walks in Central Park.

There were many reasons to return to France—the Marquis de Cuevas's ballet based on *Hadrian*'s Antinoüs was opening in mid-May, Yourcenar's 1939 novel *Le Coup de grâce* had been reissued, *Électre ou la Chute des masques* would soon be staged in Paris—but the couple's first stop would be England, a country they both loved and had not yet visited together. They would sail from Halifax, Nova Scotia, aboard the SS *Newfoundland* on July 21, arriving in Liverpool a week later.

Once again they were on the trail of a certain emperor, prompting Natalie Barney to quip, "Your card from Hotel Hadrian amused me. Is it he who pursues you or you him?"[1] The pair traveled almost immediately to Hadrian's Wall,

FIGURE 26. Portrait of Marguerite Yourcenar by Ina
Garso ïan, 1953. Reproduced by permission of Nina G.
Garso ïan.

staying near Hexham. They remained there for five weeks, exploring the wall,
making day trips, and visiting the archaeological excavation under way at Cor-
bridge.[2] From Hexham they headed south toward Port Sunlight, whose Lady
Lever Museum housed a stunning early second-century statue of Antinoüs.
En route to the west coast they stopped in Brontë country, which Grace had
visited twenty-five years earlier. Both she and Marguerite loved the Brontës.
When asked to identify her important female predecessors, Yourcenar once said,
"[Looking back] we see quite a few women poets who expressed their emotions and a few women novelists who recounted the sentiments and emotions
that moved them most deeply. I believe that the greatest among them, those
whom one can cite with the most admiration, are the Brontë sisters."[3] Back
home in Maine the couple would place images of Charlotte, Emily, and Anne
Brontë on the bureau in one of their guest bedrooms.

It was during their leisurely visit to England, where the women could travel in relative peace, that two "unforgettable" images of Grace, the first already noted, imprinted themselves in Yourcenar's memory. As the author reminisced near the end of her life about that British tour,

> I see a young woman, with a young Sibyl's features, sitting on one of the gates that separate the fields from the pastures over there; we're at the foot of Hadrian's Wall; her hair is waving in the wind from the mountaintops; she seems to embody that expanse of air and sky. I see the same young woman in a four-poster bed in an old, run-down house in Ludlow talking about Shakespeare, whom she imagines rehearsing with his actors, or rather speaking to him as if she were there.[4]

Grace was eager to show Marguerite the Norman fortress at Ludlow, which had acquired an Elizabethan cast when held by the Crown. She had first seen that medieval castle, east of Birmingham, in 1937 after visiting Margaret Symons in Wormelow. It held literary as well as historical interest for her, reputed as it was to have provided a venue in the sixteenth and seventeenth centuries for traveling performances of Shakespeare, Marlowe, and Milton.

From England the couple made their first trip to Scandinavia, a region that would hold a special place in their hearts for the rest of their lives. They were drawn to Denmark, as to Sweden, Norway, and Finland, by the promise of paid lectures. At Copenhagen's French Institute, Yourcenar's topic was "The Novelist Confronting History." She also lectured during that tour on the mythical character Electra, subject of her soon-to-be published play.

On October 22 they took a train ferry to Stockholm for a round of luncheons, book signings, and interviews. While based in Stockholm they traveled for two days to Oslo, where Yourcenar spoke at the Nobel Institute. On November 15, with Grace nursing a sore throat and Marguerite coming down with a cold, the women left for Finland on the SS *Bore II*. Still under the weather, they spent the next morning in bed deciphering four Finnish newspapers using the Finnish translation of *Hadrian* as their Rosetta Stone![5]

Back in Stockholm, where they spent another month, they got their first taste of Sweden's lavish holiday festivities. On December 6 they rode through the Old City to watch the Saint Nicholas celebration in the streets. In the square near the Royal Palace and on the palace bridges there were beautiful illuminated spruce trees. Christmas itself they spent back in Copenhagen before returning to Paris on December 28. On New Year's Eve, declining two dinner invitations, they had supper by candlelight alone in their hotel room "skolling" the new year à deux.[6]

That New Year's Eve turned out to be the calm before the storm. Throughout their Scandinavian travels, both Yourcenar and Frick had devoted considerable work time to the long-delayed *Présentation critique de Constantin Cavafy*, which Gallimard grew more and more impatient to publish as Cavafy's literary executor, Alexander Singopoulos, grew less and less cooperative with regard to the project. Sets and costumes were also being designed for Yourcenar's *Électre*, which would turn into another battle royal. But the worst cataclysm occurred on March 15, 1954, when Yourcenar's American passport was summarily canceled. Both women had renewed their passports without difficulty in Rome two years earlier. Frick sailed through the process this time, too. Had Yourcenar's celebrated novel about an emperor's love for an adolescent boy earned her more than a literary reputation?

As we saw in chapter 9, an American era of suspicion had already begun back in 1941, when a consular official in Montreal inexplicably delayed the approval of Yourcenar's new visa. By 1954 McCarthyism was in full swing. As Patricia Palmieri has noted, "Attitudes and policies toward professional women narrowed throughout the 1950s and early 1960s. In the era of the Cold War, any form of social deviance was threatening."[7] Homosexuals, in particular, were seen as both sexually and politically subversive, and witch hunts were conducted by congressional committees throughout the 1950s and 1960s.

Progressive Sarah Lawrence College was targeted by several investigations. The writer and activist Muriel Rukeyser, a member of the literature faculty, and the sociology professor Helen Merrell Lynd were both accused by the American Legion of communist involvement.[8] Lynd was questioned by the Senate Subcommittee on Internal Security. Years later Yourcenar would say that students "were very much aware of McCarthyism, with its attendant persecution of foreigners and foreign-born Americans. Many of the students in the school where I taught felt as threatened as I and other teachers did."[9] Altogether, eighteen faculty members were pursued by congressional committees, one of whom invoked the Fifth Amendment and resigned.

Another member of the faculty, Margaret Barratin, was in Paris in the spring of 1954 serving as director of the college's Students in France program. Her husband had been dismissed from the United Nations "as a sympathizer with persons unfairly investigated" by a Senate committee.[10] Barratin immediately leapt to the support of her colleague, who had given two lectures to Sarah Lawrence students over the previous few weeks.[11]

Two days later Grace Frick vouched for her companion's residential and professional ties to the United States in more extensive detail.[12] Yourcenar's even more explicit letter in her own defense, also written on March 22, goes all the way back to her birth in 1903. Not content to place the letter in the mail, Yourcenar delivered it to the embassy in person.[13]

Frick's real sentiments about the matter were expressed, with considerably more vehemence than in either of the couple's pleas to the consulate, in another letter written on March 22, 1954. It was addressed to the first member of the U.S. Congress who dared to publicly denounce the tactics of McCarthyism, Margaret Chase Smith.[14] In June of 1950 the senator from Maine had distinguished herself, in a speech known as her Declaration of Conscience, by decrying on the floor of the Senate the character assassination, intimidation, and bigotry being practiced by her Republican colleagues. Frick had attended a talk that Smith gave at the Northeast Harbor High School in 1952.[15] She knew her words would not fall on deaf ears.

At issue was the Immigration and Nationality Act of 1952, also known as the McCarran-Walter Act. President Harry S. Truman vetoed this legislation, believing it to be inconsistent with American values, but Congress overrode his veto. In 1952 the author Mary McCarthy characterized this "unjust law" in a manner pertinent to Yourcenar's plight, evoking "the many absurdities and cruelties of the McCarran Act," among them "the arbitrary refusal of visas without any kind of due process."[16] Grace Frick, for her part, told Margaret Chase Smith that she found the act's language "antithetic to all individual cultural endeavor not affiliated with some recognized institution or agency," calling its methods "terroristic."[17]

The passport debacle, ironically, was resolved not by Senator Smith but by the expatriate lesbian Natalie Clifford Barney, whose mere phone call to embassy officials cleared the impasse. Grace, still appalled by the injustice, thanked her "dear and vigorous friend" on March 23: "I am desolated to think that such a routine and clearly-defined case could not be settled without pressure from above. What of the hundreds of people who have not a Natalie Barney to fight for them by telephone, and early on Monday morning, the very first business day after our defeat? Though born of a Republican family I am becoming more and more a Jeffersonian Democrat."[18]

Yourcenar never forgot the service rendered her by Barney that March. She spoke of it no fewer than three times in her future correspondence with the famed *salonière*. In 1962, for example, she wrote to thank Barney for a gift bestowed on her and Grace, adding, "Nor have I forgotten, especially, your assistance when I found myself confronted at the American Consulate by an ignorant McCarthyist official who refused even to read my passport."[19]

Natalie and Grace shared a desire to be of service to others generally and to Marguerite Yourcenar in particular. Their mutual friendship and affection, keen from the very beginning, deepened in the wake of the passport episode. That April Natalie brought her longtime lover Romaine Brooks to tea with Grace and Marguerite at their hotel. She had asked to bring her old flame the Duchesse de Clermont-Tonnerre—to whom Barney remained devoted all her life—and a Baroness Gautier, but Frick and Yourcenar apparently preferred to meet Romaine alone.[20]

They would soon be leaving France for a four-month stay in Germany, but even while they were still in Paris they kept in touch with their generous friend by way of notes and postcards. On May 6, 1954, Marguerite informed Natalie that preparations were under way for a performance of Électre but that she was looking forward to leaving all that behind for a while. Yourcenar had loved Paris, its museums, its parks, its musical and theatrical offerings, since she was a child, but the attraction of the city was beginning to be dimmed by the ever more numerous professional obligations that always awaited her there. With regard to the work involved in finding a venue and choosing cast members for Électre, she wrote, "It is all extremely tiring, and I am delighted to be leaving and not to have to start again until September."[21] It was not until seven months later, in the rural calm of Fayence, that Yourcenar could say that "the Parisian fatigue is slowly going away."[22]

Natalie's notes and letters, which she often signed "Yours in tender friendship" or "Ever yours with love," were frequently flirtatious in tone, and there is no doubt that the women's friendship was tinged with a certain romance. Not surprisingly, given her candor regarding her sexual preferences, Barney often tried to engage her friends in lesbian-oriented topics or activities. It was with Natalie, as we have seen, that Marguerite and Grace attended the European premiere of Four Saints in Three Acts. It was also Natalie who lent a copy of Gertrude Stein's "coming out story" to the couple early in their acquaintance. Barney liked nothing better than to sprinkle her letters with allusions to Sappho, Gide, or other literary icons of a certain persuasion. She tried repeatedly to put Grace and Marguerite together with a bisexual English friend who had written an erotically charged lesbian novel that was published by the Hogarth Press in 1949. Dorothy Bussy's Olivia told the story of an adolescent's passion for the headmistress of an exclusive girls school very much like Les Ruches in Fontainebleau, which both Bussy and Barney had attended.[23] Before Marguerite and Grace left for Germany, Natalie wrote to tell them that a film based on her "old schoolmate's" novel was being shown in New York under the "fallacious title" *The Pit of Loneliness*.[24] Fallacious, that is, not only because it was chosen to echo the title of Radclyffe Hall's *Well of Loneliness* but also because Hall's novel was so obviously based on none other than Natalie Barney and her literary salon on the rue Jacob.[25]

Marguerite would sometimes respond in playful ways to Natalie's lesbian gambits, as she did shortly after she and Grace arrived in Heidelberg that spring. Knowing the Amazon's love of horseback riding, and having heard the story, by this time legendary, of a youthful Natalie dressing up as a page boy to seduce a notorious Parisian courtesan, Yourcenar and Frick sent Barney a postcard image from the *Manesse Codex*, a medieval illuminated manuscript of poetic ballads and "portraits." The one chosen for Natalie depicts a red-cheeked young knight kneeling at the feet of his lady love, a colorfully draped steed impatiently tied to a tree at his side.[26] There is no mention of the

FIGURE 27. Illustration from the *Manesse Codex* of the thirteenth-century poet Schenke von Limburg.

image in Yourcenar's short note, but the unspoken message was undoubtedly received by the postcard's witty addressee.

In early June 1952, the year they all first met, Barney had suggested that Yourcenar and Frick might like to hear the nightclub owner Suzy Solidor read from *The Songs of Bilitis*.[27] This collection of lesbian erotic poems was supposedly written by a contemporary of Sappho's and translated from the Greek for the first time in the late nineteenth century by Pierre Louÿs. In fact, Louÿs wrote the poems himself. Before their spring 1954 departure from Paris, as it turns out, Frick and Yourcenar took in a performance of the operetta *Bilitis* at the Théâtre des Capucines—without inviting Barney to join them. Yourcenar mentioned the event on the front of a postcard that can only have been chosen with Natalie in mind. Sent from the spa town of Bad Homburg, it bore the image of a wood and ivory carving of a naked girl swimming behind and holding onto a duck. This astonishing artifact from

FIGURE 28. *Cuiller en forme de nageuse*, Egypt, fourteenth–fifteenth centuries BCE Louvre Museum. © RMN-Grand Palais/Art Resource.

the Louvre, entitled *Cuiller en forme de nageuse* (Spoon in the form of a girl swimming), appears to have been an Egyptian makeup spoon. Underneath the image—that is, on the front of the postcard—Yourcenar wrote, "Grace and I saw *Bilitis* by chance at the Capucines: it was dreadful and not even amusing."[28]

On the other side of the same postcard, sent in late June, Yourcenar finally answered a question that Barney had been asking her since April: Would she be willing to advise her regarding a play she had placed with a friend's theater agent?[29] Barney called it such "a very hazardous enterprise and subject" that she didn't "quite like to think of even a Parisian audience's reactions to it," so one can imagine its provocative, probably autobiographical subject matter. In early June she mentioned it again: "Lacking your advice on whether you considered it 'jouable' [possible to stage] I asked my old friend Paul Geraldy to read it, and he found it a new but dangerous subject for anything but an 'elite.'"[30] Two weeks later Barney reported that Geraldy was going to offer her dangerous play to the Capucines or to the Mathurins next door, and she thus once more pleaded with Yourcenar to read the script: "If you find my play sufficiently interesting, perhaps I would do better to publish it than to expose it to such affronts? But do you ever have the time to read it and advise me? Or even for us to meet again?"[31]

Yourcenar, whose artistic ideals bore little resemblance to Natalie's, responded in a way that engaged with her friend's request for counsel while evading the main issue: "I will read the play with great interest, but I can already caution you not to give it to the theater—unless you find an *exquisite little stage*. That sort of thing is made for small theaters with an eighteenth-century decor à la Prince de Conti or Gustave III and not for the Capucines. The 'light' genre runs even more risk than the tragic; do not imprudently expose Psyche's wings."[32] Yourcenar's metaphorical comment about the wings of the Greek goddess who, after being married to Eros, came to serve Aphrodite was undoubtedly inspired by the wings of the Egyptian carving pictured on the front of the postcard.

Grace and Marguerite never did manage to see Barney that summer. The manuscript of Natalie's play languished at 20 rue Jacob, from which location she offered to have her assistant deliver it to Yourcenar in late September.[33] Not until the following June did Barney write to say that she had given up on having her play mounted.[34]

When Barney got a bee in her bonnet, she could be extremely persistent. This was equally true, if not more so, when she was offering advice as when she was seeking it. Indeed, a tendency to blur the line between helpfulness and meddling is yet another characteristic that Frick and Barney shared. When Grace was translating *Hadrian*, for instance, Natalie made several suggestions that, judging from the silence with which they were met by their recipients, were somewhat less than welcome. In one letter Natalie cautioned Grace somewhat cryptically, "Don't rush out your tinsnips with too much 'fervour' is the advice of this old amazon who bears you both so much keen interest and sympathy!"[35] She repeatedly urged Grace to seek translation assistance from André Gide's close friend and English translator Dorothy Bussy or Elizabeth Sprigge, biographer of Ivy Compton-Burnett.[36] Frick and Yourcenar finally succumbed to Barney's insistence that they visit Bussy at her villa, La Souco, in Roquebrune, but they did so only after the *Hadrian* translation came out.[37]

Barney's many questions about Frick's progress were, of course, an expression of interest in her friends' life—"I'm so glad that the translation is progressing 'admirably.' And without too much strain and stress? When do you expect it to appear? This should prove somewhat liberating." "And will you be heart whole and translation free to return to us in Paris this coming spring?"—but they were also a subtle means of taking sides.[38]

Barney trod on more dangerous ground with regard to another of her insistent queries, issued primarily when Yourcenar and Frick were back in Maine: "When, oh when, will you return?"[39] "When will you come back to us?"[40] "When are you both returning to France, and to me?"[41] "Are you coming this summer? In the fall? On what season may we pin our hopes of seeing you?"[42] "Come back to me soon."[43] That she considered Grace responsible for Yourcenar's much-lamented absence from Paris is intimated in a letter from the spring of 1955. Natalie had decided that Yourcenar should receive the French Legion of Honor and had begun plying her various connections to French officialdom with an eye toward achieving that end. She had apparently become concerned that Yourcenar's U.S. citizenship might pose an obstacle to the receipt of that award:

> May that worrying passport, making you and not leaving you an American, not stand in the way of this, nor of your return to us after Grace's U.S.A. Xmas. . . .
>
> But wouldn't it be more convenient to regain your French passport, for if you intend to spend most of your time out of the U.S.A. you could always return there for 3 months at a time as tourist lecturer or teacher?[44]

Although Natalie did allow that dual citizenship would be "the best solution," Grace undoubtedly viewed Barney's suggestions regarding her partner's nationality as an incursion into her territory. It was around this same time—perhaps not coincidentally—that Natalie signed two of her letters to the couple in a curious manner. On June 20, 1954, it was "And give Grace my friendship, so well differentiated between the two of you, as ever and ever your admirer and aff[ectionate]."[45] Ten months later, she signed off with "faithful and diversified love."[46]

Frick did not hold a grudge against Barney, however. Her letters continued to be warm and engaged. Yourcenar, for her part, tended to sidestep the issue of her residency, writing Barney, for example, from Petite Plaisance in July of 1955 that "in a way, I feel as close to my friends here as I did in Fayence, or even at the St. James, for I think of them often and especially of you."[47] Creative work, moreover, always provided an unassailable reason for remaining at Petite Plaisance. In a Christmas note to Barney that same year, Yourcenar wrote, possibly referring to Grace's translation of *Le Coup de grâce*: "You ask when I'll return to Europe. As soon as it's possible to, but the book will have to be completed first."[48] She signed that letter, "I embrace you affectionately. Grace does, too." As if to prove it, Frick adds a postscript in her own hand: "We are sending you a whole battery of photographs, apart, which will probably recall to you the pines of Maine as you knew them. Love to you, Grace."

CHAPTER 21 ✥ Continuing the Journey
1954–1955

> Much have I travell'd in the realms of gold,
> And many goodly states and kingdoms seen.
>
> —John Keats

ON MAY 9, 1954, GRACE Frick and Marguerite Yourcenar left Paris on the Orient Express bound for Stuttgart. Yourcenar was unwell for several weeks in Germany, which she ascribed to fatigue and heavy German food. How difficult parts of the summer were may be judged by what she wrote to Constantine "Didi" Dimaras, her Cavafy translation collaborator. She had hoped to see Dimaras in Athens but wrote in June to ask if they could meet somewhere closer to her current location. "I envy you Olympia," she wrote, "one of the most beautiful places in the world. I would gladly trade the whole Rhine River for one drop of water from the Alfeiós."[1]

Yourcenar's health had improved by early July, when she and Frick took a train ride along what Grace called the "magically beautiful valley" of the Main River heading toward Würzburg in northern Bavaria.[2] They arrived there just in time to hear the last concert of the Mozart festival, which was given out of doors in the torchlit Court Gardens of the lavish Würzburg Residence, now a UNESCO World Heritage site. Most of the rest of the summer was spent in Munich, where Yourcenar finished writing "Oppian, or the Chase" and "That Mighty Sculptor, Time."[3]

Near the end of their long stay in Germany, the couple treated themselves to several outings in southern Bavaria. Having spent so much time in big cities over the previous year, they were eager to seek respite in nature. Indeed, it was in the mid-1950s that they both began to feel that the natural world was under threat.[4] On the morning of September 5, 1954, the women traveled by train for a lakeside "breakfast-lunch" in the village of Starnberg. From there they proceeded to the alpine lakes high above Mittenwald.[5] They were so taken by the beauty of the lakes, by day or by shimmering moonlight, that they returned to cross Lake Starnberg several times.[6]

Close to midnight on September 10 back in Munich, the women were setting off on foot to mail a batch of galley proofs to New York. Just as they were leaving their hotel, a car pulled up outside. The man in the front seat was having a heart attack, and his companion was crying out for help. Grace dropped her package and rushed to the car, dispatching Marguerite to get some brandy. It was the actor and director Reinhold Schünzel, best remembered as the sinister scientist in Alfred Hitchcock's *Notorious*. His wife Lena was in such distress that Frick went with her to the hospital and escorted her back to her home. Reinhold could not be revived.[7]

Frick and Yourcenar left Germany for Paris via night train on September 22 to oversee the mounting of Yourcenar's play *Électre ou la Chute des masques*. They immediately found the actress Jany Holt unfit for the part of Electra. The actor chosen to play Orestes was equally objectionable. New auditions were held for these big roles, but the casting changes Yourcenar insisted on never got made. As relations with the play's director, Jean Marchat, and the theater owner, Mme Harry Baur, grew increasingly adversarial, Yourcenar withdrew all support, filing suit against Marchat and the Théâtre des Mathurins. Thus began the "*Electra* affair." Not until March of 1956 was the lawsuit decided in the author's favor—to the tune of 500,000 francs in damages.[8]

With high hopes of enjoying a break from the demands of Paris, the couple boarded a night sleeper for the Mediterranean resort town of Saint Raphael on December 10. It was not an ideal time of year for a vacation on the French Riviera. Both women were exhausted, and Marguerite fell ill in their poorly heated room at the Hôtel Continental. Grace set off on her own in a taxi for Fayence, where Chick Austin had offered them use of a home he owned in that Provençal village about twenty-five miles northwest of Cannes. According to Austin's biographer, the four-story villa in Fayence was located "at the top of the hill in the town, near the hôtel de ville and the local café."[9] Frick was struck by the beauty of the sparsely furnished home, but how would they heat it? Her companion, seeing the place for the first time three days later, was less favorably impressed.[10] After checking out rental options in Saint Raphael, they nonetheless decided to accept Austin's offer.

As when Grace and Marguerite had moved into Petite Plaisance four years earlier, the first thing they did was to buy a gas stove for their new dwelling.

That appliance, a batch of groceries, and the couple's two trunks and eighteen suitcases would be delivered to Fayence by the hardware store in Saint Raphael. On December 19 they themselves took the 4:30 p.m. bus to their new lodgings. Things did not go smoothly at first. It was very cold, running water at the villa was intermittent at best, and there was no water service whatsoever at night for the entire first week of their stay. To make matters worse, the bone-penetrating mistral was afoot. As Grace wrote in the daybook on December 22, the "mistral began howling in the chimney in the early morning hours, and shrieking through the windowless houses adjoining and in back of us." There was a "terrifying clatter of shutters banging and broken tiles hurled from roof tops all around us." Finally the weather calmed, and Marguerite began to recover from what turned out to be a bout of bronchitis.

On Christmas Day, their first full day of warmth, the women began exploring Fayence. Dating back to the tenth century, the village is perched on a promontory and features steep, narrow streets. On their first outing, so that Marguerite would not have to do much climbing, they ventured only as far as the Château du Puy, built in the previous century. The next day, feeling more sure-footed, they followed a goat path to the highest point in Fayence and its old bell tower, from which they had a panoramic view of the surrounding countryside. Everywhere they went they went on foot, with Grace sometimes scoping out routes in advance to be sure they would not be too strenuous for her partner. One evening, with an iron roasting spit in need of repair, they walked the half mile or so to Tourrettes seeking out the local blacksmith. Frick's description of that errand gives a glimpse of the kind of community the couple had decided to inhabit for a time. They found Monsieur Perrimond working at his forge, "very handsome in the evening light, and Madame finishing her laundry over the open air fountain. Her boiler kettle was still steaming over the small fire, and the dog lay comfortably before the blaze. Madame used cinders to whiten her linen, preferring the old process to boiling or bleach."[11] Sometimes they would stop by the forge after dark to help blow the fire, an act that can hardly have failed to resonate in the mind of an author who soon would start writing the story of a sixteenth-century alchemist-philosopher-physician. But what they most enjoyed on their walks were encounters with the flora and fauna. "Wild anemone, violets, a kind of gentian, golden buttercup, narcissus, grape hyacinth, iris, and three tiny wild blooms" they could not identify were the bounty of one country stroll. On a trek to nearby Lacoste, they saw a "wonderful cascade of sheep flowing down the steep sides of the ravine to drink from the stream. Many black and dun brown in the flock, and many lambs, pink ears raised high."[12] They often returned from their walks carrying stray pieces of furniture borrowed from nearby homes or cypress boughs broken off by the wind. Though they had lived in Fayence for only twelve days by New Year's Eve, they kept up the tradition of an eggnog party, attended by local residents, workmen, and children whom they had already befriended. Reading Frick's daybooks about the months spent in Fayence, one feels the women decompressing in that village whose night sky was a riot of stars.

As at Petite Plaisance, village children were always about. Troops of them would appear when the couple got a load of firewood, eager to carry the logs up the stairs and stack them in convenient wood boxes. Grace and Marguerite entertained them with "candle-light and shadows," compensating them with cookies bought in Saint Raphael, where they went by bus to do their shopping. One sunny day all was quiet "except for tempestuous little boys mounting the wood and acting plays in the salon."[13] On another occasion, using saucepans and colanders for shields, the boys played "Caesar landing at Fréjus and defeating Vercingétorix (who rode in upon a stick of wood)."[14]

In addition to the neighborhood children, the women acquired an Irish setter named Mirah, "whom we seem to have adopted, collar bell and all." Describing Mirah in the daybook, Grace mentions the superb German shepherd they befriended on Mount Desert Island before they bought Petite Plaisance: "She is not so beautiful as our Terry of Seal Harbor summers (the forester's dog) but she has charms of her own, particularly at table, where she likes to sit high on her chair."[15] Next to dining with her adoptive mistresses, Mirah liked nothing better than to accompany the couple on their tramps about the countryside.

While they were based in Fayence, Grace and Marguerite also received a few grown-up human visitors: Yourcenar's publisher at Éditions Plon, Charles Orengo and his wife, for example, and Alexis Curvers and his wife, Marie Delcourt. Curvers would soon find himself on the receiving end of one of Yourcenar's lawsuits, but for now he was just a Belgian poet and printer who had come into the couple's orbit the previous year.

One of Yourcenar's projects that winter was an article commissioned by the French publisher Martin Flinker for a volume honoring Thomas Mann on his eightieth birthday.[16] While Yourcenar was finishing her essay in mid-February, none other than Herr Mann himself was writing her a laudatory letter about Électre ou la Chute des masques, an inscribed copy of which she had sent to him several months earlier. Forwarded from Paris by Flinker, Mann's handwritten letter reached Fayence on February 28. Frick described it as "giving very fine commentary on the play from a humanist point of view, and corresponding exactly to the author's own views, to her great joy. Best of all, this letter was written by Mann before he could know of her article on him." Relying on her graduate-school German, Grace roughed out a first translation of the text. The visiting Marie Delcourt later helped with some difficult words in the original and wrote out the whole letter in French.[17] So precious was Mann's expression of regard that the couple had multiple photostats made of both the letter itself and the envelope it came in.

Next on the guest list in Fayence were the Russian-born artist Élie Grekoff and his painter friend Pierre Monteret. Frick and Yourcenar went all out preparing for Grekoff's five-day visit and Monteret's shortly thereafter: cleaning and washing, shopping and cooking, borrowing or buying household items they would need. The timing was less than ideal: Marguerite was just recovering from another bout of bronchitis, Grace had a stubborn skin infection, and the mistral was gearing up for a weeklong assault. Grekoff arrived on February 16, and Marguerite made a pork roast that evening to welcome him. Grace describes what happened the next day in her daybook, mentioning two village boys whom she and Marguerite had taught to make crepes: "We had intended to have cold meat the next night with artichokes and crêpes, but Élie announced emphatically that he did not like crêpes, so we had to forgo them, although we allowed Robert Dei and Georges Brun to amuse themselves and us by making a big crêpe over the fire."[18]

Grace had come up with the idea of asking Grekoff to design a bookplate for her partner based on one of Marguerite's own drawings. As Sue Lonoff de Cuevas has explained, Yourcenar made at least five sketches over several decades beginning in 1922 of the traditional character Pierrot hanging from a gibbet and identified as "Pierrot Pendu."[19]

No two drawings are exactly alike, but they all feature books lying underneath a scaffold and the following mostly Latin verse, which provides an apt sentiment for a bookplate: "Aspice Pierrot Pendu / Qui librum n'a pas rendu / Si librum redidisset / Pierrot Pendu non fuisset" (Behold the gibbeted Pierrot / Who did not return the book; / If he had given the book back, / He would not have been hung). So Yourcenar sketched a "Pierrot Pendu" for Grekoff, who, according to Frick, "immediately began to transform what should have been a wistful, rather naïve figure (based on medieval sculpture) into a pseudo-sophisticated, elaborately staged hanging of a modern pantomime figure. Not that he drew the figure itself, but in a rapid sketch he succeeded in eliminating most of what was wanted, particularly the books, which he said would be 'very tedious' to draw." Alone in their room that

FIGURE 29. Pierrot Pendu, sketch by Marguerite Yourcenar, in *Cahiers—Poèmes grecs*. Petite Plaisance Archives.

night, Marguerite said to Grace resignedly, "He can never do that design with the simplicity required," and Grace decided to withdraw her request.[20]

Grekoff caught a cold the next day and was ill for the rest of his stay. When he left on the afternoon of February 21, Marguerite "took to her bed," worn out and somewhat dispirited. Hoping to relieve their feelings, Grace made popovers for tea!

Less than two weeks later, Pierre Monteret arrived in town, bearing a "disgruntled" letter from Grekoff to Frick, which they read aloud together. We don't know the contents of that letter, and it is nowhere to be found in the archive at Harvard University. Grekoff may have resented the withdrawal of the bookplate request. There was obviously a certain testiness in the relationship between him and Frick at that time. The following year he would call her "an angel despite the appearance sometimes of something diabolical in her angelic intentions." Grekoff also had the strange habit, which may have been his way of gendering his friends' couple, of referring to the two of them in French in the masculine plural, thus tagging one of them as male; once he even addressed a letter to "Chère [feminine] Marguerite, cher [masculine] Grace, thereby reversing the gender roles that some might imagine them conforming to.[21]

The women had prepared a delicious-sounding dinner for Monteret's first night: "roast chicken, braised tomatoes, rice; salad of endive, celery, cress, mayonnaise; wine, fruit, and date pudding with crème chantilly," the latter served with lime-blossom tea.[22] "*We* thought it good," Grace reported in her daybook, but Monteret was unimpressed. His only comment was, "So you have no housekeeper of any kind?" Dinner the next night, as recounted by Grace, was nonetheless equally creative and abundant: "roast veal, braised endive, pommes de terre rissolées, salad, soufflé au chocolat (wine), infusion de tilleul, requested again by Pierre, fruit. (We forgot cheese both nights, though M.Y. had bought it specially for him. Maybe *that* is what he wanted!)"[23]

After Monteret left the next day, Grace and Marguerite climbed up to the roof of their tall building to regroup and watch the sun set. As Grace wrote in the daybook,

> We sit in wonder at our failure to stimulate enthusiasm in our house and dinner guests of the past two weeks (Elie, Pierre, Longueville).[24] (Tea guests were better.) None of them see why we like this house, in spite of the difficulty of heating it, and none of them seem to have any gusto about anything, not to mention their evident lack of interest in trying to know either the author or her work. Not a question, not an observation on her method of working, though she painstakingly inquired as to theirs.[25]

The peaceful surcease from the frenzied pace of life in Paris or Munich had given the two women a new appreciation of the value of their privacy. As Grekoff himself would note in a 1956 letter to the couple about their most recent stay in Paris—using what may be a subconscious allusion to the meals they cooked for him—they would share themselves more sparingly with others in the future: "So many people arrogantly thought that they would make a copious meal of your presence; a crowd of them came running, and you two hardly gave them a petit four."[26]

Fortunately, Frick and Yourcenar's trips to see friends around the region were more rewarding. One such was an excursion by taxi to Villefranche-sur-Mer, not far from Nice, for luncheon with Baroness Louise de Borchgrave. Borchgrave, a native of The Hague, had been a close friend of Marguerite's father and had cherished his precocious little girl.[27] In the daybook Frick calls Madame de Borchgrave "one of three daughters Stouts, a musical family whom M.Y. saw in her childhood both in Holland and on their summer visits to Belgium." Providing a rare glimpse of Marguerite as a child, Borchgrave remembered—and Frick no doubt gleefully wrote down—that she had "tyrannized" over the children of Borchgrave's sister Madeleine, "solemnly, giving them 'lessons' which they dutifully endured. She gave *dictation* to them by the hour."[28] It had been more than thirty-five years since Marguerite had last seen "Aunt Loulou." She was very fond of Borchgrave and would keep up a correspondence, carefully sending her copies of her books, until Aunt Loulou died, at the age of one hundred, in 1986.

Marguerite and Grace also saw Natalie Barney and Romaine Brooks at least three times during their four months in the Var. Barney arrived in Nice for her customary winter stay with Brooks at 11 rue des Ponchettes in late January. On Valentine's Day the couple took a chauffeur-driven car to Fayence for tea with their friends. Two weeks later Grace and Marguerite went to Brooks's beautiful apartment with its top-floor studio overlooking the Mediterranean and located next to the cliff where Nice's old château once stood. They called on Brooks and Barney again in April when they were in Nice attempting to resolve what was for once a minor passport-related difficulty. Grace took advantage of that visit to ride the elevator to the top of the cliff and tour the castle gardens.[29] Marguerite, always wary of heights, remained at ground level.

The next day the two women went by bus to the prefecture in Draguignan, hoping to iron out a bureaucratic wrinkle pertaining to the length of their stay on French soil. As Grace reports, that bus traveled "via the terrors of the Bargemon Road," which, to make matters worse, was then under repair. Still subject to sudden spells of vertigo, "Gretie clutched Grace and all things clutchable," thereby avoiding a dreaded bout of nausea. The Draguignan administrative center granted them a prolongation of their stay, but they would have to leave the country no later than April 16, one week after receiving their official papers.

On precisely that date, having sold their stove and sent their heavy luggage on ahead of them by truck, the couple left Fayence, headed for Grenoble and beyond. Two days later they would land in their beloved Scandinavia. They were delighted to find themselves again in the streets of Stockholm's Old City. It had been almost a year and a half since the couple's last visit to the region, which had ended after nine days in Copenhagen on December 27, 1953. Grace and Marguerite had gone at least twice during that previous stay to the National Museum of Denmark, where they were captivated by some Iron Age—and perhaps not coincidentally, *Roman* Iron Age—gold rings. So much so, in fact, that they arranged to have copies of those rings made by Sweden's royal jeweler, at considerable expense, during their 1955 visit to

Stockholm. Yourcenar later mentioned the rings in an unpublished travel journal called "Traversée sur le *Bathory*" about yet another trip the couple made to Copenhagen in 1964. Though several museums were closed when they arrived, "one can see the Bronze Age collections at the National Museum; we took a friendly peek at the Lurs, the garments tanned by their two-thousand-year residence in oak coffins, the Roman glass and silver, and the rings of which Grace and I wear copies made by a jeweler in Stockholm."[30] That jeweler was the renowned C. F. Carlman, and both women wore those gold rings for the rest of their lives.

The rings were fashioned to replicate Scandinavian originals dating back to the third century CE. As described by Morton Axboe, curator of

FIGURE 30. Ancient Scandinavian gold rings. Statens Historiska Museum, Stockholm, and National Museum of Denmark, Copenhagen.

Danish prehistory at the National Museum of Denmark, Yourcenar's ring was of a type "known all over Scandinavia, but not outside, and dates to the period c. 200–300 A.D."[31] Frick's was "of the type labelled 'snake head's rings,' a group of golden arm and finger rings used in Scandinavia in the 3rd century A.D. They are characterized by stylized snake's or bird's heads."[32]

The couple's love of birds is well known, and birds on the rooftops of Paris played a part in their early romance. Marguerite would remember their significance two years later, in 1957, when she inscribed a new edition of *Feux* to her partner in celebration of their twenty years together.

The title page of the morocco-bound book contains one of Yourcenar's Pierrot drawings, along with the usual poem. As Lonoff has observed, "books remain prominent at the base of the gibbet, and below Pierrot's feet a new feature has been added: rooftops, with smoke coming from two chimneys. . . . Here too, the moon and stars that appear in the other

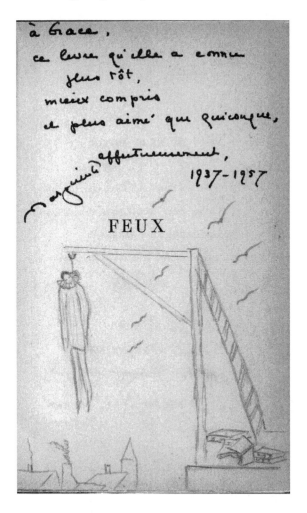

four Pierrot drawings have vanished; winging birds have taken their place."[33]

Happily, the couple's schedule in Sweden had a little more breathing space for outings than it often did elsewhere. Yourcenar had been fascinated by Sweden ever since she was a child reading French translations of Swedish legends, folktales, and short stories.[34] She and Frick eagerly set off to explore parts of the country they had not yet seen. They went to beautiful Bohuslän on Sweden's rocky west coast, so much like the coast of Maine, then traveled forty miles north to see remarkable Bronze Age rock carvings of animals, ships, and fertility figures in Tanum. At Lake Vattern they "stayed quietly alone for four delightful days."[35] They also made a trip, while staying in Uppsala, to the village of Hammarby to tour the country home and garden of Carl Linnaeus, become a shrine to that precursor of modern ecology.[36]

But it was in the iron mining town of Kiruna that the travelers would make what Kajsa Andersson has called "the most exotic and most memorable excursion" of their 1955 stay in Scandinavia.[37] Grace announced the trip, which would begin on May 27, in a postcard letter to Gladys Minear, writing emphatically at the top of the first card, "We are leaving Stockholm for the Arctic!"[38] She had always loved adventure, and she was about to have one. Traveling the entire length of Sweden to the province of Lapland, she and Yourcenar arrived in Sweden's northernmost city late that afternoon. The next day they saw Kiruna's mines, toured a Sami village, and visited a trading post and museum. Their hosts, a Dr. and Mrs. Haraldsen and their two children, then took them, as Grace reports, "to their 'kota' a genuine Lapp house which was built for them some miles from Kiruna. We went the last quarter mile on skis, in deep snow, and both of us foundered, seriously. (My first experience of being stuck, *sunk* in snow and helpless. Very edifying.)" They were so energized by the full midnight sun after dinner with their friends that they stayed up, "very excited," until two in the morning. This was the first taste for both women of an "extreme frontier" that would long retain its magic for them both. As Yourcenar later told Matthieu Galey, "I've always had a special liking for the frontier, for gateways to realms still more wild, like the Lapland region of Sweden and Norway."[39] Taking a noon train back to Stockholm the next day, they were enchanted by the "somber landscape in snow." To remember this trip which had been so exceptional for them both, they purchased two stunning lithographs of reindeer herds by the artist Nils Nilsson Skum to take back with them to Petite Plaisance. Their only wish was that they could have had more time to spend in Lapland.[40]

On June 1, 1955, after nearly two years abroad, the couple left Göteborg aboard the MS *Kungsholm*—in plenty of time, as Natalie Barney had put it, for "Grace's U.S.A. Xmas."

CHAPTER 22 ❧ Home Sweet Home
1955–1957

Ah, what is more blessed than to put cares away, when the mind lays by its burden, and tired with labour of far travel we have come to our own home . . . ?

—Catullus

GRACE FRICK AND MARGUERITE YOURCENAR arrived back home in Maine to find that hundreds of trees had been "ruthlessly" cut to the stumps in the wooded lot behind their house.[1] They mourned not only the destruction of habitat for birds and other wildlife but also the loss of a sight and sound buffer between Petite Plaisance and houses north of their property. Infuriated by the desecration, they vowed to acquire that tract of land one day. In the meantime they would concentrate on embellishing the land they already owned and refurbishing their indoor living space.

This was the beginning of a sustained period of home and yard improvement to which Frick in particular devoted her usual boundless energy. In a show of determination and style that must have raised a Northeast Harbor eyebrow or two, she often donned a pair of overalls for the purpose. (Grace once speculated that their wealthy neighbor Agnes Milliken found them neither fish nor fowl: "Apparently we fit no proper pattern of poor artist, and certainly do not fit other Northeast Harbor categories.")[2] From the "desolation" of the woodlot, she transplanted blueberries and cranberries to the grounds of Petite Plaisance. She oversaw the planting of apple trees on the west lawn and amended the soil around the Montmorency cherries to the east. She and young David Peckham struggled with a kiwi vine that would eventually grow into a leafy pergola, unique for the region, over the kitchen porch. As Yourcenar once advised the homesick young Frenchman Jean Lambert, to feel at home in America one must create, "as Grace and I

223

have done, a domain, however small it may be, governed by fantasy or one's personal wishes."[3]

Grace, again unconcerned about Northeast Harbor mores, aired the contents of the couple's storage trunks on the clothesline, on the grass, and on the front porch, "in full view of all comers."[4] Austin Furniture of Ellsworth installed bamboo blinds on the veranda overlooking the west lawn. George Korkmadjian brought a new Oriental carpet for the couple to try out. Bookshelves were designed, built, and stained for the studio; custom shelving was fitted to the chimney in the parlor; floorboards were scraped, sanded, and sealed.

Marguerite had fallen ill on returning to Halifax in June. Over the next several months in Northeast Harbor, Dr. Coffin made house calls for everything from phlebitis of a vein in the author's left index finger to intercostal inflammation. Certain foods—but which ones?—brought on "bilious attacks." One night the sculptor Malvina Hoffman and the writer Marianne Moore came for a dinner of lobster, boiled potatoes, salad, stewed plums, and cookies—and Marguerite was ill for a week.[5]

Throughout this time literary work, and its attendant battles, was plentiful for both women. Yourcenar's "Reflections on the Composition of *Memoirs of Hadrian*," already incorporated into the French version of the book, had to be appended to the English. Grace worked on that text during the summer of 1955. A complication of some kind arose, however, involving Frick's old Wellesley College classmate Florence Codman. Florence had composed her own translation of Yourcenar's original "Carnets de Notes de *Mémoires d'Hadrien*" two years earlier, but nothing had ever been done with it.[6] Did she want it used now instead of Frick's? Did she wish to be acknowledged in some way? She and Frick exchanged telephone calls about the matter in late July, and Yourcenar spent several days drafting a letter to Codman in August.[7] On completion, the couple walked it to the post office together, often a signal that something important was happening. Whatever the difficulty was, "Autumn 1955 Florence Codman" ended up on the cumulative list of Frick and Yourcenar's "historical affairs." Exceptionally, the friendship among the three women survived.

After dispatching "Reflections" to the publisher, the couple started working on the English translation of the Thomas Mann essay together in late August. It proved to be something of a moving target, as Yourcenar decided to revise the French version of the article while her partner was translating it. Over the weekend of October 22–23, for example, she added three new typed pages to the text that Frick had already translated. And she still needed "to concentrate into one discussion her previous separate discussions of the *Magic Mountain*."[8]

Almost a month later the two women did a "final" reading of the essay in English, as revised for the third time and typed for the seventh! No sooner had Yourcenar given it her stamp of approval than she decided to add another paragraph on *Joseph and His Brothers*. As Frick explained in the daybook, "Grace read her one-page addition that evening, but thought it insufficiently centered upon the main subject of the essay, *Humanism*. M.Y. admits that she had not thought of the main focus, so anxious was she to treat *Joseph* sequence as a whole, so agrees to rework this new addition." Yourcenar appreciated Frick's editorial eye. As she told a friend who had asked her to comment on his novel, "Grace Frick, to whom I am reading this letter as we sit by the fire, points out that I have offered no criticism of your book, though there are always critiques to be made (and she knows whereof she speaks, having kindly taken on the role of devil's advocate with respect to my own)."[9] It wasn't until January 28, 1956, that an overall revision of the Mann essay, tightening the focus on humanism, was completed and translated.[10] All told, there were nine or ten versions of the English translation.

Throughout all this, with the relative continuity permitted by these other projects and her tenuous health, Yourcenar was revising her 1934 collection of short stories, *La Mort conduit l'attelage*, which comprised the painterly titles "D'après Dürer," "D'après Greco," and "D'après Rembrandt." "D'après Dürer," whose main character was a "sixteenth-century adventurer in quest of knowledge," would take on a life of its own and blossom into what many readers consider to be Yourcenar's best novel. She had reached page 20 of what was still at that time a revision of "After Dürer" by June 23, 1955. Almost three more months brought her only up to page 46. About what they then began to call Le Grand Oeuvre, Grace wrote on January 29, 1956, that her companion was "feeling now well advanced and hopeful that it will be the great book that she wants it to be." Simmering on the back burner were the poems to be published by Alexis Curvers; the translations of Constantine Cavafy, subject of another legal wrangle; a new edition of *Feux*; and Frick's translation of *Le Coup de grâce*, which had been recently reissued in France.

Because Frick and Yourcenar had been out of the country for such a long time, the months after their return in June of 1955 brought a steady stream of visitors to Petite Plaisance, most of them for several days. In addition to Paul Minear, Jean and Roger Hazelton came in July with their son Mark. Gladys and the three Minear children arrived in August en route home from the Gaspé Peninsula. "The Emmas" from West Hartford, Emma Trebbe and Emma Evans, also came in August; they had been Grace and Marguerite's neighbors at 549 Prospect Avenue in what now seemed another life. Ruth Hall came with her mother in October, with Florence Codman pulling up the rear in mid-January 1956. Whatever had happened regarding her translation of "Carnets de Notes," the thank-you note she wrote to Grace after this visit makes clear that all was well between them. It also suggests from the standpoint of a sensitive third party what it was like to live on South Shore Road in winter. As Codman wrote of her departure,

> At the top of the hill beyond Somesville the snow began to spread over the hills and reached across the farms along the railroad until night fell, uniting the landscape so it could not intrude into my pondering on the past four days.
>
> They were curiously rare and intense. It was so long since we had met that time no longer counted. The empty houses at the edge of the sea isolated like a stockade in which whatever we said seemed rare and of heightened value.
>
> I need not try to describe how I enjoyed myself. It must be enough if I once more say, Thank you.
>
> Affectionately, Florence[11]

Visiting friends were an important source of pleasure for Frick and Yourcenar, but there were many others during these years of relative youth for both women, who turned fifty-two in 1955. And Marguerite's sporadic

FIGURE 32. Grace Frick and Marguerite Yourcenar in the garden at Petite Plaisance, 1955. Hazelton family archives.

ill health, ascribed by some to hypochondria but also quite likely related on occasion to anxiety, did not prevent her from enjoying herself on Mount Desert Island. In August of 1955 the couple discovered that horse-drawn carriage rides were available from Acadia's Jordan Pond Stables, established in 1953, and they wasted no time signing up for them. Sometimes they took young David Peckham or houseguests along; more often they would go alone, picking blueberries in the sun along the road near the stable or stopping for tea at Jordan Pond House. Once they walked halfway around Jordan Pond and then had "*two* popover teas each!"[12] Jordan Pond was also an ideal spot for sighting deer, whose number, age, and sex were often carefully noted in the daybook.

Mid-September 1955 brought three "heavenly" days of Indian summer, during one of which the couple sat on a nearby lawn listening to their friend Emily McKibben play Bach and Brahms on the piano. Music was one of Grace's passions—so much so that she got caught one snowy winter's night on her neighbor Ruth Jordan's front porch peering through the blinds while someone played Jordan's grand piano.[13] There was no dearth of licit concert options at hand, however, ranging from a summer chamber music festival to wintertime community concerts to performances by the high school band. Grace and Marguerite patronized them all.

When the women had a rental car or could prevail upon someone to chauffeur them, they made twilight trips to Seawall or the picturesque fishing village of McKinley (today Bass Harbor) on the island's quiet side. If the sea was fierce owing to a storm, they would drive to Thunder Hole or Otter Cliff off Ocean Drive to watch giant waves batter walls of granite. Their friend Helen Willkie was an easy mark, and she piled her four children into the family station wagon for deer-spotting rendezvous with Grace and Marguerite on many a summer's eve.

Picnics were another favorite leisure activity during these years, whether breakfast on the shore near home or supper at the Jesuit Spring, where the women watched the sun set over Somes Sound. Clams and lobsters layered with seaweed and cooked in a great pot of salt water were a treat shared most often with the Willkies, always at the same choice spot along the ocean.

The couple continued to engage with village children, with Grace in particular always trying to open their eyes to new experiences. One summer day she was so bold as to take eighteen youngsters on the early boat to Manset for a two-hour session of square dancing.[14] Several adults who were children in the 1950s recall being taken by the women on boat trips to outlying islands for picnics. "The Madame" they recall as always smiling, whereas Miss

Frick, their employer, was more strict. Richard M. Savage II, who still lives in Northeast Harbor and runs a charter boat service, vividly remembers these picnics. Frick and Yourcenar brought food "in big baskets, and there was always cheese and bread. And wine, for sure, though not for the kids. Sandwiches, but not American-type sandwiches. No bologna and cheese and tuna fish. There were cheeses and nice meats, and you ate it European style."[15]

On the night of the women's first Halloween in Northeast after their two years in Europe, Marguerite dressed up as a ghost and Grace donned a witch's hat and black robe to receive trick-or-treaters. As the years went by, in part no doubt because people did not know quite what to make of Frick and Yourcenar's household, village children were hesitant to trick-or-treat there in small numbers. Instead, eight or ten children would arrive en masse. They then went into the parlor to earn their treat by telling a ghost story, reciting a poem, or correctly answering a question related to what they were learning in school!

In the summer of 1956, attempting this time to get youngsters to engage in one of her own favorite pastimes, Frick launched a children's garden contest. On the morning of June 7—"Marguerite's birthday"!—she made the rounds of Northeast Harbor's schools to announce the competition and its handsome twenty-five-dollar first prize.[16] Miss Elizabeth Tilton of Sargeant Drive, a summer resident and garden lover, was recruited to serve as a judge. Rick Savage won first prize over five other competitors for a vegetable garden that his mother constantly pestered him to weed. But genetics may have helped him score that win: his uncle was the landscape artist Charles K. Savage, who created the extraordinary Asticou Azalea Garden.

The years after *Memoirs of Hadrian* came out were a time of high-energy, prolific literary output and mutual engagement for Yourcenar and Frick in multiple spheres of activity. On the domestic front, late 1955 brought an event long awaited by both women: a new addition to their family. On December 15 a five-month-old black cocker spaniel came into their lives, the most splendid Christmas present either woman could imagine. Both of them had been dog lovers since childhood. Grace was especially fond of cocker spaniels, having had one back in Kansas City, and Marguerite considered the breed to be just the right size for their house. They had had an eye out for a puppy as far back as 1950. During Yourcenar's spring break that year, the couple spent a few days in the White Mountain region of New Hampshire where they visited Dupont Kennels. They found "thirteen perfect cocker spaniels" there, five of them new puppies. Frick described them at the time as "the most affectionate beings ever seen." Perhaps knowing whom they need-ed to impress, the puppies "kissed and licked Marguerite from head to toe."[17]

A lot of thought went into choosing a name for the new creature. Several possibilities were suggested by the dog's scampish nature or his jet-black coat: Sprite, Devil, Imp, Scaramouche, Smokey, Blackball, and Booker T. Wash-ington (!). Food was another prominent theme: Molasses, Popover, Muffin, Plum Pudding. In the end they settled on Monsieur Popover, which eventu-ally got shortened to Monsieur.

Monsieur Popover's mistresses tracked his progress like proud parents. On January 4, 1956, "puppy" mastered the descent of the precipitous main stair-way, "squealing with fright as he goes." Grace loved regaling her young nieces, Katharine and Pamela, with accounts of his adventures and showing the girls what a lively household Petite Plaisance could be:

> It happened like this. We have two staircases, even though this is a very little house. The backstairs are so steep that some sea-captain who once lived here made himself a handrail along the wall to hoist himself up after he got around the turn. Whoever built the back stairs, and that was over a hundred years ago, did not wish to saw and plane any more boards than they absolutely had to just to go up from the kitchen, so they made as few steps as they dared, with an extra high one at the top and bottom. So it is very hard to begin the climb, even for two-legged creatures, and still harder to finish. All the little children of the village have been here at one time and another when their fathers were doing our painting or carpentering after we moved in, and the smallest tots were always the ones who loved most to go up the back stairs, hanging tight to the rope, then running through Marguerite's bedroom to the hall, and down the front stairs, sliding one hand down the banister rail. So of course this little dog would love to do just what they do.[18]

Impishness was a trait that Grace shared with her new cocker, as peo-ple who knew her often comment. Deirdre "Dee Dee" Wilson, who grew close to Grace in the 1970s, calls her "really mischievous, elf-like."[19] Robert Lalonde's fictionalized account of Yourcenar's 1957 lecture tour in Canada exaggerates Grace's devilish tendencies to the point of comic caricature.[20] Dr. Kaighn Smith, now a year-round resident of South Shore Road, asked me once—half in jest?—if I knew that Grace Frick was a witch. He will never forget the sight of her, all alone some distance down a wooded lane, dancing a spry jig in her long black cape on the night of an early first snow.[21]

One of Frick's most renowned pranks was visited on the former host and hostess of her graduate residence at Yale University, Paul and Gladys Minear. When Paul Minear became Winkley Professor of Biblical Theology at Yale Divinity School, Frick was determined to congratulate her friend in a manner equal to his accomplishment and symbolic of their shared Yale connection. In February of 1956 she wrote,

> I could think of only one fitting token to send, but it was easier thought of than procured. Over the holiday yesterday, however, I had a chance to place the small order with a local man on a visit home from Boston, and you should soon receive my congratulations in the form, if not the color, that I desire. The color should be yellow, . . . but maybe the order will come in green. Let me know, please, if you receive anything soon of those two salient possibilities.[22]

Harking back to the days when Grace partook often of the Minears' bananas at 158 Whitney Avenue, the gift arrived shortly; shipped from Boston's wholesale market, it was an eighty-pound stem of tiered bananas.

Hall Willkie, who spent lots of time with Frick and Yourcenar as a youngster, remembers Grace's playful, "childlike way": "She was so much fun to just take a walk with. Things she would point out, things she would see, and I think that's why children loved her so much, because she was not an old fuddy-duddy. She was fun and curious and mischievous, and she enjoyed intrigue a little bit." Like other young familiars of Petite Plaisance, Willkie felt closer to Frick than to Yourcenar: "I think Madame Yourcenar enjoyed us, too, but she kept us at a bit of a distance. She loved teaching us things like how to bake bread, and we would have meals together a lot, but Grace Frick would just embrace us completely." Willkie also notes how different the women were from their neighbors:

> No one really knew who they were. The local people were a little suspicious of them because they walked around in black capes. I can still see them as a little boy, and people just didn't look like that! So very odd or off-beat. And the summer people, mostly rather privileged, certainly had no understanding of them. I learned later in life that there was a lot of talk about their relationship, and people weren't happy about that at all. The lesbian relationship was suspected. I remember as a boy, people threw eggs at their door once. Things like that. People would say, "You know, *those* women . . ."[23]

Frick and Yourcenar eventually became so attached to the Willkie children, Frederick, Arlinda, Julia, and Hall, that they decided to leave them their home as a life estate. In a sense, like David Peckham, they fulfilled the couple's wish, forsaken along the way, to adopt a child of their own. Helen Willkie, mother of the brood, had come to know the women quite by chance. She and the children summered in Seal Harbor, just up the coast from Northeast, for a number of years in the 1950s and early 1960s. The housekeeper at their cottage was Bernice "Bunny" Pierce. One day Pierce noticed a copy of *Hadrian* on Helen's bedside table. As Hall Willkie reported, "Bunny told my mother, 'I know the person who wrote that book. Yes, I help take care of them, and she's a friend.' So Bunny introduced them, and they became fast friends."[24] Adding to the serendipity, Helen's brother-in-law was the antiracist presidential candidate for whom Frick had campaigned in 1940, Wendell Willkie.

When I phoned Julia Willkie in Manhattan one day to ask what she remembered of Frick, I was astonished to hear that she had a framed picture of Grace in her bedroom. "I *adored* that woman!" Julia exclaimed, adding,

> She taught us how to make French bread, how to tell what stars were what. I tell you, we were *always* at their house. I can remember sitting on their porch and snapping green beans. That kitchen was magical, with all those various jars. To me, Grace Frick was just . . . a life force! She may have been a little bossy or opinionated or whatever, but she was *a wonder*! I was always crazy about her. I mean, I always *liked* Madame Yourcenar, but . . . Well, of course she was a scholar and a writer. She was colder and more standoffish. Grace to me was kind of, I don't know what you'd call it, Yankee backbone or something, but she was a love. And she would say things like "You need to take a nap." And you did![25]

Questioned about the dynamics of Frick and Yourcenar's relationship, Julia paused for a moment before answering, "I was fairly young, but I would say Miss Frick held it all together. I would say that she allowed Madame to call the big cards. I don't think that Madame would have had the wonderful life she had if it hadn't been Grace Frick who arranged for the world to keep going so that she had the time and the luxury to do her own work."[26]

The next long trip to Europe was to take place in the fall of 1956. Yourcenar had agreed to some lectures in Holland and Belgium. Afterward she and

Frick would spend a few weeks in Paris before heading to the south of France, where they had reserved a small house for the winter.[27] The plan was to make that location in Villefranche their base of operations for trips to Italy, Spain, and possibly the Levant. As in 1953, Grace made a weeklong trip to Kansas City before they set sail. On September 25 she met Marguerite, who had traveled from Maine with Monsieur Popover, at Grand Central Station. From the start the omens for this trip were less than auspicious, with Marguerite receiving weekly "hepatitis vitamin" shots and taking liver pills.

Yourcenar had prepared several talks: "Books and Ourselves," "The Writer in the Face of History," "Europe and the Notion of Humanism," and "Greek Statues."[28] On October 12, in the Dutch city of Arnhem, she was all set to deliver "Books and Ourselves" when Frick discovered that "The Writer in the Face of History" was the advertised title for that venue. Dashing back to the hotel for the right notes, Grace made it back to the lecture hall just in time for the talk to begin without anyone being the wiser. The real face of history was soon to show itself, however.

On November 2 Frick began noting disturbing events in the daybook: "Israel takes Gaza. French and English bomb Port Said, obliterating Egyptian air force." Two days later she recorded in telegraphic haste, "News from Hungary very bad. Russians re-enter Budapest. Mass *slaughter*. Decided (M.Y. after little sleep) to return on first boat to U.S.A. because of conditions Suez and Hungary."[29]

Yourcenar, for her part, was revolted by the arrant aggression of everyone involved in these events, and by the belligerence of the British and the French in particular. She wasn't even sure that she wanted to return to France anytime soon. As she wrote to a friend in 1957, "Paris was abhorrent last year, at the time of the Suez crisis, like anyplace where madness, illusion, and willful confusion hold sway, along with deceit. I left there devastated. It seems that the alarm clock is set for the hour of disaster, and we can hear the minutes ticking by in the night."[30] To a sorely disappointed Natalie Barney, she wrote, "During that dark month of November, it seemed that fury, spite, and violence were everywhere."[31]

Josyane Savigneau has used a sentence from that letter to Barney as proof of an ongoing struggle between Yourcenar and Frick over European travel: "The further we go along, the more we note the wisdom of the resolution that brought us back here, and this despite regret at not seeing our friends from France at greater length or more frequently." According to Savigneau, Yourcenar laid down the law regarding how much America she was willing to put up with:

There is the proof, for those who might have doubts about the subject, that debate had indeed existed. But relocating in Europe would have been unacceptable for Frick. Where else but in an English-speaking country would she have found the one compensation for her self-effacement, the indispensable feeling of being absolutely necessary to Yourcenar's survival?

  . . . The compromise had perhaps been imparted to Frick couched in one of those apparently innocuous sentences that Yourcenar was so good at devising. The deceptive insignificance of those sentences was contradicted by a tone that revealed long-nurtured decisions, admitting not the slightest discussion: "We're returning to Petite Plaisance, but we'll travel."[32]

Yourcenar was indeed master of the pithy remark, but Grace had been a travel lover long before she met Marguerite, and there is no indication that she pled the case to go home in 1956. In fact, she was disappointed that their hasty departure meant abandoning trips to Aix-la-Chapelle, medieval Bouillon, and Arlon's archaeological museum.[33] The fact of the matter is that although the two women made five more trips to Europe over the next fifteen years, and did a great deal of traveling within the United States, they did not go back to France again until the spring of 1968. I strongly suspect that this was one of those times when Frick let Yourcenar "call the big cards."

Which is not to say that she was unhappy to find herself home for the holidays. The nearly monthlong series of winter festivities at Petite Plaisance got into full swing on December 13, Saint Lucy's Day. Shirley McGarr, Grace and Marguerite's near neighbor, recalls that the couple "joyously celebrated every holiday."[34] They decorated the main entrance to the house with a traditional Maine Christmas wreath, hung a sheaf of evergreens on the back door, and draped garlands of balsam or pine over both entryways. Grace also initiated a holiday tradition of her own devising. Marguerite once described it to Paul and Gladys Minear (in her original English): "We are snow-bound here, but very comfortable inside the house. Grace always puts dozens of gold, blue and red glass balls on our apple and cherry trees, so we look like having a magic orchard at Christmas."[35] When Marguerite was a child, her father would hang oranges on the branches of trees for her to pick at their villa in the south of France.[36] Whether Grace's colorful balls owe anything to that fond memory we don't know, but Petite Plaisance carries on the Christmas tradition of the "magic orchard" to this day.

Saint Lucy's Day is a primarily Scandinavian holiday that Grace and Marguerite first experienced in Stockholm in 1953.[37] They began celebrating it in Northeast Harbor in 1956. The two women had not had a tranquil

Christmas at home for five years.[38] In the interim they had made two long visits to Sweden and grown deeply attached to that country and its culture. Yourcenar often said in interviews that she had "a passion for Sweden."[39] In 1962, speaking for herself and Frick, she called Scandinavia one of their favorite places.[40] Honoring Saint Lucy's Day was a way to bring a beloved part of the world home with them.

That first celebration was a simple and intimate one. Marguerite made Swedish pastries the night before, a variation on the traditional *lussekatt*. Grace woke up the next morning, before sunrise, to the strains of her companion playing Mozart *Variations* on the spinet piano in the living room downstairs. Moments later, in the dark of dawn, Marguerite and Monsieur climbed the stairs to Grace's bedroom with a tray of hot coffee, the special buns, and a burning candle. As Grace noted years later, Marguerite would faithfully reenact this ritual every December.[41]

Josyane Savigneau has emphasized the connection between Saint Lucy's Day, a date often underlined in Frick's daybooks, and Yourcenar's beautiful Greek friend Lucy Kyriakos.[42] If there was ever any truth to that interpretation, Grace did not let it stop her from entering wholeheartedly into the spirit of the holiday. Over time, in addition to the couple's private custom, Saint Lucy's Day became a yearly event that they shared with friends and neighbors.

Shirley McGarr remembered the Saint Lucy's Day gathering: "Oh, Miss Frick! . . . I can see her coming down the stairs with the crown on her head, complete with lit candles, and dressed in a flowing white robe—very Swedish, or very Scandinavian."[43] The traditional ritual features a young girl dressed all in white; on her head she wears a crown of evergreens that holds several glowing candles. In Swedish homes the eldest daughter often donned the festive headdress and woke her sleeping father with sweet cakes and singing. At Petite Plaisance, Grace took the daughter's part, mounting the steep stairway of the house in a floor-length white garment, crown and candles on her head, and waking Marguerite in the traditional way. She then made her dramatic return to the first floor, leading revelers into the parlor where Scandinavian pastries, cakes, coffee breads, and hot beverages awaited them.[44]

In 1956 the time between Saint Lucy's Day and Christmas was largely taken up by letters and telegrams related to the "Curvers affair," the latest in a long line of battles with publishers who were viewed as having failed to honor their obligations to Marguerite Yourcenar or her work. Alexis Curvers had published Yourcenar's poetry collection *Les Charités d'Alcippe* without letting the author proofread the galleys. Predictably, the forty-page chapbook contained a variety of errors. Curvers was incensed when he found out that Yourcenar was hand-correcting the errors in every copy of the book she signed. Lawyers were consulted on both sides, and relations grew increasingly strained. On December 19 the tension was ratcheted up a few notches when Yourcenar received in the mail the copy of *Les Charités*, furiously torn in two, that she had personally inscribed to Curvers and his wife. December 21 was so thoroughly consumed by work on the conflict with Curvers that Yourcenar and Frick were up all night writing, correcting, typing, and retyping letters related to this indignity. At first light the next morning, instead of collapsing, exhausted, into bed, the two women walked down to Clarks' shore, opposite Petite Plaisance, to greet the dawn, "enjoying the purity and clarity of the air, the waning moon and the first red in the east before coming back for two hours' sleep."[45]

On Christmas Eve the couple attended a midnight worship service at the Somesville Union Meeting House, a Congregational church located near the cabin they had rented during their first summers on Mount Desert Island.[46] Christmas Day itself was marked, as it would continue to be over the years, with a traditional turkey dinner. One touching relic of Christmas in the 1970s, saved by Marguerite, suggests that the women affectionately pressed their canine companions into service as intermediaries for gift giving. It is a typical rectangular gift tag, with a red string attached to one end, bearing colorful images of Christmas bells. Beneath the printed words "Joyous Noël," Grace had written in French, "To my dear, dear Maîtresse d'Hôtel from Zoe." With "Maîtresse d'Hôtel" apparently a feminized form of *maître d'*, Zoé's gift was undoubtedly intended for the person in charge of serving her meals. Zoé obviously understood that Christmas involved giving *and receiving* gifts, however; on the back side of the tag appeared the following appeal: "I would like you to have a color portrait made of me."[47]

New Year's Eve 1956 was cold and clear. When the pendulum clock on the living room mantel struck midnight, Grace, Marguerite, and a friend named Roger Williams rang in the new year with a glass of Grace's famously spiked eggnog. Despite the frigid cold, in a throwback to ancient Greek celebrations of Dionysus, Lord of the Vine, Marguerite and Grace poured wine onto the ground from the veranda on the west side of Petite Plaisance, as Monsieur, eager to join the festivities, tried to lap it off the snow.[48] The next morning found the two women breakfasting in bed and reading aloud "The Wrath of Achilles" from the English translation of *The Iliad*. Perhaps they were looking to antiquity for inspiration in their ongoing battle with Alexis Curvers—which, of course, they eventually won.

The round of winter holidays came to an end on January 6 with the Feast of Epiphany, the last of the Twelve Days of Christmas. The customs surrounding the holiday vary by country, but special sweets and pastries are almost always center stage. At Petite Plaisance, 1957 saw the first of many gatherings for *galette des Rois*, or kings' cake, which Grace and Marguerite viewed as an appetizing way to acquaint young people with a French tradition. That first year the new French teacher at Mount Desert Island High School, Mr. Noe, brought his classes to Petite Plaisance for kings' cake and hot spiced cider. Later gatherings would include children from Northeast Harbor's Union Church as well as local students and neighbors. One year Yourcenar baked an Italian panettone for Epiphany. In 1969, when she and Grace were visiting Aix-en-Provence, they bought a bakery *galette* and had it for breakfast in their hotel room. One way or another, they never failed to observe that special day.[49]

CHAPTER 23 ❦ *Coup de Grâce*
1957

Translating is writing.

—Marguerite Yourcenar

A GREAT BLIZZARD ON JANUARY 10 found Grace and Marguerite trekking around the block on snowshoes. "Here, great Winter reigns," Yourcenar told Malvina Hoffman, "At the moment, it is snowing; yesterday and the day before, the temperature fell to 12 degrees below zero or more. This cold, still, blue, white, silver, and steel world has a marvelously pure and almost terrible beauty, like the atmosphere of certain tales and certain poems."[1]

On January 6 Frick had phoned Farrar, Straus and Cudahy to say that the English *Coup de Grâce* would be ready in two weeks. Despite that hopeful promise, she ended up devoting more time over that fortnight to correcting the proofs of *Feux* and preparing lists of reviewers for the new edition of that 1936 book than she did to translating. *Hadrian* was also coming out again in various guises, in both French and English. Entire days would pass without Grace doing any work on *Coup de Grâce*. She almost never started translating until late in the day and was lucky when she did to get to bed by midnight. On March 15 she and Marguerite left on a two-week lecture tour. Not until April 18 was the manuscript finally mailed.

That trip to Canada landed Yourcenar in the hospital with an attack of thrombophlebitis. The native Canadian writer Robert Lalonde has turned this episode into a short novel. *Un Jardin entouré de murailles* is based on a line from *Quoi? L'Éternité*: "Every great love is a garden surrounded by walls."[2] Occasionally verging on slapstick comedy, the book provides what can only be called an offbeat depiction of Yourcenar and Frick.

I happen to share Lalonde's belief in Frick and Yourcenar's love, if not precisely his characterization of the two women. Still, just as Élie Grekoff once told Grace that there might be something devilish in her angelic intentions, what "Marg" says about Grace in Lalonde's novel contains a grain of truth. Following a series of madcap adventures, the fictional author has been hospitalized after fainting on the train en route from Montreal to Ottawa. Yourcenar speaks of Frick to young Dr. Carrière, who has had a run-in or two with her strong-willed helpmate:

> Like you and me, Grace is a complex, multiple, and complicated being. But unlike you and me, she comes and goes in the world disguised as an ordinary person. Sometimes even—yes, it's true—as an utterly untamable shrew. . . . But she is an angel. Though we sometimes have doubts about angels, we know full well that they exist and that without them . . . Plus, she has marvelous courage, whereas I am no more than a forceful, obstinate beast without the slightest valor.[3]

On returning to Maine, Yourcenar was astonished to receive in the mail, as Grace wrote in the daybook, a "gift of $500 from Aunt Georgia Horner because of her illness!"[4] The episode seems to have had no lasting ill effects, and both women were soon back at their double desk collaborating on the translation of *Coup de Grâce.*

Yourcenar had composed for Frick a unique text to give her a sense of this novel's main character and a feel for the atmosphere in which he recounted his story. Almost three and a half typewritten pages long, it is called "Commentary for Grace on the Prelude to *Coup de Grâce.*"[5] Reading Yourcenar's sketch, one can't help but be struck by how vivid in her mind's eye is the image of a scene composed by her almost twenty years earlier. The "prelude" in question is set in an Italian railway station where the jaded mercenary Erick von Lhomond, injured fighting under Francisco Franco in Spain, awaits transport to Germany.

Among the soldiers gathered at the station, Erick was "one of the oldest, an officer some forty years old, but also young, with the frightening youth of an archangel. . . . His personal adventures and misfortunes are those of his era. A thousand conflicts, a thousand tensions are subtly balanced within this trim, firm body as on the tip of a sword." The two men that Yourcenar's "Commentary" depicts as Erick's audience are unfamiliar with the Baltic wars in which he took part. But they resemble him in one important way: no one need explain to them the nature of Erick's "camaraderie" with his friend Conrad. "Erick would not have started talking without a secret understanding on that point."[6]

Unlike *Memoirs of Hadrian*, written during a period of postwar euphoria when many in the West, including Yourcenar, believed that painful lessons had been learned and that enlightened leaders would build lasting world peace, *Coup de Grâce* was composed on the eve of World War II but set in the violent aftermath of the Russian Revolution in the Baltic States. Moreover, Frick translated the novel into English with the crises of Budapest and Suez still fresh in her mind.

The release of *Coup de Grâce* was greeted with profuse attention from the American press over the next several months. No major news outlet failed to review the book, and some of them did so more than once. Praise for the novel was—predictably, given its subject and tenor—more reserved than for its English-language predecessor. The earliest published critique, from the *Saturday Review*, set the tone for many to follow; it was Ben Ray Redman's "A Look in the Mirror": "American readers of Madame Yourcenar's 'Hadrian's Memoirs,' so beautifully translated by its author and Grace Frick, will take up 'Coup de Grace' with lively expectations. But if they come to it with the hope of matching the literary experience provided by the earlier translation, they will be disappointed. 'Coup de Grace' is a far less substantial book than 'Hadrian's Memoirs.'" Echoing certain American criticisms of *Hadrian* issued with McCarthyism still in full swing, Redman goes on to say that what Yourcenar does in *Coup de Grâce*, "coldly, dryly, is to draw the likeness of an absolute egotist whose character has been warped by sexual inversion."[7] In the *New York Times*, Charles Poore called Erick "a psychopathic Don Juan, a soldier of misfortune dragging his memory back through the muck and havoc of falling dynasties and rising totalitarian regimes."[8] But no one had a bad word for the translation. Herbert Kupferberg paid Frick the translator's ultimate tribute, calling her English rendering "idiomatic and graceful."[9] Even Poore's distaste for Erick did not prevent him from acknowledging Frick's gift.

Carlos Baker, a Maine native who later wrote the first biography of Ernest Hemingway, saw Lhomond in a more allegorical light. His *New York Times* review admired the "Thomas Mann–like prose" of *Coup de Grâce* and its "lucid translation," adding,

> Judged . . . as the political fable it seems basically to be, with Erick as the ver-
> itable Judas-goat of a stricken continent, a bad European leading his confreres
> toward the *coup de grace*, the novel takes on the dimensions of a parable. Its
> internal meaning will be lost on no one who has lived through the wars of our

time and has paused to meditate on that cold indifference to human values their perpetrators have displayed.[10]

William Hogan of the *San Francisco Chronicle* called *Coup de Grâce* "a brilliant novel of doom," predicting that it would become a minor classic.[11]

The most perceptive reviewer was Edwin Kennebeck, who wrote frequently for *Commonweal* and the *Nation*. Kennebeck focused not on Erick von Lhomond but on Sophie de Reval, the young woman Lhomond spurns as a lover and in the end clumsily executes: "One's first assumption might be that the 'principal character' is Erick, the narrator, but I am willing to guess that the novelist's source was 'Sophie'—her death in the story being one of those notes of completeness, of aesthetic inevitability, which real life generally does not provide."[12]

Yourcenar herself commented, in a letter to Gilbert H. Montague, on only one American review of *Coup de Grâce*. In August of 1955 Montague had invited her and Frick to a luncheon at his home in Seal Harbor along with the classicist Edith Hamilton and her companion Doris Fielding Reid. Yourcenar and Hamilton's names had been mentioned that summer side by side in the *Herald Tribune Book Review*. Two years later articles about the same two authors were again featured on the same page of the same publication.[13] In her letter to Montague, Yourcenar called the *Tribune*'s article on *Coup de Grâce* in that issue "very penetrating."[14] Its author, Virgilia Peterson, had experienced the post–World War I turmoil in northern Europe firsthand.

Marguerite and Grace had met Edith Hamilton as far back as 1946, when they were spending the summer at Dickey House on Main Street in Southwest Harbor. They already knew Doris Fielding Reid, who had been Hamilton's student at Bryn Mawr College. On the evening of September 7, 1946, they made a visit to their home in Seawall to meet Edith. Both lovers of myth and Greek antiquity, Yourcenar and Hamilton no doubt found much to discuss. Years later, on August 28, 1961, either Frick or Yourcenar mailed a copy of *Memoirs of Hadrian* to Hamilton. They received an immediate reply written in a tremulous hand on light blue stationery:

> You have given me a great pleasure, a beautiful book in an adequate setting, a text of high distinction so bound and so printed that all builds up to an ineffaceable impression of what true civilization is. You see that is the way I first read your book, a banner of civilization which does not really alter through the

ages. Thank you again and again for the way you have reaffirmed this dogma to my enlightenment and peace of mind.[15]

Hamilton was ninety-three years old.

As for the "penetrating" review, though its author was American, she had married a Polish prince and lived at his château in the years between the two world wars. They fled for their lives when the Nazis invaded in September of 1939. Peterson's "Memoirs of a 'Soldier of Fortune' " stands virtually alone in crediting *Coup de Grâce* with "the same granite integrity, stylistic skill, and underlying passion" displayed by *Hadrian* earlier that decade. Having lived in Poland, Virgilia Peterson knew whereof she spoke:

> Those unfamiliar with this cold, gray region of the world, and the proud loyalties of every segment of this feudal society will understand them better from reading Marguerite Yourcenar's story. She has detachment of spirit, economy of style and depth of understanding. The translation in which the author also collaborated, gives every word its full value. The setting and the moral problem of this brief intense book may appear strange to the American reader, but they are actually no less strange than life itself.[16]

The presentation copies of both the new French edition of *Feux* and the American *Coup de Grâce*, sent out by Frick and Yourcenar at about the same time, brought the renewal of ties in several cases with old friends not seen or heard from in years. Frick's former mentor from the Stephens College days, Louise Dudley, wrote to thank the women for her copy of *Feux* and to say she was still savoring *Hadrian*.[17] Katherine "Katy" Gatch was Grace's old friend from Wellesley and Yale, and like her partner, Marion Witt, she taught English at Hunter College. In June of 1957 Katherine thanked Marguerite for two recent mailings:

> A month or more ago, when I received from your publisher a copy of *Feux*, Marion and I had been belatedly reading your superb analysis of Thomas Mann and I believe that the thought waves our conversation sent toward Mt. Desert must have recalled us to you! Indeed, over the years (too many!) since Marion and I have seen you and Grace, we have spoken of you often, re-reading *Hadrien* with increasing delight, rejoicing in your success; gloating over the best-seller lists, but glowing over the reviews. . . .

Should anything lure you away from Mt. Desert in this direction, do please visit us. We have two guest rooms and I can think of no pleasure greater than having the two of you occupy them.[18]

A few weeks later, Frick and Yourcenar accepted Katherine's invitation to stay with her and Marion at the summer home they had recently purchased in Woodbridge, Connecticut.

On November 19 Yourcenar was scheduled to give an evening lecture at Wellesley College, "Greek Poets and Their Influence on French Poetry." Frick could not wait to show off her companion. She spent hours on November 3 contacting potential audience members: the author Helen Howe, who summered in Northeast Harbor; Emily McKibben, the pianist who regularly rented a house behind Petite Plaisance; Constantine Dimaras, Yourcenar's Cavafy cotranslator, who was staying in New York with his wife, Helen; Katy Gatch and Marion Witt; Lucille (Carpenter) White, a fellow Wellesley grad and former Kansas City neighbor, now living in Boston; Grace Hawk, a Wellesley faculty member; Martha Hale Shackford, the English professor who had written such a glowing reference letter on Frick's behalf back in 1939; Chick Austin's wife, Helen, still in Hartford; and Erika Vollger, Grace and Marguerite's seamstress friend, who lived in New York City and loved Mount Desert Island, among several others. The talk was a resounding success.

The next few days were spent with the Minears in New Haven, where Marguerite had followed Grace from France two decades earlier.[19] Knowing how the couple loved retracing their steps from the past, it is hard to imagine that they failed to walk down Orange Street, site of Frick's grad-school apartment, or to visit Yale's Gothic cathedral–like Sterling Memorial Library. Having just reconnected with Wellesley, Grace could hardly not have been contemplating where life had taken her since her college years. She had veered off the traditional academic path, but she was more than content with where she found herself now.

Eager to see her young nieces, Grace had decided to travel to Missouri for Thanksgiving—as always, sans Marguerite. On November 25, after a second weekend visit with Katy and Marion in Woodbridge, Frick left for New York, where she boarded a train for Chicago. Yourcenar, never liking to be left alone, met Erika Vollger at the station in New Haven, and the two friends headed north to Maine.

Grace Frick had much to be proud of and thankful for as 1957 drew to a close. Despite the mixed critical reaction to the American *Coup de Grâce*, the book sold briskly. As Yourcenar somewhat crankily wrote to Natalie Barney that August, "contrary to all expectations, it has earned a place for itself on this week's best-seller list, which doesn't prove a thing, least of all the reader's intelligent comprehension, but which is nice, like learning one has just won a prize in the lottery."[20] Nor was it only the critics who recognized Frick's talent as a translator. Kudos came her way from friends, former colleagues, and strangers. She was even solicited by the wife of the Hungarian-born artist and costume designer Marcel Vertès to translate the book he had just published in Paris: "We have read your brilliant, perfect translations of Marguerite Yourcenar and we would be very happy if you could translate the above mentioned book," Mme Vertès wrote.[21] Frick, who always attributed her success as a translator to Marguerite Yourcenar's assistance, demurred, but there can be no doubt that she was pleased with herself, pleased with her companion, and pleased with their prospects for the future.

Even Monsieur Popover got into the act. The two-year-old "dogster" had fallen ill the day after Christmas. "Black Monday!" Frick wrote in the day-book on December 30. "Monsieur very ill in hospital." That afternoon the cocker underwent intestinal surgery, causing his mistresses much worry. But by eight o'clock that evening, he "was coming out of anaesthetic enough to raise head and wag tail. Joy!!"[22] The couple had sent out fifty invitations to their New Year's Eve eggnog party, but the real celebration took place a few days later. On January 4 they brought Monsieur home in a taxi, "timid and thin" but healthy enough to "bark boldly at same taxi on arriving on his own doorstep." Nineteen fifty-eight was now officially "a joyous new year."[23]

CHAPTER 24 ❦ To a Far Country
1958–1959

Everyone who is born holds dual citizenship, in the kingdom of the well and in the kingdom of the sick. Although we all prefer to use only the good passport, sooner or later each of us is obliged, at least for a spell, to identify ourselves as citizens of that other place.

—Susan Sontag

NINETEEN FIFTY-EIGHT ROARED IN WITH a series of heavy rains that flooded the basement of Petite Plaisance, disabling the furnace and hot water heater. Northeast Harbor dispatched the town pump to siphon water out of the cellar into the backyard, but it seeped right back in.[1] Frick soon discovered that several nearby homes were having the same problem and, with her usual verve, proceeded to insist that the town improve the drainage along South Shore Road. The day after the second flooding, she booked passage on the SS *Constitution* to Italy. It would be her and Marguerite's "fourth trip for Europe together, not counting trips there in 1937."[2]

In New York Mrs. August Belmont, doyenne of the Northeast Harbor summer community, invited Yourcenar and Frick for tea with John Farrar and Roger Straus. After cocktails at the home of Jacques and Anya Kayaloff, they took Erika Vollger to the opening of *Tristan und Isolde* at the Metropolitan Opera.[3] The next morning the women checked a few references at the New York Public Library before sailing—with Monsieur Popover, of course—at noon.

Grace had always loved traveling by ship, however wild the weather. She once told Gladys Minear, before she and Marguerite had ever crossed the Atlantic together, "I have been in one gale at sea, one full gale, and I can still experience the wild excitement of it if I shut my eyes and listen hard for that wind, that very strange, unearthly wind, such as I had never known before."[4] To Gertrude Fay, a friend and fellow travel lover, Grace would later write that "a train—any train—or a horse, or a ship at sea in full gale are just my cup of tea."[5] She and Marguerite would soon taste that kind of excitement together.

Their ship had passed through the Strait of Gibraltar, sailing along the Spanish coast. They had been warned to expect rough weather; what they got was a violent storm that overturned chairs in the dining room and kept people up all night as Captain Valson steamed toward Cannes.[6] But the next day found the three travelers safely disembarking in Genoa and taking the train to Turin. Straightaway they hailed a horse-drawn carriage for a tour of the city. Marguerite had a sore throat the next day, but Grace was in fine fettle and spent the afternoon exploring the Egyptian Museum with Monsieur.

They would spend four months in Italy. For once, this trip abroad was more about leisure than lecturing. Two decades after their first Italian travels together, Grace and Marguerite retraced many of their early steps. In Rome they stayed again at La Residenza, in a room, Grace noted, next door to the one they shared in 1937.[7] In Florence the couple revisited San Marco's Fra Angelicos.[8] For most of May they made their base the Hotel Sirena in Sorrento, where Yourcenar had finished writing *Le Coup de grâce* in 1938.[9] This time they were working on the proofs of the Cavafy volume, which would finally come out later in 1958 after years of legal wrangling. In the Gulf of Naples they swam in the Tyrrhenian Sea. At Capri they climbed Mount Tiberius and made a leisurely visit to the ancient Roman Villa Jovis.[10] Back on the mainland they took a car to the new excavations of the ancient Greek settlement at Cumae.[11] In Paestum they saw ancient temples in sunset and twilight.[12] They took *carrozze* to the opera, cocktail parties, cafés, and museums, often noting in the daybook the names of their horses.

At the very end of the daybook for 1958, Grace made a list of the "Finest sights in Turin and Rome." Here is a small sampling of the salient entries:

March 9,   Milan, Hotel Manin, "Monsieur" seduces the chambermaid, who calls him "Monsieur Nanetto," the dwarf

[March 15], "Monsieur" peering from under the blanket at our feet, in a carriage in Borghese Gardens

March 19,   "Monsieur" flattening his belly against the grass on a cliff above Tempio, Villa Adriana

March 25,   Tuesday, "Monsieur" escaping from his parking place, at the umbrella stand, to trail us into the Bank President's office (Osio) and station himself exactly under the dog in the Antinoüs relief (*Antinoüs* of Antonianus of Aphrodisias)[13]

Leave it to Monsieur Popover to strike a pose under the image of a fellow canine in a second-century Roman bas-relief!

In mid-April Marguerite—not the hardiest of travelers—caught a cold.[14] By May 10, in Sorrento, she was diagnosed with enteritis. A month later, on June 10, the couple left Genoa for home with their twenty-three pieces of luggage. They had booked passage on a Greek ship, the TSS *Olympia*. Disappointingly for Grace, the sea was too rough for Greek dancing.

On July 9 back in Maine, Frick went to see Dr. Ernest Coffin about a change she had noticed six months earlier in the contour of her left breast. Yourcenar would later say she had "a little tumor in her breast so undefined that it was almost impossible to decide if it existed or not."[15] There was no palpable lump and no pain—until late June. What led Frick to consult Dr. Coffin as much as the very slight change in her breast was a bit of discomfort in her left arm. The news was not good. Frick had never been one to discuss her feelings at great length—Yourcenar would say she was too Anglo-Saxon for that. The furthest she went in that regard was to call July 10, the day after she saw Dr. Coffin, a "dismal" day. She who noted Marguerite's every ache and sniffle rarely spoke of her own health. On July 11 the couple went to see the surgeon, who assured them "her case would not be a serious one." Three days later he performed a radical mastectomy.

Marguerite was beside herself with worry. She knew all too well the ravages of cancer. The disease had killed the two most cherished beings of her youth, Jeanne de Vietinghoff and Michel de Crayencour. She rented a room from Lloyd Lurvey on Hancock Street in Bar Harbor, a three-minute walk from the island hospital. There she would stay for ten days during Grace's operation and recovery. Frick, of course, had always been the one to aid sick relatives and friends. This time the tables were turned. Although Yourcenar herself was being treated for a painful infection, she did everything she could to help her companion. She took charge of reporting Grace's "good result" to Aunt Dolly and sister-in-law Thelma Frick,[16] and she foiled the attempts of concerned Kansas City relations to travel to Maine to see the patient. She decorated the hospital room with flowers sent by Grace's brother Gage, Bernice Pierce, and the publishers Farrar and Straus. And she remained at Grace's side throughout the medical ordeal.

In the daybook on the date of her surgery Frick wrote with wry understatement and what one can only imagine to be humor: "Dr. Silas Coffin operates on G. to remove small tumor. No bad after-effects except for M.Y." She said almost the same thing the same day about Monsieur, who entered the "hospital" on July 14 "to have small tumor removed." By July 22, she felt well enough to quip, "Grace had stitches out one day before Doggo did." Five days later she was hosting Monsieur's third birthday party.[17]

Frick's dressing was still being changed every couple of days when "X-ray treatments" began on August 11. They were done at Eastern Maine Memorial Hospital in Bangor, fifty miles from Northeast Harbor, and would last for three weeks. Both women made the daily trips in a rented car with Frick at the wheel. They stayed in Winterport to cut down on the length of their drive.

During that first week of radiation treatment, Frick and Yourcenar, if anything, were more active than ever. On day two they invited their friends Gertrude Fay and Betsy Melcher to join them at a concert by the Polish-born classical pianist Artur Balsam in the coastal village of Blue Hill. Staying overnight at the Blue Hill House afterward, they paid a call the next morning on Adelaide Pearson at Rowantrees Pottery. At the urging of Mahatma Gandhi, Pearson and her young companion, Laura Paddock, had founded a pottery cooperative in Blue Hill in the mid-1930s. Frick and Yourcenar loved their rustic mugs, plates, and bowls made of local clay, and they eventually made Rowantrees their everyday tableware. The four women became friends, with Yourcenar once saying that Pearson and Paddock belonged "to the best type of American women of an already past era, adventurous, enterprising, unassuming, open to the whole world, and still anxious to help locally with the welfare of people."[18] Coincidentally, Adelaide Pearson was also the second cousin of Grace's longtime friend Phyllis Bartlett.

And so the days passed, one by one, with the women returning to Winterport after Frick's daily sessions in Bangor and spending weekends at Petite Plaisance. After treatment number five, alternating front and back, Frick reported, "All going well."[19] Not until the seventh treatment did she experience a radiation burn on her shoulder blade. Still, the couple continued to make every trip an outing, whether by picnicking somewhere along the way, visiting historic sites in the region, or even driving all the way to West Boothbay to see their friends Jean and Roger Hazelton.[20] In the end Frick had a total of eighteen radiation sessions without missing a beat.

Which does not mean it was easy. In the present age of breast-cancer ribbons and license plates, cancer-cure clothing and cosmetics, walkathons and races, it is hard to imagine what it was like to have cancer in the 1950s. Not once does Frick herself—or possibly even her doctors—ever actually use the dreaded term. The fact that Marguerite ignored her work and wrote almost no letters during the months of her companion's treatment is proof enough that the couple took the matter seriously. Not only could the illness be fatal, but in the case of breast cancer at a time when the wholesale removal of tissue, muscles, and lymph nodes was still standard practice, one survived only at the cost of radical disfigurement. Even as late as 1964, when Rachel Carson succumbed to breast cancer, "an individual's experience of breast cancer was still a private affair," as Ellen Leopold has written. "The disease was still an iceberg, a killer in the dark, without even a visible tip to draw attention to itself."[21]

Frick's courage and composure in confronting her plight, as well as her companion's sense of helplessness, are suggested by an astonishing statement that Yourcenar made to Élie Grekoff seven weeks after Grace's last radiation treatment. First, without going into specifics, she told Grekoff what a serious health crisis they had been through. She then informed him that Grace was "now completely well," adding, "but you can imagine the extent to which my life (more than that of Grace herself) was turned upside down."[22]

Frick had been lucky. Her scar was clean, and the radiation treatments had apparently killed any cancer cells that had not been surgically removed. She dove back into life with all the energy and zeal she was known for, and then some. Marguerite dove right in with her.

That October, on the day Frick was officially discharged from the X-ray department of the Bangor hospital, the couple headed north for a three-day camping trip. They slept that night in a cabin north of Old Town, home of the Penobscot Nation. It took them from noon until dark the next day to reach the Seboeis River Campground a few miles east of the northeastern corner of Baxter State Park. Hunting season had begun, and the first thing they saw, hanging from a tree at that campground, was a freshly killed deer. In deep distress, they turned around to head toward home, and spent the night at Millinocket's Great Northern Hotel. Yourcenar later told Élie Grekoff that their excursion to "the very beautiful mountainous region in the middle of the state was completely ruined" by hunters and their quarry.[23] The trauma was somewhat assuaged the next morning by two live deer, two moose, and two grouse the women spotted in the southwest corner of the park. They went on to hike part of the Appalachian Trail that day toward Mount Katahdin, following Nesowadnehunk Stream almost to Niagara Falls. As was so often the case for these two, they were again retracing their own footsteps: Yourcenar and Frick had made a similar trip in late September 1949. They spent their last night away at Mrs. Muzzey's Indian Hill Farm in Greenville, where they had stayed the time before.[24]

They never did end up camping out this time, but they would do so in 1959, when they stayed at Roaring Brook Campground in Baxter State Park. That year they avoided hunting season altogether by visiting the park in August. For two nights they slept in sleeping bags in a wooden lean-to. A bear cub came promptly at tea time to the trash bins not far from their shelter, looking for food. They also saw five or six brown-speckled spruce partridges, several dark-brown rabbits, a bull moose, two cows, and two calves. Most memorably, however, as Bérengère Deprez has noted, they had an encounter that found its way into Yourcenar's last work of fiction, the novella *An Obscure Man*, part of which takes place on Mount Desert Island. One late afternoon, while the two campers were hiking north of Katahdin Stream Campground, Frick reported in the daybook, "we saw a large black bear cub on the road ahead of us, who would not move out of our way. After a snarl or two he sat down and placidly ate berries, combing through them from a bush into his mouth with his two paws, in alternation. Slowly moved off into the woods as he heard the ranger's truck approaching, on its way to the dump which was his haunt."[25] In Yourcenar's fictional account, "Although bears were rare on the island, where they hardly ever ventured except in winter when the ice supported them, Nathanaël came upon one, completely alone, gathering into his great paw all the raspberries from a bush and stuffing them into his mouth with such an exquisite pleasure that the boy practically experienced it himself."[26]

It is probably not coincidental that in 1959, the year after cancer reared its head, Grace for the first time kept a second daybook, reserving it almost exclusively for observations of nature and experiences likely to feed the human spirit. In this second notebook, "Grace Frick Diary (Part 2)," she might comment on the beauty of snow in the moonlight or list the different species of birds that came to feeders at Petite Plaisance. After dinner on January 12 and again the next day, Grace and Marguerite listened together in the parlor to a recording of Schubert's Quintet in C Major. Long walks and wildlife sightings are described: on March 26, "'Jo' our chipmunk reappeared from under the porch being in strictly private quarters since November. He began working on the west side coconut feeder at once. Looks rather thin, but is as agile as ever."[27] On March 28 the northern lights blazed in the night sky on either side of the Big Dipper. Easter morning found Grace and Marguerite playing a Russian requiem mass on their spinet piano. Then they set off together on foot, in fur coats and rubber-soled shoes, for the Somesville Meeting House almost eight miles away! They probably thought it was a safe bet that someone they knew would pick them up; happily, both ways, someone did.

Frick and Yourcenar had always been attuned to the natural beauty surrounding them on Mount Desert Island, but Grace's observations in this second daybook make clear that she was paying more attention than she ever had before, realizing at some level how fortunate she was to still be there to take it all in. In September of that year, as if to prove to herself how healthy she was, Grace started horseback riding again. Before long she was clearing hurdles at a trot, with and without stirrups. Eventually she would talk Marguerite into joining her.

The women were also redoubling their attention to their own patch of nature. Paul and Gladys Minear had sent them bulbs from Holland, which they got into the ground before winter. Grace wrote to thank them in November, mentioning also the Austrian pine that Paul had planted on their property in 1951. "Marguerite often says, 'Our garden is full of Minears!' You would never believe how passionate she is about digging into the soil around this two-by-four house."[28] Yourcenar was particularly proud of their rare cherry trees, which would often yield a bountiful harvest. To Élie Grekoff she wrote in July about "the ever courageous 'Angel'" Grace: "Right now she is picking Montmorency cherries (for the first time) from the young cherry trees in the garden. And since she is wearing a toile de Jouy dress purchased in Capri with big cherries painted on it, she makes a rather gay figure against the green background."[29]

As the women reconnected with the earth, they were also reviving old friendships and opening up to new ones. Frick joined the Eastern Maine Wellesley Club and attended her first meeting at the Pilot's Grill in Bangor, taking Marguerite along with her.[30] She would make a point of attending her thirty-fifth reunion in June of 1960. The couple renewed ties as well with a man they had known since their 1945 summer stay in Southwest Harbor, Alfred "Alf" Pasquale, who was naturalized as an American in 1957. He and his companion Chuck Curtis had brought Grace bouquets of cosmos to celebrate her recovery from surgery. The two couples often went for picnics, boat rides, and moonlight drives together on the "quiet side" of Mount Desert Island.

In mid-September 1959 Frick and Yourcenar showed up unannounced on the doorstep of the artist Chenoweth Hall and the author Miriam Colwell, having just seen an exhibit of Hall's paintings and sculpture at the Northeast Harbor Neighborhood House.[31] They were on a weekend jaunt up the coast in a rental car. Chenoweth Hall was a transplant from New York City who had moved to Prospect Harbor, where Miriam Colwell was postmistress, in 1939. Hall had read *Memoirs of Hadrian* and could not believe her eyes when its author appeared at her door. The two couples developed a friendship, having tea and sharing meals at each other's homes. They even spoke of going abroad together, though the plan never came to fruition.[32] They had a lot in common in addition to their various kinds of creativity. Like Grace and Marguerite, Miriam and Chenoweth had met and come together in the late 1930s. Both couples were dog lovers. Both loved art and travel. When Chenoweth died in 1999, she and Miriam had shared a home for more than fifty years.[33]

In mid-December 1959 Grace and Marguerite set off on a new trip overseas aboard the TSS *Olympia*, sailing from New York to Portugal. The seas were very strong on that voyage, resulting in a heavy roll that lasted three straight days. For Monsieur and Marguerite, both a bit delicately constituted, it was a long and queasy crossing. For the gale-loving Grace, as much at home rolling in the deep as on the back of a galloping horse, it was pure bliss.

CHAPTER 25 ✂ Travels and Travails Foreign and
Domestic
1960–1962

The magnificent Mississippi, rolling its mile-wide tide along, shining in
the sun.

—Mark Twain

THOUGH MARGUERITE HAD A BAD cold, she and Grace spent several
consecutive late nights enjoying fado music in Lisbon's smoky bars. After
midnight mass on New Year's Eve at the Estrela Basilica, the pair were mes-
merized for hours by the plaintive strains of Herminia Silva at Bairro Alto.
Once Yourcenar had recovered from these overindulgences, she and Frick
visited a few other parts of Portugal: Tomar, Batalha, Aljubarrota, and Óbi-
dos.[1] Their trips often had a literary purpose. One important destination was
the centuries-old pilgrimage site of Santiago de Compostela, to which the
character Zeno would be headed at the opening of *L'Œuvre au Noir*.

This tour of the Iberian Peninsula was very much like the couple's 1958
trip to Italy: carriage rides, social encounters (notably, with Isabel García
Lorca, sister of the assassinated antifascist poet Federico), Roman ruins, long
walks, and museums. Yourcenar gave at least six lectures in Portugal and
Spain, the latter being where the women moved their base of operations
in late March. In Madrid they made five long visits to the Prado, where
they were particularly struck by the early Flemish paintings of Hieronymus
Bosch, Pieter Brueghel the Elder, the Master of Flémalle, Hans Memling,
Joachim Patinir, Rogier van der Weyden, and Jan van Eyck.[2] They were fascinated in April by the events and processions of Holy Week in Seville. On
May 11 they sailed for home.

Awaiting them in Northeast Harbor was Natalie Barney's *Souvenirs indiscrets*, whose author would be eagerly anticipating commentary from her
friends. Yourcenar read the book aloud to Frick in front of the fire. On June
5 she wrote Barney a long and laudatory letter congratulating her friend on

her tact, gentle humor, and perceptiveness regarding those she knew and loved. Alluding to their early discussions of Henry James, Yourcenar playfully imagines the young woman Natalie was when she first saw Belle Époque Paris as "a younger, less chaste sister of Daisy Miller and Isabelle Archer tossed into the Parisian labyrinth of love and society life." In closing, she called their recent European trip "enormously enriching despite an almost constantly rainy winter, even on Madeira, and a case of bronchitis that now seems to be for me a sort of inevitable tribute to the winter months. Here we are back home, I to work on a book, Grace to translate, and both of us to cultivate our garden."[3]

Cultivating their garden was something Frick and Yourcenar took seriously. They were already composting and gardening organically in the 1950s, long before the practice became fashionable. In 1960 they nearly doubled the size of their property, and began to develop a woodland garden, when they finally succeeded in acquiring the lot behind Petite Plaisance.[4] Barney later sent them a one-thousand-dollar gift—a sort of inheritance before the fact— and they decided to credit her with purchasing the coveted half acre. Frick's thank-you letter suggests how much the parcel meant to her companion:

> Marguerite had set her heart on having it after she saw the slashing of the trees there which occurred during one of our absences, and since we have owned it, she has worked between stretches at her desk to cut paths through the brambles and to clear the brush while leaving havens for the birds and ample space for the return of the native ferns, blueberries, and white-flowering bunchberry which grows so low to the ground, as you may remember. Although her health is much better than when we first came up here, she does not take the long walks or climbs for which the Island is best known, so it is of real importance to her to have this bit of wildland so accessible to her, and her own, to do as she wishes with it.[5]

On returning from Europe, it never took the women long to get back into the swing of island life. Summer 1960 brought many get-togethers and outings with friends, among them the Willkies; Agnes Milliken; Mrs. Belmont; Alf Pasquale and Chuck Curtis; Erika Vollger; Elliot and Shirley McGarr; Hortense and Wyncie King; the orchestra conductor Max Rudolf and his wife, Liese; Gertrude Fay, just back from Ireland; Bob and Mary Louise Garrity, at whose lodge on Indian Point Grace and Marguerite enjoyed going for a swim; and various young people who stayed over at Petite Plaisance after dances at the Kimball House a few doors up the street.

Ledlie Dinsmore and her brother Clem, who summered with their family on Greening Island near the mouth of Somes Sound, were among the latter youth. Grace and Marguerite had known their great-great-aunt Henrietta Gardiner, a passionate promoter of social causes, since the 1940s. Always eager to befriend young people, they were happy to help out. Whenever Ledlie and Clem could not row home in pea-soup fog, they spent the night in the guest rooms of Petite Plaisance.

In early September 1960 Grace, who had recently been scaling cliffs in Portugal, fell down the steep stairway at Petite Plaisance in the middle of the night, breaking her left shoulder blade and a bone in her left hand.[6] Almost immediately she began having severe intercostal nerve irritation on the injured side of her body, "much like the pain M.Y. feels above the heart region."[7] By September 20 she had also contracted shingles in her mouth and jaw.

Two changes in the content of the daybooks may relate to her health and state of mind. One involves the level of detail provided by those yearly agendas, which begins an overall decline in 1960.[8] The other concerns a few sharp comments Frick made that October, while she was still receiving treatment for injuries related to her fall. On Sunday, October 30, for example, the women hosted a party for twenty junior high schoolers who were collecting donations for the United Nations Children's Fund. On Halloween the next day Grace wrote irritably, "Ten or twelve smaller children in cheap, foolish costumes came to door. Three repeaters from Sunday were refused as too old for trick or treat." She and Yourcenar hated waste of any kind—and commercially manufactured Halloween costumes would have fit that bill for them both—but Frick loved children, and remarks like that were not typical for her.

Both women were back in high spirits by Christmastime, however, when what Grace called "a bodyguard of ten little boys" paid them a visit with a long-eared friend. Yourcenar described the event at the end of a letter to Jacques Kayaloff, with whom she had spoken by telephone on December 26:

I'm sorry if I may have seemed a bit distracted during our phone conversation last Monday. . . . But nine or ten boys from the village had just come clattering up to our door with a very charming gray donkey named Ebenezer. He was all decked out in ribbons, and hung around his neck was a letter for us (to thank us for sending him a barrel of carrots for Christmas). Monsieur and a dog belonging to one of the boys were barking to their hearts' content. We were serving treats. The donkey was eating peanuts, shells and all. The children were munching on candy. So you can see how hard it would have been, perhaps even unwise, to abandon our guests even for a moment.[9]

Nineteen sixty-one would be a year of American travel and lecturing during which Yourcenar would receive her first honorary doctorate. Grace Frick's friend Charles Hill had been trying for quite some time to get Smith College, in Northampton, Massachusetts, to bring her to campus as a speaker.[10] Hill had served in various capacities at Smith, including dean of the faculty, assistant to the president, and chairman of the English department. André Gide's former son-in-law, Jean Lambert, whom Yourcenar had known for several years, was also teaching at Smith, and Ledlie Dinsmore was a sophomore there that year.

Yourcenar gave three lectures at Smith: "Hellenic History as Seen by the Poets," "Functions and Responsibilities of the Novelist," and "Marcel Proust."[11] Frick and Yourcenar also made a point of seeing Ledlie several times while they were in Northampton. Ledlie eventually moved into Dawes House, Smith's Maison Française.

The most interesting aspect of Frick and Yourcenar's time at Smith may, however, have been what was going on in the background while they were there—namely, as Charles and Ruth Hill called it, the Dorius Affair. It had been only a few months since an infamous McCarthyist scandal had erupted in Northampton involving Newton Arvin, a respected scholar of American literature who had taught at Smith for nearly forty years. Arvin had won the National Book Award for nonfiction and published widely admired biographies of Herman Melville, Walt Whitman, and Nathaniel Hawthorne. On September 2, 1960, he was arrested for obtaining through the mail what was deemed homosexual pornography: photographs of male models that an article years later in the New York Times likened to Calvin Klein underwear ads.[12] To add insult to injury, Arvin was a member of the National Committee for the Defense of Political Prisoners. He was also a close friend of Truman Capote.[13]

Arvin was found guilty of possessing obscene materials, sentenced to a year in jail, and fined twelve hundred dollars. His jail sentence was suspended, apparently in exchange for the names of two Smith colleagues who also collected pornography.[14] One of them was Joel Dorius, who had taught Elizabethan drama at Yale University for nine years before coming to Smith. Among the offensive materials in his possession were photographs of Etruscan wall paintings.[15]

Unlike Newton Arvin, Dorius did not have tenure at Smith and, along with Edward Spofford, he was fired before a verdict on his case was even rendered in court. While Yourcenar and Frick were in Northampton, Smith's trustees were holding heated special sessions related to these two faculty members in which Charles Hill was an active participant. Hill held Dorius's work in high regard, characterizing him to his visiting friends as "a Shakespeare scholar of marked ability."[16] Both he and Ruth felt strongly that Dorius should be reinstated by the school. He would tell Grace in a letter written the day after her departure how much he regretted "the interruptions and tensions which 'L'Affaire Dorius' brought into my existence during your sojourn." At the end of that same letter, he lamented, "Incidentally, our trustees reached a decision which hasn't been announced. I'm afraid I fear the worst."[17] Both Dorius and Spofford were permanently sacked.

I initially wondered if it might have been more than mere coincidence that Yourcenar and Frick, for the first time in their more than two decades together, were lodged in separate quarters during their three nights at Smith. But that unusual fact turns out to have been caused by discrimination of another sort: Frick stayed with Ruth and Charles Hill because the Maison Française, which hosted Yourcenar, did not allow dogs.[18]

In 1963 the Massachusetts Supreme Court overturned the obscenity verdicts against Arvin, Dorius, and Spofford. Smith acknowledged in 2002 that all three professors were wrongfully terminated and created a fund for the study of civil liberties, a lecture series, and an annual American studies stipend in their names.[19] When Yourcenar and Frick returned to Northampton in June of 1961 for Yourcenar's honorary doctorate, the author stayed at the home of Smith's president Thomas Mendenhall, and Frick bunked again with Ruth and Charles Hill.[20] Just around the corner from the Hills' residence on Crescent Street, two stately old homes stood side by side that would soon be taken over by Smith to serve as dormitories. They would be named after the renowned medievalist Eleanor Duckett and her novelist companion Mary Ellen Chase, who were a professorial force to be reckoned with at Smith for forty years. In subtle homage to the lifelong companions, Duckett House and Chase House were architecturally united in 1973.[21]

Yourcenar's talks at Smith College were just the beginning of a long tour during which the author gave lectures in Connecticut, Pennsylvania, Virginia, and Kentucky. Subjects included "Christian Thought in French Literature," "The Universe of Proust," and "Attitudes toward War in French Literature." On March 25 Frick left Yourcenar and Monsieur at Louisville's Watterson Hotel and departed for a week in Kansas City. On March 29 a Dr.

McDonnell in that city informed her that two nodules in her right armpit must be "promptly" excised. But the only thing Grace did promptly was return to Marguerite in Louisville, where the two would board the *Delta Queen* on April 2 for a trip down the Mississippi River.

The weather was very fine that day, and when the boat stopped in Paducah, Kentucky, the women got off to see the hardware store where Uncle George LaRue had been working when he married Aunt Dolly. In Memphis and again in Natchez the azaleas were in bloom, and the couple were treated to the sight and song of the mockingbird. In New Orleans they explored the French Quarter and caught a show at the fabled Club My-O-My, known despite laws against female impersonation for "the world's most beautiful boys in female attire."[22] It was *the* place to be in mid-twentieth-century New Orleans for both locals and tourists. A highlight of the rest of their stay was Audubon Park, with its hundreds of wading birds. By the time they got off the *Delta Queen* in Cincinnati on April 21, they had spent almost three weeks on the Mississippi or exploring ports of call along its banks.

The river cruise made a lasting impression on both women. Years later Yourcenar would remember it in the preface to *Blues et gospels*:

> It was slow and beautiful. In the evening we would sometimes moor at the edge of small, half-submerged islands haunted by the songs of birds. The crew and the staff were black and, in our regard, full of the kindness particular to people of color as soon as they sense sympathy rather than condescension. We were invited to the evening religious service on the little rear deck that was reserved for them. The river flowed in waves, sometimes rapid, sometimes sluggish and murky, reddened by the setting sun. "*Deep river, dark river.*" Those warm voices, whose cracks and discordances I was just beginning to get used to, seemed to arise from the depths of a temperament, of a race, at once present and past.[23]

During this descent into the South, both women found themselves face-to-face with what Yourcenar would later call "the misery of the Blacks and their fight for integration."[24] As the 1960s unfolded, that fight became increasingly important to them.

Finally, on April 26, almost a month after Dr. McDonnell found two suspicious lumps on her chest, Frick was hospitalized in Bar Harbor to be operated on, as in 1958, by Dr. Silas Coffin. Amazingly, Monsieur went to the veterinary clinic the same day to have two warts removed. Dr. Coffin used a local anesthetic. Dr. Cameron, the veterinarian, put Monsieur lightly under and flushed the channels of his ears. Frick's nodules were duly removed, and she was kind enough to mention in the daybook, despite giving more detail about the dog than herself, that the pathology report came back clean. There was no malignancy.

In the late summer of 1961 Marguerite momentously decided to join Grace in one of her favorite pursuits, horseback riding. On the afternoon of August 30 Marguerite had a brief lesson at the same Jordan Pond stable from which she and Grace regularly took carriage rides in Acadia Park. Under the tutelage of a fifteen-year-old instructor named Lynn Ahlblad, a horse lover whose family ran a shop in Bar Harbor, Yourcenar rode Dallas that first day. Not everyone was convinced that she was cut out to be a rider. As her friend Shirley McGarr once said,

> I've told you what a marvelous horsewoman Grace was, just wonderful. And of course Madame Yourcenar couldn't care less about that, that was not in her world. But she did it to be with Grace. . . . Grace looked *great* on a horse 'cause she was tall and angular, but Madame Yourcenar was just plunked there, you know? And I'm not meaning that in a derogatory sense. That's the way her body was built. She was not built for a horsewoman. But she did it, and she'd sit there and she'd kind of grin, you know, that grin she had . . . But she would do things that Grace . . . that meant a lot to her.[25]

Lynn Ahlblad remembers the experience vividly—and well she should, since Frick had invented "the scheme" of having the poor girl teach Yourcenar how to ride in French! Ahlblad speaks of "Madame" wearing the same beatific smile that Shirley McGarr mentions in describing her horseback riding efforts. She also recalls that both women, who of course invited her to Sunday tea, were "very interested in kids, and *very* generous and gracious." Chuckling at the memory, Ahlblad adds, "Sometimes Grace could be a little overbearing, but, you know, it's always nice when children have that connection with brilliance."[26]

Yourcenar continued to take lessons that fall and eventually caught the riding bug. It's not hard to imagine, given how much she loved horses, with her and Grace never missing a chance to visit ones they knew around the island. By mid-October Frick was driving Yourcenar to Bangor for more advanced lessons with Alejandro Solorzano at the Forward Seat School of Horsemanship. Altogether, before winter set in, Yourcenar took ten lessons with that former member of the Brazilian Olympic team.[27]

FIGURE 33. Grace Frick and Marguerite Yourcenar in the saddle, early 1960s. Petite Plaisance Archives.

It cannot have been easy for someone with Yourcenar's sense of personal dignity—to say nothing of her stature as a writer—to attempt a pursuit that, while second nature to her partner, was not at all natural for her. Yourcenar did not have the build of an equestrian. Nor had she ever been an athlete. Her general health, moreover, was not vigorous. Yet it is clear from all reports that, knowing how much it meant to Frick, she gave herself over to riding with humility and grace. For her trouble, as she wrote a few years later, she would gain "one of the most profoundly lived parts of my life."[28]

In the space allotted to January 1, 1962, at the end of the 1961 daybook Grace made a note to herself: "Apply for new passports." She and Marguerite had decided, contrary to their usual practice, to take a monthlong cruise to their beloved Scandinavia that also included stops in Iceland and, most intriguingly, the Soviet Union. After spending a night with the Minears in New Haven, they would board the SS *Argentina* in New York City on June 11. The cruise was so thoroughly packed with activities—one is tempted to say antics, judging from the photographic memorabilia—that Grace merely listed them in the daybook. But they did see some spectacular fjords and waterfalls along the way in this season of the midnight sun.

Yourcenar later wrote about the trip to her Italian translator, Lidia Storoni Mazzolani: "This year we contented ourselves with a cruise to Scandinavia; it was the first time we took a chance on this mode of transport, which is hardly made for serious travelers. I'm quite sure that it will be a one-time experience; nonetheless, it provided us a few admirable days along the coast of Norway and Iceland, and the pleasure of spending a few days once again in two cities that are very dear to us, Copenhagen and, especially, Stockholm."[29]

What intrigued Frick and Yourcenar about this particular cruise was the possibility of spending three days in Leningrad. They viewed it as a chance to get a sense of the new Russia before deciding whether to make a longer journey there. Yourcenar's letter to Mazzolani, written shortly after the Cuban Missile Crisis of 1962, attracted a lot of attention when it was published after her death—she forbade it to appear during her lifetime—because of its extremely frank assessment of the USSR. Her and Frick's short stay in Leningrad, said Yourcenar,

> had an effect on me (and also on Grace) that I had not anticipated; all in all, as far as I'm concerned, it was one of immense discouragement. What had I hoped to find? I certainly had not counted on a glimpse of Eldorado. But, reacting no doubt against America's stupid anticommunist propaganda, with its infantile clichés, no doubt I believed I would at least encounter a newer world, perhaps a more "vital" one, even if that world were hostile or foreign to us. What I found, from the moment at dawn on the first day when we caught sight of the Russian officials boarding the boat in the fog until the sleepless night of the third day . . . was quite simply the Russia of Custine, that eternal mixture of bureaucratic routine, suspiciousness of strangers, an already Oriental nonchalance, and prudent mistrust; and that inert and almost suffocating sadness that so often appears in Russian novels, which I did not expect to find there still.[30]

Not surprisingly, she and Frick decided not to return to the Soviet Union.

CHAPTER 26 ❦ The Wages of Success
1962–1964

> Then, rising with Aurora's light,
> The Muse invoked, sit down to write;
> Blot out, correct, insert, refine,
> Enlarge, diminish, interline.

> —Jonathan Swift

SINCE THE BRIEF HIATUS FROM normal life occasioned by Grace Frick's cancer in 1958, much had been accomplished in terms of new writing, translations, and the revision or reissue of previously published books. *Présentation critique de Constantin Cavafy*, containing Yourcenar's essay on the Greek poet and the poems jointly translated with Constantine Dimaras, was finally published at Gallimard in 1958.[1] Her examination of the *Gita Govinda* came out in 1957, and Frick began translating it into English the same year.[2] Entitled "The Legend of Krishna: Notes on Erotic and Mystical Themes," the translation appeared in the British-based literary magazine *Encounter* in December 1959.[3] A "definitive" reworking of the 1934 *Denier du rêve* was also released in 1959. Two years later Yourcenar published a play based on this antifascist work entitled *Rendre à César*.[4] She had begun taking notes for her essay on the eighteenth-century Italian artist Giovanni Battista Piranesi's *Carceri d'invenzione*, in the late 1950s. "Le Cerveau noir de Piranèse" would appear for the first time in 1961 as the preface to a book of reproductions of the *Carceri* and was then included in the 1962 collection *Sous bénéfice d'inventaire*. Frick began translating "Ah, mon beau château" from *Sous bénéfice d'inventaire* in August 1961 and *Denier du rêve* two months later.

Marguerite told Natalie Barney later that year that Grace was resuming her translation of *Denier*, which she had interrupted the previous spring: "With the energy you're well acquainted with, she wears herself out working, which is very bad, but how can one stop her? (Then again, I am doing pretty much the same thing.)"[5]

Having enjoyed writing dialogue for *Rendre à César*, in late 1962 Yourcenar put the finishing touches on the two plays she had written during her first summers on Mount Desert Island. The Parisian theater director Maurice Jacquemont wrote asking for permission to mount *Le Mystère d'Alceste* in 1963, and Yourcenar granted him rights to the work for two years. Both that play and *Qui n'a pas son Minotaure?* would be published by Éditions Plon in June of 1963. A revised edition of *Nouvelles orientales* came out that year, too.

Yourcenar also received a few honors in the late 1950s and early 1960s. *Les Charités d'Alcippe*, the source of so much discord when it was published by Alexis Curvers, garnered Natalie Barney's Prix Renée Vivien—unanimously, it seems—on June 30, 1958. Created to honor women poets writing in French, the prize was named for one of Natalie's early lovers, the British-born poet Pauline Tarn, whose pseudonym was Renée Vivien.[6]

Further homage came in the form of a plaster bust created in 1962 by Malvina Hoffman. A telegram from "Grace and Marguerite" announced, "statue just arrived and safely/very very fine the finish and color both sympathiques/very happy to possess a bit of you/our love and gratitude."[7] Marguerite's thank-you letter to Malvina elaborates on the same theme. She and Grace had installed the bust in the parlor of Petite Plaisance:

> That image of myself interests and touches me enormously; at times it seems so much wiser and stronger than I am. I suppose that's the great gift that sculpture gives us. I am going to attempt to make myself resemble it.
>
> Grace tells me that she has learned more about sculpture by circling that head, and no doubt by comparing it to its model, than she ever did over many years spent visiting museums. And since, no matter how faithful is the artwork to its model, artists always put a bit of themselves into their works (Leonardo da Vinci knew this), we are happy to possess a bit of Malvina's mind along with the work of her hand. And, once again, I am infinitely moved that the kind attention of that mind settled for a moment on my face.
>
> All our affectionate thoughts and our gratitude to the two of you,
> Marguerite[8]

Rounding out this midcareer spate of honors was the Prix Combat. That prize was awarded in February of 1963 for *Sous bénéfice d'inventaire* and the entirety of Yourcenar's oeuvre.[9] All the while Yourcenar was conjuring her next major work, *L'Œuvre au Noir*.

She was also engaged in what ended up being a drawn-out epistolary exchange about Natalie Barney's *L'Amour défendu*, which the feminist scholar Blanche Wiesen Cook has called "a celebration of lesbianism."[10] As Barney wrote to "My Dears" in late 1960, "I am preparing a new book with the half that Flammarion suppressed in my 'Souvenirs,' and how valuable your advice would be concerning my essay on 'l'amour défendu' in it. And also on my chapters about Gide etc."[11] The following July, she sent the page proofs of her essays seeking Yourcenar's "approval or disapproval."[12]

Yourcenar no doubt read the essays to Frick, as she had *Souvenirs indiscrets*. It is likely a measure of her discomfort with Natalie's offhand approach to "a subject that is all in all so serious" that she took so long to respond:

> Full of shame for having let a month go by without answering you, I am finally returning your proofs, which I have hung on to unpardonably. . . . Very dear Friend, you do not need my *imprimatur* . . .
>
> Viewing things from your point of view, it seems to me that you would do better to publish the essay, first because you evidently wish it to appear, and second, especially, because its content is so essentially your own. From my own point of view, which you request, but which in this case surely matters much less, I would on the contrary hesitate. . . . Not on account of the ideas or opinions that the essay contains, about which on the whole I agree with you (though it seems that I see the same facts in a slightly different way and in a different light), but because the tone is not what I would rather have seen you choose.[13]

Yourcenar did not discuss her sexuality publicly, in part for fear of being pigeonholed. But no matter the topic at hand, she almost always went directly to the heart of it. To one persistent interviewer's questions regarding same-sex love she exasperatedly replied, "But what is love? This kind of ardor, of warmth, that propels one inexorably toward another being? Why give so much importance to a person's genitourinary system? It does not define a whole being, and it is not even erotically true. What matters, as I said, concerns emotions, relationships."[14] Barney, for her part, did not answer Yourcenar's letter until Christmas 1961: "Marguerite quite won me over with her way of criticizing my 'Amour Défendu.' But the public would hardly welcome a serious and less flippant way of presenting that still ridiculously 'taboo' subject."[15]

More than a year later, perhaps not so won over after all, she brought the matter up again: "I have . . . had the weakness to let the 'Mercure de France' print those pages on 'l'amour défendu' etc. which you, Marguerite, so wisely condemned! I could perhaps have faced that subject with less frivolity, as my life represents it! . . . I have never had to struggle against myself—hence probably my flippancy and your just reproaches!"[16]

Yourcenar may have disappointed Barney again by refusing to contribute to a special issue of the London-based literary magazine *ADAM International Review* entitled "The Amazon of Letters: A World Tribute to Natalie Clifford Barney."[17] Though she declined the invitation to join in that public salute, she read the result and wrote to Barney about it in July of 1963:

> I refused, not for the reason given by Janet Flanner, but as I have always done since the essay honoring Thomas Mann. That text was supposed to be just a few lines, but it ended up dragging me through forty-five printed pages and into themes as muddled as art and life, eroticism, humanism, occultism. . . . Incapable as I am of the short view, of the brief and telling remembrance for which you, on the contrary, are gifted, if I had accepted this gentleman's proposition, I would rapidly have found myself stopped dead in my tracks, or on the contrary I would have foundered in drawers full of notes, beneath reams of paper and torrents of ink, indeed everything one would need to write the "Memoirs of Natalie" or "The Dark Brain of Natalie," which I am not, however, qualified to do.[18]

Yourcenar's reluctance to participate in the Barney tribute likely also had to do with a wish to keep her distance from the kind of flippancy on the topic of lesbianism that she found in *L'Amour défendu*. But the memories of Natalie that she was disinclined to voice publicly she willingly communicated privately. Yourcenar had known *of* Barney long before the two women met:

> During the years 1929–1939, I had heard a lot about you from Edmond [Jaloux], and also from Jean Royère, who published some of my poems around that time and who saw you from more of a distance, with the somewhat naïve simplifications of a poet seeking myths everywhere rather than human beings. You amazed the one and enchanted the other; and the *pavillon* on rue Jacob, which would later grow amiably familiar to me, seemed through their eyes and those of a few others as fabulous as the one in *The Girl with the Golden Eyes*.[19]

Later in her letter, Yourcenar praised the woman she now knew firsthand: "I have been particularly grateful to you for having escaped the intellectual viruses of this half-century, for having been neither psychoanalyzed, nor an existentialist, nor busy performing gratuitous acts, but for having remained faithful on the contrary to what your mind, your senses, and indeed your good sense told you."[20]

It wasn't until later that fall that a rather apprehensive Natalie Barney responded to Yourcenar's letter of personal remembrance, addressing her own lengthy missive, with what one suspects to be wheedling intent, to "Dear great writer and precious friend." Barney, it turns out, had shown Yourcenar's thoughtful remarks about her friend to the author Yvon Bizardel, who she feared might wish to use them in an article about her, and to Jean Chalon, a journalist for *Le Figaro littéraire*, who did just that. Chalon, who later became Barney's biographer, published in *Le Figaro* Yourcenar's comment about Natalie having avoided the intellectual viruses of the twentieth century, which Barney "had had the indiscretion to show him." "Am I forgiven," Natalie asked, "for sharing with others your letter about me? It seems a shame for that piece of writing not to have, aside from myself, the public it deserves. If perchance you could give your consent?"[21] Two days later, on November 16, Natalie mailed Grace another check for a thousand dollars! Doubtless seeking absolution, Barney wrote, "Grace dear, I thank you for making me homesick for Mount Desert—where I never faced winters such as you most

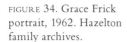

FIGURE 34. Grace Frick portrait, 1962. Hazelton family archives.

excellently describe! Are you again to weather it? . . . Do allow me to send
you and Marguerite this little gift—a token of my admiration and friendship
and with love, Natalie."[22]

The excellent description of winter on Mount Desert to which Barney
refers was Grace Frick's only known foray into published writing in her own
name. It was the foreword to the 1963 seasonal social register known as the
Island Red Book.

These forewords, known as "Greetings," were occasionally written by island notables such as the historian Samuel Eliot Morison (in 1952) or the
TV personality Garry Moore (1974). Like all *Red Book* forewords, Frick's
composition addresses "people from away" who either own summer homes
or vacation in Northeast Harbor or Seal Harbor. It offers at once a lively picture of the island in winter, a paean to the natural beauty of that season, and
a subtle plea to readers to protect island flora and fauna:

> "What is it like here in winter?"
>
> Well, this was a winter worth asking about, worthy of "the year of the
> eclipse," and almost as impressive as that event! Our final snowstorm, on May
> 11, lasted twenty-four hours and added one more record to those already set
> for depth and duration of snowfall in this area. You will see traces of the early
> storms for some time to come, for trees were uprooted by the hundred here and
> on the outlying islands. May we learn from the havoc to take better care of the
> woods which are still left standing.
>
> During even the worst blizzards, however, we could see the blink of the
> snowplows or hear the comforting chug as they burrowed their way, often
> after midnight, through the drifts which our roads had become; linemen and
> power crews answered our calls at all hours; school buses strained through their
> rounds, with rare exceptions. The mailboat plied its daily course to and from
> the Cranberries, sometimes on spectacular seas, and wind permitting, the hum
> of a lobsterman's motor could always be heard offshore. Innumerable meetings
> and social gatherings were held as usual, if not always on the exact date sched-
> uled! Church services seldom had to be cancelled; rummage was collected
> and sold by the bale, fair upon fair ushered in Christmas. Concerts (local and
> imported), theatricals, competitions, all were warmly attended. Merchants and
> deliverymen, office and laboratory workers, teachers, hospital personnel and
> volunteers took the hazards of transit in their stride (or in their slide, according
> to the manner and condition of their locomotion), and most of the services
> listed in this book, along with many others, were kept going in some form
> throughout the long months of what was extreme cold for this coastal region.

Caretakers, though freed of their garden duties, fought their way through tree-blocked drives to reach cottages banked in snow, and to shovel excess weight from roofs built originally for far lighter wear. Saturdays and Sundays were busy days on McFarland Hill, where two of our residents already fully employed have long given free lessons in skiing, and where more than one father has donated his spare hours to keep the ski-tow running. Bird feeders required constant refilling, but more than paid for their cost in suet and sunflower seed when redpolls and Eastern evening grosbeaks added their flashes of color to our year-round tenants, the chickadees and purple finches. The deer of the island are still officially protected inhabitants, but are the subject of pending legislation, and it is up to us all to consider with care the bills which would open this traditional haven to checked jackets and guns which stalk the whole state of Maine elsewhere in November and December.

Along with the difficulties and some actual hardships, but certain triumphs, too, which are a part of wintering on an island in Maine, there are also beauties unique to the season. Would that more of our summer residents and guests could see these mountains under blankets of snow. (Some few migrants manage to do so each year, and report that they feel well rewarded.) On sunny days, which are frequent even in severe cold, the light is brilliant and all contours change; the shadow of the spruce woods grows more intense against the veritable sea of white. In November, after the deciduous trees are finally stripped of their leaves, the great boulders stand out plainly on every summit, and the deep rich tones of the varied granites come into full play. Then, perhaps overnight, all color is gone beneath the sky: stony crest and needled pine or spruce alike are rounded over with a strangely soft substance which wholly transforms the known world. Sea-spray dashed on the rocks of Ocean Drive freezes before it alights, and Sargeant Drive's cliffs fairly gleam with frozen cascades. Nothing is wholly silent, though it may seem so at first. The thud of heavy snow is heard falling as the resilient branches free themselves one by one; now a creak and then a rumble like some subterranean noise comes from the ice along the shore; and from out in the middle of the Sound, where they love to congregate in vast assemblies for days and weeks at a time, rises the incessant chatter of the old squaws, most talkative of our migrant sea duck. These are only a few of the subtler rhythms of winter on Mount Desert. May you enjoy the summer the more for the mysterious period of suspense, and we hope enrichment, which the island has gone through.[23]

During the summer heralded by Frick's foreword, one of South Shore Road's seasonal families held a noteworthy social event. The invitation to it was sent to "Monsieur, c/o Miss Frick" by Grace and Marguerite's canine next-door neighbor:

> Dear Monsieur,
>   Please come to my birthday party, Friday at 5:30.
>   Supper will be served. Please bring leash.
>   Teddy Rosengarten[24]

Yourcenar, not Frick, answered the apparently bilingual hound in French on Monsieur's behalf:

> Dear Sir and Friend,
>   I am delighted to accept the invitation to celebrate the day of your birth on Friday, August 23, at five-thirty. (I have to admit that I have already dined on your provisions, yesterday, without telling you, having found a delicious bone on your kitchen porch, which I rapidly and silently took home with me.)
>   As you request, I will bring my two mistresses along with me on a leash and will do my best to ensure that they behave appropriately.
>   Your faithful neighbor,
>   Monsieur the Black[25]

By mid–October Monsieur the Black's mistresses were making reservations for a grand tour of Egypt and the Levant, where neither of them had ever been. Grace spoke of their plans in her thank-you letter to Natalie Barney:

> Dear and very generous Natalie,
>   Your gift to Marguerite, with our two names on it, was cashed without difficulty by the local bank and deposited promptly in the "travel fund," from which it will soon be drawn for use on the high seas. Marguerite has not as yet gone east of Smyrna (except for one voyage on the Black Sea) and she has long planned to visit Beirut and Israel, so this seems to be the winter. We had taken passage for this very day on the passenger-cargo boat, *Excalibur*, but recently postponed it for a December sailing, owing to the pressure of desk work here.[26]

Events were soon to take a less desirable turn on more than one front. On November 22, 1963, John F. Kennedy was assassinated in Dallas at the age of forty-six. His death was devastating for both Frick and Yourcenar, who had voted for the promising young senator with the French-speaking wife three years earlier, seeing in his youthful dynamism, progressive vision, and growing commitment to civil rights the makings of an effective national leader. They who had been members of the Mount Desert Island Committee for Peace since the previous March, and who soon would join the Civil Rights Committee then forming, saw Kennedy as embodying their hope for social justice.[27] Yourcenar told Barney a week later that she had been on the verge of sitting down to add her thanks to those of Grace, when

> a neighbor called us with the dreadful news of the shooting that cost President Kennedy his life, and, like the rest of the world, we spent the three days that followed near the television set or the radio, full of horror for this stupid act of violence and pity for that man cut off in mid-career, who seemed to be on his way to becoming a great statesman. . . . Moreover, we are stupefied by the "tough-guy," crime-thriller aspect of the murder of the man accused of the crime, and by this "good-guy" dance hall manager taking into his own hands the vengeance of a chief of state (and eliminating thus forever, deliberately or not, the possibility of learning more about the authors of the murder and the causes). Just as Proust marveled that Rasputin's death was such a "Russian" crime, we cannot get over the fact that the details of the tragedy in Dallas are so "American."[28]

Grace echoed her companion's remarks in a letter to Gladys Minear in early December: "In the desperate self-questioning of the first days, asking ourselves what has been our failure, each of us, that the nation should burst into sympathy for a brave widow and children, yet accept as legitimate, apparently, the night club operator ever in cahoots with the police (accepted for three generations now in the crime stories of every newsstand and grocery store bookstand)."[29]

Four days after the assassination, Frick and Yourcenar staged a "Greek and Roman Exhibition" for the sophomore history class at the high school that Grace proceeded to describe to Gladys. This impromptu event was inspired by a neighbor boy's keen reaction to a television program he had just seen on classical Greece. No doubt feeling that it was a way to reconnect with first principles amid the chaos of the previous days, the women "stopped all work in progress to invite the class down for a session." They put all their Greek artifacts in the parlor to the left of the front door and everything Roman in the living room. Frick then

> shot the boys and the instructor into the parlor for M.Y. to speak on Greek things, and I began with the girls on Rome, the door seriously shut between

our two voices. After some fifteen minutes I shifted my group to the kitchen, where we had laid out a Greco-Roman repast, planned to instruct rather than to delight (!!): yellow-eyed beans, boiled with bits of braised bacon added, red kidney beans boiled and dressed with olive oil and a little vinegar, all eaten with a spoon, Roman fashion—with two small silver spoons to show which are copies from the Museum in Pompeii; olives, bread (dark) without butter, but with chunks of honey in the comb; radishes; a basket tray of fruit and vegetables as near like a Roman mosaic as we could get it; "wine," made of grape juice, water, lemon juice and honey, heated, which went down with immense satisfaction, we noted; cheese and dark rye bread with sesame seeds.[30]

The girls were then sent out the kitchen door toward the parlor for Greece, while the boys took over the food.

A few weeks later Yourcenar read *Seeds of Destruction* by the peace and justice-minded Cistercian monk Thomas Merton. In the journal she was keeping at the time, she transcribed a passage from Merton's "Letters to a White Liberal" regarding the racism associated with the Kennedy assassination: "It has been said often enough, but not too often, that the President had already been killed a thousand times over by the thoughts and the words, spoken or printed, of the racists." Neither Kennedy nor most Americans had understood, in Merton's view, that "where minds are full of hatred and where imaginations dwell on cruelty, torment, punishment, revenge, and death, then inevitably there will be violence and death."[31]

Yourcenar did not need convincing on that score. Soon she would be tracing, in *Fleuve profond, sombre rivière*, the "immemorial chronicle of violence and exploitation of the Negro."[32] As Bérengère Deprez has noted, Yourcenar's examination in the mid-1960s of the plight of U.S. blacks was one "non-violent way of taking part in the civil rights struggle."[33] And struggle we must, as Frick took it upon herself to tell a Canadian admirer of *Hadrian* who wrote seeking "advice on intellectual life":

I can only wish for you as a very young person still, the thrill of finding the universe grow more wonderful every day, and your own life the richer therefore, and the determination to fight what is bad in our humankind to the detriment of what is good. Lest you think that I deal in mere abstractions, let me say that I have had an unusual number of phone calls today, all ostensibly on domestic or social matters, but that two of them dealt with problems of civil rights on the local level, one with the question of the U.N. and Cyprus, and four on a matter of laziness and error on the part of a local reporter. All involved protest against errors already committed, but the protest was made in order to cut down the same error, if possible, in the future. We both feel strongly about the power of the minority to guide opinion, and about the duty of the minority to [bear witness].[34]

As Frick once wrote to her niece Kathie, "I firmly believe that even one person can move mountains if he starts up the machinery."[35]

On December 1, 1963, Grace and Marguerite were having tea at Petite Plaisance with their Prospect Harbor friends Chenoweth Hall and Miriam Colwell and excitedly describing their imminent voyage to the Middle East. The next day Frick was at the doctor's office having two small lumps removed at the site of her original incision. They turned out to be malignant.[36] There would be no trip to Spain or Egypt or Lebanon. Instead of exploring Barcelona or Beirut, Grace—joined again by Marguerite—began a new round of radiation treatments on December 20. On Christmas Eve, after driving to Bangor in a rented car for her third treatment, the couple went to Blue Hill to attend a "Live Nativity pageant" that was held on the town green that evening.[37] It was a bitterly cold but beautiful night. They stayed to see the pageant twice, "in the open air, so moving it was with live figures and a live sheep chewing peacefully in the manger."[38] From that day through the next five X-ray sessions, Frick went alone or with a Northeast Harbor neighbor to Bangor, Yourcenar having caught such a terrible chill at Blue Hill that she was ill for over a week. Frick weathered both the cold and the radiation treatments with her usual vigor. Yourcenar was finally well enough to accompany her to her tenth and final treatment. On January 14, 1964, word came from a laboratory in Philadelphia that a suspicious-looking X-ray taken in December was normal. As Frick confidently wrote in the daybook, "This good report closes a bad episode."[39]

That same day she sent a night letter to the American Export Lines hoping to secure a spare berth on the SS *Exeter* for a February crossing to Poland. In the end she and Yourcenar would instead leave in April on the *Bathory*, reviving a plan they had made the previous year. Grace, it almost seems, could not conceive of being ill; and being alive, for both her and Marguerite, meant sailing the high seas.

CHAPTER 27 ✿ Three Crossings
1964–1965

The irreversible begins at every corner we turn.

—Marguerite Yourcenar

"SOMETHING SEEMS TO HAVE HAPPENED to my mind!" Grace Frick wrote to Gladys Minear a week after her radiation treatments ended. She had announced her clean bill of health to a long list of people but neglected to inform the Minears. "I was evidently expecting you to get our good news by osmosis!!" As Frick went on to say, "this minor flurry involved quite a bit of inquiry at other hospitals. . . . Naturally, having bothered everyone from here to Houston, Texas, I had to write to give a final report, medically speaking, and can only be grateful that it could be a good report."[1]

Marguerite Yourcenar wasn't convinced. With Frick on her usual trip to Kansas City before sailing to Europe, she expressed her concern to Natalie Barney: "Grace is feeling well, and still has her extraordinary energy (she is traveling at the moment in the Midwest) but an acute alarm was sounded this winter—a recurrence of the cancer we thought cured for more than five years. The treatments checked the spread of the disease, but the doctor and I remain worried. All we can do is live from day to day with ardor and with wisdom (such wisdom as we have) and tell ourselves that days placed end to end make up months and weeks, and hope that they make years."[2]

From the moment they left Northeast Harbor heading for Quebec and the ship that would take them to Europe, Yourcenar worried that Frick was over-exerting herself. We have a detailed, sometimes poignant description of this trip to Denmark, Poland, Czechoslovakia, Austria, Italy, and Spain thanks to Yourcenar's unpublished "Traversée sur le *Bathory*." Uncharacteristically, it contains a few personal remarks, for example, about Grace buying herself a pair of walking shoes or "some chocolate and two rolls" for them to share.

One of the text's major themes, a theme not unrelated to Frick's health, is the precariousness of human connection.

Departing on April 3, 1964, the couple drove the nearly three hundred miles to Quebec City on frozen roads through the still-wintry forest of northwestern Maine and eastern Canada. Their rental car was soon covered with muddy stalactites, and the icy roadway made for a nerve-racking ride. They arrived, wrote Yourcenar, at the very last minute to find that all the other passengers—Poles, Danes, Hungarians, a "soft and effeminate Englishman," a "sick old Ukrainian"—had been on board for hours already. Frick and Yourcenar traveled first class along with five others. Since the pet quarters below deck were "disgraceful," they kept Monsieur in their cabin.[3]

After disembarking in Copenhagen, the women traveled to the Polish town of Sopot on the Baltic Sea, where they found a good chauffeur to show them around. They were struck here as they had been in Russia by the lack of concern for public spaces. Children played in rubble left over from the war. A "sordid pile of overflowing garbage cans" adorned the courtyard of a lovely old home near Sopot's town hall; trash had not been collected for weeks.[4]

The friendly driver pointed out the concrete building where he shared two rooms on the fourth floor with his wife and son. There was no elevator, he explained, but they had running water and heat. This was a source of pride and a feeling that progress was being made. In "Traversée," however, Yourcenar is skeptical:

This fragile progress, exposed to the bombardments of the future, itself depends on an industrial concentration and human overproduction equally harmful to the earth and to man. They gave no more thought here than in Sicily or Provence to forming a strong agricultural society in harmony with a healthy region. What was, and was bad, by which I mean the great territorial domains of absentee landlords with no regard for the prosperity of the peasants, was neither reformed nor improved upon but destroyed in favor of artificial and totalitarian societies such as they all are today that have broken off contact with life and with things. There is nothing political about what I'm saying: the same reflections would come to mind on the outskirts of Paris or in Bangor, Maine. To an often despicable past we have substituted an unsustainable present.[5]

This brokenness at the level of society is echoed by the tenuousness of human bonds:

We had promised to send some geographical maps to the [chauffeur's] handsome child, who collects them. Regrettably, G lost the notebook containing his name and address: the boy must think we have forgotten him. This little incident is for me a new example of the precariousness of human relations that I think about so often. The beings whom we meet and leave become lost in the multitudes like fish in the sea and the dead in death. . . . The irreversible begins at every corner we turn.[6]

As if to pass in review some of Yourcenar's broken connections, "Traversée" then enumerates the various Poles with whom the author has crossed paths: the child Maria, once her playmate on a Belgian beach; Theodore de Wyzewa, a translator of Russian novels, and his wife, Isabelle, who had taught French literature in New York; Bronislaw Malinowski and his wife, Valetta. But the Pole recalled most vividly is a woman from Marguerite's Mediterranean-traveling past:

Then there was Sashia Baldovinetta. (Where did she get that graceful, Italian-sounding last name—from an ancestor come to Italy in the entourage of a Jagiellon? Perhaps it was a nom de guerre . . .) I had met her in Athens, where she performed in a little nightclub. She had no talent, but she was a blond girl with laughing blue eyes, at once slim and round, who had the charm of a young German farm girl. By chance, we met again on a crossing to Venice, I coming from Athens (or was it Rhodes?), she from Alexandria. She had had success as a prostitute in Egypt and quietly put money aside for her good mother in Warsaw and to set herself up for the future in Poland when she "would marry to someone." A little wife with an uneventful life. We parted in Venice after having presented each other with gifts—she giving me a string of red cut glass hearts, and I her a necklace of blue cut glass. And since that time? Had she become a heroine of the Polish resistance? Or, continuing to ply her little trade with German officers, had she turned into one of those women whose heads were photographed by the Nazis' anthropometric service and who gaze at you unforgettably from the walls of Auschwitz, almost unidentifiable, their faces all alike with those clear, wide-open eyes and features sharpened by hunger?[7]

Knowing Yourcenar's early tendency to base her fictional characters on people she knew and felt strongly about, one can't help but wonder whether Sashia may have been a model for the prostitute Lina Chiari in Denier du rêve. One might also be justified in speculating that there's more to the story of Sashia than Yourcenar is letting on.

Although the link between Baldovinetta and Chiari is mere conjecture, there is no doubt about the connection between this trip to Central Europe and *L'Œuvre au Noir*. Yourcenar's published essay on composing that book, "Carnets de notes de *L'Œuvre au Noir*," informs us that "it was in June 1964 in Salzburg, as I was attending mass (kneeling on the flagstone floor) in the church of the Franciscans, that I saw for the first time a complete vision of the character of the Prior of the Cordeliers. Until then I had only caught sight of the environs (the mentions of the Prior in 'Return to Bruges')."[8] In the essay "Mirror-Games and Will-o'-the-Wisps," from 1975, Yourcenar remembered things a bit differently: "In 1964, as I was working on the third section of *The Abyss* during a stay in Central Europe, I saw in my mind's eye, in the church of the Franciscans in Salzburg, the character of the Prior of the Cordeliers appear, who was utterly unforeseen until that moment and whose introduction partly changed the direction and meaning of the work."[9]

These recollections, with their varying emphases, point to the role of spontaneous inner vision in Yourcenar's process of writing and highlight the way this author seemed almost to be traversed by her most important characters and plots rather than consciously creating or even intentionally summoning them. Another reflection related to *The Abyss* illustrates these points even more vividly. In the "Carnets" Yourcenar calls her initial portrait of Zeno, written in 1924 and published ten years later, "awkward and naïve." At the age of twenty she had conceived of her sixteenth-century intellectual as someone who knew all the answers. That early version of Zeno evolved over the decades into the exceptional protagonist of the author's creative maturity. One of the most important aspects of his development, and indeed of the narrative more generally, impressed itself upon Yourcenar's consciousness one evening in Southwest Harbor, across the mouth of Somes Sound from Northeast, when she and Frick were visiting their friends Alf Pasquale and Chuck Curtis. "The principal change occurred," writes Yourcenar, in "one evening at Alf's around 1958: while we were listening to a series of works by Bach, I composed entirely in my mind, six or seven years before its *real* composition, the conversation between Zeno and the canon that took place a few hours before Zeno's death. Once the music had stopped and the evening came to an end, I completely forgot that dialogue. But I knew I would find it again one day."[10]

Frick and Yourcenar were back in Northeast Harbor on July 2, 1964. Yourcenar later reported on their voyage more positively than in her private musings in a letter to Natalie Barney: "Our life has been very full these last few months: after the trip to Poland, then a very delicious stay in Austria and northern Italy, we came back here in July for a cold summer darkened by politics." As she went on to say,

> I worked this morning at removing some bushes surrounding a beautiful young birch tree whose bark is already turning white (since birches, like seagulls and like the beautiful white horses in the stables of Vienna, are born gray and spotted before becoming immaculate).
>
> Today we went up to the garden kept by the Rockefellers at the top of the hill where their father once lived. The great bronze Buddhas imported from Japan and Korea, which sit cross-legged underneath the pines, are already covered with their winter veils, but one can still pray to them through the fabric for a world that is more and more in need of peace.
>
> Grâce is well, which is a great joy. We both send you our faithful and friendly good wishes.[11]

Yourcenar obviously decided to remove from this typewritten letter to Barney a more somber and poignant remark, itself partially crossed out, that appears in its first draft. It follows directly the description of the birch trees above and alludes no doubt at once to Grace Frick's health and to the dark political scenario already mentioned: "Whatever happens, I will never forget this long intimacy which has been mine with the American earth, or rather the Indian earth, a much older one that I hope will survive our agitation and madness."[12]

While Yourcenar was creating a fictional alchemist-philosopher-physician whose increasingly perilous self-realization enacts a challenge to the prevailing powers of his chaotic century, she and Frick were vigorously engaged in the peace and civil rights struggles of their own era. The daybooks from the mid-1960s are peppered with meetings of the Mount Desert Civil Rights Committee, Concerned Citizens about Vietnam, and the Mount Desert Peace Committee, which presented concrete ways for the pair to engage in the struggle for racial justice and against the Vietnam War. They attended lectures and panel discussions related to these vital causes on the island and the mainland. They circulated petitions urging President Johnson to negotiate an end to the war. They propagandized musically on open-house Sundays, playing protest songs by Pete Seeger, the Freedom Singers, Bob Dylan, and Woody Guthrie on their new "Hi-Fidelity Record Player."[13] They even donned antiwar sandwich boards on the village green in Bar Harbor.[14]

Frick and Yourcenar also participated in at least two silent vigils for peace. The first occurred in coordination with the great national demonstration of November 15, 1969, in Washington, DC. The second was held on December 13. According to the *Bar Harbor Times*, about forty people participated in the December event, which was sponsored by the Mount Desert Island People for Peace in Vietnam NOW, to which Frick and Yourcenar belonged.[15]

Frick, in particular—ever the educator and possessed now of the knowledge that youth all over America were rising up to protest segregation and acts of terror against blacks in the South—took pains to provide her young friends with the fruits of her own extensive research, conducted both out of fervor for the cause and in support of Yourcenar's work on *Fleuve profond, sombre rivière*. Paul and Gladys Minear's son Larry, a high school teacher, received a lengthy historical synopsis from Frick in April of 1964 that intertwines her perceptions, for example, of Booker T. Washington and W. E. B. Du Bois with those of her companion.[16] Frick sent those four single-spaced pages of typewritten notes, parts of which she copiously underlined in ballpoint pen for emphasis, thinking that Larry "might wish to quote them at some time." Larry went on to become a widely published expert in the field of humanitarian intervention in sites of armed conflict.[17]

Early in 1965 another opportunity arose to act locally. A state representative from Southwest Harbor, David Benson, introduced four bills in the 102nd Maine Legislature pertaining to hunting and fishing. One of them, LD 155, sought to open Mount Desert Island to a bow-and-arrow deer hunting season. The *Bar Harbor Times* railed against the bill, evoking "Tammany Hall of the 1920's."[18] LaRue Spiker, who had a weekly column in the paper entitled "Don't Bother Me with the Facts," urged like-minded islanders to circulate petitions opposing LD 155. Frick was a willing recruit. Not only did she and Yourcenar detest hunting, they loved deer.

As Grace noted in her daybook on February 6, not one resident of Mount Desert Island had been present at the January 28 legislative hearing on the deer-hunting bill. The measure, she wrote, "actually passed the House on February 2 and the Senate on February 4, unknown to anyone on Mt. Desert Island, although it pertained wholly to this Island." The next day, a Sunday, Grace and Marguerite had breakfast at the home of their peace activist friends Beth and Nathan Kaliss on Seely Road in Bar Harbor. Later that day Grace gathered signatures on and around South Shore Road. Neighborhood sentiment, according to her unofficial poll, was "wholly against" the proposal to open the island to hunting.[19]

On Monday, February 8, Frick and Yourcenar sent a telegram to Governor John H. Reed, asking him not to sign the bill until the citizens of Mount Desert Island could voice their opinion on the matter. They also telephoned their state senator about the legislation. By Thursday, February 11, Frick had collected nearly fifty signatures on her first petition.[20] That same day she sent the petition directly to Governor Reed, via registered mail, asking him to pass the document along to "our two Hancock County men." Indeed, Grace devoted all available energies throughout that week to antihunting petitions and appeals. By Saturday she had lost her voice to laryngitis.[21]

Yourcenar, meanwhile, was composing a letter to the editor of the *Bar Harbor Times*. It was published on February 11, 1965, under the heading "Democratic Procedure." This antihunting campaign was not Yourcenar's first foray into political activism—she and Frick had fought for passage of the Wild Horse Annie Act protecting wild mustangs from motorized hunters out West—but it provides early evidence of her progressively more fervent advocacy on behalf of animal welfare. Anyone who has read Yourcenar's "Fur-Bearing Animals" or "Who Knows Whether the Spirit of Animals Goes Downward" will find in her letter a familiar description of animal suffering:

To the Editor:

As a naturalized citizen of the [United States] I have just had occasion to [observe] a completely undemocratic procedure in our local government, passage of the bill LD 155 to permit, without submitting to referendum vote of the residents concerned, a season for hunting deer by bow and arrow on the island of Mount Desert. . . .

How is it that one man can put a bill through the state legislature without advance consultation with his constituents, whereas a substantial number of signatures is needed to get a single article in a . . . warrant of any town government?

As to the hunting of deer by bow and arrow, the only argument advanced openly for it is that it will reduce the herd. But it will not achieve a reduction sufficient to justify the dangers to all concerned, according to all competent biologists and hunters. Petitions are being circulated against the bill, unfortunately too late to have any effect on the house or senate vote, due to the conspiracy of silence described above, and a great number of the signatures on these petitions are from hunters themselves. What this bill will not fail to produce is untold suffering for the animal slowly dying of festering wounds made by weapons demanding highly specialized skills in the hands of inefficient hunters. In the limited area of this Island, even though shooting is prohibited in the national park, the public using the trails and the roads of Mount Desert during the autumn months of the proposed season (October and November) will be dangerously exposed to random shots (and, what is worse, from a silent hunter).[22]

As a result of all this pressure, Benson's bill was amended to require a referendum vote on hunting at the regular town meetings of the island's four municipalities the following spring.[23] In polls held on March 7 and 21, 1966, bow and arrow hunting was defeated by margins of 68 and 73 percent.

While the fate of Mount Desert Island's deer was being debated in 1965, the health of another four-legged creature dear to Frick and Yourcenar's hearts was deteriorating. As early as February 7, Grace reported in the daybook that Monsieur was "strangely ill: restless and confused, as if dazed."[24] Another bout occurred in early May, when she and Marguerite had taken him with them to Bangor. Later that month he collapsed after an outing to Beaver Dam Pond in Acadia National Park. The couple attributed that episode to heat exhaustion, but the situation worsened over the next few months, with Monsieur having frequent convulsions.

A large proportion of the entries in the 1965 daybook pertain, in meticulous detail, to Monsieur's progress or setbacks. No event in the couple's life, large or small, was recorded without noting how well or how poorly it was borne by Monsieur. Though Marguerite had an electrocardiogram in late July showing vascular weakness and impaired heart muscle function, the experience goes almost unmentioned in the calendar, sandwiched between Monsieur's low blood sugar, the forbidden bone feast in which he had naughtily indulged the previous day, and reports of him begging at teatime.

By early December his confusion and convulsions became so severe that medications had to be delivered by injection. Surprisingly, Yourcenar administered them. On December 4 the cocker spaniel was behaving so wildly that he needed an emergency shot. After spilling the first spurt, Yourcenar succeeded at injecting the poor creature with a few cubic centimeters of a tranquilizer. Later that day they delivered him to the veterinarian.

On the morning of December 6, Saint Nicholas Day, Monsieur died in his sleep at the Ellsworth Animal Hospital. Speaking as she and Marguerite sometimes did of the grounds around their home, Grace wrote in the daybook, "We dug the grave ourselves in Grande Plaisance and buried him about 6⁰⁰ p.m. in pale moonlight on early, light snow. Very peaceful and pretty when we brought him home from the hospital. Apparently his heart gave out, following a tranquillizer and anesthesia on Sunday evening."[25] A few days later they traveled to Veazie, near Bangor, to purchase a stone for Monsieur's grave in the wood garden, providing a mockup of what it should say. They brought the heavy granite marker home on December 16 in the front seat of their rented car, where it lay on the floor under Marguerite's legs. In addition to the years of Monsieur's birth and death, it bears a line from "The Scholar's Dog" by the English poet John Marston: "And Still My Spaniel Sleeps."

CHAPTER 28 ✿ Battling over *L'Œuvre au Noir*
1965–1968

In war, resolution.

—Winston Churchill

NATALIE BARNEY HAD BEEN WRITING to Marguerite Yourcenar for years about the changes occurring at Librairie Plon, where *Mémoires d'Hadrien* was published in 1951. Barney knew something of the inner workings at Plon because her novelist friend Germaine Beaumont was published there. In early 1960 she heard that Yourcenar's trusted friend and editor at Plon, Charles Orengo, did not see eye to eye with the firm's president.[1] Later that year she wrote, "I saw your *Denier* in the bookstores here, but I hear from Germaine Beaumont doubtful news of Plon—which even Orengo has left. Who are you confiding your new works to?"[2] Yourcenar underlined these sentences in red pencil as she was reading Barney's letter.

By August of 1965, with *L'Œuvre au Noir* essentially completed, Yourcenar was telling Barney that the book had cost her "as much research and reflection as *Memoirs of Hadrian*, or perhaps even more" and that she had put "as much if not more" of herself into it. She was exhausted.[3] Though the situation was not (yet) as dramatic as *Hadrian*'s had been, Yourcenar had lost confidence in Plon. Who would publish *L'Œuvre* she did not yet know.

Written on the same day as Yourcenar's friendly letter to Barney—and residing, oddly, in the same folder at Houghton Library—is the carbon copy, torn in half, of a blazing letter to Orengo's replacement at Plon, Georges Roditi. It details how shabbily Plon has handled dealings with Italian publishers and how repeatedly the house has failed to reissue Yourcenar titles that had gone out of print.[4] Meanwhile, letters and telephone calls were circulating back and forth between Yourcenar, her Parisian attorney Marc Brossollet, and Charles Orengo, now at Librairie Hachette, regarding her dissatisfaction with Plon and the possibility of legal action. As relations with Roditi deteriorated, Yourcenar filed suit, seeking to recover the rights to *L'Œuvre au Noir*, the book that mattered more to her than any other. The outcome was anything but certain.

Sometime in the mid-1960s Yourcenar and Frick met John Olin, a student at Fordham University.[5] As young people often did at that time, Olin was hitch-hiking around the Northeast during his summer vacation. He had come to Maine often with his family as a child, but this time, a backpack inscribed with a Walt Whitman quote on his back, he was on his own. He spoke with me about meeting the two women in the living room of Petite Plaisance in 2009:

> I was standing on the mainland side of the Trenton bridge before you cross over to Mount Desert, and a car stopped. It was an old model, late forties sedan, and there were what I, as a young man of twenty or twenty-one, would have called old ladies in it, which was very unusual. So I climbed in the back seat and noticed that, indeed, they were rather unusual ladies. The passenger was wearing a scarf, a head scarf, and I think she was dressed in black, and the driver was Miss Frick. The passenger was Marguerite Yourcenar. And they asked me where I was going. I didn't really have a destination, I was just coming onto the island. Often I traveled that way, and I'd find a place to stay and find a little job raking leaves or whatever during the summers in the sixties. So they said something to the effect that we can't have that, you have to have a place to stay tonight. Miss Frick sort of took charge. So before I knew it, I was on my way to Northeast Harbor.[6]

After a brief stop in Somesville, everyone arrived at Petite Plaisance. "They settled me in," Olin recalled. "I had a room upstairs. It's always nice when you're on the road to find a warm hearth and something to eat. And they were charming. They were interested in me, and I was certainly interested in them." Pointing to a green armchair, one of three around the fireplace at Petite Plaisance, he continued: "I remember sitting here. I can't remember exactly how we arranged these three chairs. But we would sit here after dinner and read Shakespeare. And we would have different parts. And then once we all got in the car and went over to Bar Harbor to see Lawrence Olivier in *Hamlet*." Frick helped Olin find a place to stay and a job. An aspiring writer himself, John valued his connection to Petite Plaisance. He came back often over the years to see "Madame and Miss Frick."[7]

On February 14, 1966, Grace and Marguerite acquired their second canine companion, Valentine Lady. She was a seven-week-old blond cocker, born on Christmas Day the previous year. "Vallie" was not as much of a scamp as her predecessor, who was not above stealing cakes off people's plates when there were guests for tea. Indeed, she was renowned for her beauty and sweet nature. But that did not stop her from falling into the pond behind Petite Plaisance when she was two months old, from which dunking she extracted herself "smelling like a sewer rat" to receive her first bath. Two days later she did it again.[8]

By mid-November Frick and Yourcenar were preparing to host Grace's elder niece, Kathie Frick, for Thanksgiving. Kathie was a sophomore at Wheaton College in Norton, Massachusetts. Her father and her Uncle Fred both thought it too risky for her to attempt a drive to the wilds of coastal Maine in late November, but Kathie was determined to try. Grace admonished her niece to use utmost care on the road and to be sure to bring "a robe or extra coats for the car, so that you can keep warm if you are stalled without a motor going for heat. . . . And have some really protective boots or galoshes to keep you dry in rain." Nighttime driving was vehemently not to be advised. Grace also insisted that her niece try to bring a fellow student, possibly someone on scholarship or else too far from home to return for only a few days. Or perhaps she could give a ride home to a girl living somewhere in Maine.[9]

Kathie arrived much later than her aunt thought wise in the evening of November 23 with a friend from Colorado, Sherry Nicola. The next day Grace took the girls to Beech Cliff, one of her favorite spots in Southwest Harbor. Then they took a boat to Cranberry Isle. Thanksgiving dinner, prepared by Marguerite, was served in the parlor at seven o'clock. The next day Richard Harwell, head of Special Collections at the Bowdoin College Library, came for luncheon. On Saturday everyone dined on lobster together at Seawall, a shore meal being de rigueur in Grace and Marguerite's view for anyone coming to visit them in Maine. On Sunday morning, in plenty of time to get back to school before dark, Kathie and Sherry departed.[10]

Alas, neither Aunt Grace nor Marguerite got the impression from Kathie's four-day visit that scholarship was the young woman's highest priority. Grace wrote despairingly to brother Gage,

Kathie worries me so. She admits to having not really read the books assigned, reading too hurriedly in high school, if at all, and skimming through notes rather than text in her college literature courses. She does not seem to be aware that college courses can be really enjoyed. She is getting none of the art, music, or theater which life in the Boston area affords, and she seems unaware of all the supplements to course work, like outside lectures brought to the college, which make for enrichment of her studies.[11]

But Kathie had other goals in mind. Despite the hopes of both her father and her aunt, she left Wheaton at the end of that academic year and transferred to the University of Colorado.

As 1966 came to an end, Yourcenar's attorney Marc Brossollet and Plon's attorney in Paris were still battling over *L'Œuvre au Noir*. With Éditions Plon convinced of its ironclad claim to the novel, the matter gave every sign of dragging on. Natalie Barney, always yearning to have Yourcenar and Frick return to Paris, wrote, "At last news of you! I heard, indirectly, that Plon had reedited your *Hadrien* and one of their young editors informed me that you [had filed suit]. This Guy Deschamps, who used to look like a Japanese is now a stout looking China man and his advice: that you should come over to Paris to see to your affairs with them! If you decide to do so I would gladly finance your trip, and greatly rejoice in seeing you. . . . "[12]

Eager though she certainly was to see her book liberated from Plon, Yourcenar had no desire to muddy the waters by making an appearance in person:

> I do not think that my presence in Paris would be useful to my "suit," quite the contrary. I know Paris all too well, and the inevitable society chitchat with people who mix everything up while assuring you they've understood you to say what you never said, and the newspaper interviews that almost always twist what you have tried to say, and, worse still, the "business" conversations with people who have mastered the art of procrastination, who tell you yes today only to say no tomorrow and make promises with no intention of keeping them.[13]

On March 15, 1967, an important article was published in *Le Monde* whose headline, "Sven Nielsen: Above All a Salesman," referred to the Danish founder of the publishing conglomerate that had acquired Librairie Plon in 1966.[14] Ten days later Charles Orengo called to say that Plon's lawyer for the first time was advising Nielsen to work out an arrangement regarding *L'Œuvre*.[15] On October 14 Yourcenar got word from Brossollet that an agreement had been reached. In legal limbo for two and a half years, *L'Œuvre au Noir* had been released. Grace and Marguerite celebrated the victory with "champagne, steak, and mushrooms for dinner!!"[16] Yourcenar was free to publish her novel wherever she chose, and she chose Gallimard. As for the English translation, no fewer than five publishers were vying for the book by early 1968.

The couple sailed for France on April 17, 1968. They arrived five days later in Cherbourg, as a young Grace had done thirty-one years earlier, unaware of what awaited her in Paris. They would stay for a whirlwind six weeks, the first eight days of which were spent in northwestern France. They visited Mont-Saint-Michel, the Breton walled village of Dinan, Carnac and its menhirs, and the medieval city of Angers. They strolled along the banks of the Loire.[17] At Fontevrault Abbey near Chinon, the couple paid their respects to Eleanor of Aquitaine; it was their second pilgrimage to the tomb of the fabled twelfth-century queen.[18]

In Paris, Natalie Barney could not wait to host a reception in honor of her friend's important new book. She would hold it on May 17 in her beloved *pavillon* at 20 rue Jacob. It had been twelve years since Frick and Yourcenar's last trip to France, and the first two weeks of their stay were awash in newspaper, radio, and television interviews, book signings, dinners with critics, and reunions with old friends. But as cramped as the pages of Frick's daybook already were with appointments at all hours, they soon became virtually illegible as the "events" of that revolutionary month thwarted most of their plans.

Students in the famed Latin Quarter had been protesting the rigid French education system since early May, holding antigovernment marches, and occupying the Sorbonne. The security forces of Charles de Gaulle's government responded with tear gas and violence. On May 13, the tenth anniversary of the coup d'état that had toppled the Fourth Republic and put General de Gaulle back in power, labor unions joined students in calling for a nationwide strike. Grace reported in her daybook on that date a "manifestation of students and other groups in sympathy, march of 500,000 to 1,000,000 from Left Bank, Place de la République, to Denfert-Rochereau." That same day a six-hour strike of the electrical workers shut down, among many other things, the elevators at her and Marguerite's hotel. On May 16 students took possession of the Odéon, one of France's national theaters. Soon train stations, airports, buses, the Metro, post offices, banks, and all the state museums would close in solidarity with the young people's cry for reform.[19]

Ironically, as Janet Flanner noted in her May 16, 1968, *New Yorker* "Letter from Paris," "the intellectual capital of Europe" had been chosen as the site for peace talks intended to end the war in Vietnam. Delegations from the United States and North Vietnam arrived in a French capital strewn with burned-out automobiles, hastily mounted barricades, shock troops, tear gas canisters, and fighting in the street. "If the Champs-Élysées represented the road to peace last Monday morning," wrote Flanner, "it was almost devoid of transportation."[20]

Grace and Marguerite, staying at the Hôtel Saint-James across the Seine from the Latin Quarter, had no choice but to walk to Natalie's reception. Barney's biographer has described the scene in *Wild Heart*: the Sorbonne was closed, Paris was paralyzed, riots were still going on in the streets, but "These circumstances did not prevent Natalie from holding her Friday, as planned, on May 17, to celebrate publication of Yourcenar's *L'œuvre au noir*. Informed that taxis were avoiding the area, Natalie remained unruffled. Her guests, she said, would come on foot. And they did, arriving in various states of exhaustion and terror. Sipping champagne and eating Berthe's cucumber sandwiches, they could hear loud explosions a few blocks away."[21]

Like everyone else, Natalie's young journalist friend Jean Chalon had to make his way on foot to 20 rue Jacob. He remembered crossing the Pont de la Concorde, which was occupied by "a crowd of CRS," or riot control forces, and purchasing a bunch of blue flowers near the corner of the rue du Bac and the boulevard Saint-Germain:

> In addition to the flowers, I brought Natalie all the graffiti I had collected from the walls. "It is forbidden to forbid," repeated the enchanted Amazon, who wondered if she hadn't written that herself somewhere in her *Reflections* or the *New Reflections*. We were about to start looking up this maxim, when the large white lace jabot of Marguerite Yourcenar appeared, together with the white foxes of her translator, Grace Friks [*sic*]. These ladies had come on foot from the rue de Rivoli. As the Pont du Carrousel was blocked by the CRS, they had decided to come by the more peaceful Pont des Arts. Natalie approved of their caution.[22]

Chalon concludes his account of the Amazon's last party, after pointing out the presence of "Mary McCarthy, rakishly dressed as if for battle," with this parting shot: "Suddenly Marguerite Yourcenar appeared, to whom I gave up my place for her to say to our hostess: 'Really, the eighteenth century is your time, much more than la Belle Epoque. How young you are Natalie, for a contemporary of Madame du Deffand and Rivarol.'"[23]

When *Portrait of a Seductress* first came out in 1976, Yourcenar did not hesitate to set Chalon straight on a few "sartorial" details, after thanking him for sending her the book and complimenting him on it. "Grace," she writes, points out to me that she has never worn white foxes, which would have been superfluous on a stormy day in June [*sic*]. M.Y.'s large white lace jabot was a white nylon jabot of modest dimensions; I have it still. Nor do I believe that I told Natalie that she was very young for a contemporary of Rivarol; I *wrote* that to her in one of the letters that are going to appear in the Doucet catalog, and that's where you will have read that sentence, which I surely did not reuse that evening. In any case, nothing serious.[24]

The worst days of the insurrection followed, with de Gaulle giving what Grace calls a "long-awaited but empty speech on television" on May 24.[25] She and Marguerite took advantage of the situation to go three times to the guignol puppet plays in the Tuileries Garden, sometimes staying for several performances.[26] They even took a horse-drawn carriage ride to Notre-Dame one night before a late dinner at the Restaurant Voltaire.[27]

Before the women set sail for home, Marguerite confided in a letter to Jean and Roger Hazelton,

I leave Paris with great sadness. The students (despite a few excesses) and the workers are by and large in the right, and the provisional triumph of the bourgeoisie whose members got scared and were reassured by de Gaulle's use of force (dangerous in itself) is hideous in its superficiality and stupidity. Nothing is definitively resolved. In the midst of all that, Paris remains very beautiful, and the common people are nearly always the essence of kindness and grace.[28]

When *L'Œuvre au Noir* finally appeared, on May 8, 1968, the timing turned out to be surprisingly good. The character at the crux of the book whose quest for knowledge rendered him heretical in the eyes of the Catholic Church was engaged in just as ardent a revolt against the dogma of his era as were the young people protesting on the streets of Paris in that extraordinary month of May. Despite the extreme disruption that the demonstrations represented for the commercial promotion of a dark and challenging novel, *L'Œuvre* sold out its entire first run of twenty-five thousand copies by July.[29] It was hailed by the critics as a masterpiece.

Before they left Paris, Frick and Yourcenar made "a long call at 20, rue Jacob," paying homage to Barney, their ninety-one-year-old friend, who had never missed a chance to further Yourcenar's career since the three women first met in 1951.[30] On June 3 the couple traveled to Rotterdam to catch their boat home. The *Nieuw Amsterdam* had called at Dublin and put out to sea when word came over the radio that Robert F. Kennedy had been shot and killed in Los Angeles. Shocked by the loss of JFK's progressive younger brother, who supported social justice for both black and poor Americans and sought to end the Vietnam War, Grace and Marguerite attended a hastily organized shipboard memorial service.[31] Only two months earlier, they had mourned the death of Martin Luther King Jr., the eloquent crusader for nonviolent resistance to oppression, poverty, and war. As Yourcenar wrote to a French friend shortly after King was shot, "The murder of this great pacifist adds another link to a chain of violent acts of which there is no end in sight."[32] With the slaying of Senator Kennedy following so closely on the chaos of Paris, it must have seemed to both Yourcenar and Frick that their world, like that of Zeno, was engulfed "in a circle of flames."[33]

CHAPTER 29 Dear Departed

1968–1969

Fond Memory brings the light
Of other days around me.

—Thomas Moore

ON JUNE 15, 1968, MARGUERITE Yourcenar received an honorary doctorate, her second, from Bowdoin College. Kathie Frick was getting married three days later on Cape Cod, and Grace would leave Marguerite at their hotel in Yarmouth, Maine, while she went alone to the ceremony.[1] Four months later Frick's aunt Dolly LaRue died in Kansas City at the age of ninety-five, leaving her niece a substantial bequest.[2]

Concerned about her own health, Grace wanted her affairs to be in order. Her lymphedema was worsening, and the increasing weight of her swollen left arm was causing other problems.[3] Before she and Yourcenar left again for France, Frick changed her will.

Grace now had only one elderly close relative to worry about, her paternal aunt Carrie Fricke in Bloomington, Illinois. To her she left 20 percent of the quarterly earnings from her trust for as long as Carrie might live. She remembered Ruth Hall with a gift of books. Foremost in her mind, though, as always, was Frick's concern for her partner's welfare. To Yourcenar she left not only all her personal and household possessions but both the revenue and, if needed, the principal of her trust estate to use as she saw fit until the end of her life:

> It is my intention and desire that the payments made shall provide a comfortable income for her during her life and, so far as may be possible, shall be sufficient to meet any special emergencies by reason of ill health or otherwise that may arise, even though the Trust Estate may eventually be exhausted by such payments and my Trustees are expressly directed to resolve any doubts in

this connection in favor of Marguerite Yourcenar rather than in favor of any contingent or final beneficiary hereunder.

Should there still be funds in Frick's residuary or trust estate after Yourcenar's death, they would be shared equally between the William Rockhill Nelson Gallery of Art in Kansas City and Frick's beloved alma mater, Wellesley College.[4]

Another crucial obligation before going abroad was to vote in the 1968 presidential election. Political matters had taken on increasing importance for Frick and Yourcenar as the 1960s unfolded. They were both early supporters of the most passionate antiwar candidate, Minnesota senator Eugene Mc-Carthy. Their opposition to the Vietnam War even spilled over into holiday greetings. Grace expressed to Gertrude Fay in December 1967 a sentiment Marguerite shared: "In this troubled world it has been hard to send Christ-mas cards, and the headline of the Bangor Daily News, 'Christendom Pauses to Observe Holy Day,' which preceded the Vietnam dispatches (!), was little short of mockery. Soberly yours, Grace Frick."[5] Three months later, with McCarthy having made a strong showing in the New Hampshire primary, Frick told Fay, "It takes intrepidity to face the chaos of our own country to-day. It seems to me that McCarthy is the only one who is really facing it, and we are both heartily glad that factory hands and defense workers, thousands of them, in New Hampshire spoke out. That takes courage when one out of every ten employed persons in the land is engaged in some occupation con-nected with the war."[6]

College students in that era, many of whom challenged middle-class val-ues with their style of dress, personal hygiene, and countercultural lifestyles, were so committed to McCarthy that they cut their hair and made them-selves presentable to go door to door on his behalf. As Frick notes in a letter to the poet Hortense Flexner, the campaign "was conducted with dignity and conviction, not only by McCarthy but by the students who worked so hard for him—no hippy costumes or long hair, but instead, the slogan, 'Clean for Gene.'" She was thrilled when a new minister came to Northeast Har-bor preaching "the necessity for Christians, here and now, to face up to the horrible *wrongness* of this war."[7] But with the Democratic Party divided on the issue, the nomination went to Hubert Humphrey. Of the 211 presidential votes cast in Northeast Harbor that year, 119 were for Richard Nixon, 89 for Humphrey, and three for George C. Wallace. Four days later, with heavy hearts, Frick and Yourcenar left for France. Adding to their distress over the election, they got to New York City too late to see their friend Erika Vollger, who had come to the pier at West Forty-Eighth Street to see them off. Three weeks later, attacked by a mugger, she would be dead.

Vollger, as Frick and Yourcenar almost always called their friend, had moved to New York from her native Switzerland in 1906 at the age of sixteen. She fell in love with the Maine coast while employed by a family named Barcy. Later in life she worked in the alterations department of Franklin Simon and Company, a women's clothing store, from which she retired at the age of seventy-one.

Frick and Yourcenar knew Vollger from way back. The three were already great friends by the time Grace first started keeping a daybook in January 1944. They shared all manner of activities, sometimes joined by Vollger's friend Rose Chessin: berry picking, swimming, sailing, picnicking, hiking, and climbing, to name a few. As Grace notes on August 17, 1944, with a playful twist, "Vollger persuades Grace, against her better judgment, to climb Champlain Mountain that day. Beautiful climb, but Vollger lost in cranberry bog on return. Ina [Garsoïan] for dinner grasped nothing of the tragedy." On the back of one photograph taken in front of Hysom Cottage, Marguerite wrote, "Grace and Erica [sic] Vollger, the Swiss dressmaker and saint." In her later years Vollger lived alone in New York, and her friends in Maine were always concerned for her safety.

In June of 1968 Vollger had fallen and fractured her hip. She was hospitalized for more than a week and had a difficult, probably incomplete recovery. On November 9 at 10:00 p.m. she left a note for "My Dears" at the pier from which their ship, the SS *Bremen*, would sail for France: "Patiently I waited from 8 o'clock, but you will probably arrive at 11:45. Bon voyage and my best wishes, Vollger." On November 29 she wrote her friends in Paris to say that she'd received a "lovely long letter from Miss Frick" and to congratulate Yourcenar on the success of *L'Œuvre au Noir*: "I am so happy for you."[8] The next communication, on December 7, was a telegram from Rose Chessin: "regret to inform erika vollger deceased."[9]

The women were stunned and heartbroken. Grace had sent Vollger a check with which to buy herself a badly needed pair of eyeglasses. She had gone to the bank to deposit it and to withdraw funds from her Christmas Club account. Vollger was attacked in her apartment by a man who had followed her home from the bank. Her landlady heard her scream and went to see what was wrong, but the thief had already broken a window and escaped. He was never caught. Vollger died in the intensive care unit of a New York hospital with Rose Chessin at her side.[10]

Stormy seas caused the *Bremen* to land in Southampton rather than Cherbourg, and the couple took advantage of the circumstance to tour the Winchester and Salisbury Cathedrals and visit Stonehenge again. Crossing the Channel, they traveled to Amiens and several towns in French Flanders before heading into Belgium. In 1980 Yourcenar shared "the most lovely story of G.F." from that time with Jerry Wilson. As he wrote in his journal,

> They were traveling in Belgium on the way to Bruges and stopped to visit a church with a statue that Mme Y. wanted G.F. to see. Arriving just at closing time, there was no one and only a few candles for light. Not to be deterred, Miss Frick took a candle and walked to the back of the church, alone, to see the statue—in that light, it was a beautiful scene and one of Mme Y's fondest memories.[11]

During the summer of 1984, Mme Yourcenar shared with me another warm remembrance in which light played a prominent role. This one, which I noted in my journal on July 13, involved both Grace and Jerry: "One of her 'fondest memories' is coming home late one night after going off on some expedition that got her home much later in the evening than she had planned on. Jerry and Grace Frick had stayed home cooking and she finally drove up to the house (it seems as though a boat might have been involved), and G.F. and J. opened together the door of the house, and the sight of those two loved people near one another (and worried about her), wrapped in a halo of light, was precious. She calls this an 'intimate memory.'"[12]

In Paris the all-important literary prizes were awarded in November. *L'Œuvre au Noir* was bound to receive one. Josyane Savigneau notes that Gallimard's press attaché had even tried—unsuccessfully—to get Yourcenar to move up the date of her transatlantic crossing so as not to miss a possible promotional opportunity for the novel.[13] She and Frick arrived in Bruges on November 22, intending to stay there for at least a week. As had happened in 1952, when *Mémoires d'Hadrien* received the Vacaresco Award, the couple had to change their plans and make their way to Paris when the publisher told them that *L'Œuvre* would win the Prix Femina. Yourcenar would be the first unanimous honoree since the prize was founded in 1904.

The day before the public announcement of the Femina Prize, they celebrated with the housemaid and companion of Marguerite's youth, Camille
Letot, in Gosselies, Belgium. It was a chance to meet Camille's family and
in particular Yourcenar's godson, Albert Letot. Camille sent the two women
off with leftover tarts from the meal they had shared, and it was thanks to
those tarts, consumed on the train, that the prize-winning author arrived, as
she wrote in an affectionate bread-and-butter letter, "not entirely famished
in front of fifty photographers' flashbulbs!"[14]

As Frick wrote in a pithy note to Helen Howe, the big French literary prizes are clustered together near the end of November, with media at the ready:

> The radio and television gear is all set to grab the winners, in whatever condi-
> tion they may arrive, and some of the poor souls, the journalists told us, were
> simply left speechless before the microphone.
>
> Thanks to the editor's warning, Marguerite had a little notice, but we were
> simply furious to cut short the few days saved for Belgium and northern France
> in order for her to be marched from the railway station on November 25 to the
> blaze of projectors which separated her from the waiting women, all twelve of
> them! I was not present, but heard later that it was a mob, both there and at the
> Gallimard cocktail which followed. People whom she swears she has never seen
> before rushed up to kiss her and called her "Marguerite" while the cameras
> clicked (you know the charming French expression, "M'as-tu vu?"), not one
> of whom has been seen since![15]

Though she did not attend the Gallimard cocktail party on the evening
of the Femina announcement, Grace cheerfully hosted a reception in honor
of the prize at the Hôtel Saint-James et d'Albany in mid-December. Held
from five to seven o'clock in a salon on the hotel's second floor, a room
with two large mirrors facing each other, the event was attended, among
others, by Femina jury member Germaine Beaumont, Emmanuel Boudot-
Lamotte, Marc Brossollet and his wife, the film actress Pauline Carton, the
journalist Jean Chalon, Natalie Barney's new young friend Mme Lahovary,
the critic Robert Kanters, the French diplomat and U.N. delegate Jean Chau-
vel, the French historian Pierre Nora, a few members of the Orengo family,
Yourcenar's old friend Anne Quellenec, the writer Diana Forbes-Robertson
Sheehan, the critic Patrick de Rosbo, Princess Hélène Schakowskoy, and
the Marquis de la Villa Rocha. Jean Chalon described the party to Josyane
Savigneau in the late 1980s and to me in 2007. He recalls being the only

man at that "very feminine" gathering. To Savigneau he portrayed Grace as resembling the French cartoon character L'Espiègle Lili, adding that she bustled about making introductions and making sure that everyone got a chance to pay homage to the guest of honor.[16] To me, perhaps by way of finding an American counterpart of Mischievous Lili, he wrote, "Grace was very feminine, very bouncy; sometimes she made me think of Minnie Mouse, Mickey's companion. The Yourcenar-Frick couple was very upper-class, even a bit bourgeois. An example of bourgeois dignity in Lesbos."[17]

Chalon obviously picked up on Frick's mischievousness, which many who knew her have noted. But that a woman of her age—she and Yourcenar were both sixty-five in 1968—and level of accomplishment should be likened to a comic strip mouse, even one whose real name was Minerva, hints at a kind of denigration that in Grace's case would only become more pronounced. Jean Chalon meant no malice toward Frick—he also said that she was always very kind to him and "a perfect hostess"—but his comment subtly partakes of a prevalent phenomenon where the partners of prominent cultural figures are concerned. Do we put the author we revere on a pedestal so high that no spouse or helper could possibly belong up there with him or her? Do we feel such a strong connection to the artist we admire that we can't bear the thought of someone being even closer? Or do we simply want our idols to be totally autonomous, forging their unique creations without ever needing to rely on someone else?

On December 18, determined to get away from Paris before Christmas, Frick and Yourcenar eagerly went south. They had originally planned to go to Spain, possibly sailing home from there on a freighter. As Grace wrote to Paul and Gladys Minear,

> A friend wrote us of cargo boats on the Spanish American (or Atlantic?) Line, from Bilbao, but they are cargo boats without a physician aboard, and Marguerite is a poor enough sailor to hesitate about them. Dramamine usually takes care of her in transit, but our November crossing was so dramatic (tables and chairs a-lurch, and several passengers with fractures as a result) that all her old fears are revived, and she dreads the crossing as much as I enjoy it, and about as much as I dread the drive to and from New York.[18]

In the end the "state of exception" declared by dictator Francisco Franco in January 1969, and reports of the brutal suppression of Basque and student protesters by the regime, caused the two women to abandon all thoughts of traveling to Spain.

By December 27 the couple had reached Aix-en-Provence, where they made a long stay at the Hotel Riviera. It was unusually cold in Aix that winter, and on January 6, after king's cake and chocolate for breakfast, Grace injured a rib attempting to close a heavy shutter in a windstorm. Dr. J.-C. Vidal examined Frick's chest two weeks later and found a lump at the edge of her mastectomy scar that later proved to be malignant.[19] X-rays taken in Aix revealed calcified filaments extending from the apex of her scar into her right lung.[20] It was at this time that seepage began along the edges of Frick's surgical scar.

Two months later, on March 7, the women arrived in Perpignan and checked in at the Grand Hôtel. They had invited Grace's younger niece, Pamela Frick, who was studying in Switzerland that year, to spend the weekend with them there. She did not want to.[21] Though a highly intelligent young woman, Pamela did not necessarily share her aunt's zest for scholarly pursuits. But her father, Gage, insisted, and she reluctantly complied. What Aunt Grace viewed as trying to impart to her nieces her own love of learning the girls themselves often experienced as unwelcome criticism of their educational choices and interests.

Pamela arrived in Perpignan before her aunt did and, probably hoping to build some privacy into the long looming weekend, took a room, as Grace wrote in the daybook, "at Hotel Halder instead of going to our hotel!" The next morning Grace and Marguerite hired a car to take their guest to the seaside town of Collioure on the Mediterranean, and then to explore the Romanesque cloister in the village of Elne. Grace was determined to make Pamela's visit as culturally enriching as possible.[22]

The next day everyone headed northwest, with the same driver, to the fortified city of Carcassonne, taking a diagonal route through the Corbières Mountains and returning to Perpignan via the ancient Roman city of Narbonne. Before Pam's departure on March 10, with the Palace of the Kings of Majorca disappointingly closed, the couple settled for a tour of the renowned altarpieces of Perpignan's Saint Jacques Church. Frick was not convinced, seeing Pamela off at the train station, that her niece had taken full advantage of the educational experience she had organized for her over the preceding three days. The high-spirited, nineteen-year-old Pamela, for her part, had

had her fill, among other things, of historical lectures on the melding of French and Spanish culture inspired by the wrought-iron grillwork of Perpignan's many balconies.[23] The future would nonetheless prove that she and her aunt shared at least two lifelong passions: a taste for travel and a love of horseback riding.

CHAPTER 30 ✤ Grace Bashing Begins
1969–1971

> You can't prevent it, despite yourself, you will not escape history.
>
> —André Gide

FRICK AND YOURCENAR WERE NEVER more united than when they were fighting a literary battle together, and Éditions Plon continued to fall short of Yourcenar's expectations for her work. As Frick noted in November of 1969, Plon's "reprints" of *Denier du rêve* and *Alexis* turned out to be "recompositions incredibly massacred as to text, and even as to format (type mixtures, irregular lines and spacing)."[1] The reissue of Yourcenar's translation of Virginia Woolf's *The Waves* was not much better. "Preparing the case against Plon" cost the women eight full days of more productive and creative work. They were still firing letters back and forth to attorney Marc Brossollet about the "Plon affair" in May of 1971.[2]

Frick had started work on *The Abyss*, whose title derives from Zeno's meditations in the central chapter of *L'Œuvre au Noir*, sometime in the mid-1960s. In late August 1967 she was translating at night after helping Yourcenar correct the French manuscript of the novel during the day.[3] As always, literary tasks were woven into daily life. One work session on the French text took place at Jordan Pond House while the couple sipped tea and watched "fantastic mist descending on the Bubbles," two of Mount Desert Island's rounded mounts.[4]

There was great interest in Yourcenar's new book on this side of the Atlantic. On August 18, 1968, Robert J. Clements of the *Saturday Review* traveled to Petite Plaisance to interview Frick and Yourcenar about *The Abyss*.[5] It was not an easy text to render in English—Yourcenar once referred to the "weighty task" of translating this dense novel—and progress was slow.[6] According to the daybook, it was not until October 30, 1969, that Frick mailed chapter 8, "The Fuggers of Cologne," to Farrar, Straus and Giroux. With thirteen chapters yet to go, she was only one-third of the way through the book.

These were busy years for both women. Yourcenar's French translation of Hortense Flexner's poems, including the thirteen "for Sutton Island" off Mount Desert, came out in October of 1969.[7] The following month Yourcenar gave a talk on André Gide at Smith College commemorating the centennial of Gide's birth. Other speakers included the renowned American scholars of French literature Germaine Brée of the University of Wisconsin and Wallace Fowlie of Duke University.[8] Yourcenar went last, on Saturday, March 22, having attended the other two speeches. She had composed her talk in advance and was planning to deliver it from a few pages of notes. But the lectures of Brée and Fowlie had been so cautious and scholarly that she doubted whether students understood them. Hoping to say something they could grasp, Yourcenar tore up her notes and spoke instead "*about* Gide."[9]

Perhaps with Newton Arvin on her mind, she said first that the author whose career the Smith community had gathered to celebrate was homosexual. Her improvised lecture, entitled "André Gide Revisited," later appeared in the *Cahiers André Gide*. It is hard to imagine that Yourcenar did not think of Grace Frick when she told her audience what Gide once said to his wife, a woman she described as "extremely discreet, extremely self-effacing, never wanting to let herself be put first, never wanting to be talked about": "You can't prevent it, despite yourself, you will not escape history."[10]

Yourcenar's success was beginning to catch up with her and Frick. On March 18, 1970, the Belgian Royal Academy of French Language and Literature elected Yourcenar to its honorary ranks. She would be inducted the following year. The French critic and admirer Patrick de Rosbo wished to do a series of radio interviews on Yourcenar's work and arranged a late-summer 1970 trip to Northeast Harbor.[11] He arrived just three days after Yourcenar was released from the Bar Harbor Hospital, where she had four or five (benign) breast tumors removed.[12] Rosbo was scheduled to arrive the day before, September 2, but he telephoned from Bangor to say he had no money for a taxi.[13]

The interviews began September 3, with Yourcenar still weak and fatigued. The next day, after hosting Rosbo from ten in the morning until eight-thirty at night, Frick drove him to three restaurants before he found a menu to his liking. Both women took him for tea at Jordan Pond House. They had him stay for dinner more than once after long days of recording. One day he stayed until 10:30 p.m. Marguerite and Grace were both exhausted. Finally, on September 9, he went back to France. Upon leaving

Northeast Harbor, Rosbo left a trail of unpaid bills and personal loans, even trying—unsuccessfully—to convince the proprietor of the Harborside Inn to let him check out without paying for his stay.[14]

The radio broadcasts aired on France-Culture in January 1971. The following year Rosbo published a transcription of the interviews that Yourcenar had substantially revised and augmented.[15] He then set about repaying the author and Frick for their hospitality by way of a defamatory article about his week at Petite Plaisance, "Huit Jours de purgatoire avec Marguerite Yourcenar," in the new arts magazine *Gulliver* that calls his week at Petite Plaisance "eight days in purgatory with Marguerite Yourcenar." Rosbo chose to focus most of his venom on Frick, first attacking her physical appearance: "I caught sight of a little, bony face. A shrunken head? The mummy of Ramses II? Her gray hair, sparse and messy, reminded me right away of a little old man, very thin with emaciated features, of some much older sister of Nathalie Sarraute's, of some woman artist from the twenties, also in a way of André Gide's little wife. I wasn't sure which sex." He then sketched a scurrilous account of his conversation with Yourcenar:

> A table separated us, on which were placed our two microphones. Off to the side, the Confidante was keeping watch: silent, vigilant, a shade within the shadows. Without letup and insistently, Marguerite Yourcenar's gaze turned toward her, consulting her, seeming to seek her tacit approval or support. The comedy of the supposed dialogue unraveled, losing its consistency from minute to minute, veering into farce. I had before me nothing more than an anxious profile straining toward its own dark night and making no effort to disguise its dependence.
>
> "Madame," I asked brusquely, "could you occasionally make an effort to turn toward me, to look at me? Would that not give more life to our exchanges?"
>
> "I could not possibly take my eyes away from Grace's . . ."[16]

Yourcenar was appalled by the vileness of Rosbo's assault. To her Parisian friend and occasional doctor Marthe Lamy, she wrote that Rosbo had attacked Frick for "attempting to defend me, knowing that I did not have the strength to do it myself."[17] She immediately started to compose an indignant response to Rosbo's screed with help from an equally disgusted Charles Orengo. As she wrote to Brossollet in February 1973, Rosbo had already taken aim at her by way of a third party the previous September, when an article appeared in *Les Lettres françaises* depicting her as "avaricious of heart." The text in question was Josane Duranteau's review of Rosbo's published interviews, which alleged that Yourcenar had refused to play by the rules of a spontaneous conversation. "There is something a bit comical in this blockage, this rigidity, this incapacity to let oneself be grasped by the other. It must not be pleasant to dance with Marguerite Yourcenar."[18] Yourcenar, for her part, decided not to dance with *Gulliver*, recognizing the wisdom of her lawyer's advice that she let the matter drop.[19]

By July of 1970 Frick had translated six more chapters of *The Abyss*. Yourcenar had begun the first volume of what would eventually become a family trilogy, *Le Labyrinthe du monde*, inspired while writing *L'Œuvre au Noir* to delve into her Belgian and French Flemish roots.[20]

On February 10 and 11, 1971, Frick, Yourcenar, and the cocker spaniel Valentine Lady got their vaccinations for yet another trip abroad. On March 8, they boarded the SS *Michelangelo* in New York City, bound for Spain. Unlike their previous crossing, this one was smooth, the weather was good, and no one fell ill.

Traveling by train first to Madrid and then to Burgos, León, and Astorga in Spain, the couple did some sightseeing before heading to Brussels for Yourcenar's Belgian induction. In Astorga they were particularly moved to find themselves in a town that was a major stopping point on the pilgrimage route to Santiago de Compostela.[21] In describing their day there, Frick makes a comment suggesting that she too was not immune to treating Zeno, as Yourcenar so often did, as if he were a real person. Remarking on the extraordinary Renaissance architecture of the Astorga town hall, Grace notes that it had probably been built "after Zeno's time there, as he was young. It was where Zeno went with Don Blas to see four Jews and one Spanish heretic executed in the Plaza of Ayuntamiento." Back in Burgos on March 24, they saw Hadrian's inscription in honor of his Spanish tribe at the museum of the Casa de Miranda.

Once Grace and Marguerite reached Brussels they were caught in the academy whirlwind. Right after they arrived at their hotel, Paul and Gladys Minear's twenty-eight-year-old daughter, Anita Fahrni, appeared, having traveled from her home in Switzerland to represent her family at the induction. Pamela Frick, who was studying that year at the Sorbonne, would also attend. That first evening, a Friday, the Belgian Baroness Vaxelaire gave a celebratory dinner for thirty guests. As Fahrni recalled, the formal servers wore white gloves. The tables were adorned with orchids. Among the guests was the Quebecois novelist Anne Hébert, who would receive a prize the next day given jointly by the French and Belgian Academies. Next to Yourcenar sat

Marie Genevoix, wife of the Académie française's perpetual secretary Maurice Genevoix, while Frick's place was beside the evening's hostess. Among the others present were the novelist Suzanne Lilar and her husband, the Count and Countess d'Aignan, and Duchess Edmée de la Rochefoucauld.[22]

The main event took place on Saturday afternoon at the Belgian National Theater. Mme Lilar, an academy member since 1952, presided. After Anne Hébert received her prize, the distinguished Belgian poet and novelist Carlo Bronne spoke of Yourcenar's life and literary work. In her response Yourcenar discussed the American professor whose academy chair she was taking, Benjamin Mather Woodbridge. A descendant of the influential early New England Puritans Richard, Increase, and Cotton Mather, Woodbridge had taught romance languages and literature at Reed College in Oregon.

That evening Frick and Yourcenar dined at the Hotel Amigo with Anita Fahrni and two friends come from Paris for the induction, Charles Orengo and Jeanne Carayon, Yourcenar's valued proofreader. Sunday would be a day of rest, which in this instance meant a taxi ride to the eleven-thousand-acre Sonian Forest on the outskirts of Brussels. Now protected as an endangered ecological site by the European Union, that great woodland was once described by May Sarton as "the magnificent Forêt de Soignes, miles and miles of soaring beeches pruned and cherished ever since it had been set aside as a hunting forest for the Dukes of Burgundy."[23] Grace and Marguerite took Anita Fahrni with them on this outing, thanks to whom we have photographs of the women together in their late sixties.

After touring the house of Erasmus, dining with Aunt Loulou de Borchgrave, and visiting with Yourcenar's half nephew Georges de Crayencour, Grace and Marguerite jubilantly left Brussels for Zeno's medieval Flemish birthplace of Bruges. There they would enjoy the rare luxury of staying in one place for five weeks. Marguerite took Valentine every day for her morning walk, retracing the steps of her protagonist in the cobblestone streets with Valentine Lady at her side. Together they brought her to the country home of Lucienne de Reyghere just outside Bruges amid blooming jonquils and narcissus. As Grace noted in the daybook, the elegant cocker was "full of joy to run free on the grass!"[24] The couple also haunted the Gruithuis Museum and its "superbly exhibited" holdings, which ranged from medieval and Renaissance sculpture to kitchen tools, medical instruments, and a guillotine.[25] They went to vespers and a mass at the Béguinage.[26] They visited the English Convent of Bruges, staying twice for the evening service there.[27] During a leisurely day-trip with Dominique Willems to Ostende, they were treated

FIGURE 35. Grace Frick and Marguerite Yourcenar in the Sonian Forest, 1971. Minear family archives.

to the sight of a "group of horses and riders on the sand, silhouetted against waves and wet sand at sunset."[28] It was a scene that could have come from *The Abyss.*

All the while there was a steady stream of literary work. In addition to the proofs of the new paperback version of *L'Œuvre au Noir,* the eighth French edition of *Memoirs of Hadrian* was coming out, as were the new or reissued works *Rendre à César, Denier du rêve, Théâtre I,* and *Discours de réception,* a published version of the speeches given at Yourcenar's Royal Academy reception. Both Yourcenar and Frick scoured first and second proofs of each title with meticulous application. Not surprisingly, no progress seems to have been made on either Frick's translation work or Yourcenar's family memoir over the course of this European sojourn.

On May 5, 1971, the women left for a twelve-day Botel cruise in Holland that took them from Amsterdam to Arnhem, Dordrecht, Gouda, Leyden, and back to Amsterdam. En route to the Dutch capital from Bruges they visited a nature reserve on the North Sea at Zwin which, with its sand dunes, sea lavender, and richly varied population of owls, herons, storks, ducks, and geese, was a revelation for these lovers of birds and the sea. They then spent three and a half weeks in Paris, during which Yourcenar was finally appointed to the French Legion of Honor, a national tribute for which Natalie Barney had campaigned as far back as the 1950s.[29] Barney had been forced to leave her beloved *pavillon* and Temple of Friendship on the rue Jacob in 1970 after living there for sixty years. The property, which she rented, had been purchased by a former official in Charles de Gaulle's government who wished to renovate the building. Natalie would stay at the luxurious Hôtel Meurice while waiting to return to her home.[30]

On November 17 that year Barney had written to Marguerite and Grace to say how much she looked forward to seeing her friends: "I hope soon to have news of your return to Paris—dog and all!"[31] The couple made a point of visiting Barney the following June in her suite a few doors down from the Saint-James. They would never see her again. Barney died in early 1972 at the age of ninety-five without ever returning to rue Jacob. As Yourcenar wrote to Jean Chalon about her and Frick's last visit with their friend, Natalie had already seemed at that time to be "a light and charming ghost who was lingering among us. Now she has entered her realm once and for all, her legend already begun."[32]

On June 12, 1971, Frick and Yourcenar left Paris for Le Havre, where they would board the SS *Alexander Pushkin* for the trip home. They were delighted when the purser upgraded them to a larger cabin on the ship's top deck. It would be easier to walk the exuberant Valentine. The extra space also turned out to be useful for another reason. Exercising Valentine after dinner that first night, Grace tripped over a guy wire and ruptured a tendon in her left knee. The ship's Russian surgeon stabilized the injured joint with a loose cast and ordered complete bed rest. Both women took all of their meals for the rest of the trip in their stateroom.[33] Frick recovered quickly, but being confined to a cabin for an eight-day ocean crossing was not easy. The accident also prevented Grace, as she wrote to her niece, from seeing "every beam and timber of the vessel."[34] It was her last crossing.

Back home there were no immediate alerts on the health front for either Yourcenar or Frick. They both went to the Bar Harbor Hospital for various tests on July 30, 1971, with no report of bad results. A humorous incident that occurred a few weeks later suggests that despite their health challenges, both women still had plenty of spunk.

Ann (Fullan) Gilkes, whose family began summering up the street from Petite Plaisance in 1965, told this story in 2010 when she was a vigorous ninety-one years old. Frick, as was her habit, had welcomed the Gilkeses to the neighborhood when they arrived in Northeast, and a friendship involving both parents and children ensued. Frick and Yourcenar were fond of syllabub in the mid-1960s, an old English dessert of thickened cream harking back to the Tudor dynasty, and they treated Ann and young Jane Gilkes to the concoction in the garden of Petite Plaisance shortly after the Gilkeses moved in.[35] Visits back and forth between the two houses, whether for tea, cocktails, or the occasional meal, became part of summer life. Ann Gilkes never forgot what Grace had told her early on about meeting Marguerite in Paris: "She was in the dining room or the salon of her hotel, and 'I saw this magnificent woman with sparkling blue eyes, and I was fascinated. So I went up and introduced myself to her. She knew more about Keats and Shelley than I did!'"[36] Grace never tired of recounting how intensely she was drawn to Marguerite the first time she laid eyes on her.

As it happens, Ann Gilkes had a sister who had the same effect on people. In September of 1971 Amelia Mohan came to Northeast Harbor for a visit. Charming, worldly, and adventurous, Mohan was a lovely fifty-seven years old. Ann Gilkes brought her over to Petite Plaisance on the afternoon of an open-house Sunday.[37] Amelia liked to stir things up. "She got Grace and Marguerite's number," Ann recalled, "the minute she walked in"—and she decided to have a little fun. Amelia sat down next to Grace and started chatting away with her flirtatiously. Grace was undoubtedly flattered. She wasn't used to being sought out by newcomers. Ann took a seat next to Marguerite. After a minute or two, Amelia felt a pair of eyes boring down on her with fierce intensity. If looks could kill! Well aware she was the target of Marguerite's displeasure, Amelia poured the charm on even thicker, going so far as to stroke Grace's knee. Grace did not protest. This was more than Marguerite was willing to put up with. She rose from her chair and marched across the room to assert her place. Grace was obviously not displeased with Amelia's attentions. Whether Marguerite knew it or not, she dropped by the Gilkeses' Blanchard Cottage several times while Amelia was in town.[38]

Amelia Mohan was living at that time in Southern Pines, North Carolina. Despite her playful high jinks that September Sunday in 1971, she had traveled north to see the Gilkeses because she had throat cancer. She could have submitted to a procedure that would have left her with an artificial voice box, but she didn't want to go through life that way. So she had come to say goodbye. Six weeks later, back home in North Carolina, she died.

CHAPTER 31 ✿ Round Two
1971–1973

So long as he lives a guest should never forget a host who has shown him kindness.

—Homer

UNLIKE GRACE FRICK, MARGUERITE YOURCENAR did not revel in Maine's hard winters. She did go so far as to say she didn't mind them once, it being "difficult to find a good climate in the winter. Paris is beastly, also."[1] But both women gloried in the beauty of autumn, with its brilliant blue skies, trees ablaze with color, and luxurious warmth of Indian summer. On just such a day in October of 1971 Marguerite took Valentine Lady to pick the last flowers of the season along a South Shore Road blissfully devoid of summer traffic. Overjoyed, Valentine darted down a leaf-strewn path, "her little paws sturdy on the golden foliage." Heading toward the sea, the cocker disappeared in the bushes of a neighbor's garden. Marguerite called out to her gaily, taking pleasure in the sound of her name. Instead of bounding toward her mistress, Valentine ran toward the road. "Through the bushes," Yourcenar recalled,

> I vaguely watched a car to my left moving down the street at a very leisurely pace. A second later, a voice called out to me, "Is it your dog that I have hit?" I took a few steps back, toward the road—Valentine was stretched out on the ground, dead. She must have thrown herself against the car and bounced off like a ball. There she lay, her neck broken. I had the very strong feeling that vibrations of life were pulsing from her still warm body and disappearing into space. I fell (or threw myself) onto the ground and heard myself crying, "They have killed our dog!"[2]

The village woman whose car had hit Valentine was beside herself. "I'm awfully sorry," she kept repeating, "I can buy you another dog." Dazed, Marguerite replied, "You see, we loved her so much."[3] As she recalled elsewhere,

At that moment Grace arrived, coming from the back of our woods, and, once again, I heard myself crying, "They have killed our dog!" All together we approached the little one, still inert: Grace bent over and felt her heart still beating very faintly; I felt it, too.

"Go get a little milk, some cognac . . ."

I ran into the house, poured a bit of milk into a measuring cup, and took the little flask of cognac that we keep in case of an accident. But I thought that if by chance she was still living and had internal bleeding, we shouldn't give her this cognac. I remembered the day, on a street in Munich, that I went to get a whole bottle of brandy in a nearby bar to try and revive a stranger who was dying of a heart attack in his car. The veterinarian? Twenty miles away, and his office closed on Sunday. But when I knelt down with my ridiculous measuring cup of milk, I realized again that she was beyond all help.

"Her heart completely stopped beating under my hand," Grace told me.[4]

With the help of near neighbors Elliot and Shirley McGarr, the couple buried Valentine in their wood garden, lining her grave with ferns that autumn had already turned to gold.

Once they were back inside the house, Emily Brzezinski knocked at the door. She and Zbigniew summered up the street, and they had happened by just after the accident. In Emily's hands were the roses Marguerite had intended to pick "and a tender little note evoking Valentine bounding about 'in Elyseum fields.'"[5] Her epitaph would be a verse from the sixteenth-century poet Pierre de Ronsard, "Portant un Gentil Coeur Dedans un Petit Corps [Bearing so brave a heart within a little body]."

There was no time to dwell on grief. Two days after Valentine's death, the advance guard of a seven-man television crew arrived from Paris to begin a week of filming. That same day, October 5, Frick and Yourcenar got a new cocker puppy. They named her Zoé, the Greek word for "life"—whether as an affirmation or a plea.

The 1970s were a decade of ever increasing media attention and various honors. October of 1971 brought the first visit of the Parisian literary critic Matthieu Galey, who would host a televised documentary about the author: at home baking bread or typing in the studio, shopping for Indian corn at the Pine Tree Market, atop Mount Cadillac.[6] Galey would make several more pilgrimages to Northeast Harbor, collecting the wide-ranging conversations that became *With Open Eyes*.

In October of 1972 another French camera crew, headed by Michel Hernant, came to Petite Plaisance to talk with Yourcenar about her play *Dialogue dans le marécage*. Later that month Colby College followed Smith and Bowdoin in bestowing on Yourcenar an honorary doctorate of letters. Frick's old friend Mary Marshall from Yale University was teaching at Colby that year. In December of 1972 Yourcenar received the Prince Pierre de Monaco literary prize for her entire body of work, though she was too ill to attend the ceremony. Two years later, she would get the Grand prix national de la culture.

In addition to the radio broadcast of *Dialogue dans le marécage*, other Yourcenar plays were being brought to life on French stages: *Le Mystère d'Alceste* premiered in Rennes on March 21, 1973. *Dialogue dans le marécage* was mounted on May 24, 1973, at the Vincennes Festival. The students of Pierre Valde put on *Électre ou la Chute des masques* on March 19–21, 1974, at the National Conservatory in Paris.[7] In August of that year Radio-Canada sent Françoise Faucher to interview Yourcenar for five days.[8] The following month brought a Belgian TV crew for a week and the renowned photographer Gisèle Freund.[9]

While the media attention brought new readers to Yourcenar's work, it also brought inopportune callers to her door. In June of 1972 Yourcenar received a breezy letter from a would-be visitor who breached Frick and Yourcenar's defenses.[10] Elvire de Brissac, a young French writer, announced that, "opera glass in hand," she was off "to take the profile of the universe." She would be touring the United States that summer, and she would like to visit Petite Plaisance. Enclosed with her letter was a note from the French author Paul Morand, who had commented very favorably on Yourcenar's first published novel, *Alexis*, in the pages of the *Courrier littéraire*.[11] No doubt it was Morand's note that caused the author to receive the young woman. She even reserved a hotel room for her.[12]

Brissac arrived on September 6, two days earlier than planned. Grace in particular took pains to make her feel welcome. Within minutes of Brissac's arrival at the Asticou Inn, Frick appeared at the venerable old hotel's reception desk. As Brissac would write about her trip in the book *Ballade américaine*, "The Asticou Inn was not a motel that one enters and leaves after paying the bill and Miss Frick . . . was not a person like everyone else."

"Then again, yes," Brissac goes on to say,

> like one other: the same braid around her head, the same sneeze-contorted face,
> defying the laws of nature, nose to the right, tongue to the left, arms hanging
> down to her bobby socks; lumpy as an Italian palace; the same fundamental

independence, with inconceivable single-mindedness, the same irreverence for intermediaries, wanting to talk all the time and send you to hell.

I was there.[13]

Brissac then proceeds to reveal, in a long, stream-of-consciousness paragraph, that the "one other" person whom Grace Frick resembled in her life was the no-nonsense, seen-it-all "Parigote" nanny who raised her and her brother, the thought of whom amused her just as much as Frick did when she first saw her.[14] Miss Frick "rolled me up like a spitball, threw me into her car and out of her car, into the arms of a Caucasian who repaired carpets at the Met, onto all fours to catch a glimpse of the seals."[15]

Yourcenar would later describe Brissac's portrait of Grace as taking up "where Rosbo left off in its rudeness and indelicacy." The author was incensed by what she saw as Brissac's relentless harassment—indeed, "trampling"—of Frick, whose only conceivable sin toward Rosbo and Brissac was "an excess of goodwill."[16] She was also infuriated by the fact that the red band attached to *Ballade américaine* for display in bookstore windows used *her* name as a marketing ploy. Moreover, she had recently completed a long essay on the Swedish novelist Selma Lagerlöf for Éditions Stock, publisher of Brissac's book. She could not believe that Stock's director, André Bay, who had worked with her on the Lagerlöf, would stoop so low. How could he have allowed her life to be "indecently evoked" in a book from his house without letting her read and consent to the publication?[17] Bay replied lamely that Brissac's memoir had been produced by a section of Stock with which he was not involved.[18] A letter to Stock from Yourcenar's attorney Marc Brossollet nonetheless got Yourcenar's name removed from the advertising banner.[19]

Jean Chalon made the mistake of publishing a favorable review of *Ballade américaine* in *Le Figaro*. Though he put a positive spin on the Petite Plaisance chapter, his article did not fail to draw Yourcenar's ire. Brissac had set out, wrote Chalon, to encounter two "giants" of world literature in the United States, Henry Miller and Marguerite Yourcenar. She was unimpressed with Miller, but her visit to the "monumental" Yourcenar went better: "Elvire de Brissac portrays very well the imposing royalty that emanates from the author of *Memoirs of Hadrian*: 'She was waiting for me on two steps, I had the impression of climbing the grand staircase of the Paris Opera . . .' And what a performance awaited her! Yourcenar preparing a bite to eat. Ah, that Elvire was a lucky one to be invited to the home of the incomparable Yourcenar!"[20]

Yourcenar was deeply offended by Chalon's enthusiasm for Brissac's book, and she didn't shrink from saying so. After dispensing with the notion that the four birchwood steps of her front porch bore any resemblance to the grand staircase of the Paris Opera, she scolded, "But everything about this little essay seems to strike you as perfect. In fact, the snickering caricature of Grace Frick, of which most of it consists, calls to mind the gleeful chortling of hooligans flinging to the ground and trampling underfoot some nameless passerby—with this one difference, entirely to the credit of the hooligans, that the latter, to begin with, had not sought an invitation to their victim's home."[21]

Chalon was crushed by this letter, which Yourcenar signed "With changed regards." To his journal he confided, "A terrible letter from Yourcenar has . . . fallen on my head. She has withdrawn her esteem and friendship because I dared to praise a book by Elvire de Brissac that contains one or two disagreeable paragraphs about Grace Fricks [sic], Yourcenar's friend. As far as blunders go, one couldn't do much better. I am king of the blunderers."[22]

Despite the undeniably disrespectful aspects of *Ballade américaine*, I don't think Elvire de Brissac set out to insult Frick and Yourcenar. In fact, she found a sense of "absolute security" in their company that she hadn't known

FIGURE 36. Grace Frick and Marguerite Yourcenar with young American friends at Rockefeller Gardens, July 1972. Elvire de Brissac met Frick a few weeks after this photograph was taken and described the braid around her head in *Ballade américaine*. Petite Plaisance Archives.

since childhood. Her description of a drive along the Loop Road in Acadia
Park has all the elements of a family road trip. Frick is at the wheel of a rental
car, Brissac is beside her in the passenger seat, and Yourcenar, in the back, is
doing her best to keep Zoé from biting and scratching the car window.

> While Miss Frick drove, with one finger in a splint, I traveled passionately,
> docilely down two routes: the blinding cliff road, where we were going to
> perish thanks to the extreme fantasy of Miss Frick's manner of driving an
> automobile—stopping abruptly or on the left side of the road, starting up again
> in reverse to show me a cove—and the no less astonishing road that led me far
> into the past, to the scene of my earliest childhood in Brissac, where, seated
> between Mazelle and Nénin, nothing, I mean absolutely nothing, could hap-
> pen to me.[23]

Unlike Patrick de Rosbo, Brissac was clearly fond of Frick and Yourcenar.
Her transgression was to subordinate the two of them to the purpose of her
personal memoir. No pardon would be issued for that blunder.

Another presidential election was coming up in November 1972, and Grace
Frick was recruiting votes for the antiwar Democrat George McGovern. To
her niece Kathie Peryam she mailed a heavily annotated 1971 campaign letter from the South Dakota senator's office. "I find it excellent, sober, factual,
and sincere," wrote Frick. "Any vote cast for him, whether or not he finally
wins, will inevitably influence the next Administration."[24] As Election Day
drew nearer, Grace asked Richard Minear, "Are you pulling for McGovern?
We are. . . . Nixon seems to me increasingly unprincipled. The devious strategy of the anti-busing campaign, the growing encouragement of corporate
White Africa and Rhodesia, et al. Truly a pernicious man in power, and
self-righteous to boot. Furiously yours, G.F."[25] Nixon nonetheless won by a
landslide, only to leave office in disgrace in August 1974.

As America's political health took a sharp turn for the worse, Frick and
Yourcenar's physical health was also declining. In an "inventory" written
the next month in one of her notebooks, Yourcenar was seeing everything
through a glass darkly:

> Heart failure with angina—
> Bronchial allergies and rheumatism—
> Physical heaviness—

Fluctuating blood pressure, sometimes too high.

G's physical state bad and getting worse.

Total disorder in the financial and fiscal situation.

The translation of *L'Œuvre au Noir* almost three years behind. . . .

A possibly irrational but desperate need of change.

Too unwell to travel alone—possibly soon to travel at all—and Grace too exhausted to see traveling as anything other than drudgery.[26]

Grace, for her part, had been hospitalized for dilation and curettage of her uterus and removal of a polyp in April of 1972. Lab tests on that tissue were fine, but her luck turned a few months later when nodules were excised from the scar on her chest.[27] Cancer had begun its relentless return. Yourcenar's mysterious ill health nonetheless got most of Frick's attention throughout this period. On October 26 Marguerite began suffering from what seemed to be a bad allergy. She soon had a fever, chills, and "violent perspiration." Three weeks into these symptoms, doctors were calling them some type of influenza. Marguerite was so sick that Grace had to cancel her own medical appointments to stay home and care for her. By Thanksgiving, as her malady entered its fifth week, Yourcenar could barely come downstairs from her bedroom to the kitchen for a meal. She finally entered the hospital on December 30, and Grace Frick slept from midnight until noon the next day, her first full night of rest in a week.[28]

Yourcenar underwent every imaginable test "with no result but exhaustion and pain and months of recovery," as Frick noted with frustration in the daybook. Grace went to see her every day of her nearly two-week stay, sometimes spending the entire day at the hospital. On January 12 a "very weak and much underfed" Marguerite Yourcenar was discharged with no better idea of what was wrong than when she entered the hospital. Both women tracked Marguerite's night sweats, temperature fluctuations, and daily medications for months. Bouts of perspiration often required the use of a hair dryer. Marguerite was sweating so profusely in the wee hours of one February morning that Grace spent half an hour massaging her, then administered a cup of hot cocoa.[29] The patient was well enough to have breakfast that day. Shortly thereafter Frick wrote to Helen Howe that "M.Y. is improving and downstairs some half the day, being now nearly off the third and last drug (a digitalis) given by Gilmore since August 12. This makes three wrong drugs from him and one from Gerdes, the latter for six weeks, the former for *months*. Inexcusable." She signed that letter "Grace Frick, nursemaid."[30]

Shortly after Yourcenar first fell ill, a delegation came to Petite Plaisance from Colby College, in all its academic regalia, to present her honorary doctorate. Frick described the event in a letter to her brother Gage:

The Colby College Honorary Doctorate was awarded her by the President and two Trustees in person on October 29th (with a delegation of nine, in all, coming from Waterville, solemnly robing themselves in cap and gown in our small house, and going through the exact platform ritual, as they apparently had to do to award it legally. What with two brilliant red doctoral gowns of the Dean of Students and his wife (also a Professor there), from Leland Stanford, it was quite a colorful occasion.

I had invited a few people from the village with whom we had literary connections, so we were some twenty in all, and we served a buffet of (donated) lobster and American champagne. Marguerite came down from bed a half-hour before the ceremony, probably distributed a few germs while making her acceptance speech, but managed to stay up till they left, some hours later; but the price in fatigue was heavy. This is the first time I have not had to battle with her to keep her from working when she has fever. She has really been *down*. Happily, the naughty puppy is a great diversion.[31]

It was not until April of 1973—minus the offending drugs—that she finally began to recover.[32]

Grace and Marguerite both turned seventy that year, and most of their friends had retired. A steady stream of them made a point of visiting the couple through the middle of that decade. Mary Marshall, retired now from Syracuse University, spent a weekend with her friends in September of 1971. They took in all the traditional Mount Desert Island sights: Ocean Drive, Mount Cadillac, Bass Harbor Light, and Seawall, among others.[33] Ruth and Charles Hill drove up from Northampton, Massachusetts, for five days the following October, staying at the Asticou Inn. The couple's one-time deer-spotting friend Helen Willkie, who had lived abroad for a time in the 1960s, came right after New Year's in 1973, while Marguerite was in the hospital. With Grace spending days in Bar Harbor with her partner, Helen stood in as hostess of the open house one Sunday while she was there.[34] Grace's oldest friend, Ruth Hall, whom she had not seen since 1964, also spent a week visiting the couple that year.[35]

One person who did not come was Grace's closest friend from Wellesley, Phyllis Bartlett. Phyllis had retired early from the English department at

Queens College on account of ill health. Her husband, John Pollard, had died of a heart attack in 1968, and Phyllis was living alone in the apartment they had shared on East Fiftieth Street in Manhattan. She and Grace had spoken with each other by phone at Thanksgiving time in 1972. Five months later Phyllis died. According to a small article in the *New York Times*, "The police reported that Dr. Bartlett had been found dead of burns near her kitchen sink, where the water was still running, in a flammable synthetic fur-piled bathrobe and that there were indications that she had been cooking."[36] Grace was devastated by the news, which came to her from another Wellesley classmate. Try as she might, phoning friends all over the country, she was unable to learn anything further about Phyllis's startling demise.

At Petite Plaisance, through it all, progress continued on the semiautobiographical *Souvenirs pieux*, delving into Yourcenar's maternal lineage. On March 16, 1973, Grace went early to Mount Desert Island High School to photocopy the first 294 pages of the manuscript.[37] Frick was more involved in work related to this book than has generally been recognized. Many pages of research notes in her hand are preserved at the Houghton Library. She prepared a detailed portrait of Yourcenar's cousin the Baron de Cartier de Marchienne, for example, a onetime Belgian ambassador to the United States and to Great Britain, whose death merited an obituary in the *New York Times*.[38] She also annotated a very old list of the siblings of Fernande de Cartier de Marchienne for her companion's use. Yourcenar may have felt particularly appreciative of her assistance with that project, calling Grace with affection rarely shared with a third party "my very precious friend and collaborator" in a letter to Georges de Crayencour.[39] And this despite the still unfinished translation of *L'Œuvre au Noir*.

The malignant lumps found recently on Frick's chest were metastases from her original breast tumor. She had already had radiation twice, and treatment options were few. As she explained to her brother Gage, "The Bangor clinic has nothing to suggest except a possible hormone treatment, but I have always been leery of that, even in mild form. Admiral Morison's wife elected cobalt treatment in preference to surgery, but she had a hard three-year struggle before she died this winter, gallantly accompanying Sam on his travels."[40]

To make matters worse, the summer of 1973 was excessively rainy, foggy, and cool. "In human memory," Yourcenar wrote to Jeanne Carayon on August 3, "no one here has ever seen a summer so rainy and so rich in fog." She found the almost constant lack of sunlight physically depressing.[41] Late that month, Yourcenar was hospitalized with a slipped lumbar disk for ten days of intensive treatment: traction, fomentation, massage.[42] Frick took a taxi to the hospital to escort her partner home at the end of her stay. That same day, September 7, they transacted the purchase of their joint burial plot in Somesville's Brookside Cemetery.

CHAPTER 32 ❦ Offerings to Neptune and Hermes
1974–1976

> And make your chronicle as rich with praise
> As is the owse and bottom of the sea
> With sunken wrack and sumless treasuries.

> —William Shakespeare

BY THE FRIGID, STORMY MIDDLE of January 1974, Frick was confronted with yet another malignancy, this one a small uterine tumor. While she was hospitalized for the removal of that organ, Marguerite took over the engagement calendar. Every day from eleven o'clock until six she spent at Grace's bedside in Bar Harbor; every night, fearful without her companion, she slept at home attended by a succession of local helpers, some of them nurses. Only once in eleven days, when it was five below zero and a snowstorm made the twelve-mile trip to the hospital too risky, did she fail to spend the day with Grace.[1] Six months later, on July 3, Dr. Cooper would excise another cancerous lump from one of Frick's upper ribs. But as in the early years of Grace's illness, the two women almost always found a way to make an outing of a doctor's appointment in Bar Harbor, often visiting Acadia's wildflower garden on the way home.[2]

At Petite Plaisance they had their own wood garden strewn with lady's slipper, wild lilies, and jack-in-the-pulpit, among other native plants. Both women were committed to conscientious environmental stewardship writ large and small. As Yourcenar wrote to Jeanne Carayon that August,

> we use no chemical products in our yard here, except for the least offensive fertilizers. It is a matter of protecting not only people but also our nonhuman friends, the little woodland creatures, the birds, the bees, Zoé and the dogs who come to visit. . . . The lawn and the little woods are marvelously green, and the (Montmorency) cherry harvest has been a benediction. Grace Frick up

on the ladder, and me helping delicately to bend the branches overloaded with fruit with a long bamboo pole—the kind of moment one will never forget, no matter what happens.

As the latter phrase suggests, Frick was increasingly unwell. "And, yes, I am worried about Grace's health, which requires constant monitoring," Yourcenar went on to acknowledge.[3]

Though wary of hormone treatments, Grace began taking diethylstilbestrol in late September 1974.[4] She would continue to do so for the next fifteen months. The goal was to slow or stop the spread of nodules on her chest. Although some lumps did shrink, others grew slowly larger. Her mastectomy scar began opening in spots over her rib cage where radiation therapy had thinned the tissue. None of which stopped Frick from being "priestess of the orchard," as Yourcenar once called her.[5] She continued to engage in her usual activities, but they took an increasing toll on her body. A long day spent working in the garden or hauling firewood by hand could now trigger several days of pain and tingling in her swollen left arm.[6]

Yourcenar began keeping her own gloomy record of Frick's worsening health in 1974. The first entry evokes Frick's strong connection to *Memoirs of Hadrian*:

Today, Tuesday, July 10 (it's the one thousand seven hundred thirty-sixth anniversary of Hadrian's death at Baiae), Grace has received from Dr. Cooper what seems indeed to be the news that the end toward which we all are headed is in sight for her (a new cancerous induration at the base of her sternum). The long Way of the Cross that began around June 6, 1958, along which we have been granted many temporary halts, sometimes moments of sweet respite, now seems to be nearing its final stations. Dr. Coffin, who has since retired but who treated her during the first years of her illness, told me back on March 30, when he brought the arbutus seedlings that we were going to plant in the garden: "She's a goner." I suppose he hears things from his former colleagues at the hospital. "What do you mean?" I cried out. "Such a statement means nothing without a measure of time? One year, two years, six months?" "I have no idea," he replied.[7]

Adding to the gloom, Yourcenar got word on December 11, 1974, that her trusted friend of twenty-three years Charles Orengo had died in Paris. Orengo, who had published *Hadrian* at Plon and helped her win the battle for

L'Œuvre au Noir, had called her earlier that year to read a stunning review in Le Monde of Souvenirs pieux.[8] "Something ends for me with his death," wrote Yourcenar in her journal. "And what's more, the bad news finally comes at a moment when I'm trembling for Grace. Everything is slipping away."[9]

In the fall of 1975, the poet Nicolas Calas told Yourcenar that André Embiricos had died of lung cancer in Greece.[10] In responding, Yourcenar told "Nico" how fond she had been of Embiricos, whom she had not seen since 1939, adding that "since then, he seems to have refused all contact, immersed as he was in his own writings and dreams."[11]

On December 8, 1975, Yourcenar wrote in her journal that the oncologist Dr. Parrot had discontinued Frick's diethylstilbestrol that day. Grace had distrusted the drug from the beginning, and Marguerite believed it had made her more ill. "Parrot noticed another very small induration in her right armpit. Another, more visible one was already noticed by us three centimeters from the old scar (the one that's getting bigger). Lower, near her ribs." Something had to be done.[12]

In late 1975 Frick would have her first and only break, for three weeks, from any form of medication before beginning a new chemotherapy regime called the Bonadonna protocol. It consisted of three drugs: Cytoxan, fluorouracil, and methotrexate. Very effective against recurring cancers, it became available at precisely the moment when Grace Frick's doctors would otherwise have had little to offer her. Frick had already outlived ninety-nine of her Wellesley classmates despite both creeping cancer and the assault on her body of the treatments that she had endured. But she was not well enough to attend her fiftieth reunion in May 1975. Part of the reunion came to her that June, however, in the form of Betsy Lunn, her Wellesley roommate; Rusty Corkran, her class president; and Rusty's husband, David.[13] Phyllis Bartlett's spirit cannot have been far away.

Despite Frick's worsening health, the summer of 1975 was an active one. In addition to the postreunion delegation from Wellesley, Gage Frick came to check on his sister in July.[14] Frick and Yourcenar attended almost all the chamber music concerts in the village, and Frick admonished the writer and actor Gunnar Hansen at one of them for playing the deranged killer Leatherface in The Texas Chainsaw Massacre. The R-rated film had come out the previous fall and made a lot of money, but its blood and gore went beyond what many moviegoers could tolerate. According to Hansen himself, Frick had this to say about his role in the notorious film: "Twelve people were murdered in New York City yesterday, and it's your fault!"[15] There were no hard feelings, though, as both Frick and Yourcenar agreed to read one of Hansen's first short stories, "An American Parlor," which they felt showed him to be a real writer.

Frick and Yourcenar both loved being near the sea. One of their favorite recreations, as Grace once told Gertrude Fay, was to take "two hours just plain free, to watch the surf on Ocean Drive."[16] Typically, Frick wanted to share their passion with young people. Both women were early supporters of a fledgling venture whose goal was to bring youth to Mount Desert Island to learn about the ocean and its creatures.

The Acadia Institute of Oceanography, a marine biology camp, hosted its first students in 1975. Jean Hazelton had introduced Frick and Yourcenar to the institute's founders, George and Esther Hahn, in the early 1970s. Esther Hahn reminisced about the couple and their support of the AIO in a 1994 letter to Hazelton:

> They were both environmentalists; Grace especially was interested in our camp. She was instrumental in getting someone to write about us in the Bar Harbor *Times* and Ellsworth *American*. She invited our first-year group to Petite Plaisance for a lawn party. (A mime group performed for us.) Mme. Yourcenar served the punch. Grace explained in her usual manner that one bowl of punch was for the student-campers and the other for the adults. We enjoyed her forthrightness and so did the kids.[17]

Grace Frick knew a thing or two about developing a school from the ground up, and the Hahns were grateful to her. "We bought the house across from the school when it became available and named it the *Grace* House in her honor," Hahn remembered. "We had a Grace Frick scholarship for Maine students. That was established after her death. We told Marguerite about it. She was delighted and wrote us a nice letter about how much it would have pleased Grace."[18] Helping the Hahns get their school up and running was clearly a reminder for Frick of the life she'd left behind more than three decades ago. It meant a lot to her to be able to contribute to the future of the island she loved.

In the summer of 1975 Frick may have been more focused on the Acadia Institute of Oceanography than she was on translating *The Abyss*. She also did not perform her usual meticulous reading of *Archives du Nord* before the first half of that manuscript went to Jeanne Carayon in France for proofreading. As Yourcenar notes in the letter she wrote to accompany that mailing, "This is the first time that Grace Frick, who is too busy, has not read a manuscript of mine from one end to the other before it leaves the house. I am therefore counting more on you." Not only did Frick fail to scour the current work in progress, but she wasn't translating, either. "Here things are 'okay,'" said Yourcenar to Carayon, "and I feel stronger than I did last year. The translation of *L'Œuvre au Noir* into English, which is practically finished (all that remains is a revision), has come to a halt, which is a nerve-racking situation for me because it has been six years now since the contract was signed, and I feel, with despondency, as if before a past-due debt. But one can do only what one can."[19] It seems that Frick, for once, was making something other than her partner's career her top priority. Yourcenar's resigned "one can do only what one can" suggests a kind of powerlessness in the face of this unusual circumstance. Not until six months later could Yourcenar finally tell Carayon that "the proofs of the English translation of *L'Œuvre au Noir* (*The Abyss*) are in our hands, and I am trying to keep myself available to help Grace Frick with her translator's corrections, although she is the one who must make the final decision regarding English usage."[20]

Yourcenar had been working on *Archives du Nord* since June of 1974. Her progress on that second volume of her family chronicle slowed when she agreed, in September of 1975, to preface a collection of Selma Lagerlöf's novels in translation.[21] It was a way to pay homage to the literary culture of Sweden, a country that had meant so much to her and Grace during the heyday of their European travels.

Frick later wrote to the Minears about the Lagerlöf project, informing them that *Le Monde* had published most of the preface in a full-page spread, and that "Marguerite is pleased that the extract evoked much comment about a writer to whom she felt that she herself owed a great debt." She then addressed her companion's ambivalent attitude toward feminism:

This Lägerloff [*sic*] will probably also be her only, and indirect, contribution to the feminist movement, feeling as she does that there is no difference between basic intellectual capacity in male or female, only a long-standing difference of opportunity for expression of that capacity. She has indignantly turned down offers to write, or allow reprints of her work, for this or that collection in which the word *feminine* is the distinguishing factor, though she is constantly aware of the strong pleas against injustice to women in many roles of life. She did write a brief diatribe recently against women as exploiters of their "femininity," allowing themselves to be shown in advertisements as objects of luxury in order to sell sports cars, extravagant gowns, jewelry, and fur coats, thus continuing the old trade of prostitution in a more blatant, less personal form. I forget how

the matter came up, but she was trying to suggest the many ways in which she
thought that women could work toward true liberation by being less subservi-
ent to fashion and to their own domination by masculine convention.[22]

When the long-awaited American edition of *The Abyss* was finally released
in June 1976, the summer of the U.S. Bicentennial celebration, the reviews
ranged from the dismissive to the dithyrambic. The all-important *New York
Times* published what Yourcenar herself described to Jeanne Carayon as a
"stupid" article "engaging only with the shell of the subject (but no stupider,
after all, than Cabanis's article in *Le Monde*, which had the same defect, when
it came out in France)."[23] Of course, the book was repeatedly compared with
Memoirs of Hadrian, a far more optimistic look at human prospects as seen
through the eyes of a compelling historical figure. In declaring *The Abyss*
"unfortunately . . . not level with her earlier achievement," the *Times* complains that the novel is "unevenly weighted" and that it "moves with delib-
erateness and machination, coincidence being too coincidental and surprise
almost wholly absent." It finds nothing compelling about the novel's protagonist: "All this would be supportable if Zeno were moving to us and we felt
obliged by the authority of his presence to care for him and his destiny."[24]
But he isn't, and we don't.

Other critics also found Zeno unlikable. Frank Kermode saluted Frick's
"exceptionally fine" translation of the work in the *New York Review of Books*
but, echoing Britton, called Zeno "a barely credible amalgam of the philosophical interests of the period."[25]

On the other side of the Atlantic, the *Times Literary Supplement* waited four
months before mentioning the English *Abyss* on its pages.[26] That citadel of
British literary taste had already criticized the book, with special emphasis on
Zeno, when it came out in the original French in 1968:

[Yourcenar's] primary interest in her hero . . . is intellectual: thus we do not
see him develop as a human being. He is denied warmth and fallibility. We do
not see other characters or events through his eyes; rather he remains a distant
figure for whom scenes and family ties are constructed in order to allow him an
entrance so that the discourse may begin. Zénon reminds us more of those flat,
clearly outlined and carefully painted figures that emerge towards the forefront
of a crowded Flemish painting of the period.[27]

It's enough to make one wonder whether this anonymous reviewer actually
read the book through to the end before submitting his article, since Zeno's

evolution from arrogant youth to near secular sainthood is a major thrust of
the novel. That first British article ends with a backhanded flourish citing
one of "the most vivid passages" from *L'Œuvre au Noir*. Central to it is the
description of a curly-haired hunting dog relieving himself.

Six years later, in 1974, the English historical novelist Mary Renault's
glowing front-page survey of Yourcenar's work in the same publication
called Zeno "a dazzling evocation of North European Renaissance man" and
lamented the poor treatment his French creator had received in Great Britain.[28] Apparently by way of repetition compulsion, the *Times Literary Supplement* heralded *The Abyss* with a mere paragraph quoting from Renault's
earlier piece.[29]

The author told Jeanne Carayon that neither the bad nor the good reviews
of *The Abyss* affected her much one way or the other:

> in my eyes, the book has too real an existence for me to take much of an in-
> terest in those commentaries. I was very touched, though, by the letter I re-
> ceived from a philosophy student who had the impression he had found there
> an implementation of his own ideas and sustenance for his life; this kind of
> testimony, which occurs more frequently than one might dare hope, makes one
> feel that one's time has not been completely wasted. But Grace remains rightly
> discouraged by the fact that the publisher did not wait for her final corrections
> and that he charged a considerable sum for the ones he included. What is worse,
> he made unauthorized, and stupid, corrections on the first proofs and did not
> eliminate them from the second proofs, as he should have done, contractually.
> She is not satisfied with the title *The Abyss*, either, which seems fine to me since
> it is the title of the central chapter, given the impossibility of translating the
> alchemical term used in the French title.[30]

Frick knew how important this novel was to her companion's status as
an author in the English-speaking world; naturally, she wanted everything
about it to be perfect. She never got over her annoyance regarding the American title. In 1994 the Harvill Press of London issued an edition of the book
under the less somber title *Zeno of Bruges*. Grace would have approved.

Despite a belief held by some Yourcenar scholars to the effect that *The
Abyss* is not as well rendered into English as *Memoirs of Hadrian*, no professional reviewer had anything but praise for the translation. Even some who
didn't like the book itself complimented Frick's work. The American critic and author Lewis Gannett may have said it best, with regard to a novel

structured by the three-stage process of alchemical transformation, when he called the book "beautifully transmuted into English by Grace Frick."[31]

One of the first reviewers to recognize both Frick's achievement and Yourcenar's was Peter S. Prescott in the popular weekly magazine *Newsweek*, of all places. Prescott salutes Frick's translation and comments, in contrast to the disparagers of Zeno, that "to have chosen for a hero not a ruler or a warrior or a feckless adventuring youth, but a man who is credibly represented as one of the leading intellectuals of his time, was a daring undertaking that Yourcenar has brought off triumphantly."[32] He is not a lone voice. Naomi Bliven penned a detailed and admiring review in the *New Yorker*.[33] *Choice*, a publication of the Association of College and Research Libraries, calls *The Abyss* "a superb novel by the author of *The Memoirs of Hadrian*," one whose "English version has the impact, unity of style and control of the original French."[34] Robert Taylor of the *Boston Globe*, citing Frick's "meticulous" translation, dubs *The Abyss* an "extraordinary work, the finest historical fiction in years," adding that "Mme. Yourcenar's novel may well be one of the few in our time to merit the designation 'classic.' "[35] Stephen Koch's superb analysis, "In a Circle of Flames," for the *Saturday Review* zeroes in on the conclusion of the novel, Zeno's taking of his own life to avoid being burned alive in the public square for his heretical writings: "This final passage must surely be accounted one of the most powerful and profound in the fiction of the last two decades." Understanding, unlike several American critics, what was at issue for contemporary readers in Yourcenar's depiction of a violently factionalized sixteenth-century Europe, Koch concludes passionately,

> "Our worst century yet" has not been an age of humanism. Almost the whole of modern thought—to say nothing of modern experience—runs against the positions, and the forms, that Yourcenar defends. (It would be most instructive, for example, to contrast her archeology of knowledge with Foucault's own very brilliant, but hardly humanistic, meditations.) Well, that doesn't matter. The books exist, and the crucial faith they embody is alive and real in their pages. Our own abyss is becoming painfully familiar, but Mlle. Yourcenar has at least lit us a beacon—all facts and fire and light—there on her island off the coast of Maine.[36]

By the time *The Abyss* finally came out in mid-1976, its translator was entering a new stage of her illness. Certain changes in her physical, mental, and emotional state were beginning to suggest that Grace Frick would not withstand forever the ill effects of everything she had been through since

1958. Sometime in July 1976 an astrologer named Jean de Walque looked into Marguerite Yourcenar's future using the Chinese Book of Changes, or I Ching. Marguerite reported the result in her journal: "Three years sitting beneath a dead tree, in a state of indigence." Consulting the text herself, the author noted that it said, "more picturesquely, 'bare-assed.'" She then added, "Do not forget: three years. Persevere."[37]

CHAPTER 33 ✥ One More Midnight Sun
1976–1977

I have seen sidereal archipelagos! and islands
Whose delirious skies are open to the sea-wanderer . . .

—Arthur Rimbaud

WITH THE ACADIA INSTITUTE OF Oceanography off to a good start and
The Abyss finally translated, Grace Frick resumed her usual routine of combing through manuscripts before they were sent off to France. Yourcenar's
health had improved after a months-long bout of bronchitis followed by seasonal hay fever. Frick's was being monitored more and more closely; the
Bonadonna drugs upset her digestion, caused eye fatigue, and made her painfully sensitive to bright light. Both women went to Bar Harbor together
every week for Frick's blood test. As Yourcenar told Jeanne Carayon, they
took advantage of the trip "to enjoy beautiful landscapes on the way over
and back, run a few errands, bring a picnic with us in the car or take tea in a
lakeside pavilion."[1]

In early April 1976 Frick and Yourcenar's forty-year-old housekeeper Ramona Turner lost her husband. Ramona had been working for the couple
since sometime in 1974. As Yourcenar related to Jeanne Carayon, she was at
Petite Plaisance when the phone call came about the death: "Her pain was
very Racinian: a little cry, a few suppressed sobs, then 'I have to go right
home.' Grace Frick exclaimed that she was going to accompany her, even if
it meant coming back by whatever means chance might provide. While she
went to get their two coats, Ramona, sitting next to the telephone, continued
sobbing quietly while with one hand she stroked the head of Zoé, who had
put her two front paws on her knees."[2]

On September 30, en route to Southwest Harbor in a friend's car, Grace
asked to be dropped off at Brookside Cemetery in Somesville to weed her
and Marguerite's burial plot. Yourcenar wrote in her journal three days later,

This symbolism "We are leaving her in the cemetery" distresses me. But we are always wrong to let ourselves be taken in by traditional symbolism. When we came back to get her two hours later, she was lying in the good sun on what will be her grave pulling up weeds, and the caretaker of the cemetery, Mr. Preston, was galloping along the lanes with our dog, whose gold and mahogany coat was glistening gaily. The atmosphere was divinely lighthearted.

But what did she think about during those two hours? Along those lines, she has nothing to say. I can only guess.[3]

Things were not going well overall, however. With her immune system compromised by the drugs she was taking, Frick was increasingly subject to opportunistic infections. In mid-September she had an acute attack of erysipelas, a painful rash accompanied by itching and fever, that made her very ill. By early October Dr. Cooper had begun to notice certain mental "short-circuits" that Yourcenar herself and Ramona had been aware of for a few months. "Sometimes her memory fails or gets everything terribly *confused*; other times her imagination goes galloping dangerously far from the facts," Yourcenar wrote in her journal. Speaking of Dr. Cooper, she added, " 'It's classic,' he tells me, with a doctor's practical wisdom." Incapacitating weakness, horrible nightmares, alternating sleeplessness and somnolence, extreme irritability, indifference toward matters of importance: these were some of the debilitating symptoms that were making Frick behave in ways that were often out of character, sapping her legendary energy and eroding her usual conscientiousness. Yet she could also snap out of it, wrote Yourcenar, and be "almost her old Self."[4]

Amid all this, Volker Schlöndorff's adaptation of *Coup de Grâce* came out in late 1976. A private showing of the film at the cinema in Ellsworth was attended by sixty-five or seventy invited guests on New Year's Day 1977 despite near-zero-degree cold.[5] An unsigned review in the *Soho Weekly News*, sent to Yourcenar and Frick by Alf Pasquale, begins, "Marguerite Yourcenar is not an easy read, either in the original French or the excellent translations by her long-time companion, Grace Frick. Her prose is dense, rich, extraordinarily complex: Every sentence is loaded with oblique references and understatements, and the meticulously honed prose style may be a labyrinth of subtlety and allusions, but it's also a goldmine of ideas and sensitivity." The reviewer then goes on to say that *Coup de Grâce* "is one of the most magnificent 'little' novels ever written, and Margarethe von Trotta and Volker Schlöndorff have captured it with an astounding faithfulness in their film of the same title."[6]

Yourcenar disagreed with the latter sentiment, but critics, moviegoers, and other directors—from Vincent Canby to Ingmar Bergman—found the film to be exceptional in every way.

By February 1977 Frick was going "rapidly downhill."[7] For months she had daily fevers ranging from 99.5 to 101 degrees. Time and time again she asked her doctors why her temperature was always elevated, and no one would give her an answer. She had also developed a persistent shallow cough. "Perfectly all right," Dr. Cooper repeated after each exam. Frick felt that she was being treated like a child. Only when she "raised the roof" one day did Dr. Cooper finally admit that her symptoms could be caused by the Bonadonna drugs.[8] The next time Frick saw him, he was a "changed man."

On February 7, having developed an acute case of shingles in her groin, Frick saw a new young physician, Dr. Haynes, who was particularly knowledgeable about herpes zoster. He and Dr. Cooper put her in the hospital immediately and kept her there for a week. Antibiotics and three daily packs of a special soap solution gradually gave her some relief. Yet another chest X-ray revealed suspicious streaks in the lower right lung. Young Dr. Haynes then ordered a gallium X-ray and took specimens of her sputum. Finally, someone was taking Frick's symptoms seriously. As always, Marguerite went every day to the hospital, braving frigid weather, storms, and icy roads. Every night Grace called home from the pay phone on her unit. For once, Marguerite was managing to spend the night alone. In the morning, Ramona was there.[9]

On February 14 Grace returned from the hospital to find "Valentine Blessings Especially For You" waiting in her bedroom. On the inside of the commercial card, spread over two pages, were the printed message "A word bouquet / On Valentine's Day / For you . . ." and the image of a big bouquet of roses surrounded by the words "Thanks, Praise, Appreciation, Faith, Hope, Joy, Peace, Gladness, Blessings, Love, Happiness, Memories." On the right-hand side, Yourcenar had drawn a brown heart and, below it, a red one, labeling the sketches "Zoé's brown heart" and "Marguerite's red heart" and playfully signing the card, "Your Two roommates."[10] Grace was back home, and, for a while at least, all seemed to be well.

Word soon came that there were cancer cells in Frick's sputum. On February 22 she would start a new chemotherapy regimen called the Cooper protocol. Along with Cytoxan, fluorouracil, and methotrexate, Grace would get a weekly shot of vincristine to inhibit cell replication and daily oral prednisone.[11] As Yourcenar wrote to Jeanne Carayon, they would make the best of it: "We went to Bangor yesterday, some 80 kilometers from here, for a doctor's appointment. I thought it inhuman to subject her to this little trip on such a cold day in these conditions, but her courage was not daunted by it. Happily, we had a lovely day—freezing, certainly, but sunny and clear, and my thermoses of tea and my basket of sandwiches did not go to waste."[12] Frick, for her part, told Gladys Minear, "Bernice Pierce drove us to Bangor on our first sunny day, and Marguerite went along, against my advice, and said that she enjoyed it, though now *she* is worn out from a kind of letdown after too much worry."[13]

Marguerite had always done the cooking for Grace and herself, having learned to cook back when they were living in Hartford. As Grace's health declined, it became Marguerite's primary way of caring for her partner. In 1974, when Françoise Faucher asked Yourcenar if cooking was a symbol for her, she replied, "It may be more than a symbol. In rather pompous terms, you could almost say that it is a calling. You could say, for example, that when you offer food to friends, when you offer it to your family, it is a form of love. It is a way of sustaining life, your own of course, and that of those you love."[14] By early 1977 Frick was losing her taste for solid food. From her hospital bed in Bar Harbor, she wrote to Gladys Minear, "I am quite content to go on with clear liquids forever, I am just that tired of food."[15]

It wasn't long before Grace had also had enough of the devastating side effects of the Cooper protocol. At her doctor's office in Bar Harbor on April 8 for her usual blood count she announced that she was quitting the regimen.[16] Five days later she was back in the Mount Desert Island Hospital.[17] There she stayed until April 21, when she was transferred to the Eastern Maine Medical Center.[18] The oncologist there, Dr. Parrot, put Grace on Tamoxifen, a drug that had just been approved to combat late-stage breast cancer. When she went back to Bangor on May 23 for her second checkup after leaving the hospital, she was doing so well that Dr. Parrot gave her permission to realize a decades-old desire.[19]

Grace had dreamed of seeing Canada and the Pacific coast with Marguerite ever since she had gone alone to British Columbia and Banff in 1947 after visiting "Aunt George." In Victoria and Vancouver Frick was fascinated by the totem poles carved by the indigenous peoples of that region.[20] Arriving in Banff, she found the town decked out in ice-coated "glittering moose, elk, and bear carved out of snow" for the winter carnival.[21] In front of Frick's hotel and all along the main street, frozen statues were lined up as if to guard the entrance to a crystal fortress on whose battlements flew gay British flags.[22]

On February 4 Grace began composing several postcards of a snow-draped Banff to Marguerite. In the first she quotes the title of a popular song, conveying no doubt how she was feeling after two months away from her companion: " 'Show me the way to go home' but let it be through snow, like this. The train ride across southern Canada from Victoria is reputedly one of the most beautiful in the world in summer, but in winter it is a Paradise. Every minute's view from the train beautiful all day, and tonight full moon."[23] Whenever she found herself surrounded by beauty in moonlight, Grace longed to share it with the woman she loved.

On that same moonlit night, Frick decided to hike up a canyon near Banff in search of resident wildlife. As she wrote in a multi-postcard "letter" to Marguerite, it was nearly midnight when she set off:

> I decided to be prudent for once and ask at a lighted house nearby if it were wise to go on alone. . . . The house belonged to the guardian of the fish hatchery adjoining, and he and his wife had the most beautiful Indian things imaginable, given them by Indian friends over twenty-five years ago when they lived in the West Coast of Vancouver Island, above Victoria. The very things I had been carefully studying for three days in two museums, only more beautiful and far more interesting.[24]

On the way back from this remarkable encounter in the woods, Frick met two elk "just ambling around looking me over with great unconcern."[25] It was a thrilling experience in every respect.

When Grace got back to Hartford, Marguerite was overjoyed—and quite possibly relieved!—to have her partner back. On February 15, 1947, the date of Frick's return, she drew an enormous shining sun in the daybook, so large it took up almost the whole page.[26]

By 1977 much had changed. Not only were Grace and Marguerite Yourcenar thirty years older—well into their seventies—but the health of both women was far from robust. Frick had been living on borrowed time for years. Yourcenar, worn out by worry and the daily disruption of Frick's repeated hospital stays, was "feeling very ragged and anxious." She did not dare to set off on such a long voyage without help.[27] As Grace wrote to her niece Kathie, Marguerite "held up well during my three hospitalizations of a week each, but after I won my battle to get off the highly toxic drugs, and began to revive with a new treatment, she was near collapse, and was afraid to take off (all reservations being then already made!)."[28]

Yourcenar did not in fact dare to go without a helper, and both women thought it would be nice for the recently widowed Ramona to have a change of scenery. Ramona said she'd go, but then she changed her mind five or six

days before everyone was to depart. Finally she relented—as long as she could
have the entire month of July off "to rest up after her return"![29]

The three women boarded the Trans Canada Railway at Montreal, heading west, on May 31. They would then make a round-trip cruise from Vancouver north along the coast on a ship aptly named in light of what this trip
meant to Grace: the MS *Renaissance*. They did not return to Mount Desert
Island until June 20.

FIGURE 37. Grace Frick and Marguerite Yourcenar aboard the MS *Renaissance*, 1977.
Petite Plaisance Archives.

One description of this expedition appears in the Pléiade chronology:
"Grace Frick, after a grueling stay in a medical clinic, decided to undertake
a month-long voyage to Alaska, preceded and followed by a train ride across
Canada from east to west, and vice versa. Marguerite Yourcenar accompanied her on that trek and visited with her two of Canada's great national
parks, those of Banff and Jasper, along with the coast of the Inland Sea and
the Klondyke [*sic*] Trail."[30] The one-thousand-mile Inside Passage weaves a
course through channels and straits between the mainland and various islands

from Puget Sound to Skagway, Alaska. With its towering glaciers, forests of hemlock and spruce, abundant sea birds, whales, polar bears, and other forms of wildlife, the region is a sea and nature lover's paradise.

Frick, for her part, was elated because, unlike the night in 1947 when she saw elk and a deer but not a single bear, she and Marguerite had the great good fortune to see a grizzly during their one day in Banff on the trip west. Also, as she wrote to her niece Kathie, Marguerite saw "a moose emerging from a pond by the railroad track just before we reached Jasper, and therefore the whole trip is proving a great success for her."[31]

Five years later Yourcenar would once again cross Canada by rail, following in her and Frick's footsteps. This time she was headed, in the company of a young Jerry Wilson, to California, Hawaii, and Japan. Several of the essays in the posthumous collection *Le Tour de la prison* recount the various stages of that journey. One of them dwells at some length on the voyage with Frick. Borrowing its title from Rossini's *The Italian Girl in Algiers*, the essay begins as Yourcenar's train wends its way toward the Canadian west coast in the fall of 1982. It is night, and the author is ensconced in her sleeping car:

Rossini's trills, roulades, and vocal phrases accompany me throughout the night between Ontario and Manitoba, in my capsule-like compartment, a cassette player resting on my pillow.[32] The rocking of the train merges with the music and creates the impression one is hearing it with one's entire body. The music is lighthearted, cheerful, bathed in the untroubled sensuality and charms of easy love that Italy has long been reputed to impart, in which the virtuosity of voices that entwine and pull apart corresponds to the interplay and loving art of bodies. Surrendering to them here in this abstract, moving place, this convoy crossing the forest that knows nothing of the pleasures of nineteenth-century Naples and Paris, beneath the square of pale, almost white night that fills the windowpane and will last until dawn, has the charm of incongruity. My reclining body, my ears bathed in sound abandon themselves to that charm in a space all their own. Rossini's *spumante* dispenses neither violent intoxication nor sublime exhilaration. Nothing but a warm and innocuous sensual delight. Delicious relaxation.

I had once seen Vancouver in the light of summer, during the precarious lull of a "remission" in the fatal illness that for ten years had tortured the friend whose existence I shared. The disease went further back, but the first ten years had been an almost uninterrupted triumph over it. This time, following a heart attack due to the effects of chemotherapy, one of her habitual bursts of energy had made possible this trip to Alaska, which she had contemplated for a long time. In that land of mist which sometimes turns to fog, we had a month of perfect blue skies. Navigation on the Inland Sea was a long sliding between mountain crenellations hooded with snow, still sufficiently devoid of history to seem new and pure. Blocks of ice fell into the water with a muffled sound. It was not the broad daylight of the Arctic summer, but the length of the evenings and the sun's rays obliquely slipping between the chaise longues already hinted of the midnight sun. We would not leave the deck till after midnight, surrounded by twilight. Reclining next to that woman who lay beneath her covers on a deckchair parallel to my own, I gazed with her on a long lingering red sky, feeling, as one always does when traveling by sea toward the far north, that we were at the prow of the planet. Nothing will ever have seemed sweeter to me than moments of stillness such as these spent sitting or lying beside beings diversely—or similarly—loved, as we look not at each other but upon the same things, our bodies remaining for various reasons supremely present (I had surely not forgotten, in the present instance, the long weeks of hospitalization), but with the illusion of being for a moment only two matched pairs of eyes.[33]

As biographers and other commentators have noted, travel was for Yourcenar the corollary of love.[34] The cruise to Alaska that Yourcenar remembers in this passage was the last sea voyage she and Frick took together—indeed, the only one taken during the eight years of worsening illness that preceded Grace's death. It is not by mere chance that the sensual strains of Rossini with which "L'Italienne à Alger" begins, recalling as they do the coming together of bodies engaged in the art of love, evoke the country of the couple's first passion.

Marguerite Yourcenar well knew, as she lay on that deck chair beside her companion, that Grace Frick had entered the twilight of her life, stepping into what Carlos Castaneda, an author Yourcenar enjoyed, once called "the crack between the worlds."[35] Frick and Yourcenar's close friends in Northeast Harbor, Connecticut, and Paris had been deeply concerned about the wisdom of embarking on a long, strenuous trip with Frick's health so precarious. But she insisted, and Yourcenar could not help admiring her for it. For Grace, the trip was both the fulfillment of a long-held desire and a palimpsestic return to the enchanted time when she and Marguerite first discovered Scandinavia, the midnight sun, Saint Lucy's Day, and other joyful customs that they brought back to Maine and observed every year in their own home.

Writing to Jeanne Carayon on their return, Yourcenar spoke of the "indescribable" beauty of the glaciers, the sea, and the forested islands that she and Frick had feasted their eyes on, linking the particular quality of the subarctic twilight to the most subversive inhabitant of her fiction: "The weather was so lovely and mild that we could spend nearly entire days on deck, which is to say also part of the night at that latitude where darkness barely falls. It was not yet quite the midnight sun that I so loved in the Scandinavian North, to the point of giving it to Zeno for his last vision and a symbol of immortality, but the sunset went on and on in an all-pink sky, reflected by the glaciers till eleven-thirty and beyond."[36]

Marguerite Yourcenar guarded her personal life with considerable vigor. She almost never spoke directly of Grace in her work or in media interviews, for reasons no doubt complex and multiple. The fact that she chose, some four years after Grace's death, to offer in an essay an intimate glimpse of their couple, in a moment of respite from a cruel time, is extraordinary in and of itself.[37] That she chose to cast upon that moment a crepuscular glow suggestive of the midnight sun also forges a delicate link between her real-life companion and the fictional character of her own creation whom she loved and admired above all others.

CHAPTER 34 🎔 Surcease
1977–1978

> I have seen on the sand
> an empty seashell.
> I have seen on the waves
> the trembling birds.
>
> —Marguerite Yourcenar

WAITING ON THE KITCHEN TABLE when the couple returned to Petite Plaisance from their Alaskan adventure was a letter from the Académie française. On June 15, 1977, while they were away, that learned body had unanimously chosen to give Marguerite Yourcenar its Grand Prix de littérature. The prize, created in 1911 and entailing a cash value of fifty thousand French francs, crowned the entirety of an author's oeuvre. Congratulations had already arrived by telegram from old friends Élie Grekoff and Pierre de Monteret—"WE ARE HAPPY FOR YOU BOTH"—and more would soon flow in.[1] *Archives du Nord* would come out to wide acclaim later that summer. Suddenly, everyone was talking about Yourcenar joining the academy, an honor never granted to a woman—not Madame de Staël, not George Sand, not Colette, and certainly not Simone de Beauvoir—in the three-and-a-half-century history of France's preeminent institution.

Jean Dausset of the Académie des sciences, a friend of the Académie française's perpetual secretary, came to Petite Plaisance with his wife urging Yourcenar to consider a three-month annual residence in France to enhance her eligibility.[2] Jean d'Ormesson, the youngest "Immortal," had already broached the topic with his colleagues. Claude Gallimard telephoned to pass along what by January 1978 would become, according to Frick's daybook, the "further insistence" of the academy that Yourcenar present her candidacy.[3] Thérèse de St. Phalle of Librairie Flammarion wrote to tell the author how eager academy members were to receive her into their illustrious company and to express her own arguments in favor of that possibility:

> Perhaps in considering the idea, you could tell yourself that all the women who have written since the beginning of time would be entering along with you. You are our first chance. No one would dare vote against you out of misogyny. If you were to say that you might be able to come spend three months a year in Paris, for example, I am sure their doors would open, to you and to all the women writers you would represent, whose standard bearer you would be![4]

Yourcenar's reaction to that letter can be gauged by how thickly she underlined the phrase "come spend three months a year in Paris" in turquoise Flair pen. Which is not to say that she failed to make her feelings plain in responding to similar pleas. There would be no question of her making courtesy calls on sitting academy members to solicit their votes or of her spending several months a year in Paris. She was not even willing to commit to coming frequently to France. By her lights, moreover, the possibility of admitting a woman to the academy was generating altogether too much commotion.[5] To make matters worse, as she reported to Jean d'Ormesson, she had let her French citizenship drop when she became an American.[6] Only citizens of France could join the Académie française at that time.

Yourcenar also mentioned to d'Ormesson the "personal circumstances" that, along with her literary work, had kept her away from Europe longer than might otherwise have been the case. But Frick's health had improved quite dramatically since April 1977. Dr. Parrot called her progress on tamoxifen "fantastic." She had gained weight, her tumors had shrunk, her cough had disappeared.[7] Finally realizing her dream of taking Marguerite to the Pacific Northwest had also given Grace a big lift. By November of that year, for the first time since the spring of 1974, Frick was on only one medication. Incredibly, she was coming back to life.

In mid-November Yourcenar wrote to Jeanne Carayon about a possible return to France in the spring, though fearful of the demands it would bring. Of life at Petite Plaisance she went on to say that Grace was back working in the garden. She had

> completed the abundant apple harvest by herself, one of my bouts of laryngitis accompanied by a touch of bronchitis having kept me indoors for the past ten days. Earlier, we picked the plums from our lone plum tree (they are small, but I counted almost two hundred of them). And we found time, which is very

rare, to take two shore walks on nearby properties, storing up all the gold of autumn; then another walk along the rocky coast of the island, where we caught a glimpse of a beautiful blue heron and watched the wheeling flight of a mother seagull and her child, who was learning to fly; the little one, all wobbly, would come back now and then to his mother, literally, to kiss her.

Yourcenar nonetheless knew that Frick's remission might not last, as Dr. Parrot had made clear: "We are living somewhat in the moment, like seagulls on the crest of a swell."[8]

Grace was enjoying every minute of her remarkable reprieve. Her Wellesley roommate Betsy Lunn spent three days at Petite Plaisance in mid-July.[9] Ruth and Lucy Hall came for four days in August. From the top of Mount Cadillac to Ocean Drive to the island's quiet side, sights were seen and shown. Now that Grace had regained her taste for food, there was also Jordan Pond House, The Moorings, Abel's Lobster Pound.[10]

In December the couple decided to take a leaf from Natalie Barney's book and start making some monetary gifts to certain friends while they were still living. Inside their Christmas card to Paul and Gladys Minear, who were flying off to a family reunion, was a sizable check and a note:

> Do not be baffled, in the present rush, by the enclosed check. Simply endorse and deposit it by mail. It comes as a result of our decision to begin some bequests now, gradually, after talks with our lawyer, Ruth Hall, who was here on a visit from Kansas City this summer. Once, you know, we wanted to will you our house, but your joint establishments in Vermont seem so much better suited to your needs that a property this far away in Maine would only be an encumbrance, we realize. Besides, this is a year in which you could surely use some extra cash, and I think that you should use this check right now, and not travel too economically for your comfort and health. . . .
>
> Much love from both of us to all of you,
> Grace[11]

The improvement in Frick's health that had allowed her to resume the work she so enjoyed around the grounds of Petite Plaisance was also showing up in the form of energy devoted to literary work. During the first few months of 1978, Frick was hand-correcting the manuscript and later the proofs of a new edition of *Sous bénéfice d'inventaire*, tracking the successive publications of the Selma Lagerlöf essay, and helping Yourcenar with professional correspondence.[12] She was also making advance arrangements for a growing number of media personalities, and hosting them during their sessions at Petite Plaisance.

Among the latter, most momentously, was the first trip to Northeast Harbor of the French television host Maurice Dumay with a crew that included Dumay's "friend," Jerry Wilson. It was on April 30, 1978, that Grace Frick wrote in the daybook, "First week in May, May 3–6, French Television coming to Northeast Harbor FR3, Paris: Producteur, Maurice Dumay (friend, Jerry Wilson =) Photographer." Late in her life, Yourcenar reread the daybooks and put three big crosses in the slot for April 30. On May 1 she wrote, "Maurice Jerry."[13] Dumay would return to Petite Plaisance the following November with Jerry, to do a bit more filming and recording.[14]

Speaking of Jerry years later, Yourcenar would say that he had spent his early years in Louisiana, where his family owned a fifteen-hundred-acre farm along the Mississippi River. The farm was sold when Wilson's grandparents died, and the family then moved to Arkansas. At the age of twenty-two, Jerry went to Paris, knowing not a word of French, to become a tennis instructor. He subsequently met Jean-Marie Grénier, a videographer for Air France, thanks to whom he became a professional photographer. Since his youth he had had a passion for American black music of all kinds.[15]

Grace Frick and Jerry Wilson became immediate friends, a fact often ascribed to their common Southern heritage.[16] But Frick was not a Southerner. What she and Jerry shared was their love of music, their sympathetic respect for African Americans, and their opposition to racial injustice. Grace had always been a lover of young people and a tireless if occasionally overzealous promoter of their intellectual development. Jerry was a handsome, soft-spoken twenty-nine-year-old when he first came to Northeast Harbor that May. Frick likely saw him as someone whose future she could help to shape.

One way or another, Frick and young Wilson grew warmly attached to each another. Jerry later told a friend that between Frick and Yourcenar, Grace was "the kinder of the two."[17] He even made the long trip to Northeast Harbor in August or September of 1979 solely to call on Frick when she was gravely ill.[18] Jerry Wilson may have been the last in a long line of young people, going back to Norah Tapley at Hartford Junior College and including Larry, Richard, and Anita Minear, David Peckham, and Julia and Hall Willkie, among others, with whom Grace formed strong bonds of mutual affection over the years. I have already mentioned Yourcenar's memory of Grace and Jerry standing side by side in a halo of light, their affection for each other spilling over onto her.[19] Sometime in 1981 she told a friend that "Grace and Jerry were one of the most beautiful harmonies of my life."[20]

Nine days after Dumay and Wilson finished their assignment in Northeast Harbor and flew back to Paris, Frick's by that time yearlong spell of exceptional well-being came to an end. On May 15, 1978, Grace was on the south porch of Petite Plaisance when a high wind sent the kitchen door flying and knocked her to the ground.[21] She had broken the humerus in her left arm. After four days in a cast at the Bar Harbor Hospital, she was transferred to the orthopedic unit of the Eastern Maine Medical Center. There they fit her with an arm sling and swath to immobilize her shoulder, itself broken eighteen years earlier in another bad fall.[22]

What might have been simply an unfortunate accident for someone whose underlying health was stronger dealt Frick a major blow. On June 20 Grace began doing pendulum exercises for her shoulder, which increased the swelling of her already bloated left arm.[23] We can judge how devastating her injury was by the importance it acquired in the daybook and by how long it remained prominent there. Every Monday for four straight months, until September 4, 1978, Frick noted how many weeks it had been since the accident. Between August 6 and December 8, she reported a total of fifty sessions of physical therapy at the Mount Desert Island Hospital in addition to the exercises she had done during the first two months after she fell. But, as always, Grace was determined to recover; when the couple's friend and neighbor Maria Giulia Vitelli broke her hip on June 21, Grace was at her house the next day—and for the next three days in a row—doing everything she could to help.[24]

Nor did Frick's compromised state keep her from following through with a plan she and Yourcenar had made to see the "Pompeian exhibit" at Boston's Museum of Fine Arts, a reminder of the years spent bringing *Hadrian* into the world. *Pompeii AD 79* featured artifacts from the day in August 79 when Mount Vesuvius erupted, burying Pompeii and Herculaneum in volcanic lava and ash. Mary Jordan, owner with her husband of Northeast Harbor's Pine Tree Market, drove the couple to Boston on July 7, an extremely hot and humid day. They stayed at the Copley Plaza. After exploring the exhibit for five hours that afternoon and evening, the women dined in the Plaza Bar and Dining Room, with its rich oak paneling and walls lined with books. The next morning they were back at the museum for several more hours—of Japanese, Chinese, and Egyptian art this time. Since they had a willing chauffeur in Mrs. Jordan, they stopped on the way home at the Portland Museum of Art to see early French and American impressionists. They even made a detour to coastal Wiscasset to have dinner with the Hazeltons.[25] When Marguerite reread the daybooks late in her life, she put five large crosses next to

Frick's description of this trip, the largest number of these symbols of pleasure ever used all at once anywhere in the engagement calendars.

By mid-July it had been two months since Frick's fall—and twenty years, as she noted in the daybook, since her mastectomy.[26] Nurses had begun coming three times a week to help Frick exercise by holding her heavy left arm away from her body. Eventually, they would fit her with a Jobst sleeve in an effort to counteract the swelling. Sometime during that same year, in what one hopes was a very private location, Yourcenar added some current remarks to a sheaf of notes she had composed about *The Abyss* between 1965 and 1968. They would eventually be published in a second, posthumous Pléiade edition of her fictional works. Comparing herself to Zeno, and alluding to the titles of the second and third major parts of that novel, she wrote,

> My immobility dates back almost ten years. (1978)
> In certain respects, "prison" rather than "immobility," since it is no longer up to me to walk through the open door.
> Obsession with illness observed in another.[27]

Whether Frick ever read these comments we don't know, but they suggest, among other things, the kind of atmosphere that reigned at Petite Plaisance when Frick was overwhelmed by the challenges with which she had no choice but to contend.

It was likely in the summer of 1978 that an incident occurred which may show how bad things could get. John Olin stopped by Petite Plaisance one day, as he had many times over the years since Frick and Yourcenar had befriended him in the mid-1960s. This time, as he would later recall, things took a startling turn:

> Here's what happened, and this has always been . . . one of the unresolved questions of my life. I came back . . . for my summer visit, and I had a wonderful talk with Madame, I thought. She was warm as ever. And I guess Grace was there, she was bringing the tea things and here and there, but I remember mostly Madame. Um . . . And then when I left, I walked out the kitchen. And I . . . I was on the little porch, on the step landing, and Grace turned to me, and almost turned *on* me and said . . . she said some terrible things to me. I . . . I was totally taken by surprise.

Olin could not recall Frick's exact words, but he remembered her calling him selfish and telling him not to come back.[28]

What caused Frick to attack John Olin that day we will doubtless never know. The man I met at Petite Plaisance some thirty years later was a warm, thoughtful, and considerate person. He was also a writer whose connection with an author like Marguerite Yourcenar had meant a lot to him. As a result of Frick's remarks, that connection was severed. Olin himself had the idea after learning from a Yourcenar biography how much Frick suffered in the last years of her life, that "perhaps she was not well toward the end of the seventies and maybe was concerned about who would be in Madame's life after her."[29] Indeed, in Jerry Wilson, she may already have anointed her successor. It is also possible that John became the unwitting target of anger that had nothing to do with him. We have already seen Yourcenar speak of the mental "short-circuits" and unusual irritability to which her companion was subject as early as mid-1976. It was incredibly frustrating for Frick, after enduring for years a treatment regime that kept her alive but in nearly unrelenting distress, to have finally regained a measure of her customary vigor only to be laid low again for months on end. Frick had been walloped by her own back door in the midst of a miraculous reprieve from her illness. Olin may have been collateral damage.

Almost thirty years later an old friend of Jerry Wilson's who once traveled with Yourcenar late in her life would propose another theory. "Perhaps out of jealousy," asserted Jean-Marie Grénier, "Grace had for a long time driven away visitors who struck her as troublesome. Especially if a certain friendship might be born of the encounter. Jerry continued that tradition; he even created new taboos to protect the great lady. The frequent meals she had at my place occurred in the strictest privacy: on those rare occasions when there were guests, their names had to be submitted for his approval."[30]

If in fact the gregarious Frick was in the business of fending people off at that time of her life, she wasn't doing a very good job of it. Old friends and new acquaintances were constantly coming to Petite Plaisance that summer and fall. One Sunday in August, eleven adults and three children came to call between noon and nine at night. The person the couple saw the most of that summer, though, was Gertrude Fay, the octogenarian world traveler who unfailingly brought Frick and Yourcenar a gift she knew would please them. This time it was an English translation of François Villon's *Poems*.[31] Gertrude came to Petite Plaisance for tea or supper with her friends at least once a week well into the fall of 1978. For Gertrude's ninetieth birthday, Grace, perhaps inspired by Villon, composed a poem in Fay's honor, "Portrait of a Non-Jamesian Lady":

Who wears a weary air
And yields to dull despair
When "tout reste à faire"?
Not Gertrude!

Who is it that has said,
"The book's too *long* to be read.
This poem's over my head"?
Not Gertrude!

Who minds the plane's confines,
Or fellow tourists' whines,
Or lack of food or wines?
Never Gertrude!

★ ★ ★

Who never takes her ease
The best chair for to seize?
Emits nor cough nor sneeze
(*Not even in the Hebrides*)?
'Tis Gertrude.

Who is that lady fair,
With smooth, undistraught hair,
Sniffing the desert air
To track the lion to his lair?
Behold, 'tis Gertrude!

Who may this paragon be,
Of virtues rare to see,
This spirit of sheer energy?
'Tis none but *GERTRUDE!!!*[32]

Gertrude Fay turned ninety on November 24, 1978. On that same date Grace Frick stopped taking tamoxifen.[33] Had the drug stopped working, as Dr. Parrot once warned her it might? No explanation is given in the daybook. As Grace wrote to Gladys Minear that month, she and Marguerite were planning to keep "very quiet for both of the coming holidays," though the president of Harvard University and his wife would be coming by on Thanksgiving afternoon to meet Marguerite. Realizing perhaps at some level that her prospects for the future might be dimming, Grace signed off from this friend of nearly fifty years on a rare note of wistfulness: "Now goodnight, until 1979, with love from your New Haven, Whitney Avenue, acquaintance. It never seems very long ago to me, the calendar notwithstanding."[34]

It had been a custom for a few years now that Frick and Yourcenar shared Christmas dinner with island friends Mary Louise and Robert Garrity. The author later told Matthieu Galey about the Christmas of 1978 by way of illustrating that one encountered indifference and hostility in a Maine village "somewhat less often" than in New York or Paris. Though Frick "'went out' very little" at that time in her life, Yourcenar said,

> it was agreed that the four of us would have dinner together and that no other guests would be invited, in order to avoid tiring our ailing companion. On Christmas morning I picked up the telephone and heard the sound of Mrs. G's voice. "In the village this morning," she said, "I ran into the man who sweeps the streets. It's no secret that his wife has just left him and their fourteen-year-old son. I invited both of them. I hope you won't mind and hope that Grace won't find them too tiring." Of course we didn't mind, and that night all six of us shared a fine Christmas dinner in front of the fireplace, enjoying a warm feeling of friendship.[35]

It was Grace Frick's last Christmas.

CHAPTER 35 ❦ Coda
1978-1979

> Hope is the thing with feathers
> That perches in the soul,
> And sings the tune without the words,
> And never stops—at all.

> —Emily Dickinson

AS FEARLESSLY AS SHE ONCE denounced a fraudulent Pendergast voter in 1930s Kansas City, or swam so far out to sea that she frightened her friends, or marched up to the likes of Marguerite Yourcenar in a Paris hotel, or admonished academic officials who rejected her junior college girls on account of their race or religion, or plunged into a Canadian forest in the middle of the night hoping to encounter a bear, or found a way by sheer force of will to see the midnight sun again with her partner of four decades, Grace Frick set off alone in the dead of January 1979 on a desperate seven-hundred-mile journey to one of America's foremost cancer-treatment centers. At the Roswell Park Memorial Institute in Buffalo, New York, she would receive photodynamic therapy, a technique that uses intense forms of light to destroy cancer cells.[1] The American Cancer Society describes the treatment today as having no long-term side effects when properly performed, with little scarring once targeted sites have healed.[2] That would not be Frick's experience, however.

Marguerite did not go with Grace to Buffalo. Frick insisted on traveling alone.[3] The trip, by bus and by train, took twenty-four straight hours in a raging blizzard.[4] The treatment was administered for ten days. As Yourcenar later reported, by the time Frick went to Roswell Park, her cancer had spread everywhere. "All she accomplished was getting third-degree burns all over her body, which only made her suffering worse."[5]

Grace was still not ready to give up, and Marguerite did accompany her on another medical expedition shortly after she returned from Buffalo. The destination this time was Dr. Kaighn Smith's office in Philadelphia. Dr. Smith and his wife, Ann, had purchased a summer home near Petite Plaisance in 1968. One day, Ann remembered, they came home to find on their porch a wooden berry basket "filled with sweet grass, almost like a little bird's nest. And there were a variety of things in there: some quail eggs, a little salt cellar, some sweet-smelling ferns, with a little, almost like a little poem: Salt from the sea / Eggs from the birds / Grass from the earth, apropos of the Easter season bringing hope and renewal."[6] There was no indication of who had left it there, but the culprit of course was "Miss Frick."

Dr. Smith had an obstetrics and gynecology practice in Philadelphia. He was not a breast cancer specialist, but he was a friend. Frick and Yourcenar had attended his daughter Gay's wedding a few weeks earlier.[7] "She came down to see me in Philadelphia," Smith recalled. "'Madame' was with her, and they took the bus. . . . She had a messy tumor, there's no question about it."[8] But there was nothing Dr. Smith could do to help.

Frick's skin had broken down so badly from the laser treatments that her chest was oozing serous fluid. Every day until the end of her life, her dressings had to be changed to staunch the flow. The dressings were soaked in Clorox, as Ruth Westphal explained: "You just dip the sterile dressing in the solution and lay it on the chest, to cover it, and then you change it again. It was done twice a day, and it was kind of sweet. They always had the fireplace burning, so we would burn her dressings afterwards. When I came in the afternoon, it was maybe my last visit of the day, and sometimes they would insist I stay for tea."[9] When the operation was done, Grace simply rose from her bed and carried on with the day. "She was so brave," Dee Dee Wilson recalled, "I just can't tell you how brave she was. . . . We just kept care of her chest, with kindness really. She never complained. She never, ever complained."[10]

And there were reasons to. The months that followed Frick's last-ditch attempts to stop the cancer raging through her body brought a constant stream of Parisian journalists to her door. Unable to control her disease, Frick put her ever more feverish energies into protecting her companion from collapse at the hands of the French media. As she wrote to Gertrude Fay in mid-February about Matthieu Galey, "[Marguerite's] interviewer from *L'Express*, Paris, is here for the week, and started in the day you called, recording steadily from 2:00 to 7:00 p.m., with only a break for one cup of tea. She was nearly dead from fatigue and *hunger*, and I from anxiety for her. Today I packed him off at 6:00, and will hold him firmly to that schedule."[11] Galey's recording sessions were so exhausting that Yourcenar wound up in the hospital. Galey even went so far as to appear at her bedside there to extract from his hapless interlocutor the conclusion of an interview interrupted by the author's chest pains![12]

Things went even worse with another Parisian journalist, Jean-Paul Kauff-mann, who wrote for *Le Matin.* Kauffmann came to Northeast Harbor on May 9 or 10, 1979, and as Grace wrote (in French) in the margin of one of Marguerite's letters to Jeanne Carayon, "He stayed for five hours, and I had to throw him out!!"[13] Not satisfied with Yourcenar's answers to his ques-tions, Kauffmann sent the author an additional list of queries the day after their meeting, which Yourcenar duly corrected for its errors of grammar and incivility. The most annoying of Kauffmann's seven questions, judging from the length of Yourcenar's response, seems to have been, "Is it your taste for perfection that prevents you from opening up completely?" Yourcenar did not try to conceal her annoyance:

> The response to such a question is difficult, because the question itself creates the effect of a magma of errors.
>
> a) The taste for perfection and the desire or the will to "open up completely" have nothing in common, with the result that the question has the effect of a leap in logic, if not a jump from pillar to post.
>
> b) By what measure do you judge that a person whom you do not know "is not opening up completely"? My personality, like my house, is open to every-one, and I believe that is the case for most authentic personalities.[14]

Whether Galey or Kauffmann or some other importunate journalist was responsible for inaugurating the tradition, these months of relentless media attention may have been what prompted Yourcenar to start using prearranged signals to Frick that the time had come to show their guest to the door. Dee Dee Wilson was one of the few people who had an intimate acquaintance with the couple's household at that time. In light of the negative things that have been said about Frick by so many French journalists and authors, I asked Wilson once what she thought about Frick's gate-keeping role. "It took me a while to realize that no matter what Grace did, Marguerite was in charge," Dee replied. "And if she were rude to someone, she was allowed to be rude to that person. She told them, 'It is time for you to go, Madame Yourcenar is tired.'"[15]

Dee Dee also had occasion to learn that Frick could be full of the devil. "Oh, she was," Wilson remembered. "When I had the wonderful experience of getting to know her, I found her really mischievous, elf-like. And it was wonderful to find this trait in a woman who was so formidable in town and had been to me. You know, eyes twinkling and covering her face with her hand to keep from laughing out loud so someone downstairs with Marguerite wouldn't hear."[16]

Wilson, whose longtime home in Northeast Harbor could be quickly reached by a path through the Petite Plaisance wood garden, also witnessed moments of intimacy between Yourcenar and Frick, even in the latter months and weeks of Frick's life. When I mentioned that Robert Lalonde had tried to convey the women's love *and* their playfulness in *Un Jardin entouré de murailles*, Wilson answered, "Yes! Well, I've *seen* that. They had voice signals . . . If Grace was upstairs and Marguerite was down and Grace wanted her attention, she'd go . . . ," at which point Dee Dee made a high-pitched, rhythmic sound in the back of her throat. "And Marguerite would respond in kind. It was just a little singsongy call. But it was intimate, and sweet. Being in the house so much, you found out all these little habits they had. It was endearing."[17]

Sometimes when Dee Dee came to care for Grace after dinner, she would find the two women lying together on the bed in Marguerite's room. In 2005, she recalled the first occasion: "I went at my regular time, early evening, to bathe Grace, do her dressings, and so on, and they were in there reading out loud. I can't tell you which one was reading. They smiled at me, read another few lines, and it was very natural, no embarrassment, just very, very natural."[18] A few years later, Wilson commented, "There they were, you know, snuggled in the same bed side by side, reading a book, sharing a book. What could be more beautiful? . . . It was a lovely, loving scene between two women who *did* have a love affair."[19]

Dee Dee's affection for Grace was all the more meaningful—and all the more unlikely—in that relations between the Wilson family and Frick had been strained for years when Wilson first became Frick's nurse. They had reached the breaking point one day after an incident involving the Wilsons' German shepherd. Dee Dee and her radiologist husband, Robert, had gone out for dinner one evening, leaving their six children in the care of young Elizabeth Kelley. When they returned, Dee Dee reported,

Beth was in a dither. Once again Grace had invaded our home and suggested things that should be done or weren't done. What happened was, she'd gone around back and emptied the dog's water dish and come inside to refill it at the kitchen sink. And she complained to Beth about how we didn't take care of this wonderful dog, for shame, and quite frankly was certain that my husband was a vivisectionist. And all the children were around, . . . and my husband was *infuriated* to be called a vivisectionist!

In the windup, "Grace wrote a letter to him that didn't apologize but alluded to the fact that indeed she did come into the house and *may* have said this. Doesn't recall. And he forbade her to set foot on our property here."[20] And that is where things stood for a very long time between the Wilsons and Grace Frick.

Then one Sunday morning Dee Dee spotted Frick making her way slowly on foot past the Wilsons' house on Rock End Road headed toward Union Church. Bent over as she was on account of her spine and her enormous left arm, her head bobbing up and down as villagers often recall, she looked so weary that Wilson offered her a ride, fearing that Frick would angrily refuse. Instead, she said, "Thank you very much," and got in. As Dee Dee remembered, "That was the first contact I had after the dog episode. But she was willing to get in the car. In other words, she was very forgiving. . . . I hesitated as to whether to stop. Of course, I was so glad I did."[21]

Wilson started seeing Frick professionally as a favor to Ruth Westphal, her colleague at the Northeast Harbor Nursing Service. Ruth had borne the burden of Grace's dressing changes seven days a week in addition to her full-time job. Wilson agreed, though she did not think Frick would accept her in the house. "Well, I went in, and Grace was in bed upstairs. I said, 'How are you this evening, Miss Frick?' and she said, 'My name is Grace.' It was a wonderful breakthrough, and we became friends, and she was a wonderful patient. Sweet and funny and elfin-like and mischievous. And to think that she accepted me was to me quite exceptional."[22]

Of the several journalists who came from Paris in the spring of 1979, one finally managed to find favor with both denizens of Petite Plaisance, and he returned it in kind. Over the course of only two days in mid-May, Jacques Chancel recorded everything he needed for a week's worth of hourlong programs, and then some, to be broadcast in France the following month. It was with the sympathetic Chancel that Yourcenar for once publicly gave way to—or simply could no longer hide—her emotions with respect to Grace as she told the story of the Dutch translator who, many years earlier, had seen in Frick "the visage of fidelity."

The most personally revealing—indeed, shocking—part of Chancel's conversation with Yourcenar was never broadcast, however, no doubt because the author forbade it. But the exchange was published in a little volume containing a partial transcription of the Yourcenar *Radioscopies*. The conversation began when Chancel posed a question alluding to the death of Yourcenar's mother and the unusual upbringing Marguerite had as a result. Yourcenar had heard far too many such questions, and she did not try to conceal her impatience:

M.Y. . . . I've forgotten nothing about the girl I once was, that Mademoiselle de Crayencour about whom critics constantly harass me. Like her, I can say about those who were around me then, and those who pester me still with their curious questions: I don't love as they love, I don't live as they live. I will die as they die. My end will not be a rupture, I am preparing myself for it. Besides, I have at my side the most exalting example of courage there could be, my friend Grace, my lifelong companion, who knows she is condemned to death. The cancer chips away at her, destroying her. Her hands are nothing more than little trees stripped of their leaves, yet she lives and she loves as if eternity were promised to her.

J.C. I profess my admiration. Rarely have I seen, or encountered, such an attentive friend. I can tell that Grace, at every moment, would like to offer us even more precious assistance, Grace who has already done everything within her power as a sick woman, but it is hard for her even to hold a simple cup of tea. And yet she never complains. And sometimes, pardon me, I am surprised by your cold indifference toward her, as if everything she does were your due.

M.Y. I could never have imagined that you would criticize me this way. That arrow straight to my heart is hard to bear, but we have agreed to be totally frank. You can be assured that I am never in a state of indifference, though I know that my voice and my carriage sometimes bear witness against me. I have a certain aptitude for uttering my words and raising my head. It is the old reflex of an old woman who has forged herself a carapace, of a lifelong reader who lives with ghosts. I may strike you as remote from daily matters, as taking refuge in a kind of arrogance. Yet I am sensitive to every detail, however slight or momentous. And Grace, to return to her, represents the essence of my life as a woman. Of course I will have to come back to my dear Zeno, in *The Abyss*, which I consider my best novel: "I am one, but multitudes are in me." Grant me the possibility of losing my way.[23]

That Yourcenar's conversation with Chancel should have taken such an unlikely and circuitous route from an allusion to the loss of Fernande de Crayencour to an acknowledgment of Frick's utter centrality to who Marguerite Yourcenar was *as a woman* is a phenomenon about which one could write volumes. And this, not only because the author for once was able to verbalize in no uncertain terms the primacy of Grace in her life, even as the structure of the couple's relationship was crashing into the abyss of Frick's decline, but also because this passage shows that Yourcenar knew, though she was almost never able to admit, that her formidable self was built around a core of profound vulnerability. Yourcenar had indirectly revealed that vulnerability in the past, during the 1920s and 1930s, in such youthful self-reflections as the lost and lovelorn Pierrot or the moonstruck Sappho of *Fires*, "a trapeze artist, too winged for the ground, too corporal for the sky."[24] Grace's multifaceted love for the woman and the writer in her partner is what made it possible for Marguerite to become "Yourcenar."

Despite the unusual turn that her conversation took with Jacques Chancel, Yourcenar was very pleased with the interview overall. On May 14, 1979, she told Georges de Crayencour all about it and about Grace's now almost continual suffering.[25] Two weeks later, apparently forgetting her previous letter, she wrote again to her half nephew, "things are not running very smoothly here. The state of Grace's health has gotten rather worse since the beginning of the year, and there are times when she experiences quite a lot of pain. But her energy never gives out completely. She spent part of the night Saturday to Sunday making a great loaf of bread worthy of the finest baker."[26] Yourcenar also reported to Crayencour again on her sessions with Jacques Chancel.[27]

On July 20, according to Yourcenar's journal, a new phase in Frick's illness began. It was around that date that her bouts of nausea became more frequent and that Grace began refusing most nourishment and drink. Only with great effort could Marguerite get her partner to consume a few hundred calories and a quart of fluid a day.[28] The time had also come when Frick began lashing out at the person to whom she had been devoted for more than half her life.

After one particularly difficult doctor's visit in early August that year, when Frick had vomited once on the bed in the examining room and again in the car, she surprised Yourcenar and the driver, Mary Savage, by asking to stop at Rockefeller Gardens on the way home. Neither Marguerite nor Mary could imagine her having the strength to make the round of the large garden. Nonetheless, aided by a cane and by Mary, that is exactly what she did. Yourcenar, meanwhile, visited her favorite spots in the garden alone, paying her respects to the great cross-legged Buddha in the pines and placing an oleander flower she found on the ground in the cavity at the base of the statue. "During all this time," Yourcenar later wrote, "Grace was taking her slow walk on Mary's arm. She has more confidence in Mary than in me, now that the illness has lodged in her a kind of irritation toward me—and it didn't begin yesterday. The doctors and nurses assure me that 'it's in the normal course of things.'"[29]

By this time Frick was taking methadone, a powerful sedative that caused her to sleep for long periods every day.[30] Lacking strength for anything not utterly essential, she had given up most of her usual activities, epistolary, horticultural, literary, and administrative. Nonetheless, as Yourcenar noted in her journal, "she still dresses for the visitors who come, stops moaning in their presence, covers the sprawling crab on her neck with a large scarf and her open sternum, which constantly drips blood."[31] The great difficulty, as Yourcenar told Georges de Crayencour, was "to keep her nourished, which I am striving my utmost to do, not always successfully."[32]

Frick did not share with her companion what she was thinking at the Rockefeller Gardens that day or her innermost thoughts about her plight. But she may have revealed them inadvertently one day. As Yourcenar wrote about Grace on August 3,

> This afternoon, sitting on the veranda where she lay on a chaise longue, bundled up in a blanket and trembling with fever—I heard her murmur distinctly the word "Epilogue."
>
> "Why epilogue?" I asked in as steady a tone as possible.
>
> "I don't know. There is the word prologue. There is the word epilogue."
>
> And that was all. She fell back into her half-slumber.[33]

Frick's ill humor toward Yourcenar got progressively worse as time went on. Everyone who was close to the couple remembers how kind Grace was to others throughout the last stage of her illness—and how unkind she was toward her companion.[34] Dee Dee Wilson will never forget how shocked she was one day to hear Grace, whose bedroom she had entered to begin a change of dressings, scream at Marguerite, sitting quietly near her, "Get out, my nurse is here!"[35] It did not seem to matter what Marguerite did to try to help or ease Grace's suffering, it always seemed to go wrong. As Wilson once speculated about Frick's treatment of Yourcenar, "People who are very, very ill turn on a beloved because they know that beloved won't lash back at them.

And so Marguerite, unknowingly, was a whipping post. It isn't unusual at all, but it was very difficult. And Marguerite was very hurt and bewildered and tried all the time to make her comfortable. . . . Marguerite was just defeated, no matter what she tried to do."[36]

Shirley McGarr, in a similar vein, remembered the time Marguerite called her to come by if she wanted to see Grace while she was still well enough to enjoy a neighborly visit. McGarr came right over, climbed the steep main stairway just inside the front door, and turned left into her friend's bedroom. Grace's face lit up with pleasure at the sight of her, then instantly contorted with anger: Marguerite had followed Shirley into Grace's room.[37]

To me Mme Yourcenar once described Frick's state of mind toward the end as a kind of murderous fury. Shirley's husband, Elliot McGarr, had told me a story one day in 1985 about Grace asking him to get rid of a pair of red squirrels that had moved into Petite Plaisance. According to McGarr, Yourcenar hadn't known about the operation in advance and she was angry when she learned of it. But that was not at all the case, according to the author herself. "I remember that episode very well," she said. "It revealed to me a fundamental brutality in Grace Frick—she was already ill—that I had never been aware of before. It was a kind of killing rage, the way they were enraged against the Jews. But perhaps she could find no better way to vent her own rage against death than to unleash it on those two red squirrels."[38]

By mid-October, Yourcenar was describing Frick to the solicitous Georges de Crayencour as having lost all sense of time and place, needing oxygen to breathe, and no longer capable of reading the lovely letter that Crayencour had written her. "Perhaps it is good," she wrote to her half nephew, "that a being should cast off all moorings before departing, but the awful thing here is that the worse the illness gets, the more she wants to live, denying even that she is ill, or continually asking, like a child, why she is suffering. Neither the nurses nor I know what to say, realizing that she does not have the strength to face the facts as they are."[39] But Dee Dee Wilson strenuously rejects the idea that Frick had lost touch with reality.[40] "She was always in her right mind," Wilson has insisted. "Anyone as ill as Grace would bitterly complain and even deny their illness, and say, 'Why me?' It's all normal." What she did have very late in her debility, however, was the implausible conviction that somewhere in North America she could find a treatment that would cure her. When Marguerite and Dee Dee broke the news to her together that there was no more hope, she was furious.

Grace died on a Sunday, November 18, 1979, after two or three days of drifting in and out of consciousness. For a week or two, one of the nurses had been staying overnight so that Marguerite would not be alone with her. Dee Dee was on duty that evening, and she knew the end was near. The two women sat side by side next to Frick's wooden bed, its tall headboard adorned with a painted scene depicting an ancient sailboat with a bird's-head prow heading into port, its white sail catching the wind. The room was quiet except for the sound of Grace's shallow breathing. As hearing is the last sense to go for the dying, Dee Dee urged Marguerite to speak to Grace. Instead, the author got up from her chair, walked down the hall to her own room, and came back with a small round music box made of cherry or another dark wood. Marguerite wound it up and played *Till Eulenspiegel's Merry Pranks* by Richard Strauss, holding the device close to Grace's ear. When the notes ran out, Yourcenar rose from her chair, took the music box back to her bedroom, and resumed her vigil at Frick's bedside.[41]

According to Dee Dee, a great lover of opera and classical music who remembered Frick's death in vivid detail, Grace had given the music box to Marguerite. As a gift it was particularly apt, since the many tales about the folk hero Till originated, like Frick's ancestors, in medieval Germany then made their way into the Flanders of Yourcenar's paternal lineage.[42] Musically, *Till Eulenspiegel's Merry Pranks* is a kind of duet, featuring the interaction between two primary instruments, a horn and a clarinet. The piece also contains sections suggestive of a galloping horse—Till is often depicted in the tales as riding through the countryside on horseback, as Grace herself so loved to do. It is hard to imagine a more fitting musical accompaniment to the final moments of "the lady on horseback" who once rode all over Mount Desert Island searching for, and finally finding, the house in which she now lay dying.

Like the last tinkling notes of Strauss's tone poem, Grace's respirations slowed and finally came to a stop. Dee Dee removed her oxygen mask. The ordeal was finally over. Following the ancient folk tradition, Yourcenar went to one of the windows overlooking South Shore Road and the sea, opening it wide to set Frick's spirit free. "Grace was just lovely when she died," Dee Dee remembered with affection. "All the pain and suffering left her face, and she looked like a beautiful young girl. Her face just got younger and younger. She was transformed after the long years and even more grueling final weeks of suffering."[43]

Marguerite Yourcenar had accompanied her partner through every crisis of a decades-long illness. With the help of three devoted nurses who all became dear friends, she had also accomplished the admirable feat of making it possible for her to die at home, in her own bed, in the presence of love. Ruth

Westphal, whom Dee Dee had called to say the end was near, arrived right after Frick died. Then came Dr. W. R. Horner to certify the death. Ruth remembered how good Dr. Horner had always been with Grace and how kind it was of him to come out that night and "pronounce her" in person.[44] Then the funeral director and his assistant arrived from Somesville. They covered Frick's body with a sheet and strapped her to a stretcher for the precarious climb down the steep stairway leading to the front door. Marguerite followed the body down the stairs and to the hearse that was waiting out front. Finally, Frick's third regular nurse, Ella Young, arrived from Seal Harbor to spend the night with Marguerite, who, as Dee Dee said again and again, "*could not be alone, simply could not be alone.*" "Many, many, many nights" would go by before Yourcenar would be able to spend the night alone at Petite Plaisance.[45]

Here is what she wrote in the daybook that evening, and over the next few days:

November 18, 1979 (Sunday)
   The death (9 o'clock in the evening beneath a beautiful starry sky)
   November 23, the ashes are returned to the earth on a beautiful misty, sunny morning
   November 26, the memorial service.[46]

There would be no embalming of the body and no viewing. Grace Frick's remains would be cremated and her ashes buried in the small cemetery next to the cottage where she and Marguerite had spent their first summers on Mount Desert Island. In the obituary she wrote for the *Bar Harbor Times*, Yourcenar called Frick "a brilliant and accurate translator" who would be "remembered for her translations of 'Memoirs of Hadrian,' 'Coup de Grace,' and 'The Abyss,'" adding that "many will remember even more her generosity, her kindness and deep sympathy for all she met and knew, her interest in humanitarian, environmental and educational causes and her courage in her long illness."[47]

Ruth Westphal remembered the burial. Except for the undertaker Tom Fernald, who had dug the small hole for Frick's ashes in advance, only she and Dee Dee were present at the cemetery with Yourcenar. "Madame had an Indian basket, and she lined it with a silk scarf. She and Grace always saved rose petals, which they kept in a wooden trough at the top of the stairs on the right-hand side. It was like a little tradition. Whenever they got roses, they put them in there and saved them. And she spread rose petals in the basket, and then we put the ashes in."[48] Marguerite then scattered a handful of petals into the grave, wrapped the sweet-grass basket in silk scarves, and lowered it into the hole. No one spoke. Once the hole was filled with earth, Marguerite Yourcenar raised her hand as if to wave and said simply, "Goodbye, friend."

EPILOGUE ✂ In Memoriam

NORTHEAST HARBOR'S UNION CHURCH WAS full to bursting for Grace Frick's memorial service. Her brother Gage Frick and his adult daughters, Katharine and Pamela, had traveled to the island for the ceremony. Villagers turned out in force to pay their respects. Deirdre "Dee Dee" Wilson later remembered thinking, "If only Madame would look around this church and see all the people who came out for Grace, she would know how much everyone loved her. But she couldn't; she was immersed in her own grief."[1] Reverend William Bigelow began the observance by stating that the bereaved had chosen not to have a standard Christian service, although several of the texts were from the Bible. It consisted of the following readings:

Saint Matthew V, The Sermon on the Mount

Saint Paul, I Corinthians XIII

Saint Francis, Canticle of Living Creatures (followed by five minutes of silence)

Chuang-Tzu VII.6

Chuang-Tzu VI.6

The Four Buddhist Vows

A poem by the nineteenth-century Japanese nun Rye-Nen: "Seventy-six years have these eyes beheld the changing scenes of autumn. / I have had time enough to admire the moonlight. Ask me no more: / Only listen to the voice of pine and oak trees, when hardly any wind stirs."

The statement made by Michel de Crayencour about the death of his wife, Fernande: "We must not complain because this person is not anymore with us; we must rejoice that she has been with us so long."[2]

Shortly after Frick's death, Yourcenar handwrote a note, in English, requesting exactly the same service and burial for herself as was used for her companion. She addressed it jointly to the Somesville funeral directors, Dee Dee Wilson, and Ruth Westphal. No step is left to chance:

> In case of my death, I wish to be creamated [sic], and the method of burial to be the same as for Grace Frick:
>
> Take the ashes away from the plastic bag.
>
> Place them in the Indian Basket left for that purpose on the first floor of my house, over the large linen cupboard along the stair railings.
>
> —line the Basket with the two scarves already in it and use one large scarf in my scarf drawer, in my room to wrap all.
>
> —Use the dry flowers in large [sic] with desk over white chest upstairs as done for Grace Frick.
>
> (All my thanks in advance to Didy [sic] and Ruth)

In the left margin, Yourcenar wrote vertically:

> Burial hole to be dug some four or five feet north of Grace Frick, that is, at middle or end of plot away from stream.
>
> Dec. 11, 1979, Marguerite Yourcenar[3]

Before Frick's funeral had even been held, Yourcenar was designing identical grave markers for Grace and herself, originally foreseen to be in bronze.[4] She felt strongly that both plaques "should be undertaken at the same time by the same artist in order not to be disparate."[5] For Frick's epitaph, Yourcenar chose the phrase "hospes comesque" from the poem with which *Memoirs of Hadrian* begins and ends.[6] In those lines the poet, believed to be Hadrian himself, calls his soul "hospes comesque corporis," "guest and companion of my body." He feels affection for that "gentle and drifting" little being full of playfulness, as Clayton Koelb observes, one so intimately bound to the self. Koelb also notes how important the phrase "hospes comesque" was in Yourcenar's portrait of the emperor: "Early in the *Memoirs* she has Hadrian invert the figure of the poem by describing his body as 'my faithful companion and friend, truer and better known to me than my own soul.'"[7] The inversion is particularly pertinent with regard to Frick and Yourcenar because *hospes*, like the French *hôte*, means both "host" and "guest," implicitly establishing an equivalence in the role each woman played for the other. As Yourcenar once wrote in her personal journal regarding the small offerings she made to the bronze Buddha at the Rockefeller Gardens, "But remember that you yourself are at once the one who offers, and the offering, and the one to whom everything is offered."[8]

Grace and Marguerite had carefully designed and landscaped their gravesite together over the years, integrating into it mosses, bunchberry, ferns, and other native plantings. It was important to Yourcenar that the site be maintained according to her wishes. On the day after Christmas that year, she sent a check for ten thousand dollars to the Brookside Cemetery Society, "as a memorial for my friend Grace Frick," requesting specifically that the two linden trees near the stream be replaced in the spring. Yourcenar had already arranged to plant two trees on their lot, "either cedar, yew, ginkgo, or white pine, on each side of the rock already in place."[9] By the time I knew Mme Yourcenar in the 1980s, the two trees on the site were birches with twin trunks, and they needed replacing. In discussing them with the gardener one day, the author repeatedly emphasized that the new trees must be just like the old ones. No doubt to signify, as I wrote in my journal at the time, the two women "growing together."[10]

Perhaps the most poignant expression of condolence that Yourcenar received regarding Frick's death came from the man with whom she had been conversing at the Hôtel Wagram on that February day in 1937 when she and Frick met, Emmanuel Boudot-Lamotte. Composed on stationery from Capri's Minerva Hotel, the letter is dated October 4, 1980, suggesting that it took some time for Nel to find the courage to write. "I did not dare speak to you of Grace," he said,

> but thought about it all the more. My sister met the challenge, quite naturally. You responded in kind. Do know at least that when you would like to speak of her, I will always lend you an attentive ear, and more. I had associated her with Céler, the faithful friend all the way to Baies, and yet, you were Céler, too. When I see you, I will see her again.
>
> I wait for you with my old admiration and my deepened affection.
> NEL[11]

Yourcenar, who had learned to ride a horse because it meant so much to Frick, saved this letter comparing both her and Grace to Hadrian's faithful steed. At the top of it she wrote, "To Keep / Grace Frick." Obviously, Nel had struck a chord.

On March 6, 1980, Mme Yourcenar was finally elected to the Académie française. Congratulatory messages came pouring in. One was from Katherine Gatch, Frick and Yourcenar's Woodbridge, Connecticut, friend whose companion by then had also lost her life to breast cancer. "You will know," said Gatch, "that I also thought about Grace and of the unbearable irony that she was cheated by so short a time of the final triumph of accompanying you to Paris. Not the least of your achievements is what you did for her life."[12] The unbearable irony, of course, had to do with what Frick had done for Yourcenar's.

Acknowledgments

One does not make an omelet without cracking a few eggs. This biography is an attempt to rectify the prevailing perception of Grace Frick and her relationship with Marguerite Yourcenar. In the process of so doing, it criticizes writers and scholars whom I nonetheless highly respect and for whom, in certain cases, I have great affection. They know who they are, and I hope they will forgive me.

It is simply not possible to sufficiently acknowledge in the space of a few pages the debt of gratitude I owe to the dozens of people who have contributed to this project. My heartfelt thanks go first of all to the archivists, librarians, and historians who have so nimbly facilitated my access to unique archival documents, hard-to-find volumes, or historical information crucial to the content of this book. I am especially indebted to Amy Cummings of the Maine State Library's interlibrary loan department; Susan Halpert, reference librarian of the Houghton Library, Harvard University; Alan Havig, professor emeritus and archivist of Stephens College; Céline Hirsch, lay archivist for the Congrégation de Notre Dame de Sion in Paris; and Sean Parke of the Archives and Special Collections of the University of Hartford for services beyond the call of duty.

I have also received valuable assistance from the following archivists, librarians, or researchers: Pauline Adams, Jasmin Agosto, Morton Axboe, Rich Boulet, Emmy Chang, François Chapon, Mike Churchman, Annie Cough, Astrid Cravens, Patricia Cusick, Isabelle Diu, Maude Frechette, Celia Fritz-Watson, Ian Graham, Willie Granston, Amanda Gustin, Tina Hawes, David M. Hays, Micah Hoggatt, Jane Hornsby, Rachel Howarth, Paul Huffman, Shannon Julien, Karen Kukil, Bill Landis, Abby Lester, Margaret Mair, Anne Morddel, Theodora B. Newlands, Marie-Dominique Nobécourt Mutarelli, Hervé Pagnier, Heather Paxton, Amanda K. Rector, Deborah Richards, Judith Ann Schiff, Stephanie Schmidts, Catherine Seemann, Daniel Smith, Emily Walhout, Kay Walkup, and David Warren. I am grateful to them all.

Many friends, students, scholars, neighbors, and admirers of Grace Frick and Marguerite Yourcenar gave generously of their time, their knowledge, and their talents in support of this endeavor. Special thanks go to Yvon Bernier for his helpful comments on an early version of the manuscript and to the following individuals for their poignant remembrances of the two women: Professor Emerita Jane Bond, Mme Yourcenar's onetime student at Sarah Lawrence College; the late author Miriam Colwell; South Shore Road neighbors Nancy Ho and the late Bob Ho; the writer John Olin; and three childhood favorites of Miss Frick and Mme Yourcenar: David Peckham, Hall Willkie, and Julia Willkie. I am similarly indebted to Kerry Aguilar, Lynn Ahlblad, Elly Andrews, Stephen Bartlett, the late C. Ronald Bechtle, Ledlie Dinsmore Bell, Ann Birstein, Emily and the late Zbigniew Brzezinski, Joan Stroud Blaine, Jean Chalon, Cheryl Chase, Patrick Chasse, Hope Cobb, Élyane Dezon-Jones, Susan Dumont-Bengston, Anita Fahrni, Colette Fellous, Eugene Gaddis, Nina Garsoïan, Marilyn and the late Donald Harris, Daniel Hazelton, Mark Hazelton, the late Ann Fullan Gilkes, the late Gunnar Hansen, Suzanne King, Donna M. Levinsohn, Leonor Lobo De Gonzalez, Jacques Loeuille, Jean and Durlin Lunt, Richard Lunt, Jo Markwyn, Jay McGarr, Phoebe Milliken, Beth and Larry Minear, Richard Minear, Kay Tracy Moore, William Mosely, Joelle Nolan, the late David Nolf, the late Bernice Pierce, Beth Pfeiffer, Susanna Porter, the late Elaine Higgins Reddish, Elizabeth Renault, Sophie and Charles Rieuf, Katharine and Alex Rosser, Mimi Salsbury, Michèle Sarde, Will Schwalbe, Jeff Seroy, Claude Servan Schreiber, Kaighn and Ann Smith, Dan Stevens, Joan Van der Grift, George Weeks, and Pamela York.

Stephanie Williams and Deanna Davis of the marketing department at the University of Missouri Press have done their job with remarkable speed and thoroughness. My editor at the press, Mary Conley, could not have been more of a pleasure to work with. I don't know how often she has had to guide authors through eleventh-hour traumas, but she handled mine with thoughtfulness and grace. My copy editor, Brian Bendlin, did his best to keep me on the straight and narrow. I salute him for his professionalism, patience, and good nature—and for saving me from a couple of bloopers!

This biography would not exist without the incredible kindness shown to me by, and the extraordinary assistance I have received from, Charles C. Butt. Janneke S. Neilson has been both an early supporter of this venture and a champion of preserving Petite Plaisance as a literary landmark. Words are not adequate to thank either of them. Heartiest thanks go as well to the

Alliance for the Arts of New York for a travel grant that funded several visits to out-of-state archives and to John de Cuevas for his many good offices on my behalf.

For their keen interest, constructive criticism, and friendship, I particularly want to thank Bérengère Deprez, Achmy Halley, Claire L. Malarte-Feldman, Françoise Provost, Françoise Roy, Jane Gilkes Straßgütl, and Sharon Thompson. I am deeply indebted to the late Jean Hazelton, Shirley McGarr, the late Gladys and Paul Minear, and Deirdre "Dee Dee" Wilson, five of Grace Frick and Marguerite Yourcenar's closest friends. Their willingness to share precious memories has meant the world to me.

Last but the opposite of least are three people whom I thank from the bottom of my heart. Marguerite Yourcenar's literary coexecutor and friend Yannick Guillou not only read and commented warmly on an earlier version of my manuscript but, with typical generosity, helped me navigate the complicated labyrinth of international permissions. Sue Lonoff de Cuevas probably rues the day she ever thought of writing a book about Marguerite Yourcenar's drawings, but she has unfailingly provided me over the course of many years with a perfect balance of kudos, critical comment, and sage advice. My partner, Jayne Persson, whose dedication to this project may exceed my own, has read and thoughtfully improved every version of every chapter in this book. By whatever quirk of fate, the blessing of her presence in my life, and that of her lovely daughter Sara, coincided with my early stints of serving as a docent at Petite Plaisance. A lifelong reader, Jayne understood right away the importance of Marguerite Yourcenar's home as a site of literary pilgrimage. In 2012, despite long-standing health challenges, she took it upon herself to create the Petite Plaisance Conservation Fund, thereby exemplifying Grace Frick's belief that "one person can move mountains if he starts up the machinery." For these and many other gifts that Jayne brings to my life, I am thankful every day.

Notes

Preface

1. Yourcenar, *Le Tour de la prison*.

2. Paul Minear to the author, December 22, 1993. At the top of this three-page, single-spaced typewritten letter, Minear indicated that the document was "not for publication." I obtained permission to quote from it only what I've quoted herein when I interviewed Paul and Gladys Minear, April 5–6, 2004.

3. Jean Hazelton, interview with the author, August 8, 2006. See also GFAB, November 22, 1951.

4. Ibid., Hazelton links the comments quoted here to pages 198, 206, 207, and 318 of Savigneau's *Inventing a Life*.

5. Jean Hazelton to Gladys Minear, November 26, 1993, Hazelton family archives.

6. Stephen Goode, review of *Marguerite Yourcenar: Inventing a Life*, by Josyane Savigneau, *Washington Times*, October 31, 1993.

7. Review of *Marguerite Yourcenar: Inventing a Life*, by Josyane Savigneau, *Publishers Weekly* 240, no. 36 (1993): n.p.

8. L. Peat O'Neil, "Invent Your Life—Lest Someone Beat You to It," *Belles Lettres: A Review of Books by Women* 9, no. 3 (1993–94): 22.

9. See, e.g., Yourcenar, *Lettres à ses amis*, 50–60.

10. Savigneau, *Inventing a Life*, 121.

11. Savigneau, *L'Invention d'une vie*.

12. Michèle Goslar, quoted in Elisabeth Mertens, "L'Esprit et la chair," *Le Vif/ L'Express*, June 6–12, 2003, 75. See also Goslar, *"Qu'il eût été fade."*

13. Rousseau, *Yourcenar*, 10, 14.

14. Sarde, *Vous, Marguerite Yourcenar*, 247, 274. Sarde's book, written entirely in the formal second-person plural as if addressed directly to Yourcenar, is not technically a biography. The text is one side of an "imaginary dialogue" containing novelistic elements. It has a biography's heft, however, along with a traditional scholarly apparatus based on published and unpublished sources.

15. Malcolm, *Two Lives*, 205, 206.

16. Joan Acocella, "Becoming the Emperor: How Marguerite Yourcenar Reinvented the Past," *New Yorker*, February 14 and 21, 2005, 246.

17. The Guppy interview is preserved at the Houghton Library, MYC (856). There were so many changes to the original transcript that Yourcenar recopied by

hand most of the amended text before returning it—slowly—to Guppy. She was not happy with this interview from the beginning, and she eventually wrote to Guppy that she had to "forbid completely the text of this interview, in any form, and, as usual, send a copy of it to my lawyer." Yourcenar's subsequent death may have been the only reason that the interview made it to print.

18. Guppy interview. "The usual story"? I suspect that many would not consider this arrangement "usual" at all. As for being "of a certain age," Marguerite was thirty-three, and Grace had just turned thirty-four. They were hardly fossilized.

19. P. N. Furbank, "The Time of Her Life," *New York Review of Books*, October 19, 1995, 53.

20. Marguerite Yourcenar to Natalie Barney, July 18, 1956, MYC (1032). There is some question about whether this letter was ever mailed to Barney, but the sentiment remains the same either way.

21. Marguerite Yourcenar, interview by Jacques Chancel, *Radioscopie*, France Inter, Wednesday, June 13, 1979. Over the course of two days, Chancel taped ten hours of conversation with Yourcenar, only five of which were put on air. At least some of the material that was not broadcast has been provided in Chancel's *Marguerite Yourcenar: Radioscopie*.

22. Yourcenar, *Quoi? L'Éternité*, 278.

Prologue

1. I contacted Harris at Ohio State University in 2009, hoping that he would have a copy of Frick's original translation of that play. He did not, but he had something much more precious: a forty-five-minute tape recording of Frick made on November 27, 1977, now in the HFA.

2. Frick recording, November 1977; Grace Frick, handwritten note from 1934, PPA.

3. February 1937 register of the Port of Cherbourg, Cherbourg Communication Service.

4. McKenna, *The Secret Life of Oscar Wilde*, 53.

5. Frick recording, November 1977. I have omitted *uh*'s and *um*'s and made a few other minor changes to the transcript of Grace's oral account for the sake of readability and clarity. Ellipses points (. . .) mark pauses in Grace's remarks, while bracketed ellipsis points ([. . .]) indicate my own omissions. Because this recording was made during a car ride around Mount Desert Island, ellipsis points often mark locations in the spoken text where Grace was giving directions or commenting on points of historical interest.

6. Grace first visited her cousin Nancy (aka Sister Marie Yann) on February 5, 1937. Sister Yann died two days later. Archives of Notre Dame de Sion.

7. Frick recording, November 1977.

8. Savigneau, *Inventing a Life*, 115.

9. Savigneau, *Inventing a Life*, 115, 116, 117. Savigneau describes Codman, now deceased, as "an editor, an intellectual, and a Francophile, who was Jane Bowles's friend" (115).

10. Frick recording, November 1977.

11. I assumed at the time, though I can't be certain, that Mme Yourcenar was talking about a lesbian nightclub. Josyane Savigneau, in *Inventing a Life*, 91, speaks of Yourcenar's "dissipation" at this time in her life, "meaning alcohol (a little), men (no doubt a few), and women (a lot, beyond a doubt)." Florence Tamagne similarly notes in *The History of Homosexuality in Europe*, 186–87, that Yourcenar "led a dissipated life including many love affairs until she met the American academic Grace Frick, in 1937, with whom she shared the rest of her life. She was a regular on the Paris lesbian scene, at the Thé Colombin, rue du Mont-Thabor, and Wagram, 208 rue de Rivoli, and she was a mainstay of the local night life." Thé Colombin was right around the corner from the Hôtel Wagram, and it possessed the signal distinction of having been mentioned several times in Marcel Proust's monumental *In Search of Lost Time*.

12. Frick recording, November 1977.

Chapter 1

1. Alice May Self was born in Fort Wayne, Indiana, on January 1, 1872. John Henry Frick was born in Bloomington, Illinois, in October 1871. His last name was originally spelled Fricke. John Henry apparently dropped the *e*, a change that was made legal by his children. His younger sister Carrie, by contrast, kept it.

2. "Samuel M. Jones," Ohio History Central, http://www.ohiohistorycentral.org/w/Samuel_M._Jones.

3. Information about John Henry's employment obtained from U.S. Census Bureau, 1900 U.S. Census of Toledo; Toledo City Directories of 1898–1903; and FFA.

4. Grace Frick, biographical questionnaire, 1942, WCA. Alice May Self received teacher training at either Warsaw or Fort Wayne, Indiana, probably attending an ad hoc institute. The training itself was apparently quite rudimentary, and the examinations were extremely tough. Failure rates sometimes topped 50 percent.

5. Marguerite Yourcenar to Georges de Crayencour, April 20, 1976, in Yourcenar, *Lettres à ses amis*, 501. Yourcenar's letter also noted that there was no relation between Grace's family and that of the wealthy Pennsylvania industrialist.

6. "Horrible Accident," *Fort Wayne Daily Gazette*, July 9, 1885.

7. This description of George A. LaRue is based on his obituary in the *Kansas City Star*, April 21, 1943.

8. "Kansas City," *Encyclopedia Britannica*, https://www.britannica.com/place/Kansas-City-Missouri; and "Paris of the Plains: The Jazz Age in Kansas City, 1920–1940," University of Missouri–Kansas City, http://library.umkc.edu/spec-col/parisoftheplains/webexhibit/page2.htm.

9. Charles O. LaRue had established his printing business in 1896; Stevens, *Centennial History of Missouri*, 4:977–78.

10. U.S. Census Bureau, 1900 U.S. Census of Toledo. Katharine and Anna's parents emigrated from Ireland.

11. Obituary of Marion C. Self, *Fort Wayne Journal Gazette*, February 22, 1916, 13.

12. Information about the LaRue family residences, the Frick-Bacon marriage, and George W. Bacon comes primarily from public records, annual directories of Kansas City, 1908–19, and U.S. censuses.

13. Mme Yourcenar later said that Frick loved her uncle "passionately." Marguerite Yourcenar, conversation with the author, July 13, 1983.

14. Marguerite Yourcenar, in Pierre Desfons, dir., *Saturday Blues*, a 1984 documentary made for broadcast on the French television station TF1.

15. Seymour, ed., *History of the American Field Service*, appendix G, "Roster of Volunteers of the American Field Service in France, 1915–16–17," http://net.lib.byu.edu/estu/wwi/memoir/AFShist/AFS3l3.htm.

16. "Frederick C. Frick Wins the French War Cross for His Bravery," *Westport Crier*, December 19, 1917.

17. Palmieri, *In Adamless Eden*, 31.

18. "Indiana, Marriage Index, 1800–1941," Ancestry, https://search.ancestry.com/search/db.aspx?dbid=5059.

19. Bowery Street has since become Fleming Avenue.

20. U.S. Census Bureau, 1900 U.S. Census of Newark, New Jersey.

21. U.S. Census Bureau, 1910 U.S. Census of Newark, New Jersey.

22. *Fort Wayne Gazette*, April 4, 1886, 8.

23. U.S. Census Bureau, 1920 U.S. Census of West Paterson, New Jersey. "John J." is the name given for Cora's husband in all the censuses. The age and ancestral birthplaces given in 1920 also match up with previous records.

24. U.S. Census Bureau, 1930 U.S. Census of Kansas City, Missouri, identifies the LaRues' youngest charge as Nancy G. Gallagher, with the "G." presumably standing for Grace.

25. National Register of Historic Places, nomination form for Mineral Hall, http://www.dnr.mo.gov/shpo/nps-nr/76001112.pdf.

26. Frick, biographical questionnaire, 1942.

27. Designed by the prominent architect Frederick C. Gunn, the building is included in a walking tour of Kansas City's Library District; see Kansas City Public Library, "Library District Walking Tour," http://www.kclibrary.org/district-tour.

28. Anonymous typewritten document, FFA.

29. "Now Take a Man of His Type," n.d., FFA.

30. See, e.g., the website of the Westport Historical Society, http://westporthistorical.com; and "A Brief History of Westport," http://www.westportkc.com/history.php.

31. "Battle of Westport," http://www.battleofwestport.org; "Missouri Civil War," http://www.missouricivilwar.net; and American Battlefield Protection Program, "CWSAC Battle Summaries: Westport," http://www.nps.gov/hps/abpp/battles/mo027.htm.

32. Juana Summers, "Westport High School Alumni Look Back on Decades of History," *Kansas City Free Press*, June 2, 2010. The school closed its doors forever in 2010.

33. Daniel Smith (Kansas City historian), e-mail to the author, August 15, 2010.

34. "Club Notes," *Westport Crier*, January 5, 1921.

35. Quotations are from the 1921 Westport High School *Herald*.

36. "Conference of High School Journalists at Lawrence," *Westport Crier*, December 1, 1920.

37. *Westport Crier*, February 2, 1921.

38. *Westport Crier*, January 5, 1921.

39. See the 1921 Westport High School *Herald*, 89–91. Highest distinction was accorded those with a minimum of thirty academic E's. Four of the 167 female students achieved that status in 1921, as did one of the 114 male students, all of whose names preceded those of the school's female students in the *Herald*'s class roster.

40. Marguerite Yourcenar, conversation with the author, July 4, 1983. Cushman McGiffert, retired president of the Chicago Theological Seminary, and his wife came for tea on the lawn at Petite Plaisance on June 30, 1983. While Mme Yourcenar was inside the house answering a telephone call, Dr. McGiffert ventured to tell me that Miss Frick was "a contemporary woman" who got involved in all sorts of causes and local controversies, whereas Mme Yourcenar was more oriented toward the past. When I mentioned the comment to Mme Yourcenar a while later, she called the observation "absurd," adding that both she and Grace Frick were engaged in causes such as conservation, civil rights, protesting the Vietnam War, and so on, and that Grace's favorite literature was Elizabethan poetry.

41. The wealthy and fabled American dressmaker Nelly Don lived across the street from the new LaRue residence, but her fashion sense probably didn't rub off on Grace. Judging from the comments made by friends and acquaintances, neither Grace nor Marguerite paid a great deal of attention to her attire. As Dee Dee Wilson once remarked, Mme Yourcenar was convinced that anything a Frenchwoman wore was automatically stylish.

Chapter 2

1. Shirley McGarr (longtime friend of Frick and Yourcenar), interview with the author, September 4, 2005.

2. Goslar, *"Qu'il eût été fade,"* 135.

3. Frick's most extensive chronology of her life dates back only to 1925, the year she graduated from college. See GFC.

4. Palmieri, *In Adamless Eden*, 102–3.

5. In the second decade of the twenty-first century, Wellesley has remained the highest ranked of the now Five Sisters according to the yearly analysis of American liberal arts colleges compiled by *U.S. News and World Report*. See the rankings for 2018 at https://www.usnews.com/best-colleges/rankings/national-liberal-arts-colleges.

6. Latimer, *Women Together/Women Apart*, 30.

7. Michelle Gibson and Deborah T. Meem, "Introduction," in Gibson and Meem, eds., *Lesbian Academic Couples*, 4.

8. Palmieri, *In Adamless Eden*, 137–39.

9. Grace E. Hawk, "A Motto in Transit," in Glasscock, ed., *Wellesley College, 1875–1975*, 212.

10. Ibid., 212–13.

11. Palmieri, *In Adamless Eden*, 246, 148.

12. "Westporter Tells of Student Life at Wellesley," *Westport Crier*, January 5, 1921.

13. Eleanor Wallace Allen, "Greetings from Twenty-Fifth Reunion Class," 1, WCA.

14. *Wellesley College Bulletin*, 1921–22, WCA.

15. Grace Frick, official academic transcript, obtained from the Office of the Registrar, Wellesley College, in February 2011.

16. Ibid.

17. David M. Hays, e-mail to the author, January 26, 2011.

18. WCCC, 1950, 28, WCA.

19. Palmieri, *In Adamless Eden*, 203, 183, 185.

20. Lucy Dow Cushing, handwritten history of Alpha Kappa Chi, WCA.

21. *Wellesley College News*, various dates, 1923–25.

22. Thrale, *Thraliana*.

23. Balderston died in 1979 at the age of eighty-four; see "Katharine C. Balderston, 84, Dies; Professor Emeritus at Wellesley," *New York Times*, November 23, 1979. Shackford herself died four years later, leaving a fifty-thousand-dollar bequest to Wellesley College; Palmieri, *In Adamless Eden*, 108.

24. GFAB, 1969 and 1970.

25. *Wellesley College Bulletin*, 1923–24, 111, WCA.

26. Grace Frick, student information card, obtained from the Office of the Registrar, Wellesley College, in February 2011.

27. Grace Frick, biographical questionnaire, 1942, WCA.

28. Marguerite Yourcenar, conversation with the author, July 17, 1983.

29. See, e.g., Palmieri, *In Adamless Eden*, 169.

30. Palmieri, *In Adamless Eden*, 80, 165.

31. In 1977 Grace discussed Milton's work with Donald Harris and Nadine Bicher as if she had read it the day before. Grace Frick, audio recording by Donald Harris, November 27, 1977, HFA.

32. *Wellesley College Bulletin*, 1924–25, 64, WCA.

33. Palmieri, *In Adamless Eden*, 165.

34. Fergusson, O'Gorman, and Rhodes, *The Landscape and Architecture of Wellesley College*, 84.

35. "Simplicity Keynote of Tree Day Program," *Wellesley College News*, May 28, 1925, 1.

36. *Wellesley College News*, April 16, 1925, quoted in Glasscock, *Wellesley College*, 353.

37. "Supreme Beauty Is Message of Pageant," *Wellesley College News*, May 28, 1925, 1.

38. "Academic March to Start Celebration," *Wellesley College News*, May 28, 1925, 1.

39. "Celebration Marks Fiftieth Anniversary of the College," *Wellesley College News*, June 4, 1925, 1.

40. Ibid., 1–2; "Anniversary Services for Delegates to Be in Chapel," *Wellesley College News*, May 28, 1925, 1.

41. Barbara P. McCarthy, "Anniversary Celebrations," in Glasscock, ed., *Wellesley College*, 352.

42. "Celebration Marks Fiftieth," *Wellesley College News*, June 4, 1925, 2.

43. Ibid., 3.

44. McCarthy, "Anniversary Celebrations," 357.

45. "New Point of View Given by Dr. Black," *Wellesley College News*, June 25, 1925, 1.

46. Allen, "Greetings," 3.

47. Ibid.

Chapter 3

1. Grace Frick, biographical questionnaire, 1942, WCA.

2. WCCC, 1929, 17, WCA; Frick, biographical questionnaire, 1942.

3. WCCC, 1927, 19, WCA. Horton House was and still is a large brick building at 666 Washington Street, providing rental housing for Wellesley faculty. Grace rented a small apartment there in 1926–27.

4. Pauline Adams (retired librarian and archivist of Somerville College, Oxford University), e-mails to the author, February 11 and March 7, 2011.

5. GFC.

6. Missouri Digital Heritage Collections, *Stephensophia* Collection, http://www.sos .mo.gov/archives/mdh_splash/default.asp?coll=stephens.

7. "History of Stephens," http://www.eastchance.com/uni.asp?id=2203; Stephens College, "Timeline," https://www.stephens.edu/about-stephens/timeline.

8. *Stephensophia*, 1928, 17, 19, 23.

9. "War and Reconciliation: Mid-Missouri Civil War Project," University of Missouri–Columbia School of Law, http://law.missouri.edu/bowman/index.html.

10. Sources include Alan Scher Zagier, "Mo. Corrects Record on 1923 College-Town Lynching," November 8, 2010, NBC News, http://www.nbc news.com/id/40077595/ns/us_news-life; Alan Havig to the author, February 23, 2011; Katy Bergen, "Columbia Man Works to Change Death Certificate of Lynching Victim," *Missourian*, September 12, 2010, https://www. columbiamissourian.com/news/local/columbia-man-works-to-change-death -certificate-of-lynching-victim/article_0869f547-7892-5ceb-8ecb-43c14794ef8d. html; Katy Bergen, "Benefit Raises Money for James T. Scott Headstone," *Missourian*, November 8, 2010, https://www.columbiamissourian.com/news /benefit-raises-money-for-james-t-scott-headstone/article_082899d9-b4ea-535a- 948a-bec9c18a38d2.html; and "Old Stewart Road Bridge, Site of James T. Scott Lynching," http://www.columbiamissourian.com/multimedia/photo/2010/09/12 /old-stewart-road-bridge-site-james-t-scott-lynching.

11. Alan Havig to the author, February 23, 2011.

12. Dudley also headed the English department in 1913–14. *Bryn Mawr College Calendar*, 1916, vol. 9, part 2, 36.

13. *Stephensophia*, 1932, 22, and 1935, 34.

14. *Stephensophia*, 1935, 14.

15. Stephens College, "A Tradition of Innovation," *Ideal Connection*, fall 2010, http://www.stephens.edu/alumnae/magazine/wp/?p=945.

16. Dudley and Faricy, *The Humanities*, signed copy in the PPA.

17. Dudley and Faricy, *The Humanities*, 4th ed., signed copy in the PPA.

18. *Stephensophia*, 1929, 64.

19. *Stephensophia*, 1930, 200.

20. See the letters of Louise Dudley to Grace Frick, MYC (2456). Dudley died in 1975 at the age of ninety-one.

21. Benvenuto Cellini, *Autobiography of Cellini*, trans. Thomas Roscoe (London: Simpkin, Marshall, Kent, n.d.).

22. See "Benvenuto Cellini," *Encyclopedia Britannica*, https://www.britannica.com/biography/Benvenuto-Cellini-Italian-artist; and Dino S. Cervigni, "Cellini's *Vita*, or the Unfinished Story of a Disillusioned Hero," *Modern Language Quarterly* 39 (1978): 15–26.

23. Grace Frick to Gladys and Paul Minear, August 7, 1949, MFA.

24. The bookcase next to Grace's bed at Petite Plaisance still holds an inscribed copy of William Wordsworth's *The Prelude, or Growth of a Poet's Mind*, which Helen Darbishire edited. It is liberally annotated by Grace, suggesting that she used it in her teaching.

25. Pauline Adams, e-mail to the author, February 11, 2011.

26. Ann Birstein, telephone interview with the author, April 3, 2011.

27. Chapman, *Oxford Playhouse*, 68; Jane Hornsby (of the Oxford Playhouse), e-mail to the author, February 15, 2011.

28. WCCC, 1929, 6, WCA.

29. Gaskell, *The Life of Charlotte Brontë*, Grace Frick's annotated copy, PPA.

30. Ibid., 317.

31. Wordsworth, *Wordsworth's Guide to the Lakes*, 5th ed., Grace Frick's annotated copy, PPA.

32. GFC.

33. WCCC, 1929, 11, WCA.

34. Information about Grace's ocean crossings obtained from ship's manifests, "All Immigration and Travel results for Grace M Frick," Ancestry, https://www.ancestry.com/search/categories/40/?name=Grace+M._Frick&birth=1903_Toledo-Ohio&gender=f&location=2&name_x=_1&priority=usa.

35. Grace Frick to Paul and Gladys Minear, November 15, 1949, MFA.

36. Alan Havig to the author, February 23, 2011.

37. Grace Frick, "A Survey Unit for the Study of English Literature" (manuscript), 1930, Stephens College Archives, 3.

38. Dudley, *The Study of Literature*, v.

39. Frick, "Survey Unit," 1.

40. Ibid., 4–5.

41. Ibid., 8.

42. For Frick's cross-burning experience, see Yourcenar, *Blues et gospels*, 10.

43. Frick, "Survey Unit," 6–10.

44. Ibid., 18–19.

45. Ibid., 19.

46. See, e.g., Savigneau, *Inventing a Life*, 117.

47. Savigneau, *Inventing a Life*, 116. Codman's friend, at least in the 1940s, was Margot Hill; GFAB, 1945.

48. Marianne Zerner, postcard to Grace Frick, May 12, 1933, Northeast Harbor Public Library Archives. A 1939 Yale PhD, the Vienna-born Zerner taught German at Queens College of the City University of New York. She never married.

49. Mme Yourcenar, for her part, had this to say about *The Well* late in life: "*The Well of Loneliness* garnered interest owing to its scandalous aspects (for the time), which is not negligible, but it is *very bad literature*." Marguerite Yourcenar to the author, July 7, 1986.

50. The two women intersected at Stephens in 1929–30 and, according to Rummell's aunt, Jo Markwyn, possibly also the previous year. Jo Markwyn, e-mail to the author, February 18, 2011.

51. Frederics, *Diana, a Strange Autobiography*, 139–40.

52. U.S. Census Bureau, 1930 U.S. Census of Kansas City, ward 4; Stephanie Schmidts (former principal of Notre Dame de Sion in Kansas City), e-mail to the author, April 10, 2010.

53. Frick spoke of Nancy's scholastic difficulties with Donald Harris. Grace Frick, audio recording by Donald Harris, November 27, 1977, HFA.

54. Grace Frick, graduate transcript, University of Kansas Archives.

55. Gladys Minear to the author, November 5, 2007. Both porch and lawn disappeared in 2007.

56. Gladys Minear to the author, February 19, 2007.

57. Frick recording, November 1977.

58. WCCC, 1932, 20, WCA.

59. Grace Frick, official transcript, obtained from the Yale University Registrar's Office; GFC.

60. Judith Ann Schiff (chief research archivist, YMA), e-mail to the author, July 12, 2006.

61. Wilson, *The Essential Shakespeare*, copy in the PPA.

62. Diane E. Kaplan (head of research services, YMA), e-mail to the author, December 10, 2010.

63. Marguerite Yourcenar, conversation with the author, July 13, 1983.

Chapter 4

1. Scott O'Kelley, "Boss Tom," University of Missouri–Kansas City, https://web .archive.org/web/20160322191657/http://library.umkc.edu/spec-col/parisofth eplains/webexhibit/political/pol-01.htm.

2. Arthur Holst, "The Politician and Political Machines," in Sisson, Zacher, and Cayton, eds., *The American Midwest*, 1702.

3. Grace Frick, biographical questionnaire, 1942, WCA; Lawrence H. Larsen, "Gage, John Bailey, 1887–1970," in Lawrence O. Christensen et al., eds., *Dictionary of Missouri Biography*, 327.

4. Frick, biographical questionnaire, 1942.

5. "Missouri: Vote of Confidence," *Time*, April 11, 1938, http://www.time.com /time/magazine/article/0,9171,759419,00.html.

6. Scott Bekker, "Pendergast's Ghost: Fifteen Indicted in Two Years in Missouri," *Austin American Statesman*, November 29, 1996; John E. Hansan, "The Pendergast Machine of Kansas City, Missouri (1900–1939)," Social Welfare History Project, February 28, 2011, http://www.socialwelfarehistory.com/eras/pendergast -machine; "Tom Pendergast: Boss of Kansas City Ages, and Turn of Fortune Changes," *Newsweek*, March 21, 1938, 10–11.

7. Frick family documents, FFA.

8. Brian Burnes, "Women Defeated Kansas City Machine Rule," *Kansas City Star*, March 30, 1996.

9. Bekker, "Pendergast's Ghost"; Hansan, "The Pendergast Machine."

10. Celia Fritz-Watson (director of alumnae[i] affairs), Notre Dame de Sion High School, Kansas City), e-mail to the author, April 13, 2010.

11. Notre Dame de Sion, "Jerusalem—150 Year [*sic*] of Presence," http://www .notredamedesion.org/en/news.php?caso=view&id=7.

12. "Kansas City's Historic Hyde Park," https://web.archive.org/web/2010 1214083318/http://hydeparkkansascity.retrosites.com.

13. "George LaRue Dies," *Kansas City Star*, April 21, 1943.

14. Grace Frick, audio recording by Donald Harris, November 27, 1977, HFA.

15. Patricia Cusick (London archives of the Sisters of Sion), e-mail to the author, May 28, 2010.

16. Information on Sister Marie Yann from the Archives of the USA/Canada Province of Notre Dame de Sion, received from Catherine Seemann (archivist for Notre Dame de Sion's Canada/USA Province) and Stephanie Schmidts via e-mail, April 9, 2010.

17. Céline Hirsch (lay archivist for the European Province of the Sisters of Notre Dame de Sion in Paris), e-mail to the author, May 5, 2010. Hirsch explained the likely provenance of Nancy's religious name.

18. The other three hotels were the Continental, the Grand, and the Ritz. Nancy's address, that of Sion's mother house in Paris, and "Grandbourg (country place)" constituted the remainder of Grace's notes.

19. GFC.

20. Yourcenar biographies have located this convent in Fontainebleau, as Frick did in her chronology, calling it a country house or château. Notre Dame de Sion has never owned a property in Fontainebleau, and archival records of the Sion Sisters preserved in Paris clearly indicate that both the novices and the postulants went on retreat at Grandbourg in August 1934. Céline Hirsch, e-mail to the author, April 30, 2010; Catherine Seemann, e-mail to the author, March 17, 2011. Information about the family's comings and goings here and in subsequent paragraphs come from GFC; and ships' manifests, "Passenger lists," Ancestry, https://search.ancestry.com/search /category.aspx?cat=112.

21. WCCC, 1935, 18, WCA. The Piccadilly Theatre copy of the Sangster play resides on the bookshelf next to Grace Frick's bed at Petite Plaisance, along with many other volumes related to the Brontës.

22. GFC.

23. Grace Frick, alumni information sheet, May 13, 1935, YMA.

24. Margaret Bottral to Grace Frick, December 21, 1934, MYP (1185).

25. Patricia Cusick, e-mail to the author, May 28, 2010. Issy became a retirement home for Sion Sisters in the 1960s, closing its doors for good in 1997; Céline Hirsch, e-mail to the author, April 26, 2010.

26. Frick recording, November 1977.

27. Sontag, *Illness as Metaphor*, 35.

28. Sionian letter from the mother house, January–March 1937, received via e-mail from Catherine Seemann, March 3, 2011.

29. House journal, Issy-les-Moulineaux, February 7, 1937.

30. Sionian Letter from the mother house, January–March 1937.

31. House journal, Issy-les-Moulineaux, February 9, 1937.

32. Céline Hirsch, e-mail to the author, April 20, 2010.

33. *Independent: Kansas City's Journal of Society*, March 6, 1937, 4.

34. Celia Fritz-Watson, e-mail to the author, April 16, 2011.

35. Emily Sophian to Grace Frick, [second half of] February 1937, MYP (1230).

36. Ibid.

37. Hirsch e-mail, April 20, 2010.

Chapter 5

Epigraph: According to the 1922 Wellesley *Legenda*, 185, WCA, "Incipit Vita Nova" [The new life begins], by a Wellesley College freshman, appeared anonymously in the *Atlantic Monthly* (date not given in the *Legenda*). Here is the whole poem:

> Chained by enchantment to the spot.
> My being throbs with palpitating joys;
> Yet I am stilled.
> A thousand lovely fancies
> Play upon my mind,
> A thousand lovely words
> Spring to my lips;
> Yet I am dumb.
> I stand spellbound,
> Chained by enchantment to the spot.
> I have just seen
> My Village Senior.

1. Yourcenar, *Feux*, 9–10, quoted in Savigneau, *Inventing a Life*, 104.

2. Marguerite Yourcenar, "Notre-Dame-des-Hirondelles," *Revue hebdomadaire*, January 2, 1937, 40–49; Marguerite Yourcenar, "Mozart à Salzbourg," *Revue bleue* no. 3 (1937): 88–89.

3. Marguerite Yourcenar, "Le Lait de la mort," *Les Nouvelles littéraires*, March 20, 1937, 1–2.

4. Woolf, *Les Vagues*. Coincidentally, Woolf appeared on the cover of *Time* magazine on April 12, 1937; the article calls *The Waves* her masterpiece.

5. See, e.g., Savigneau, *Inventing a Life*, 98; and Sarde, *Vous, Marguerite Yourcenar*, 175.

6. Marguerite Yourcenar, conversation with the author, July 12, 1984. What I wrote in my journal on July 13, 1984, was actually the following: "M.Y. was living with the man of the seven-year relationship at the hotel when she met G.F." We had been discussing the beginnings of her relationship with Grace.

I realize that readers are likely to see André Fraigneau in Mme Yourcenar's description of a difficult man, and I cannot dismiss that possibility outright. But Fraigneau himself has made clear that he never reciprocated Yourcenar's passion for him. Certainly he would not have been "living," or even staying temporarily, at the Hôtel Wagram with Yourcenar in early 1937. Indeed, the 1936 work *Feux* leaves one with little doubt that whatever level of intimacy there may ever have been between Yourcenar and Fraigneau was a thing of the past.

In contrast to Fraigneau, Yourcenar did acknowledge, throughout her life, having had a relationship with Embiricos. As a Greek national, Embiricos may also have had reason to frequent the Hôtel Wagram. Though Fraigneau was both a writer and an editor, Embiricos was also a writer—the very one, in fact, who was by Yourcenar's side day and night when she was working on *Feux* and *Nouvelles orientales*. In March 1935, shortly before he took Yourcenar cruising on the Black Sea, Embiricos had published a volume of surrealist prose poems, similar in form if not in content to the texts of *Fires*, entitled *Blast Furnace*. Knowing how the group of literary friends with whom Yourcenar associated during the 1930s often discussed their works in progress with—and drew inspiration from—one another, one would be hard pressed not to see at least a superficial connection between Yourcenar's "fires" and Embiricos's "furnace." Yourcenar was hardly a surrealist, but *Feux* was the closest she ever came to being one.

Biographers have been reluctant to say whether Yourcenar's relationship with Embiricos, whom she always called a "friend," included sexual intimacy. The information that is available to us now about the Greek writer and psychoanalyst strongly suggests that he would not have spent three months sailing virtually alone with her if it had not. Yourcenar, for her part, was then and would remain throughout her life, as she preferred to say, "sensually adventurous."

Finally, a document composed by Yourcenar not long before her death lends further credence to the hypothesis that Embiricos was "the man of the seven-year relationship." It is the small, red, hardcover book in which Yourcenar jotted down the provenance of objects at Petite Plaisance that she had acquired over the course of her life. Speaking of the modern print that hangs over her bed, she wrote (in the telegraphic style she used for this volume), "A charming drawing in itself, but trivialized by too many reproductions, by a contemporary Chinese painter whose name escapes me. Represents a horse, outlined in black on a white background. (In my mind the legendary horse that flies into the sky every 1,000 years.) Gift of André Embiricos who had just bought it in a boutique on the quays *during our last meeting in Paris (1937)*." PPA, emphasis added.

7. Marguerite Yourcenar, conversation with the author, July 7, 1983.

8. Marguerite Yourcenar, conversation with the author, July 12, 1984.

9. Savigneau, *Inventing a Life*, 114–15.

10. First published in July 1937 in *Nouvelles littéraires*, "Une Visite à Virginia Woolf" was later incorporated into "Une Femme étincelante et timide," *ADAM International Review* 364–66 (1972): 16–17, and reprinted in *En pèlerin*, 107–20, and *Essais et mémoires*, 490–98.

11. Goslar, *"Qu'il eût été fade,"* 136.

12. Documentation accompanying the Image Works photographs supplies the date of February 5, 1937.

13. Fernande, born on February 23, 1872, and Grace's Aunt Dolly, born on February 24, 1873, almost shared a birthday.

14. Alberto Manguel would later translate that story, "Our-Lady-of-the-Swallows," and others into English in *Oriental Tales*.

15. Jerry Wilson, personal journal, February 28, 1980, quoted in Savigneau, *Inventing a Life*, 115.

16. Sarde, *Vous, Marguerite Yourcenar*, 226–27.

17. Marguerite Yourcenar, conversation with the author, July 13, 1983.

18. Fraigneau, speaking in 1989 and quoted in Savigneau, *Inventing a Life*, 102.

19. Woolf, *The Diary of Virginia Woolf*, 5:60–61. Edmond Jaloux, the French critic who had saluted a major new talent when *Alexis* came out in 1929, was an admirer of Woolf. He may have been the one to suggest that Yourcenar translate *The Waves*. The Margeries were a family of diplomats well known in both Paris and London.

20. Marguerite Yourcenar, "Une Visite à Virginia Woolf," later incorporated into "Une Femme étincelante et timide," and reprinted in *En pèlerin*, 116 (first published in Savigneau, *Inventing a Life*, 114).

21. WCCC, 1937, WCA.

22. GFC; GFAB, 1966. See also WCCC, June 1937, 19, WCA.

23. Savigneau, *Inventing a Life*, 118.

24. Charlotte Musson to Marguerite Yourcenar, December 22, [1970s?,] MYP (755).

25. Deirdre Wilson, telephone conversation with the author, January 21, 2010.

26. Marguerite Yourcenar, conversation with the author, August 14, 1983.

27. Marguerite Yourcenar, immigration papers, MYC (569).

28. Grace Frick to Paul and Gladys Minear, November 13, 1949, MFA.

29. Marguerite Yourcenar, "Karagheuz et le théâtre d'ombres en Grèce," 1938, in *En pèlerin*, 17.

30. Marguerite Yourcenar, "Marionnettes de Sicile," in *En pèlerin*, 36, 37, 39.

31. The Elymi were identified by the Greek historian Thucydides as being a people of Trojan origin.

32. See, e.g., "Segesta," Trapani Sicilia, http://www.trapani-sicilia.it/english /segesta.htm.

33. Yourcenar, *With Open Eyes*, 262.

34. Historical information about sites in Sicily comes from "Segesta," *Encyclopedia Britannica*, https://www.britannica.com/place/Segesta; and "Taormina,"

Encyclopedia Britannica, https://www.britannica.com/place/Taormina. Information on places visited by Frick and Yourcenar comes from GFC; and GFAB, 1966.

35. Yourcenar speaks of "Hitler ranting in Naples (I hear him to this day) flanked by two rows of eagles in simulated stone" in *How Many Years*, 129. "D'après Greco" was one of three short stories published together in 1934 in *La Mort conduit l'attelage*. It later became *Anna, soror . . .*

36. Grace Frick, postcard to Ruth Hall, July 19, 1937, PPA.

37. Yourcenar, *With Open Eyes*, 262.

38. Marguerite Yourcenar, "Objets à Northeast Harbor" (manuscript), PPA.

39. Yourcenar, "Karagheuz," 20.

40. Caïmi, *Karaghiozi*, inscribed copy in Frick's bedroom, Petite Plaisance.

41. According to the passenger list for that New York–bound crossing, Yourcenar boarded the *Conte di Savoia* with Frick and then returned to shore before the ship set sail. Curiously, Yourcenar is identified as "M," married, on that ship's manifest. Five weeks later, when she traveled from Le Havre to New York, she is classified as "S," single; but on the passenger list from October 1939, when Yourcenar sailed from Bordeaux to New York, one finds a "D," for divorced, next to her name! Intriguingly, Yourcenar told Bernice Pierce, her and Frick's housekeeper for many years on Mount Desert Island, that she had once been married; Bernice Pierce, interview with the author, June 20, 2010.

Regarding her marital status, Yourcenar also made an ambiguous comment to attorney Ruth Hall in the early 1950s on a questionnaire related to the disposition of her papers in the event of her death. To the question "Have you ever been married?" she responded, "No. The Mme. generally used is the French usage for women writing, etc [*sic*]; like the Miss for the married actresses in England. Also of a long, but not legal, attachment, now nroken [*sic*] for many years." Financial Papers, Will of Marguerite Yourcenar, 1943–1953, MYC (562). If Yourcenar's explanation had ended after "attachment," it would be unequivocally general; the "now [b]roken for many years" seems to particularize it, however. There is reason to wonder whether she means to refer to the "seven-year relationship" in which she once spoke of having been involved during the 1930s.

42. Sandomenico, *Il "viaggio di nozze" di Marguerite Yourcenar.*

43. Between 1934 and 1944, the national symbol for Italian gold and silver was the fasces, a bundle of rods with a protruding ax blade that, among its other historical uses, was the emblem of Mussolini's Fascist party. The symbol for Arezzo, one of four main centers for Italian gold jewelry, is AR. The symbol for Uno a Erre in that city is 1. Both symbols, along with the fasces, are present on the inside of Grace and Marguerite's rings.

44. Sue Lonoff de Cuevas discusses the provenance of this bookplate in her perceptive study *Croquis et griffonnis*, 52–53.

45. Alesch, *The Other/Reader*, 148, notes that hands are "closely associated with life, and even with the soul" in Yourcenar's oeuvre.

Chapter 6

Epigraph: This stanza of the poem "Human Life" is highlighted in Grace Frick's copy of Matthew Arnold's *Poems*, 174, PPA.

1. Cecil Miller, quoted by his son John Miller, e-mail to the author, June 13, 2012. Regarding Frick's 1937 visit with Symons, see GFAB, September 22, 1953. Her name appears under various spellings in Frick's notes.

2. Margaret Symons to Grace Frick, MYP (1225). Chepstow was one of the first Norman keeps in Glamorgan.

3. Savigneau, *Inventing a Life*, 115–16.

4. Yourcenar's U.S. visa, stamped "3/2 Prof.," was issued in Geneva on September 3, 1937, and was valid for a period of one year. It gives her last permanent residence as the island of Capri.

5. Marguerite Yourcenar to Joseph Massabuau, September 29, 1937, in Yourcenar, *Correspondance avec Joseph Massabuau*, 146–49.

6. "Notes of Social Activities in New York and Elsewhere," *New York Times*, October 9, 1937.

7. Marguerite Yourcenar to Emmanuel Boudot-Lamotte, November 16, 1937, in Yourcenar, *Lettres à ses amis*, 48. Atala is the mixed-race title character of an 1801 François-René Chateaubriand novella that was published after its author had visited the United States.

8. Deprez, *Marguerite Yourcenar and the USA*, 61.

9. GFC.

10. Alice Parker to Grace Frick and Marguerite Yourcenar, October 14, 1956, MYC (3429).

11. Marguerite Yourcenar to Miss Sibley, February 2, 1962, MYP (1043).

12. Mary H. Marshall, "Memories of Marguerite Yourcenar," *Syracuse Library Associates Courier* 25, no. 2 (1990): 31, 35, 41.

13. Ibid., 33.

14. Marguerite Yourcenar to Joseph Massabuau, February 5, 1938, in *Correspondance*, 153–54.

15. Marguerite Yourcenar to Joseph Massabuau, January 14, 1935, in *Correspondance*, 67. Yourcenar wrote no fewer than seven letters to Massabuau in that month of January alone, complaining of her "tragic" situation (55) and further noting, "Everything is so bleak for me. If I don't manage to recover were it even half the amount due, I do not know how, with the income I have left, and all the obligations with which I am still burdened until the termination of the lease, I am going to get through the year" (65).

16. Marguerite Yourcenar to Joseph Massabuau, January 27, 1938, in *Correspondance*, 150–52.

17. Marguerite Yourcenar, quoted in John R. Wiggins, "Famous French Author Lives in Northeast Harbor," *Ellsworth (ME) American*, April 11, 1974.

18. Yourcenar, *Memoirs of Hadrian*, 321.

19. Willa Cather to Alexander Woollcott, October 15, 1931, MS Am 1449 (246), Houghton Library, Harvard University. Published with the permission of the Willa Cather Literary Trust.

20. Stock (publisher), letters and telegrams to Marguerite Yourcenar, MYC (3804).

21. M. Delamain to Marguerite Yourcenar, May 4, 1938, MYC (3804).

22. Willa Cather to Ferris Greenslet, August 23, 1945, MS Am 1925 (341), Houghton Library, Harvard University. Published with the permission of the Willa Cather Literary Trust.

23. Constantine Dimaras, quoted in Savigneau, *Inventing a Life*, 108.

24. Françoise Pellen, "Translating Virginia Woolf into French," in *The Reception of Virginia Woolf in Europe*, edited by Mary Ann Caws and Nicola Luckhurst (London: Continuum, 2002), quoted in Bosseaux, *How Does It Feel?*, 55.

25. Whenever Yourcenar's "euphonious inaccuracies" strayed too far from Woolf's text, Pierre Nordon, the editor of Virginia Woolf, *Romans et nouvelles, 1917–1941* (Paris: Librairie générale française, 1993), footnoted the passages in question and provided alternate translations. See Bosseaux, *How Does It Feel?*, 104–7.

26. It is even worth noting that Yourcenar's working title better reflects the verbal nature of Cather's *Death Comes . . .* than does the one chosen by Stock's replacement translator, the French equivalent of *Death of the Archbishop*.

27. Andrew Jewell, abstract of "'Curious Survivals': The Letters of Willa Cather," *New Letters* 74, no. 1 (2008): 154–75, http://digitalcommons.unl.edu/libraryscience/132.

28. Cather, *La Mort de l'archevêque*.

29. WCCC, 1948, 28, WCA.

30. Yourcenar, *Blues et gospels*, 5. Deprez discusses Yourcenar's relationship to American forms of protest and dissent in *Marguerite Yourcenar and the USA*, esp. chap. 2.

31. Pierre Desfons, dir., *Saturday Blues*, a 1984 documentary made for broadcast on the French television station TF1.

32. Yourcenar, *Blues et gospels*, 5–6.

33. Yourcenar's settlement amounted to approximately $10,128.00 when she got it, the equivalent of more than $172,000.00 in 2018; see "Foreign Exchange Rates," *Federal Reserve Bulletin*, May 1938, 418, https://fraser.stlouisfed.org/files/docs/publications/FRB/1930s/frb_051938.pdf.

34. Yvon Bernier, "Marguerite Yourcenar: Le Québec et le Canada," in Goslar, ed., *Les Voyages de Marguerite Yourcenar*, 169–91.

35. Marguerite Yourcenar, quoted in Bernier, "Marguerite Yourcenar: Le Québec et le Canada," 171, 172–73.

36. Ibid., 174.

37. Lonoff, *Croquis et griffonnis*, 16–17. With the author's generous permission, passages cited here and elsewhere are in her original English, although the page numbers referenced are from the French text.

38. Lonoff, *Croquis et griffonnis*, 17.

39. Marguerite Yourcenar, "Kali Beheaded," in *Oriental Tales*, 119. The word "pointed" was omitted from the published translation.

40. Lonoff, *Croquis et griffonnis*, 17–18.

41. Ibid., 19.

42. Stein, *Paris France*, 109.

Chapter 7

1. Bill Landis (archivist, YMA), e-mail to the author, July 17, 2017.

2. Savigneau, *Inventing a Life*, 119.

3. Ibid., 7–8.

4. I have made some minor punctuation and word choice changes here to my translation of this letter as it appeared in Savigneau, *Inventing a Life*, 129. It is worth noting that Grace used the informal *tu* form to address Marguerite in this letter, as the two women did in life. This was a rare expression of familiarity for Yourcenar.

5. Yourcenar, *Les Songes*, in *Essais et mémoires*, 1540–41. Donald Flanell's translation, *Dreams and Destinies*, leaves out the preface. Technically, Yourcenar's twenty-eighth year began on June 8, 1930, and her thirty-third year ended on June 7, 1936. But it's more likely that she means between the ages of twenty-eight and thirty-three.

6. See, e.g., Yourcenar, *Les Songes*, in *Essais et mémoires*, 1586, 1598, 1602.

7. Marguerite Yourcenar, "Chronologie," in *Œuvres romanesques*, xx.

8. The lines from Donne's poems cited here follow Frick's sometimes slightly wayward punctuation and spelling.

9. Bloom, *John Donne*, 15.

10. She made several trips in and out of Switzerland that summer, crossing the border at Domodossola. See Yourcenar's passport from that era, MYC (569).

11. This novel "was inspired by an authentic episode from the years 1918–1919 that had been related to her a few days earlier, in Switzerland, by a friend of the principal character." Yourcenar, "Chronologie," xx.

12. Yourcenar, "Chronologie," xx.

13. Goslar, *"Qu'il eût été fade,"* 141.

14. See chapter 18 of the present volume.

15. Yourcenar, *Coup de Grâce*, 138.

16. Ibid., 150–51.

17. See, e.g., Savigneau, *Inventing a Life*, 122–27; Goslar, *"Qu'il eût été fade,"* 141–45; and Sarde, *Vous, Marguerite Yourcenar*, 199, 221–22, 226.

18. Savigneau, *Inventing a Life*, 124.

19. See the discussion in Howard, *From Violence to Vision*, 141–45.

20. Frick's inscribed copy of *Coup de grâce*, call number FC9.Y8850C 1939, is preserved at the Houghton Library.

21. Marguerite Yourcenar to Charles Du Bos, August 6, 1938, in Yourcenar, *Lettres à ses amis*, 60.

22. Du Bos, *Approximations*, 117.

23. Yourcenar, *With Open Eyes*, 71.

24. Ibid., 142.

25. Elisabeth Frick to Grace Frick, July 24, 1938, MYP (1193).

26. Marguerite Yourcenar to Charles Du Bos, July 14, 1938, in Yourcenar, *Lettres à ses amis*, 59.

Chapter 8

1. For this description of Château de Muzot, see GFAB, August 26, 1951.

2. Marguerite Yourcenar, "Chronologie," in *Œuvres romanesques*, xxi.

3. Yourcenar, *Réception de Marguerite Yourcenar à l'Académie royale*, 43. The date of Calderon's election comes from Jean-Claude van Aerde (Belgian Royal Academy of French Language and Literature), e-mail to the author, May 15, 2008.

4. Savigneau, *Inventing a Life*, 130, and fig. 18.

5. Sarde, *Vous, Marguerite Yourcenar*, 229.

6. Yourcenar evokes Fernande de Cartier de Marchienne's schoolgirl "love affair" with Jeanne de Vietinghoff in *Dear Departed*, 262–65.

7. Information on Lucy's age comes from Marguerite Yourcenar, conversation with the author, August 15, 1983.

8. Nikos Calamaris, like André Embiricos and Odysseas Elytis, was a Greek surrealist writer.

9. Constantine Dimaras to Marguerite Yourcenar, November 24, 1937, MYP (212).

10. The French verb used by Dimaras is *se volatiliser*; one might go so far as to say that Lucy was "going down the drain."

11. Savigneau, *Inventing a Life*, 109.

12. Marguerite Yourcenar, conversation with the author, July 10, 1983. With regard to the word "friend," I noted in my journal at the time, "remember the care with which she uses this word."

13. Information on Kyriakos's and Yourcenar's skiing abilities comes from Marguerite Yourcenar, conversation with the author, July 10, 1983.

14. Savigneau, *Inventing a Life*, 130. It is highly likely that the baron's last name was actually Gutmausthal. On November 5, 1966, a Herm[ ] Gutmausthal wrote to Yourcenar from Vienna regarding a possible visit with her in Maine. MYP (339).

15. "New Year's in Kitzbühel, in the Tyrol. Marguerite Yourcenar ventures into Bavaria, then in March leaves Austria, already plunged in the prewar shadows, and finds herself in Athens"; Yourcenar, "Chronologie," xxi.

16. "Easter 1939," in *Autobiographie III* photo album, PPA.

17. Marguerite Yourcenar to Emmanuel Boudot-Lamotte, April 17, 1939, in Yourcenar, *En 1939*, 79.

18. Ibid. Yourcenar wrote to Boudot-Lamotte from Athens three times in February, beginning on the third of that month; once in March; twice in April; and once in May. Some of the Cavafy translations, along with Yourcenar's essay on the poet, were published in the journal *Mesures* in January 1940.

19. A previous long stay in Greece (two months)—also spent in Athens at the Petit Palais—ended on September 30, 1936. For the detail about traveling to France on a freighter, see Yourcenar, *En 1939*, 81.

20. Marguerite Yourcenar, conversation with the author, August 15, 1983.

21. Marguerite Yourcenar, "Self-Commentary," in Savigneau, *Inventing a Life*, 453. The maiden voyage of the *Nieuw Amsterdam* had actually occurred in 1938.

22. SS *Manhattan*, ship's manifest, October 15, 1939, "New York, Passenger Lists, 1820–1957," roll 641, Ancestry, https://www.ancestry.com/interactive /7488/NYT715_6411-0475?pid=1005897362&backurl=https://search.ancestry .com/cgi-bin/sse.dll?indiv%3D1%26dbid%3D7488%26h%3D1005897362 %26tid%3D%26pid%3D%26usePUB%3Dtrue%26_phsrc%3DZcZ1%26_ phstart%3DsuccessSource&treeid=&personid=&hintid=&usePUB=true&_phs- rc=ZcZ1&_phstart=successSource&usePUBJs=true.

23. On June 18, 1939, she wrote to Jean Ballard from the Wagram; in Yourcenar, *Lettres à ses amis*, 62.

24. Marguerite Yourcenar to Emmanuel Boudot-Lamotte, July 19, 1939, in Yourcenar, *Lettres à ses amis*, 63.

25. Yourcenar, "Self-Commentary," 455.

26. Ibid.

27. GFC; Bill Landis (archivist, YMA), e-mail to the author, July 17, 2017.

28. Grace Frick, alumni information sheet, June 1, 1939, YMA.

29. Marguerite Yourcenar, conversation with the author, July 10, 1983.

30. "German-American Bund," *Encyclopedia Britannica*, https://www.britannica .com/topic/German-American-Bund.

31. Rosalind Rosenberg, "Virginia Gildersleeve: Opening the Gates," Living Legacies, http://www.columbia.edu/cu/alumni/Magazine/Summer2001/Gilder sleeve.html.

32. *Wellesley College News*, June 4, 1925, WCA.

33. Yourcenar, "Chronologie," xxi–xxii. The lecture tour did not take place until the fall of 1940.

34. Blanchet-Douspis, *L'Influence de l'histoire contemporaine*, 20. "European Diagnosis" is a highly pessimistic historical and cultural analysis that was written when Yourcenar was very young. It was published in 1928 in the *Revue de Genève*.

35. Yourcenar, *With Open Eyes*, 157.

36. Marguerite Yourcenar, in Pierre Desfons, dir., *Saturday Blues*, a 1984 documentary made for broadcast on the French television station TF1.

37. Yourcenar, *Blues et gospels*, 7.

38. WCCC, 1950, WCA.

39. The English translation of Tristan L'Hermite's poem appears in Johnson and Stokes, *A French Song Companion*, 121.

40. Marguerite Yourcenar, postcard (never sent) to Lucy Kyriakos, Easter 1940, MYP 372 (1076). St. Georges, or Agios Georgios, is a seaside village at the northeastern tip of the island of Euboea.

41. Yourcenar, "Chronologie," xxii.

42. For both poems, see Yourcenar, *Les Charités d'Alcippe*, 18–19.

43. Marguerite Yourcenar, conversation with the author, August 15, 1983.

44. Deirdre Wilson, telephone conversation with the author, May 8, 2009.

45. Marguerite Yourcenar, conversation with the author, July 12, 1984.

46. Gladys Minear to Jean Hazelton, November 29, 1993, MFA.

Chapter 9

1. Edith A. Sprague to Howell Cheney, April 26, 1940, HCCHJCC (ARCH042), UHASC.

2. Phyllis Bartlett to Howell Cheney, April 24, 1940, HCCHJCC (ARCH042), UHASC.

3. University of Hartford, "Hartford College for Women," http://library.hartford .edu/UniversityLibraries/archspeccoll/archives1/hcw.aspx.

4. *A University for Hartford, a University for the World: A Short History of the University of Hartford*, chap. 5, "A University for the World," http://library.hartford.edu/aboutus /Publications/history/fivethre.htm.

5. Charles Hill to Helen Randall (outgoing Hartford Junior College administrator), April 28, 1940, HCCHJCC (ARCH042), UHASC.

6. Minor W. Latham to Hartford Junior College, March 21, 1940, HCCHJCC (ARCH042), UHASC.

7. Tucker Brooke to Howell Cheney, April 25, 1940, and Edith A. Sprague to Howell Cheney, April 26, 1940, HCCHJCC (ARCH042), UHASC.

8. J. J. Oppenheimer to Howell Cheney, May 2, 1940, HCCHJCC (ARCH042), UHASC.

9. Laura Lockwood to Howell Cheney, April 28, 1940, HCCHJCC (ARCH042), UHASC.

10. Martha Hale Shackford to Howell Cheney, April 26, 1940, HCCHJCC (ARCH042), UHASC.

11. William C. DeVane to Howell Cheney, April 29, 1940, HCCHJCC (ARCH042), UHASC.

12. Howell Cheney to Grace Frick, May 1, 1940, HCCHJCC (ARCH042), UHASC.

13. Howell Cheney to Grace Frick, May 8, 1940, HCCHJCC (ARCH042), UHASC.

14. Marguerite Yourcenar, "Lectures Given from February 1940 to June 1942," faculty folder, SLCA; GFC.

15. Beatrice Kneeland, audio recording, November 23, 1982, HCWC (ARCH051), UHASC.

16. Elizabeth Williams, audio recording, December 21, 1982, HCWC (ARCH051), UHASC.

17. Oliver Butterworth, unpublished history of Hartford Junior College, HCWC (ARCH051), UHASC.

18. Grace Frick to Howell Cheney, July 17, 1940, HCCHJCC (ARCH042), UHASC.

19. Butterworth, unpublished history.

20. Theodora B. "Teddy" Newlands to the author, August 5, 1991.

21. "Art Reproductions Now Adorn Walls of Junior College," *Hartford Times*, September 16, 1940.

22. Grace Frick to Howell Cheney, n.d., HCCHJCC (ARCH042), UHASC.

23. Untitled newspaper article, scrapbook of Paula Polivy, HCWC (ARCH051), UHASC.

24. Grace Frick to Howell Cheney, October 30, 1940, HCCHJCC (ARCH042), UHASC.

25. Ibid.

26. Miscellaneous newspaper articles saved by the Student Press Board, HCWC (ARCH051), UHASC.

27. Grace Frick to the Hartford Junior College Board of Trustees, January 6, 1941, in Butterworth, unpublished history, HCWC (ARCH051), UHASC.

28. Dorothy Pietrallo, audio recording, December 2, 1982, HCWC (ARCH051), UHASC.

29. Jordon Pecile, "When France's Immortal Lived among Us," HCWC (ARCH051), UHASC.

30. Marguerite Yourcenar, Christmas card to Dolly (Mrs. George) LaRue, [December 1946,] FFA.

31. Millicent Bolling Smith, audio recording, November 11, 1982, HCWC (ARCH051), UHASC.

32. Grace Frick to Howell Cheney, January 20, 1941, HCCHJCC (ARCH042), UHASC.

33. Frick not only supported her Jewish college "girls" but also sponsored a German Jewish couple's immigration into the United States during World War II. Grace Frick to Paul and Gladys Minear, August 7, 1949, MFA.

34. GFC. Yourcenar was already identified as a lecturer on art at the school in late 1940, however, in a *Hartford Courant* article dated December 30, 1940, Press Board Scrapbook, HCWC (ARCH051), UHASC.

35. Bernier, "Marguerite Yourcenar: Le Québec et le Canada," 175–76.

36. Jerry Wilson, personal journal, March 17, 1980, Wilson family archives. Yourcenar also briefly mentioned her detainment to Matthieu Galey in response to a question about whether she had gone through difficult times in America: "Well, I've done time in prison, though I must say it was a very short time." Yourcenar, *With Open Eyes*, 236.

37. Inside back cover, GFAB, 1956.

38. Pressboard scrapbook, September 1940–June 1941, HCWC (ARCH051), UHASC.

39. Kneeland audio recording.

40. "Dr. Woolley Speaker at Graduation," unidentified clipping, [June] 19, 1941, Press Board Scrapboook, HCWC (ARCH051), UHASC.

Chapter 10

1. Oliver Butterworth, unpublished history of Hartford Junior College, HCWC (ARCH051), UHASC.

2. "Hartford Junior College Now in Its Second Year," *Hartford Courant*, November 3, 1940.

3. "Joins Faculty," *Hartford Times*, August 18, 1941. Musson belonged to a school of women artists, and was known for painting members of "the smart set" of literature and the theater in the 1930s; see Musée Elise Rieuf, "Charlotte Musson: Biography," http://www.musee-elise-rieuf.org/Biography-47.html. Her painting is now owned

by the Musée Elise Rieuf in Massiac, France, whose proprietors have reliable evidence to support the approximate date given here; Sophie and Charles Rieuf, e-mail to the author, April 22, 2009.

4. "Will Teach New Art History Course Here," *Hartford Courant*, August 17, 1941. Savigneau's *Inventing a Life*, fig. 15, and Goslar, *"Qu'il eût été fade,"* 203, assign a date of "around 1936" to this photo. It's possible, but Yourcenar has on the same jacket in the picture that she wore in the Kitzbühel snapshots from New Year's 1939–40.

5. Savigneau, *Inventing a Life*, 139.

6. Sarde, *Vous, Marguerite Yourcenar*, 269–376.

7. Goslar, *"Qu'il eût été fade,"* 153–65.

8. Marguerite Yourcenar, "Carnets de notes, 1942–1948," in *En pèlerin*, 171–72.

9. Marguerite Yourcenar to Jacques Kayaloff, January 20, 1942, in Yourcenar, *Lettres à ses amis*, 73.

10. Deprez, *Marguerite Yourcenar et les États-Unis*, 9 and passim.

11. Yourcenar, *Denier du rêve*, 11–12. Dori Katz's translation of this book, *A Coin in Nine Hands*, does not include the preface.

12. Jane Marcus's introduction to the book notes that Woolf "wanted the American reader to respond to her attack on fascism because she published *Three Guineas* in the United States in a version especially for American readers with many changes, deletions, and additions." Jane Marcus, "Introduction," in Woolf, *Three Guineas*, xxxv.

13. Eleven books by Woolf still reside in the library of Petite Plaisance today.

14. Marguerite Yourcenar, "Forces du passé et forces de l'avenir," in *En pèlerin*, 55–62, and *Essais et mémoires*, 460–64.

15. Precisely when the essay was published remains uncertain. No copy of the French Consulate's bulletin has ever been found.

16. Marguerite Yourcenar, "Chronologie," in *Œuvres romanesques*, xxii.

17. Frick's translation is preserved in MYP (1322) and MYC (185).

18. The first edition of *Denier du rêve* (Paris: Grasset, 1934) was substantially revised and reissued in 1959. Halley, *Marguerite Yourcenar en poésie*, points out that Yourcenar's creative and political affinities grew more progressive over the decade of the 1930s.

19. Mann's *School for Barbarians*, with an introduction by Thomas Mann, sold forty thousand copies in the first three months of its release; see Tóibín, *New Ways to Kill Your Mother*, 202.

20. Grace Frick, typescript of "Waiting for the Barbarians," MYP (1354).

21. Constantine Dimaras, quoted in Savigneau, *Inventing a Life*, 142.

22. Marian Murray, "French Author and Teacher Pleads for Greeks, Cites Heroic Struggle of Hellenic People," *Hartford Times*, February 12, 1941.

23. Murray, "French Author and Teacher." Mytillene is the capital of Lesbos.

24. Yourcenar, "Chronologie," xix.

25. In fact, Yourcenar traveled a great deal during the 1930s to various European destinations, but her experience in Greece, like that of the emperor Hadrian, remained paramount.

26. Murray, "French Author and Teacher."

27. Marguerite Yourcenar, quoted in Murray, "French Author and Teacher."

28. Marguerite Yourcenar to Constantine Dimaras, July 1951, in Yourcenar, *Lettres à ses amis*, 87–90.

29. Regarding this lecture tour, see "Mme. Yourcenar to Lecture on French Art," *Hartford Times*, November 13, 1941; and American Association of Teachers of French, "Report of the Scholarship Committee," *French Review* 15, no. 3 (1942): 270.

30. "Reception after Lecture for Dr., Mrs. Malinowski," *Hartford Courant*, November 23, 1941; "Dr. Malinowski Lectures Tuesday at Junior College," *Hartford Courant*, November 24, 1941.

31. "War No Part of Instinct, Yale Authority Testifies," *Hartford Times*, November 26, 1941.

32. "Farmington Author Listed for Lecture," *Hartford Times*, December 3, 1941.

33. "French Vocal Program at Junior College Today," *Hartford Courant*, December 17, 1941.

Chapter 11

1. My description of Austin and the Wadsworth Atheneum draws on Lary Bloom, "Impresario's Back Story of Daring," *New York Times*, October 28, 2007, mailed to me by Frick and Yourcenar's then 102-year-old friend Gladys Minear; Steve Courtney, "Elegant European Called 'Reactionary' Hartford Home," *Hartford Courant*, August 4, 2002; Gaddis, *Magician of the Modern*; and Jane Roy Brown, "A Legacy of Firsts on Display at the Wadsworth Atheneum," *Boston Globe*, November 1, 2006, http://www.boston.com/travel/articles/2006/11/01/a_legacy_of_firsts_on_display_at_the_wadsworth_atheneum.

2. Gaddis, *Magician of the Modern*, 353.

3. Savigneau, *Inventing a Life*, 141. Goslar, *"Qu'il eût été fade,"* 158.

4. Marguerite Yourcenar, "À propos d'un divertissement et en hommage à un magicien," in *Théâtre I*, 138.

5. Le Corbusier, quoted in Gaddis, *Magician of the Modern*, 288.

6. Gaddis, *Magician of the Modern*, 353.

7. Yourcenar, "À propos d'un divertissement," 137.

8. The text of Frick's original translation has been lost, but Dori Katz's later version, *The Little Mermaid*, was published in Yourcenar, *Plays*, 149–64.

9. Marguerite Yourcenar to Jacques Kayaloff, January 20, 1942, in Yourcenar, *Lettres à ses amis*, 72.

10. "Mme. Yourcenar Writes Play on Folk Theme," *Hartford Times*, May 16, 1942.

11. Yourcenar, "À propos d'un divertissement," 145.

12. Marguerite Yourcenar, card to Truda Kaschmann, December 13, 1979, Wadsworth Atheneum Archives.

13. Yourcenar, "À propos d'un divertissement," 143.

14. See Yourcenar's note on the clipping "A. Everett Austin, Jr., Presents the Renowned Elizabethan Tragedy ''Tis Pity' by John Ford" in Printed Materials, 1937–1993, MYC 372.2 (579).

15. Yourcenar, "À propos d'un divertissement," 143.

16. Gaddis, *Magician of the Modern*, 358.

17. "Wellesley Club to Be Entertained," *Hartford Times*, February 11, 1942; "Wellesley Club to Meet at Junior College," *Hartford Courant*, February 11, 1942.

18. "The *Alcestis* of Euripides," translated by Gilbert Murray, presented by Society Alpha Kappa Chi, May 25–26, 1923, page from the handbill given out for the performance, AKX: Programs (1893–1953), WCA.

19. Society column, *Hartford Courant*, February 14, 1942, 7.

20. Financial Papers, 1943–53, MYC (562).

21. See, e.g., Grace Frick to Howell Cheney, June 16, 1942, HCCHJCC (ARCH042), HUASC; and Ella W. Shaw to Miss Frick, June 27 and July 27, 1942, HCCHJCC (ARCH042), HUASC.

22. Grace Frick, postcard to Howell Cheney, August 11, 1942, HCCHJCC (ARCH042), HUASC.

23. Gladys Minear to the author, December 14, 2008, MFA.

24. Paul Minear, in Paul and Gladys Minear, interview with the author, April 6, 2004.

25. To Matthieu Galey, for example, she said that on an island "you feel that you're standing on the border between the human world and the rest of the universe." Yourcenar, *With Open Eyes*, 103.

26. Yourcenar, *Sources II*, 273.

27. Thanks to the late David Nolf, whose mother, Marie Garrett Nolf, now owns Hysom's Cabin, also sometimes known as Hysom Cottage.

28. Elaine Higgins Reddish (proprietor of Higgins Store), interview with the author, June 15, 2002.

29. Grace Frick, audio recording by Donald Harris, November 27, 1977, HFA.

30. Marguerite Yourcenar, "Examen d'Alceste," in *Théâtre II*, 101.

31. Marguerite Yourcenar, preface to *La Petite Sirène*, in *Théâtre I*, 146.

32. Yourcenar, *Le Mystère d'Alceste*, 109.

Chapter 12

Epigraph: Grace Frick once called the Satan of *Paradise Lost* "a magnificent figure," telling Donald Harris that "Milton set out to make him a devil, but he got so fascinated with him. . . . It was harder to describe a good man like Jesus." Grace Frick, audio recording by Donald Harris, November 27, 1977, HFA.

1. Marguerite Yourcenar, interview by Jacques Chancel, *Radioscopie*, France Inter, June 11–15, 1979.

2. "Hartford Junior College Starts New Year Auspiciously," *Hartford Times*, September 22, 1941.

3. Informal history of the class of 1944, *Highlander*, Yearbook Collection (ARCH149), UHASC.

4. See, e.g., Susan Barlow, "Howell Cheney," Manchester Historical Society, http://www.manchesterhistory.org/reprints/MHS3_HowellCheney.html.

5. Howell Cheney to Grace Frick, May 8, 1940, HCCHJCC (ARCH042), HUASC.

6. This letter, on Hartford Junior College Dean's Office letterhead, is mistakenly dated 1940, at which time Frick was still at Barnard College.

7. Grace Frick to Howell Cheney, February 17, [1940,] HCCHJCC (ARCH042), HUASC.

8. Howell Cheney to Grace Frick, July 1, 1941, HCWC (ARCH051), HUASC.

9. "Local Junior College Names Secretary," *Hartford Times*, March 23, 1942.

10. Grace Frick to Howell Cheney, May 5, 1942, HCCHJCC (ARCH042), HUASC.

11. Grace Frick to Howell Cheney, June 16, 1942, HCCHJCC (ARCH042), HUASC.

12. Ibid.

13. Oliver Butterworth, unpublished history, HCWC (ARCH051), HUASC.

14. Marguerite Yourcenar to Christine Lyman (Hartford Junior College employee), n.d., HCCHJCC (ARCH042), HUASC.

15. "Junior College to Show Mexican, French Movies," *Hartford Courant*, February 8, 1943, 12.

16. Howell Cheney to Clement C. Hyde, January 22, 1943, HCCHJCC (ARCH042), HUASC.

17. Howell Cheney to Grace Frick, January 25, 1943, HCCHJCC (ARCH042), HUASC.

18. Elizabeth Rogers Payne, ed., "Wellesley in the World," *Wellesley*, March 1943, 160.

19. Frick family documents, FFA.

20. Grace Frick to Howell Cheney, April 2, 1943, HCCHJCC (ARCH042), HUASC. Twenty-six years later, Frick had not forgotten Howell Cheney. In the spring of 1969, with antiwar and antiestablishment sentiment running high among American and French youth, Grace told Gladys and Paul Minear that she sympathized with their son Larry's "stone-age President of Ohio State," adding that "Mr. Cheney, of Hartford Junior College, was *pre*-Neanderthal." Grace Frick to Paul and Gladys Minear, March [n.d.], 1969, MFA.

21. Grace Frick to Howell Cheney, January 27, 1943 (not received until April 13, 1943), HCCHJCC (ARCH042), HUASC.

22. Howell Cheney to Grace Frick, April 20, 1943, HCCHJCC (ARCH042), HUASC.

23. Death certificate of George A. LaRue, Missouri State Archives.

24. Jerry Wilson, personal journal, March 26, 1980, Wilson family archives.

25. GFAB, February 8, 1945.

26. See Stephen Trachtenberg to Marguerite Yourcenar, September 8 and 15, 1980, MYC (3928); and Stephen Trachtenberg to Jean Lunt, June 17, 1981, MYC (3928).

27. Marguerite Yourcenar to Stephen Trachtenberg, September 9, 1980, MYC (5304).

28. Marguerite Yourcenar to Beatrice Kneeland, May 19, 1987, Wadsworth Atheneum Archives.

29. Grace Frick to Howell Cheney, May 8, 1943, HCCHJCC (ARCH042), HUASC.

30. Howell Cheney to Ruth Houghton (Wellesley Placement Office), ca. June 11, 1943, HCCHJCC (ARCH042), HUASC.

31. Dorothy Pietrallo, audio recording, December 2, 1982, HCWC (ARCH051), HUASC.

32. "Austin, A[rthur] Everett, Jr., 'Chick,'" *Dictionary of Art Historians*, https://dictionaryofarthistorians.org/austine.htm.

33. Howell Cheney to Grace Frick, June 7, 1943, HCCHJCC (ARCH042), HUASC.

34. Students of Hartford Junior College to Howell Cheney, June 14, 1943, HCCHJCC (ARCH042), HUASC.

35. Shakespeare, *The Tragedy of Hamlet, Prince of Denmark*, Grace Frick's annotated copy, PPA.

36. Ruth Hall, Esq., to Grace Frick, January 8, 1943, MYC (562).

Chapter 13

1. Mary Marshall to Grace Frick, June 13, 1944, MYP (1214).

2. Probate Court document number 53,435, Jackson County, Missouri.

3. Financial Papers, 1943–53, MYC (562).

4. Ibid.

5. Ibid.

6. Margaret Smith to Marguerite Yourcenar, July 1, 1943, MYC (562).

7. Thomas Hughes to Marguerite Yourcenar, July 11, 1943, MYC (377).

8. Thomas Hughes to Marguerite Yourcenar, July 25, 1944, MYC (377).

9. On April 28, 1943, a document was filed by the law offices of Bowersock, Fizzell and Rhodes of Kansas City appointing Fred to take over for Gage as executor of LaRue's will. Gage was already overseas. Probate Court document number 53,435, Jackson County, Missouri.

10. Ruth Hall to Grace Frick, May 6, 1943, MYC (562).

11. Ibid.

12. Ibid.

13. Ibid.

14. Antoinette Hoffherr, "The Making of Hadrian's Memoirs," MYC (862).

15. See GFC; and GFAB, 1944 and 1966.

16. GFAB, 1945.

17. Yourcenar's salary for the year 1942–43 was $1,300; Faculty folder, SLCA.

18. Marguerite Yourcenar, conversation with the author, July 12, 1984.

19. Probate Court document number 106,774, Jackson County, Missouri.

20. Ibid.

21. Chung, *Grants for Scholarships*, 238–40.

22. George A. and Dolly F. LaRue Trust Form 990, ProPublica, https://projects.propublica.org/nonprofits/organizations/436122865.

Chapter 14

1. Kayaloff, of Armenian descent, emigrated from Russia to Paris after World War I and then to New York; "Jacques Kayaloff, 85, Is Dead; Ex-Head of Louis Dreyfus Co.," *New York Times*, September 18, 1983.

2. GFAB, January 24, 1949.

3. Ibid., 1944.

4. Ibid., 1944–46.

5. Barranger, *Margaret Webster*, 121.

6. Savigneau, *Inventing a Life*, 173.

7. Barbara Kaplan, "Becoming Sarah Lawrence," https://archive.is/5I2L7.

8. "Madame Marguerite Yourcenar," information sheet, SLCA.

9. André Morize to Dr. Duggan, February 16, 1941, SLCA.

10. Louis Barillet, comments on Marguerite Yourcenar, June 5, 1942, SLCA.

11. Gelderman, *Mary McCarthy: A Life*, 138.

12. McCarthy, *The Groves of Academe*, 64.

13. Reading list, September 15–October 15, unspecified year, SLCA.

14. Marguerite Yourcenar, conversation with the author, August 13, 1983.

15. See, e.g., GFAB, April 20, 1944.

16. Yourcenar, *With Open Eyes*, 95.

17. Marguerite Yourcenar, interview by Jacques Chancel, *Radioscopie*, France Inter, June 11–15, 1979.

18. Marguerite Yourcenar, interview by Françoise Faucher, *Femme d'aujourd'hui* (TV series), excerpted in Delcroix, *Portrait d'une voix*, 144. Yourcenar actually taught for nine academic years, fall 1942–spring 1950 and 1952–53.

19. Phyllis Rothschild Farley, conversation with Sue Lonoff de Cuevas, received via e-mail to the author, April 2, 2009.

20. Jane Bond, telephone interview with the author, February 2, 2008; J. Max Bond Sr. was dean of the School of Education at Atlanta University during Jane's two years at Sarah Lawrence. He was later president of the University of Liberia.

21. Bond interview.

22. Marguerite Yourcenar, audio recording of an interview by Maurice Dumay, March 6, 1980, PPA.

23. Charlotte Pomerantz Marzani, quoted in Savigneau, *Inventing a Life*, 165–66.

24. Donna Levinsohn to the author, October 20, 1993.

25. Donna Levinsohn, e-mail to the author, December 4, 2007; GFAB, 1944.

26. Marguerite Yourcenar, faculty report of Marianne Mosevius, March 3, 1944, DLA.

27. Marguerite Yourcenar, faculty report of Marianne Mosevius, April 25, 1944, DLA.

28. Marguerite Yourcenar, faculty report of Marianne Mosevius, October 27, 1944, DLA.

29. Marianne Mosevius, handwritten note to herself, October 26, 1945, DLA.

30. Marguerite Yourcenar to Marianne Levinsohn, February 5, 1949, DLA. The maple syrup was mail-ordered from Mrs. Wiggins's Country Store in Northampton,

Massachusetts. Yourcenar told Levinsohn she knew "the old Negro who harvests and grinds the [buckwheat flour] grains: he is a very noble personage."

31. GFAB, August 23, 1944.

32. Marguerite Yourcenar, "Chronologie," in *Œuvres romanesques*, xxii.

33. GFAB, August 22, 1944.

34. Marguerite Yourcenar, "Three Greek Myths in Palladian Perspective I," trans. Marguerite Yourcenar and Grace Frick, *Chimera* 4, no. 3 (1946): 42–51; Marguerite Yourcenar, "Three Greek Myths in Palladian Perspective II," trans. Marguerite Yourcenar and Grace Frick, *Chimera* 4, no. 4 (1946): 6–19.

35. GFAB, August 29, 1944.

36. "College Faculty Spends Summer Imaginatively," Sarah Lawrence College *Campus*, October 4, 1944. *Dramatis Personae* was a collection of three plays—*Le Mystère d'Alceste*, *Intermède d'Ariane*, and *Électre ou la Chute des masques*—that Yourcenar hoped to publish soon.

Chapter 15

1. Keeping in mind that Yourcenar was identified as "Belguin" when she sailed to America in 1939, however, it is most interesting to note that she described herself as having been naturalized "under the Belgian quota" in a March 22, 1952, letter to the American Consul in Paris, MYP (1377).

2. Grace Frick, audio recording by Donald Harris, November 27, 1977, HFA.

3. Artemis Leontis, "Eva Palmer's Distinctive Greek Journey," in Kolokotroni and Mitsi, eds., *Women Writing Greece*, 162. Yourcenar once wrote to Barney that "Mount Desert has forgotten the two nymphs, Eva and Natalie, who ran along the beaches and should be part of its legend." Marguerite Yourcenar to Natalie Barney, July 29, 1963, in Yourcenar, *Lettres à ses amis*, 189.

4. Grace Frick to Natalie Barney, December 1955, NCBC 2362.

5. As Yourcenar told Matthieu Galey, "Grace was known in the village as the 'lady on horseback who's looking for a house.'" Yourcenar, *With Open Eyes*, 104.

6. Elaine Higgins Reddish (proprietor of Higgins Store), interview with the author, June 15, 2002.

7. Jerry Wilson, personal journal, March 19, 1980. Wilson family archives.

8. GFAB, August 5, 1948.

9. Marguerite Yourcenar, conversation with the author, date unknown. Jerry Wilson mentions what is probably the same event in his journal on March 17, 1980, when he speaks of "the play acting done in the jardin imitating a tree."

10. The phone number was "Trafalgar 7-4050"; GFAB, 1946.

11. "Visitor Tells of War's Effect on European Children," *Vassar Miscellany News*, October 18, 1941.

12. In a 1942 document preserved in the SLCA, Yourcenar stated under the heading "Academical [*sic*] Degrees": "None except the French B.A. degree. Education by private tutors. As a free student, and without intention of accumulating credits, has followed courses at the universities of Aix, Geneva, and Bologna."

13. GFAB, 1944.

14. Ibid.

15. Ibid. Andrée Royon went on to practice psychoanalysis in New York City.

16. GFAB, 1945.

17. GFAB, January 10, 1945.

18. Marguerite Yourcenar, handwritten codicil to her will, November 18, 1946, MYC (562).

19. Marguerite Yourcenar to Marianne Levinsohn, February 5, 1949, DLA.

20. Ibid.

21. GFAB, March 18, 1949.

22. GFAB, August 26, 1949.

23. GFAB, August 28, 1949.

24. Yourcenar, *Memoirs of Hadrian*, 342–43.

25. Sarde, *Vous, Marguerite Yourcenar*, 310.

26. Officially, they went to Rome to start the all-important English translation of *Hadrian*—on-site, as it were. Marguerite Yourcenar to Harold Taylor, February 3, 1952, SLCA.

27. GFAB, March 8, 1952.

28. Charlotte Pomerantz Marzani, quoted in Savigneau, *Inventing a Life*, 166.

29. Marguerite Yourcenar to Marianne Levinsohn, February 5, 1949. There are no letters to or from Levinsohn in the Houghton Library's public archive. One can only hope that some will come to light in 2037, when the sealed papers of Yourcenar are released. Tragically, Marianne Levinsohn, who had been through so much in her youth, was killed in a car crash at the age of fifty-three while driving her son home from Yale University in 1975. Donna Levinsohn, e-mail to the author, December 4, 2007.

30. Savigneau, *Inventing a Life*, 392.

31. Marguerite Yourcenar, conversation with the author, August 19, 1983.

32. Author's personal journal entry, August 22, 1983.

33. GFAB, September 7, 1955.

34. Grace Frick to Pamela Frick, June 25, 1955, FFA.

35. GFAB, January 15, 1956.

36. David Peckham, interview with the author, July 7, 2008.

37. Ibid.

38. Ibid.

Chapter 16

1. Kathryn James (reference librarian at the Beinecke Rare Book and Manuscript Library, Yale University), e-mail to the author, April 19, 2006.

2. Marguerite Yourcenar to Ruth Hall, May 29, 1950, MYC (562).

3. Marguerite Yourcenar to Harold Taylor, October 23, 1949, SLCA.

4. Grace Frick to Gladys Minear, n.d., MFA.

5. Chauncey Brewster Tinker (1876–1963) had worked with Hall to create the Rare Book Room. Marjorie Wynne (supervisor of the Rare Book Room after Hall's retirement) to the author, June 9, 2006.

6. Grace Frick to Gladys Minear, n.d., MFA.

7. Ibid.

8. Ibid.

9. Marguerite Yourcenar to Ruth Hall, May 29, 1950, MYC (562).

10. Marguerite Yourcenar, conversation with the author, July 12, 1984.

11. Comptoir National d'Escompte to Marguerite Yourcenar, February 28, 1950, MYC (560).

12. Marguerite Yourcenar to Ruth Hall, May 29, 1950, MYC (562).

Chapter 17

1. Durlin Lunt, interview with the author, June 30, 2008; Elizabeth Renault, interview with the author, July 1, 2008.

2. Grace Frick to Ruth Hall, October 20, 1950, MYC (575).

3. Chancel, *Marguerite Yourcenar: Radioscopie*, 12.

4. Marguerite Yourcenar to Ruth Hall, September 13, 1950, MYC (562).

5. GFAB, 1951; Grace Frick to Gladys Minear, [August 20–27,] 1951, MFA.

6. The owners on September 29, 1950, were Cora A. Kimball (a widow), Margaret M. Kimball (unmarried), Loren E. Kimball Jr., and Marion M. Kimball (Loren's wife). Hancock County, Maine, Registry of Deeds, 466.

7. The historian is Mrs. Carl E. Kelley; Maine Memory Network, "Northeast Harbor: From Rustic to Rusticators," http://www.mainememory.net/bin/Features?f=268&n_id=5&supst=Exhibits.

8. Marguerite Yourcenar, conversation with the author, July 22, 1983.

9. Willie Granston, "Old Houses in Northeast Harbor," unpublished manuscript based on research in the Northeast Harbor Public Library Archives, 2008, courtesy of the author. Information on the wedding of Kimball and Gilpatrick came from Jim Dangel, "Gilpatrick Family Cards," http://www.dangel.net/GilpatrickWebCards/WC70_125.HTM (accessed in February 2017), though the web page is no longer extant.

10. When Acadia National Park came into being, Brown Mountain was renamed Norumbega.

11. Jean Lunt, "History of the House,"1988, PPA.

12. H. W. Small, *A History of the Town of Swan's Island, Maine*, 2nd ed., http://www.swansisland.org/small.pdf.

13. GFAB, March 5, 1951.

14. Vaun Gillmor to Marguerite Yourcenar, July 10, 1950, MYC (2050).

15. Marguerite Yourcenar to Vaun Gillmor, July 13, 1950, MYC (2050).

16. Delcroix, *Portrait d'une voix*, 204; GFAB, October 24, 1955.

17. GFAB, October 24, 1955.

18. Patrick Chasse, conversation with the author, August 8, 2009.

19. Shirley McGarr, conversation with the author, November 24, 2009.

20. C. Ronald Bechtle (George Korkmadjian's son-in-law), conversation with the author, July 26, 2001.

21. André Fraigneau, quoted in Savigneau, *Inventing a Life*, 189.

22. John Barrett to Marguerite Yourcenar, March 12, 1951, MYC (2050).

23. GFAB, March 26, 1951.

24. GFAB, January 18, 1945.

25. GFAB, April 19, 1950.

26. Levon Avdoyan, " 'Magistra Studentorum per Armeniam et Byzantium': Nina G. Garsoïan (1923–)," in Chance, ed., *Women Medievalists and the Academy*, 803.

27. Marguerite Yourcenar, 1963 list of busts and paintings of herself, MYC (563).

28. Marguerite Yourcenar to Ruth Hall, April 27, 1951, MYC (562).

Chapter 18

1. Grace Frick, alumni information sheet, May 14, 1951, YMA.

2. GFAB, July 2, 1951.

3. For the first correct mention of Yourcenar's birthday, see GFAB, June 8, 1960.

4. Marguerite Yourcenar to Joseph Breitbach, April 7, 1951, MYC (4314).

5. Marguerite Yourcenar to Jacques Kayaloff, December 31, 1960, in Yourcenar, *Lettres à ses amis*, 520–21.

6. GFAB, June 28, 1951.

7. Natalie Barney to Grace Frick, November 16, 1963, MYC (5401).

8. Grace Frick, "Notes about Barney," MYC (289).

9. GFAB, July 3, 1951.

10. Souhami, *Wild Girls*, 60.

11. Natalie Barney to Marguerite Yourcenar, June 1952 [before June 10], MYC (1032).

12. Stein, *Things as They Are*.

13. Karren LaLonde Alenier, "The Steiny Road to Operadom," *Scene4*, August 2014, https://www.scene4.com/archivesqv6/2014/aug-2014/0814/karren lalondealenier0814.html; Natalie Barney, quoted in Rodriguez, *Wild Heart*, 337.

14. Grace Frick to Natalie Barney, July 9, 1952, NCBC.

15. Ibid.

16. Natalie Barney to Marguerite Yourcenar, June 1, 1952, MYC (1032).

17. Jean Racine, *Phaedra*, translated by A. S. Kline, 2003, http://www.poetryi ntranslation.com/PITBR/French/PhaedraActI.htm: "Ce n'est plus une ardeur dans mes veines cachée : / C'est Vénus tout entière à sa proie attachée."

18. Rodriguez, *Wild Heart*, 340.

19. [Delarue-Mardrus,] *Nos Secrètes Amours*, PPA. Yourcenar also placed question marks next to lines suggesting that lesbian love was "impossible" or prohibited.

20. Regarding Barney's early trip to Lesbos, see Miron Grindea, ed., "The Amazon of Letters: A World Tribute to Natalie Barney," special issue of *ADAM International Review* 30, no. 299 (1962).

21. Natalie Barney to Marguerite Yourcenar and Grace Frick, August 10, 1952, MYC (1032), in Barney's original English.

22. Marguerite Yourcenar, postcard to Natalie Barney, August [29], 1952, NCBC 2359.

23. DeJean, *Fictions of Sappho*, 298.

24. GFAB, July 23, 1951.

25. Grace Frick, postcard to Gladys Minear, July 27, 1951, MFA.

26. GFAB, August 5, 1951. "The older Madame Finch" stayed on at Vufflens until September.

27. GFAB, September 4, 1951.

28. Savigneau, *Inventing a Life*, 213–16.

29. M. Godemart to Marguerite Yourcenar, September 24, 1951, quoted in Savigneau, *Inventing a Life*, 215.

30. GFAB, November 4 and 7, 1951.

31. Jean Hazelton, interview with the author August 8, 2006. The letter was written on October 17, 1951.

32. Ibid.

33. Emmanuel Boudot-Lamotte to Marguerite Yourcenar, December 9, 1951, MYC (2080).

34. Constantine Dimaras to Marguerite Yourcenar, August 5, 1951, MYP (212).

35. DeJean, *Fictions of Sappho*, 5.

36. Ibid., 296.

37. Ibid., 297.

38. Howard, *From Violence to Vision*, 117–49.

39. DeJean, *Fictions of Sappho*, 297–98.

Chapter 19

1. Florence Codman to Marguerite Yourcenar, January 15, 1952, MYP (170).

2. GFAB, January 19, 1952.

3. Angel Gurria-Quintana, "Collective Madness," *Financial Times*, November 13, 2004.

4. Ibid. See also Smith, ed., *The Bookshop at 10 Curzon Street*, 19–20.

5. Marguerite Yourcenar to Max Daireaux, September 11, 1951, in Yourcenar, *D'Hadrien à Zénon*, 45.

6. Bearing witness to that early stage of Grace and Marguerite's romance are two line drawings of La Residenza and, aptly enough for two women who loved a blazing fire, its fireplace logo, in Yourcenar's autobiographical albums, PPA.

7. Frick's green leather-bound 1952 edition of *Alexis* is preserved at the Houghton Library, Harvard University, FC9.Y8850.929ab.

8. GFAB, May 2, 1952.

9. Marguerite Yourcenar, "Andalusia, or the Hesperides," in *That Mighty Sculptor, Time*, 171–72.

10. Robert Ochs to Marguerite Yourcenar, June 1952, MYC (3516).

11. Yourcenar, *Réception de Marguerite Yourcenar à l'Académie royale*, 43.

12. Savigneau, *Inventing a Life*, 224.

13. Sarde, *Vous, Marguerite Yourcenar*, 315.

14. "This is the letter from Grace Frick I spoke to you about the other day," Robert Ho wrote to me in 2004. "Nancy and I have treasured it for all these years. Both of us were deeply touched by her reaching out to us at an emotionally tumultuous time—particularly for Nancy. The letter helped ease my entry into this community which is now home for me and our children. It says so much of Grace and what she valued and represented in her life." Robert Ho to the author, June

30, 2004. Bob Ho succumbed to cancer at the age of seventy-seven on February 17, 2012.

15. It may not be coincidental that it was after twelve years with Frick that Yource-nar made unity and stability, as Jeanine Alesch has emphasized, the hallmarks of Hadrian's empire. See, e.g., Alesch, *The Other/Reader*, 79.

16. Jean Hazelton, interview with the author, August 8, 2006.

17. Ibid.

18. Cather, *Willa Cather on Writing*, 109.

19. I mention Yourcenar's astrological sign, that of the restless Twins, in part be-cause she herself was interested in astrology. She had birth charts drafted for Hadrian and Zeno. Her literary oeuvre owes some of its most moving scenes to the tension between and the movement toward a resolution of seemingly irreconcilable dualities.

20. GFAB, October 11, 1952. The woman was Mrs. Reginald Allen.

21. Savigneau, *Inventing a Life*, 225.

22. Marguerite Yourcenar to Natalie Barney, October 15, 1952, NCBC 2360; Mar-guerite Yourcenar to Victoria Ocampo, December 22, 1952, MS Span 117 (791), Houghton Library, Harvard University. While translating *Hadrian*, Frick kept incredibly detailed notes on the spelling of terms and proper nouns, complete with information about the efforts she made to verify each one, the reasons why specific forms were chosen, and the places where corrections were made in the manuscript along the way. Stacked one atop the other, they would make a pile about ten inches high. MYC (236).

23. Marguerite Yourcenar to Natalie Barney, June 15, 1953, NCBC 2365.

24. Natalie Barney to "My Dears," June 21, 1953, MYC (1032).

25. Grace Frick to Mary Lou Aswell, March 3, 1953, MYC (5439).

26. Grace Frick to Roberta Todd, April 22, 1959, WCA.

27. Marguerite Yourcenar to Jeanne Carayon, October 2, 1971, MYC (4346). Quoted in Savigneau, *Inventing a Life*, 324–25.

28. Gerald Sykes, "In Imperial Rome," *New York Times*, November 21, 1954, 6.

29. Geoffrey Bruun, review of *Memoirs of Hadrian*, *New Republic* 131 (1954): 23.

30. Robert Parris, review of *Memoirs of Hadrian*, *Nation* 179 (1954): 554.

31. Frank White, "Hadrian and the World That Became Turkey," *Turk-ish Daily News*, July 21, 2008, http://www.armeniandiaspora.com/showthread .php?139107-ANKARA-Hadrian-And-The-World-That-Became-Turkey.

32. Dorothy Sinclair, review of *Memoirs of Hadrian*, *Library Journal* 79 (1954): 2, 100.

33. Geoffrey Bruun, "Hadrian's Story as That Complex Emperor Might Have Written It," *New York Herald Tribune Book Review*, November 21, 1954, 1.

34. *Memoirs of Hadrian* was on the *New York Times* best-seller list from December 12, 1954, through April 24, 1955.

Chapter 20

1. Natalie Barney, postcard to "Dear Friends," September 14, 1953, MYC (1032).

2. GFAB, August–September 1953.

3. Marguerite Yourcenar, audio recording of an interview by Maurice Dumay, March 1980, PPA.

4. Yourcenar, *Quoi? L'Éternité*, 278.

5. GFAB, November 16, 1953.

6. GFAB, December 31, 1953, entry in 1954 daybook.

7. Palmieri, *In Adamless Eden*, 263.

8. Sarah Lawrence College, "Sarah Lawrence under Fire: The Attacks on Academic Freedom during the McCarthy Era," https://www.sarahlawrence.edu/archives/exhibits/mccarthyism/.

9. Yourcenar, *With Open Eyes*, 97.

10. GFAB, December 13, 1952.

11. Margaret Barratin to the American Consul in Paris, March 20, 1954, NCBC 2374.

12. Grace Frick to the American Consul in Paris, March 22, 1954, MYP (1377).

13. Marguerite Yourcenar to the American Consul in Paris, March 22, 1954, MYP (1377).

14. Grace Frick to Margaret Chase Smith, March 22, 1954, MYP (1047).

15. Ibid. See also GFAB, September 25, 1952.

16. McCarthy, "No News, or, What Killed the Dog," in *On the Contrary*, 35.

17. Grace Frick to Margaret Chase Smith, March 22, 1954, MYP (1047).

18. Grace Frick to Natalie Barney, March 23, 1954, NCBC 2376.

19. Marguerite Yourcenar to Natalie Barney, November 10, 1962, MYC (4204).

20. GFAB, April 17, 1954.

21. Marguerite Yourcenar to Natalie Barney, May 6, 1954, NCBC 2377.

22. Marguerite Yourcenar to Natalie Barney, December 29, 1954, NCBC 2383.

23. Bussy was a member of the brilliant British Strachey family, some of whom were regulars of the Bloomsbury group. She would eventually work side by side with the founder of Les Ruches, Marie Souvestre, at Allenswood Academy outside London. Their most renowned pupil was the future American first lady Eleanor Roosevelt.

24. Jacqueline Audry directed this film based on a screenplay written by Colette. After a 1951 release in France, *Olivia* acquired its "fallacious" title in the United States, where, like *The Well of Loneliness*, it was censored.

25. Natalie Barney to Marguerite Yourcenar and Grace Frick, April 17, 1954, MYP (42).

26. Marguerite Yourcenar (writing for the couple), postcard to Natalie Barney, May 29, 1954, NCBC 2377.

27. Natalie Barney to Marguerite Yourcenar, sometime before June 10, 1952, MYC (1032); Louÿs, *Les Chansons de Bilitis*.

28. Marguerite Yourcenar, postcard to Natalie Barney, June 28, 1954, NCBC 2380.

29. Natalie Barney to Marguerite Yourcenar and Grace Frick, April 21, 1954, MYP (42).

30. Natalie Barney to Marguerite Yourcenar and Grace Frick, June 6, 1954, MYP (42).

31. Natalie Barney to Marguerite Yourcenar and Grace Frick, June 20, 1954, MYC (1032).

32. Marguerite Yourcenar, postcard to Natalie Barney, June 28, 1954, NCBC 2380.

33. Natalie Barney to Marguerite Yourcenar and Grace Frick, postmarked September 27, 1954, MYP(42).

34. Natalie Barney to Marguerite Yourcenar and Grace Frick, June 10, 1955, MYC (1032).

35. Natalie Barney to Marguerite Yourcenar and Grace Frick, September 12, 1952, MYC (1032).

36. See, e.g., Natalie Barney to Grace Frick and Marguerite Yourcenar, July 21, 1953, MYC (1032); and Natalie Barney to Grace Frick and Marguerite Yourcenar, April 21, 1954, MYP (42).

37. GFAB, December 15, 1954.

38. Natalie Barney to Marguerite Yourcenar and Grace Frick, November 1, 1952, MYC (1032).

39. Natalie Barney, postcard to Marguerite Yourcenar and Grace Frick, November 30, 1953, MYC (1032).

40. Natalie Barney to Marguerite Yourcenar and Grace Frick, June 10, 1955, MYC (1032).

41. Natalie Barney to Marguerite Yourcenar and Grace Frick, August 8, 1955, MYC (1032); Barney's original English.

42. Natalie Barney to Marguerite Yourcenar, late February 1956, MYC (1032); partially my own translation.

43. Natalie Barney to Marguerite Yourcenar, April 7, 1956, MYC (1032).

44. Natalie Barney to Marguerite Yourcenar and Grace Frick, April 6, 1955, MYC (1032).

45. Natalie Barney to Marguerite Yourcenar, June 20, 1954, MYC (1032).

46. Natalie Barney to Marguerite Yourcenar and Grace Frick, April 6, 1955, MYC (1032); Barney's original English.

47. Marguerite Yourcenar to Natalie Barney, July 5, 1955, NCBC 2384.

48. Marguerite Yourcenar, Christmas letter to Natalie Barney, [December 1955,] NCBC 2361.

Chapter 21

1. Marguerite Yourcenar to Constantine Dimaras, June 17, 1954, MYC (4459).

2. GFAB, July 3, 1954.

3. Both essays are included in *That Mighty Sculptor, Time.*

4. "Around 1955," said Yourcenar to Claude Servan-Schreiber in 1980; see Delcroix, comp., *Portrait d'une voix,* 284.

5. GFAB, September 5, 1954.

6. GFAB, September 9–10, 1954.

7. GFAB, September 10–16, 1954. Jean Hazelton recalled a less dramatic but fundamentally similar incident that occurred on the rue Saint-Honoré in Paris. She and Grace were walking toward a restaurant for lunch when an elegantly dressed Frenchwoman passed them headed the other way. Grace turned to Jean and said,

"She's *crying!*" And off she went, chasing after the sobbing passerby to see what she could do to help!

8. Marguerite Yourcenar to Natalie Barney, March 11, 1956, in Yourcenar, *D'Hadrien à Zénon*, 513. The award was not received until 1963, however.

9. Gaddis, *Magician of the Modern*, 408.

10. GFAB, December 16, 1954.

11. GFAB, January 5, 1955.

12. GFAB, March 11, 1955.

13. GFAB, January 29, 1955.

14. GFAB, February 19, 1955.

15. GFAB, March 3, 1955.

16. The volume was *Hommage de la France à Thomas Mann*.

17. GFAB, April 13, 1955.

18. GFAB, February 16, 1955.

19. See Lonoff, *Croquis et griffonnis*, 41–53.

20. GFAB, February 18, 1955.

21. Élie Grekoff to Marguerite Yourcenar and Grace Frick, November 26, 1956, MYP (332); Élie Grekoff to Marguerite Yourcenar and Grace Frick, April 26, 1955, MYP (332).

22. GFAB, March 6, 1955.

23. GFAB, March 7, 1955.

24. The double transgression of "Mlle Longueville" had been to overstay her welcome and to show no interest in Thomas Mann's letter to Yourcenar. GFAB, February 28, 1955.

25. GFAB, March 8, 1955.

26. Élie Grekoff to Marguerite Yourcenar and Grace Frick, November 26, 1956, MYP (332).

27. See, for instance, Goslar, *"Qu'il eût été fade,"* 93.

28. GFAB, January 11, 1955.

29. GFAB, April 4, 1955.

30. Marguerite Yourcenar, "Traversée sur le *Bathory*," unpublished typescript, MYC (524). Lurs are curved horns cast in bronze, six or more feet long, that may have been used to call warriors to battle.

31. Morton Axboe, e-mail to the author, June 30, 2009.

32. Morton Axboe, e-mail to the author, November 25, 2008.

33. Lonoff, *Croquis et griffonnis*, 50.

34. Marguerite Yourcenar to Mrs. Kenneth B. Murdock, August 19, 1966, MYP (546).

35. Grace Frick to Gladys Minear, May 26, 1955, MFA.

36. GFAB, May 18, 1955.

37. Kajsa Andersson, "Présence scandinave dans l'oeuvre de Marguerite Yourcenar," *Romansk Forum* 16, no. 2 (2002): 246.

38. Grace Frick to Gladys Minear, May 26, 1955, MFA.

39. Yourcenar, *With Open Eyes*, 255.

40. GFAB, May 27–29, 1955.

Chapter 22

1. GFAB, June 12 and 22, 1955.

2. GFAB, October 21, 1955.

3. Marguerite Yourcenar to Jean Lambert, September 23, 1956, in Yourcenar, *Lettres à ses amis*, 125.

4. GFAB, June 29, 1955.

5. GFAB, August 18, 1955.

6. Florence Codman to Marguerite Yourcenar, May 25, 1953, MYP (170).

7. GFAB, August 25, 1955. The letter has apparently not been preserved.

8. GFAB, October 28 and 29, 1955.

9. Marguerite Yourcenar to Henri Balmelle, April 2, 1959, in Yourcenar, *Lettres à ses amis*, 139.

10. The translation, deemed "remarkable" by Yourcenar's "Chronologie," in *Œuvres romanesques*, xxv, was entitled "Humanism and Occultism in Thomas Mann." It came out in 1956 in the *Partisan Review*.

11. Florence Codman to Grace Frick, January 19, 1956, MYP (170).

12. GFAB, August 29, 1955.

13. Deirdre Wilson, interview with the author, October 16, 2005.

14. GFAB, July 27, 1956.

15. Richard Savage , telephone interview with the author, October 2, 2007.

16. There were also prizes of fifteen, ten, and five dollars. Richard Savage, telephone interview with the author, October 2, 2007.

17. GFAB, February 19–21, 1950.

18. Grace Frick to Katharine and Pamela Frick, January 16, 1955, MYP (1200).

19. Deirdre Wilson, telephone conversation with the author, November 20, 2009.

20. Lalonde, *Un Jardin entouré de murailles*.

21. Kaighn Smith, interview with the author, September 27, 2008.

22. Grace Frick, card to Paul and Gladys Minear, February 26, 1956, MFA.

23. Hall Willkie, telephone interview with the author, June 9, 2010.

24. Ibid.

25. Julia Willkie, telephone interview with the author, June 20, 2010.

26. Ibid.

27. Marguerite Yourcenar to Natalie Barney, July 18, 1956, MYC (1032).

28. GFAB, October 12–30, 1956.

29. GFAB, November 2–4, 1956.

30. Marguerite Yourcenar to Aziz Izzet, November 27, 1957, in Yourcenar, *Une Volonté sans fléchissement*, 179.

31. Marguerite Yourcenar to Natalie Barney, December 27, 1956, NCBC 2386.

32. Savigneau, *Inventing a Life*, 227–28.

33. GFAB, November 11, 1956.

34. Shirley McGarr, interview with the author, September 4, 2005.

35. Marguerite Yourcenar to Paul and Gladys Minear, December 23, 1975, MFA.

36. See, e.g., Yourcenar, *With Open Eyes*, 4–5.

37. In Scandinavia the holiday is called Saint Lucia's Day, but here I follow Frick and Yourcenar's English spelling: "We stopped in Copenhagen to finish some

literary work and had a Danish Christmas at Elsinore, having had Saint Lucy's Day in Stockholm with crown of candles and awakening to coffee and song"; Marguerite Yourcenar to Märta Modeen, January 11, 1954, in Yourcenar, *D'Hadrien à Zénon*, 291.

38. In 1952 they spent all but the very end of December in their Scarsdale, New York, apartment, returning to Maine only briefly. In 1953 and 1954 they were in Europe. Over the holidays in 1955, the water main supplying Petite Plaisance froze three times, putting a big crimp in the festivities. GFAB, 1956 and 1957.

39. See, e.g., Delcroix, comp., *Portrait d'une voix*, 251.

40. Marguerite Yourcenar to Natalie Barney, November 10, 1962, MYC (4204): "early in the summer, we took a trip lasting nearly two months that brought us to Scandinavia (one of our favorite places: order and beauty, and great open spaces) and for a few days for the first time to Leningrad." For a Francophile, "order and beauty" is an unmistakable reference to Charles Baudelaire's famous "Invitation to the Voyage" and its invocation of luxury and pleasure.

41. GFAB, December 12–13, 1956; see also December 13, 1963.

42. Savigneau, *Inventing a Life*, 110.

43. Shirley McGarr, telephone interview with the author, November 24, 2009.

44. In a folder of holiday recipes saved by Yourcenar, MYC (228), one finds, along with other international fare, a whole page of "Swedish Christmas Food."

45. GFAB, December 21, 1956.

46. Buttons, thank-you card to Monsieur, December 24, 1956, MYP (1371).

47. Yourcenar's status as chief cook earned her another playful gift-related card in the mid-1950s. This one was a Valentine from Grace and Monsieur. The envelope is addressed "To you from your 2 boarders," and on the front are several rows of red hearts and flowers, along with the first half of the sentiment "A Valentine Gift for You 'Cause You're my Valentine!" Signing the card as if from Monsieur in helter-skelter printing, Grace wrote, "and mine, too, Wag, wag, wag!" PPA.

48. GFAB, early 1957.

49. See, e.g., GFAB, 1957, 1959, 1965, and 1969.

Chapter 23

1. Marguerite Yourcenar to Malvina Hoffman, January 15, 1957, in Yourcenar, *Une Volonté sans fléchissement*, 47.

2. Lalonde, *Un Jardin entouré de murailles*, 101.

3. Ibid., 101–2.

4. GFAB, March 21, 1957.

5. Marguerite Yourcenar, "Commentaire pour Grace," MYC (76).

6. Ibid.

7. Ben Ray Redman, "A Look in the Mirror," *Saturday Review*, July 20, 1957, 22.

8. Charles Poore, "Books of the Times," review of *Coup de Grâce*, *New York Times*, July 23, 1957.

9. Herbert Kupferberg, review of *Coup de Grâce*, *New York Herald Tribune*, July 31, 1957.

10. Carlos Baker, "A Baltic Soldier," *New York Times*, July 21, 1957.

11. William Hogan, review of *Coup de Grâce, San Francisco Chronicle*, July 22, 1957.

12. Edwin Kennebeck, "Strange Triangle," *Commonweal* 66 (1957): 574–75.

13. [Virgilia Peterson,] "The Memoirs of a 'Soldier of Fortune,' " *New York Herald Tribune Book Review*, July 21, 1957, 3; and Maurice Dolbier, "Meeting Writers on Ship and on Shore," *New York Herald Tribune Book Review*, July 21, 1957, 3.

14. Marguerite Yourcenar to Gilbert H. Montague, September 3, 1957, MYP (991). A copy of Peterson's autobiography, *A Matter of Life and Death*, still resides at Petite Plaisance.

15. Edith Hamilton to Marguerite Yourcenar, August 30, 1961, MYP (342).

16. [Peterson,] " 'Soldier of Fortune,' " 3.

17. Louise Dudley to "Grace and Marguerite," April 14, 1957, MYC (2456).

18. Katherine Gatch to Marguerite Yourcenar, June 13, 1957, MYC (2695).

19. GFC.

20. Marguerite Yourcenar to Natalie Barney, August 12, 1957, NCBC 2387.

21. Mme. Marcel Vertès to Grace Frick, December 9, 1957, MYC (5514).

22. GFAB, December 30, 1957.

23. GFAB, January 4, 1958.

Chapter 24

1. GFAB, January 7–16, 1958.

2. GFAB, February 16, 1958.

3. GFAB, February 18, 1956.

4. Grace Frick to Gladys Minear, February 8, 1950, MFA.

5. Grace Frick to Gertrude Fay, January 14, 1979, Fay family archives.

6. GFAB, February 26, 1958.

7. GFAB, March 11, 1958.

8. GFAB, April 19, 1958.

9. GFAB, May 9–29, 1958; Grace Frick to Chenoweth Hall and Miriam Colwell, March 11, 1964, Colwell family archives.

10. GFAB, May 29, 1958.

11. GFAB, June 1, 1958.

12. GFAB, May 25, 1958.

13. GFAB, undated page at the rear of the 1958 daybook.

14. GFAB, April 12–15, 1958.

15. Marguerite Yourcenar to Henri Balmelle, April 2, 1959, in Yourcenar, *Lettres à ses amis*, 138.

16. GFAB, July 14, 1958.

17. GFAB, July 14 and July 22, 1958. As usual, Monsieur's birthday party featured a raw-hamburger cake decked out with candles.

18. Marguerite Yourcenar, personal communication, 1982, quoted in Anne Olga Dzamba, "Adelaide Pearson of Blue Hill, Maine," typescript conveyed to the author by Sharon Thompson.

19. GFAB, August 15, 1958.

20. GFAB, August 28, 1958.

21. Leopold, *A Darker Ribbon*, 153.

22. Marguerite Yourcenar to Élie Grekoff, October 24, 1958, in Yourcenar, *Une Volonté sans fléchissement*, 280. Curiously, there is no mention of Grace's cancer in any of the published or archival correspondence with Natalie Barney until 1964.

23. Marguerite Yourcenar to Élie Grekoff, October 24, 1958, in Yourcenar, *Lettres à ses amis*, 279.

24. For this whole trip, see GFAB, October 20–24, 1958.

25. GFAB, "Grace Frick Diary (Part 2)," August 16, 1959.

26. Yourcenar, *An Obscure Man*, in *Two Lives and a Dream*, 18; see also Deprez, *Marguerite Yourcenar and the USA*, 55–56.

27. GFAB, "Grace Frick Diary (Part 2)," March 26, 1959.

28. Grace Frick to Gladys Minear, November 10, 1959, MFA.

29. Marguerite Yourcenar to Élie Grekoff, July 29, 1959, in Yourcenar, *Une Volonté sans fléchissement*, 367.

30. GFAB, April 29, 1959.

31. The exhibit had taken place in September. Miriam Colwell, e-mail to the author, July 23, 2008.

32. Chenoweth Hall, postcard to "G. & M.," n.d., PPA.

33. Miriam Colwell, interview with the author, July 14, 2008.

Chapter 25

1. GFAB, January 10–13, 1960.

2. GFAB, March 29–31, 1960.

3. Marguerite Yourcenar to Natalie Barney, June 5, 1960, in Yourcenar, *Une Volonté sans fléchissement*, 462–63.

4. GFAB, November 4, 1960.

5. Grace Frick to Natalie Barney, November 10, 1962, MYC (5435).

6. GFAB, September 3, 1960.

7. GFAB, September 8, 1960.

8. The daybooks dated 1948–59 contain, e.g., nearly twice as many words on average as those for 1960–72.

9. Marguerite Yourcenar to Jacques Kayaloff, December 31, 1960, in Yourcenar, *Une Volonté sans fléchissement*, 521–22.

10. See, e.g., Ruth Hill to Grace Frick, September 7, 1958, MYP (1206).

11. GFAB, February 15–16, 1961.

12. See Werth, *The Scarlet Professor*; "Arvin, Newton," Smithipedia (Smith College), http://sophia.smith.edu/blog/smithipedia/faculty-staff/arvin-newton; "Newton Arvin Papers, 1900–2001," Five College Archives and Manuscripts Collections, http://asteria.fivecolleges.edu/findaids/smitharchives/manosca36.html, accessed on February 11, 2017; and Robert D. McFadden, "Joel Dorius, 87, Victim in Celebrated Anti-Gay Case, Dies," *New York Times*, February 20, 2006, http://www.nytimes.com/2006/02/20/obituaries/20dorius.html?_r=0.

13. "The Literary Lights of Artists' Colony Cast Long Shadows to Smith College," *NewsSmith* (Smith College), summer 2009, http://www.smith.edu/newssmith/summer2009/yaddo.php.

14. McFadden, "Joel Dorius," states that "Mr. Arvin . . . named names, including those of Mr. Dorius and Edward Spoffard."

15. Smith College, "Former Smith Professor Joel Dorius Dies," February 20, 2006, http://www.smith.edu/news/2005-06/doriusobit.html.

16. Elizabeth von Klemperer, obituary of Charles Hill, *Smith Alumnae Quarterly*, summer 2000, 89; GFAB, February 17, 1961.

17. Charles Hill to Grace Frick, February 18, 1961, MYC (2857).

18. See Marguerite Yourcenar to Jean Lambert, January 23, 1961, in Yourcenar, *Persévérer dans l'être*, 38–39.

19. Smith College Office of College Relations, "Actions of the Smith College Board of Trustees regarding Issues of Civil Liberties Past and Present," March 22, 2002, http://www.smith.edu/newsoffice/releases/01-085.html.

20. GFAB, June 10, 1961; Florence MacDonald (secretary of the board of trustees of Smith College) to Marguerite Yourcenar, May 27, 1961, MYC (5203).

21. Vickery, *Smith College: An Architectural Tour*, 128–29.

22. GFAB, April 2–7, 1961; David Cuthbert, "My O My: A Legend Evoked," *New Orleans Times Picayune*, April 29, 2005.

23. Yourcenar, *Blues et gospels*, 8.

24. Marguerite Yourcenar, "Chronologie," in *Œuvres romanesques*, xxvii.

25. Shirley McGarr, interview with the author, November 24, 2009.

26. Lynn Ahlblad, interview with the author, September 6, 2006.

27. GFAB, November 30, 1961.

28. Yourcenar, *Sources II*, 273.

29. Marguerite Yourcenar to Lidia Storoni Mazzolani, Christmas 1962, in Yourcenar, *Lettres à ses amis*, 170.

30. Ibid., 171. The Marquis de Custine wrote the 1839 work *Empire of the Czar: A Journey through Eternal Russia*.

Chapter 26

1. Yourcenar's "Critical Introduction to Cavafy," the preface to the Cavafy translations, appears in *The Dark Brain of Piranesi and Other Essays*, translated by Richard Howard.

2. Yourcenar, "Sur quelques thèmes érotiques et mystiques de la Gita-Govinda," preface to Shri Jayadeva, *Gita Govinda*.

3. Marguerite Yourcenar, "The Legend of Krishna," *Encounter* 13, no. 6 (1959): 3–9.

4. Yourcenar, *Rendre à César*, later published in *Théâtre I* and, as *Render unto Caesar*, in *Plays*.

5. Marguerite Yourcenar to Natalie Barney, November 10, 1962, MYC (4204).

6. Rodriguez, *Wild Heart*, 339; Natalie Barney to Marguerite Yourcenar, June 20, 1958, MYC (1032).

7. Grace Frick and Marguerite Yourcenar, telegram to Malvina Hoffman, October 23, 1962, Malvina Hoffman Papers, Getty Research Institute, Series I.A., Correspondence 1909–68, box 11. Hoffman studied sculpture in France under Auguste Rodin.

8. Marguerite Yourcenar to Malvina Hoffman, October 23, 1962, Malvina Hoffman Papers, Getty Research Institute, Series I.A., Correspondence 1909–68, box 11. By "the two of you" Yourcenar means Hoffman and her companion Gullborg Groneng, known as Guldie. Hoffman's obituary in the *New York Times* states that "Miss Hoffman had been living at the studio with her secretary." "Malvina Hoffman Dead at 81," *New York Times*, July 11, 1966.

9. GFAB, February 18, 1963.

10. Blanche Wiesen Cook, "Women Alone Stir My Imagination," *Signs: Journal of Women in Culture and Society* 4, no. 4 (1979): 734.

11. Natalie Barney to Marguerite Yourcenar and Grace Frick, December 27, 1960, MYC (1032).

12. Natalie Barney to Marguerite Yourcenar and Grace Frick, July 20, 1961.

13. Marguerite Yourcenar to Natalie Barney, August 28, 1961, MYC (4204).

14. Shusha Guppy, "The Art of Fiction No. 103: Marguerite Yourcenar," *Paris Review* 30, no. 106 (1988): 8.

15. Natalie Barney to Marguerite Yourcenar and Grace Frick, December 25, 1961, MYC (1032).

16. Natalie Barney to Marguerite Yourcenar and Grace Frick, January 13, 1963, MYC (1032).

17. Miron Grindea, ed., "The Amazon of Letters: A World Tribute to Natalie Barney," special issue of *ADAM International Review* 30, no. 299 (1962).

18. Marguerite Yourcenar to Natalie Barney, July 29, 1963, in Yourcenar, *Lettres à ses amis*, 186–87. Flanner, author of the *New Yorker*'s "Letter from Paris" for fifty years, explained her choice not to take part in the *ADAM International* tribute as follows: "Miss Barney is a perfect example of an enchanting person not to write about"—whatever that means. Janet Flanner, quoted in Wickes, *The Amazon of Letters*, 211.

19. Marguerite Yourcenar to Natalie Barney, July 29, 1963, in Yourcenar, *Lettres à ses amis*, 187–88. Balzac's *Girl with the Golden Eyes* dealt, scandalously at the time, with issues of seduction and bisexuality.

20. Marguerite Yourcenar to Natalie Barney, July 29, 1963, in Yourcenar, *Lettres à ses amis*, 189.

21. Natalie Barney to Marguerite Yourcenar, November 14, 1963, MYC (1032).

22. Natalie Barney to Grace Frick, November 16, 1963, MYC (5401).

23. Grace Frick, foreword to the 1963 *Island Red Book*, 1–7. Today the annual volume is called *The Redbook: Directory and Handbook*; Northeast Harbor resident Cheryl Chase is the editor and publisher.

24. Teddy, card to Monsieur, August 20, 1963, MYP (1371).

25. Marguerite Yourcenar (as Monsieur) to Teddy, August 21, 1963, MYP (1371).

26. Grace Frick to Natalie Barney, November 27, 1963, NCBC 2395.

27. For these committees see, e.g., GFAB, March 26 and 30, 1963, and January 18 and April 2, 1965.

28. Marguerite Yourcenar to Natalie Barney, November 29, 1963, NCBC 2396. Yourcenar and Frick never owned a television, but on occasions such as this they would go next door to watch with the McGarr family.

29. Grace Frick to Gladys Minear, December 6, 1963, MFA.

30. Ibid.

31. Merton, *Seeds of Destruction*, 7. Yourcenar, *Sources II*, 330.

32. Yourcenar, *Fleuve profond*, 8.

33. Deprez, *Marguerite Yourcenar and the USA*, 106.

34. Grace Frick to Jean-Louis Côté, February 18, 1964, MYC (4423). The words in brackets here were mostly cut off and hard to read.

35. Grace Frick to Katharine Peryam, December n.d., 1971, FFA.

36. Frick reports the date of this new operation variously as December 2 or 3, depending on the source.

37. GFAB, December 24, 1963.

38. GFAB, December 25, 1963.

39. GFAB, January 14, 1964.

Chapter 27

1. Grace Frick to Gladys Minear, January 21, 1964, MFA.

2. Marguerite Yourcenar to Natalie Barney, March 30, 1964, NCBC 2398.

3. Marguerite Yourcenar, "Traversée sur le *Bathory*," unpublished typescript, MYC (524).

4. Ibid.

5. Ibid.

6. Ibid.

7. Ibid.

8. Marguerite Yourcenar, "Carnets de notes de *L'Œuvre au Noir*," in *Œuvres romanesques*, 857.

9. Marguerite Yourcenar, "Mirror-Games and Will-o'-the-Wisps," in *That Mighty Sculptor, Time*, 95.

10. Yourcenar, "Carnets de notes de *L'Œuvre au Noir*," 860. Yourcenar and Frick spent many evenings with Pasquale and Curtis over a period of thirty years. Only once does the daybook mention an evening of music, on October 5, 1959.

11. Marguerite Yourcenar to Natalie Barney, October 5, 1964, NCBC 2399.

12. Marguerite Yourcenar to Natalie Barney (draft), October 5, 1964, MYC (4204). She left out the last nine words in the second version of the letter.

13. Frick was particularly fond of "A Hard Rain's A-Gonna Fall" and "We Shall Overcome" from Pete Seeger's album *Little Boxes: Broadside Ballads 2*. Grace Frick to Paul and Gladys Minear, December 29, 1964, MFA.

14. Yourcenar, *With Open Eyes*, 236. Participants also sent a strongly worded antiwar letter to President Richard Nixon.

15. *Bar Harbor Times*, December 18, 1964, 1.

16. Grace Frick to Larry Minear, n.d. (probably 1964), MFA.

17. See Larry Minear, "About the Author," http://larryminear.com/about-the-author-2.

18. *Bar Harbor Times*, February 4, 1965, 1, and February 11, 1965, 1.

19. GFAB, February 7, 1965.

20. GFAB, February 11, 1965.

21. GFAB, February 13, 1965.

22. The microfilm copy of Yourcenar's letter preserved at Bar Harbor's Jesup Memorial Library contains several illegible words in the first few paragraphs. Square brackets contain the easier ones to figure out or identify. The essays "Fur-Bearing Animals" and "Who Knows Whether the Spirit of Animals Goes Downward" can be found in Yourcenar, *That Mighty Sculptor, Time.*

23. *Bar Harbor Times,* February 11, 1965, 1.

24. GFAB, February 7, 1965.

25. GFAB, December 5, 1965.

Chapter 28

1. Natalie Barney to Marguerite Yourcenar, March 1, 1960, MYP (42).

2. Natalie Barney to Marguerite Yourcenar, December 27, 1960, MYC (1032).

3. Marguerite Yourcenar to Natalie Barney, August 17, 1965, in Yourcenar, *Lettres à ses amis,* 224.

4. Marguerite Yourcenar to Georges Roditi, August 17, 1965, MYC (4204).

5. GFAB, May 23, 1965, mentions Olin being there "for two nights end of May or first week in June." Olin remembers them first meeting in 1966. He may be right, as Frick's daybook entry is less precise than usual.

6. John Olin, interview with the author, August 7, 2009. Frick and Yourcenar were making an exception in picking up Olin. The couple had sometimes stopped for hitchhikers back in Connecticut, but one day Grace had a close call that caused her to abandon the practice. Driving alone on an isolated road in a wooded area of the state, she picked up a stranger in a snowstorm. She narrowly escaped being raped. Marguerite Yourcenar, conversation with the author, July 17, 1983.

7. Olin interview.

8. GFAB, April 20 and 22, 1966.

9. Grace Frick to Kathie Frick, November 10, 1966, FFA.

10. GFAB, November 23–27, 1966.

11. Grace Frick to Gage Frick, February 16, 1967, FFA.

12. Natalie Barney to Marguerite Yourcenar and Grace Frick, December 19, 1966, MYC (1032). Although this letter was written almost entirely in English, Barney used the expression "en procès" here, and her choice of terms is reflected in Yourcenar's response. I have provided a translation in brackets that can serve in both locations.

13. Marguerite Yourcenar to Natalie Barney, January 1, 1967, MYC (4204).

14. GFAB, March 15, 1967.

15. GFAB, March 25, 1967.

16. GFAB, October 14, 1967.

17. Yourcenar, *Sources II,* 323.

18. Grace Frick to Gertrude Fay, March 10, 1970, courtesy of Fay's daughter, Hope Cobb.

19. GFAB, May 13–18, 1968.

20. Flanner, *Paris Journal,* 2:249.

21. Rodriguez, *Wild Heart,* 354.

22. Chalon, *Portrait of a Seductress*, 220.

23. Ibid., 221.

24. Marguerite Yourcenar to Jean Chalon, April 9, 1976, in Yourcenar, *Lettres à ses amis*, 497.

25. GFAB, May 24, 1968.

26. GFAB, May 19 and 26, 1968.

27. GFAB, May 29, 1968.

28. Marguerite Yourcenar to Jean and Roger Hazelton, June 3, 1968, Hazelton family archives.

29. See Savigneau, *Inventing a Life*, 304–5, for the critical reaction to this book.

30. GFAB, June 1, 1968.

31. Ibid., June 6, 1968.

32. Marguerite Yourcenar to Jean Mouton, April 7, 1968, in Yourcenar, *Lettres à ses amis*, 285.

33. Yourcenar, *The Abyss*, 139.

Chapter 29

1. GFAB, June 14–18, 1968.

2. GFAB, October 30, 1968.

3. Information about the progress of Frick's illness comes from a cancer report, written on both sides of five index cards and stapled together, that Frick sent to Gladys Minear on February 26, 1977, MFA.

4. Last will and testament of Grace Frick, executed on November 5, 1968, in Bar Harbor, Maine, MYC (566).

5. Grace Frick to Gertrude Fay, December 17, 1967, Fay family archives.

6. Grace Frick to Gertrude Fay, March 16, 1968.

7. Grace Frick to Hortense Flexner, February 14, 1968, MYC (5440).

8. Erika Vollger to Grace Frick and Marguerite Yourcenar, November 29, 1968, MYP (780).

9. Rose Chessin, telegram to Grace Frick at Morgan and Company, Paris, sent on December 7 but received on the December 9, 1968, MYP (157).

10. Four-page sequence of events prepared by Frick using letters from Chessin, MYP (157).

11. Wilson journal entry, February 26, 1980, Wilson family archives.

12. Author's personal journal entry, July 13, 1984.

13. Savigneau, *Inventing a Life*, 306.

14. Marguerite Yourcenar to Camille Letot, [November] 28, 1968, in Yourcenar, *Lettres à ses amis*, 304. *Lettres à ses amis* gives a date of October 28 for this letter, but the Femina prize was not announced until November 25. Grace Frick was deeply moved by this visit with three generations of the Letot family. She would write a lovely letter to Camille on December 10, 1969, recalling the intimacy of their gathering in Gosselies and how pleased she was to have been part of it (see Yourcenar, *Lettres à ses amis*, 336n2). To Yourcenar's earlier letter she added, "I am very happy to have met all of you, too, and to have friends in Belgium. I promise you, Madame Camille, that I will do my best to take good care of our dear Marguerite."

15. "M'as-tu vu?" or "Did you see me?"; Grace Frick to Helen Howe, January 4, 1969, Schlesinger Library, Helen Howe Repository, Container I.C. 227, Correspondence with Marguerite Yourcenar and Grace Frick, 77-M218-78.

16. Savigneau, *Inventing a Life*, 313–14.

17. Jean Chalon, e-mail to the author, March 7, 2010.

18. Grace Frick to Paul and Gladys Minear, February [15–16,] 1969, MFA.

19. GFAB, January 6 and 20 and November 3, 1969; Frick cancer report sent to Gladys Minear, February 26, 1977, MFA.

20. GFAB, February 3, 1969.

21. Pamela York, telephone interview with the author, March 29, 2013.

22. GFAB, March 8, 1969.

23. GFAB, March 10, 1969.

Chapter 30

1. GFAB, November 4, 1969.

2. GFAB, May 2, 1971.

3. GFAB, August 20–23, 1967.

4. GFAB, August 26, 1967.

5. GFAB, August 18, 1968. Clements's article from this interview was never published.

6. Marguerite Yourcenar to Gerald Kamber, October 30, 1968, in Yourcenar, *Lettres à ses amis*, 305–6.

7. Yourcenar, *Présentation critique d'Hortense Flexner*.

8. GFAB, November 21–23, 1969.

9. Author's personal journal entry, July 17, 1982.

10. Marguerite Yourcenar, "André Gide Revisited," in *Cahiers André Gide*, vol. 3, *Le Centenaire*, 22. An annotated offprint is available at MYC (19).

11. For all the Rosbo correspondence, beginning April 10, 1969, see MYC (3609).

12. Marguerite Yourcenar to Marthe Lamy, June 30, 1973, in Yourcenar, *Lettres à ses amis*, 395.

13. GFAB, September 2, 1970.

14. Marguerite Yourcenar to Marc Brossollet, February 26, 1973, MYP (864).

15. Rosbo, *Entretiens radiophoniques avec Marguerite Yourcenar*.

16. Patrick de Rosbo, "Huit Jours de purgatoire," *Gulliver*, February 4, 1973, 30–35.

17. Marguerite Yourcenar to Marthe Lamy, June 30, 1973, in Yourcenar, *Lettres à ses amis*, 396.

18. Josane Duranteau, "Avarice de soi," *Les Lettres françaises*, September 27, 1972.

19. Marguerite Yourcenar to Marc Brossollet, March 13, 1973, MYP (864).

20. As she notes in the novel's postface, some of the characters' names come from genealogies of her ancestors; Yourcenar, *The Abyss*, 370. They include Wiwine, Hilzonde, Zénon, and Adriansen. Yourcenar, *Réception de Marguerite Yourcenar à l'Académie royale*, 12.

21. GFAB, March 21, 1971.

22. Anita Fahrni, e-mail to the author, April 17, 2013; GFAB, March 26–27, 1971.

23. Sarton, *I Knew a Phoenix*, 42.

24. GFAB, April 18, 1971.

25. GFAB, April 4–5, 1971.

26. GFAB, April 6 and 25 and May 2, 1971.

27. GFAB, April 18 and 25, 1971.

28. GFAB, April 12, 1971.

29. According to the 1971 daybook, Frick and Yourcenar arrived in Paris on May 18 and left there on June 12, 1971. GFAB, 1971.

30. Rodriguez, *Wild Heart*, 361.

31. Natalie Barney to Marguerite Yourcenar and Grace Frick, November 17, 1970, MYC (1032).

32. Marguerite Yourcenar to Jean Chalon, February 7, 1972, in Yourcenar, *Lettres à ses amis*, 388.

33. GFAB, June 13, 1971.

34. Grace Frick to Kathie Peryam, sometime in the summer or fall of 1971, FFA.

35. GFAB, August 1, 1965.

36. Ann Gilkes, interview with the author, August 28, 2010.

37. Frick expected Ann and Amelia on September 12 according to the daybook, but their visit was postponed. It probably occurred on Sunday, September 19. Hardly anything is noted in the daybook for September 13–30. GFAB, September 12–30, 1971.

38. Ann Gilkes, interview with the author, August 28, 2010.

Chapter 31

1. Marguerite Yourcenar, quoted in John R. Wiggins, "Famous French Author Lives in Northeast Harbor," *Ellsworth (ME) American*, April 11, 1974.

2. Marguerite Yourcenar, "Des chiens que j'aimais," a text that Yourcenar wrote on the back pages of her paternal aunt Gabrielle de Crayencour's schoolgirl notebook, MYC (842).

3. Ibid.

4. Marguerite Yourcenar, "Tribute to Valentine," in *Sources II*, 311.

5. Ibid., 313.

6. "Une Vie, une œuvre, une voix" [A life, a vocation, a voice] aired on Antenne 2 on February 19 and 20, 1972.

7. Handbill for *Électre ou la Chute des masques*, MYC (128).

8. GFAB, August 24–29, 1974.

9. Ibid., September 7–14 and 27–29, 1974.

10. Yourcenar called Brissac's letter "scatterbrained" in a letter to Jean Chalon, February 3, 1977, in Yourcenar, *Lettres à ses amis*, 527.

11. Morand, *"Alexis ou le Traité du vain combat*, par Marg Yourcenar," *Le Courrier littéraire* 15 (1930): 158.

12. Marguerite Yourcenar to Elvire de Brissac, July 1, 1972, MYC (862).

13. Brissac, *Ballade américaine*, 180.

14. Brissac, *Ballade américaine*, 180–82. "Parigote" is a colloquial, often pejorative term for a Parisian girl or woman.

15. Brissac, *Ballade américaine*, 182–83.

16. Marguerite Yourcenar to Marc Brossollet, December 10, 1976, MYP (864).

17. Marguerite Yourcenar to André Bay, December 29, 1976, MYC (5235).

18. André Bay to Marguerite Yourcenar, January 4, 1977, ibid.

19. Marguerite Yourcenar to Jeanne Carayon, February 19, 1977, MYP (868).

20. Jean Chalon, "Sur les traces de Lolita," *Le Figaro*, January 8, 1977.

21. Marguerite Yourcenar to Jean Chalon, February 3, 1977, in Yourcenar, *Lettres à ses amis*, 527–28.

22. Jean Chalon, journal entry of February 8, 1977, provided to the author via e-mail on March 7, 2010. The passage was published in Chalon's *Journal de Paris*.

23. Brissac, *Ballade américaine*, 190–91.

24. Grace Frick to Kathie Peryam, n.d., FFA.

25. Grace Frick, postcard to Richard Minear, n.d., MFA.

26. Yourcenar, *Sources II*, 290–91.

27. GFAB, April 12–15 and November 10, 21, and 30, 1972.

28. GFAB, December 31, 1972.

29. GFAB, February 14, 1973.

30. Grace Frick to Helen Howe, February 20, 1973, Helen Howe repository.

31. Grace Frick to Gage Frick, November 30, 1972, FFA.

32. Grace Frick to Kathie Peryam, April 17, 1973, FFA.

33. GFAB, October 15–17, 1971.

34. GFAB, January 7, 1973.

35. GFAB, July 24–August 1, 1973.

36. "Phyllis Bartlett, Educator, Is Dead," *New York Times*, April 19, 1973.

37. GFAB, March 16 and 21, 1973.

38. "Baron de Cartier, Belgian Envoy, 74, Ambassador to London, Dean of Corps, Is Dead," *New York Times*, May 11, 1946, 27; Marguerite Yourcenar, *Souvenirs pieux*, documents and notes, MYC (459).

39. Marguerite Yourcenar to Georges de Crayencour, July 21, 1973, in Yourcenar, *Lettres à ses amis*, 402.

40. Grace Frick to Gage Frick, July 22, 1973, FFA.

41. Marguerite Yourcenar to Jeanne Carayon, August 3, 1973, in Yourcenar, *Lettres à ses amis*, 405.

42. Marguerite Yourcenar to Jeanne Carayon, August 31, 1973, MYP (868).

Chapter 32

1. GFAB, January 14–25, 1974.

2. See, e.g., GFAB, August 12, 1974.

3. Marguerite Yourcenar to Jeanne Carayon, August 14, 1974, in Yourcenar, *Lettres à ses amis*, 442–43.

4. GFAB, September 24, 1974; Frick cancer report sent to Gladys Minear, February 26, 1977, MFA.

5. Marguerite Yourcenar to Jeanne Carayon, July 25, 1975, in Yourcenar, *Lettres à ses amis*, 468.

6. See, e.g., GFAB, October 6–12, 1974.

7. Yourcenar, *Sources II*, 302–4.

8. GFAB, January 3, 1974.

9. Yourcenar, *Sources II*, 281–82.

10. Nicolas Calas to Marguerite Yourcenar, September 23, 1975, MYP (127).

11. Marguerite Yourcenar to Nicolas Calas, September 26, 1975, ibid. (866).

12. Yourcenar, *Sources II*, 303.

13. GFAB, June 1–2, 1975.

14. GFAB, July 25–26, 1975.

15. Gunnar Hansen, interview with the author, July 18, 2006.

16. Grace Frick to Gertrude Fay, n.d. [but most plausibly summer 1975], courtesy of Hope Cobb (Fay's daughter).

17. Esther Hahn to Jean Hazelton, December 2, 1994, MFA.

18. Ibid.

19. Marguerite Yourcenar to Jeanne Carayon, July 25, 1975, in Yourcenar, *Lettres à ses amis*, 467–68.

20. Marguerite Yourcenar to Jeanne Carayon, January 18, 1976, in Yourcenar, *Lettres à ses amis*, 486.

21. Marguerite Yourcenar to André Bay, September 21, 1975, MYC (5235).

22. Grace Frick to the Minear family, February 13, 1977, MFA. The essay Frick refers to here is Marguerite Yourcenar, "Fur-Bearing Animals," in *That Mighty Sculptor, Time*, 87–88.

23. Marguerite Yourcenar to Jeanne Carayon, July 20–28, 1976, MYP (868).

24. Arthur A. Cohen, review of *The Abyss*, *New York Times Book Review*, July 11, 1976, 7–8.

25. Frank Kermode, "A Successful Alchemist," *New York Review of Books*, October 14, 1976, 6, 8.

26. Review of *The Abyss*, *Times Literary Supplement*, October 22, 1976, 1321.

27. "Cartesian Quest," *Times Literary Supplement*, October 3, 1968, 1103.

28. Mary Renault, "Imagining the Past," *Times Literary Supplement*, August 23, 1974, 893.

29. Review of *The Abyss*, *Times Literary Supplement*, October 22, 1976, 1321.

30. Marguerite Yourcenar to Jeanne Carayon, July 20–28, 1976, MYP (868).

31. Lewis Gannett, quoted on the back of the book jacket of *The Abyss*.

32. Peter S. Prescott, review of *The Abyss*, *Newsweek*, June 28, 1976, 75.

33. Naomi Bliven, "Truth and Consequences," *New Yorker*, June 14, 1976, 109–10.

34. Review of *The Abyss*, *Choice* 13 (1976): 835.

35. Robert Taylor, "New Historical Fiction—Finest in Years," *Boston Globe*, June 29, 1976.

36. Stephen Koch, "In a Circle of Flames," *Saturday Review*, June 12, 1976, 29, 30.

37. Yourcenar, *Sources II*, 247.

Chapter 33

Epigraph: Arthur Rimbaud, "The Drunken Boat," in *Complete Works*, 135.

1. Marguerite Yourcenar to Jeanne Carayon, July 20–28, 1976, MYP (868).

2. Marguerite Yourcenar to Jeanne Carayon, April 16, 1976, MYP (868).

3. Yourcenar, *Sources II*, 304.

4. Ibid., 303.

5. GFAB, January 1, 1977.

6. Review of Volker Schlöndorff's *Coup de Grâce, Soho Weekly News*, February 16, 1978, contained in a folder of clippings in English about the film, MYC (883).

7. Frick cancer report sent to Gladys Minear, February 26, 1977, MFA.

8. On January 19, 1977, according to Grace Frick's February 1977 cancer report.

9. Frick cancer report, 1977; Grace Frick to Paul, Gladys, and Anita Minear, February 13, 1977, MFA; GFAB, 1977.

10. Marguerite Yourcenar, Valentine's Day card to Grace Frick, February 14, 1977, MYP (913).

11. Frick cancer report, 1977. The report ends here. "End of long story," she writes on the last index card.

12. Marguerite Yourcenar to Jeanne Carayon, February 19, 1977, MYP (868).

13. Grace Frick to Gladys Minear, February 26, 1977, MFA.

14. Marguerite Yourcenar, interview by Françoise Faucher, in Maurice Delcroix, comp., *Portrait d'une voix*, 148–49.

15. Grace Frick to Gladys Minear, February 13, 1977, MFA.

16. GFAB, April 8, 1977.

17. GFAB, April 13, 1977.

18. GFAB, April 19 and 21, 1977. Yourcenar, for her part, notes on pages 304 and 323 of *Sources II* that Frick was hospitalized April 3–10 and 12–17, 1977, in Bar Harbor and then April 21–27, 1977, in Bangor.

19. GFAB, May 23, 1977.

20. Grace Frick, postcard to Marguerite Yourcenar, February 3, 1947, PPA.

21. WCCC, 1950, WCA.

22. Grace Frick, postcard to an unnamed addressee, February 4, 1947, PPA.

23. Grace Frick, postcard to Marguerite Yourcenar, February 4, 1947, PPA.

24. Grace Frick, postcards to Marguerite Yourcenar, February 5, 1947, PPA.

25. Grace Frick, postcard to "The Emmas" [Emma Trebbe and Emma Evans], February 5, 1947, PPA.

26. GFAB, February 15, 1947.

27. GFAB, May 23, 1977.

28. Grace Frick, letter and postcard to Kathie Peryam, June 17, 1977, FFA.

29. Grace Frick, letter and postcard to Kathie Peryam, May 26, 1977, FFA.

30. Marguerite Yourcenar, "Chronologie," in *Œuvres romanesques*, xxx.

31. Grace Frick, letter and postcard to Kathie Peryam, June 17, 1977, FFA.

32. Traveling by train to meet Frick in Taos, New Mexico, during the first days of writing *Hadrian*, Yourcenar described herself, similarly, as "closed inside my compartment as if in a cubicle of some Egyptian tomb"; Yourcenar, *Memoirs of Hadrian and Reflections on the Composition of Memoirs of Hadrian*, 328.

33. Marguerite Yourcenar, "L'Italienne à Alger," in *Le Tour de la Prison*, 29–30.

34. See, e.g., Sarde, *Vous, Marguerite Yourcenar*, 199, and Deprez, *Marguerite Yourcenar and the USA*, 125.

35. On page 91 of her copy of Castaneda's *The Teachings of Don Juan*, Yourcenar marked the paragraph in which Don Juan says, "The twilight is the crack between the worlds."

36. Marguerite Yourcenar to Jeanne Carayon, July 6, 1977, in Yourcenar, *Lettres à ses amis*, 552. For Zeno's end, see Yourcenar, *The Abyss*, 354–55.

37. I have dated "L'Italienne à Alger" on the basis of temporal references in the text itself.

Chapter 34

1. Élie Grekoff and Pierre de Monteret, telegram to Marguerite Yourcenar and Grace Frick, June 1977, MYP (332).

2. GFAB, October 30, 1977.

3. GFAB, January 23, 1978.

4. Thérèse de St. Phalle to Marguerite Yourcenar, December 24, 1977, MYP (671).

5. Marguerite Yourcenar to Louis Pelissier, December 17, 1977, MYP (1013).

6. Marguerite Yourcenar to Jean d'Ormesson, October 24, 1977, MYC (5008).

7. GFAB, June 21, 1977.

8. Marguerite Yourcenar to Jeanne Carayon, November 12, 1977, in Yourcenar, *Lettres à ses amis*, 577–78.

9. GFAB, July 16–19, 1977.

10. GFAB, August 12–15, 1977.

11. Grace Frick, Christmas card to Paul and Gladys Minear, December 16, 1977, MFA.

12. Frick lists the publication projects in which she participated in the 1978 daybook. See also *Sous bénéfice d'inventaire*: Corrections, MYC (441 and 442); and *Selma Lagerlöf*: Préface, MYC (422).

13. GFAB, April 30 and May 1, 1978. Dumay's show was broadcast in France on June 4, 1978.

14. GFAB, November 1, 1978, a date next to which Yourcenar subsequently placed four large *X*'s in Flair pen.

15. Marguerite Yourcenar, conversation with the author, July 6, 1983. On August 26, 1985, she called Jerry Grénier's secretary.

16. See, e.g., Savigneau, *Inventing a Life*, 2, 362–63; and Goslar, *"Qu'il eût été fade,"* 299.

17. Deirdre Wilson (no relation to Jerry), conversation with the author, May 8, 2009.

18. See Savigneau, *Inventing a Life*, 376–77; and Yourcenar, Japan and India travel diary, 1977–83, MYC (196). In the latter notebook, Yourcenar mistakenly assigns to 1977 Wilson's professional trips to Northeast Harbor of May and November 1978, and to 1978 his personal visit to Grace of 1979.

19. See chapter 29.

20. Jean-Marie Grénier, "Les Derniers Voyages de Marguerite Yourcenar," in Goslar, ed., *Dix Ans après . . .* , 106.

21. GFAB, May 15, 1978.

22. GFAB, May 15–24, 1978.

23. GFAB, June 20, 1978.

24. GFAB, June 21–24, 1978.

25. GFAB, July 7–8, 1978.

26. GFAB, July 10–12, 1978.

27. Marguerite Yourcenar, "Carnets de notes de L'Œuvre au Noir," in Œuvres romanesques, 858.

28. John Olin, interview with the author, August 7, 2009. Olin was not sure when the incident occurred, most likely 1977 or 1978.

29. Olin interview.

30. Grénier, "Derniers Voyages," 104–5.

31. Villon, Poems, copy in PPA.

32. Yourcenar saved this poem, which I have slightly abridged, with her papers, MYP (1349).

33. GFAB, November 24, 1978.

34. Grace Frick to Minear, n.d. [but pre-Thanksgiving 1978], MFA.

35. Yourcenar, With Open Eyes, 192–93.

Chapter 35

1. National Cancer Institute, "Photodynamic Therapy for Cancer," https://www.cancer.gov/about-cancer/treatment/types/surgery/photodynamic-fact-sheet.

2. American Cancer Society, "Photodynamic Therapy," http://www.cancer.org/treatment/treatmentsandsideeffects/treatmenttypes/photodynamic-therapy.

3. Marguerite Yourcenar, conversation with the author, July 4, 1983.

4. Grace Frick to Gertrude Fay, January 14, 1979, MS Fr 423 (6), Houghton Library, Harvard University.

5. Marguerite Yourcenar, conversation with the author, July 4, 1983.

6. Kaighn and Ann Smith, interview with the author, September 27, 2008.

7. Gay Smith was married outdoors on the windy western shore of Somes Sound on December 23, 1978. This event was not for the faint of heart! Frick and Yourcenar attended both the ceremony, on the Jesuit Plain, and the small gathering at the Smiths' home afterward.

8. Smith interview.

9. Ruth Westphal, interview with the author, September 20, 2007.

10. Deirdre Wilson, interviews with the author, October 24, 2009, and September 23, 2007.

11. Grace Frick to Gertrude Fay, February 13, 1979, Fay family archives.

12. Savigneau, Inventing a Life, 367.

13. Marguerite Yourcenar to Jeanne Carayon, May 15, 1979, MYP (868). See also letters to Jean-Paul Kauffmann, MYP (940).

14. Jean-Paul Kauffmann file, MYP (396).

15. Deirdre Wilson, interview with the author, October 16, 2005.

16. Deirdre Wilson, telephone interview with the author, November 9, 2009.

17. Deirdre Wilson, interview with the author, December 3, 2009.

18. Wilson interview, October 16, 2005.

19. Deirdre Wilson, interview with the author, February 4, 2010.

20. Ibid. Beth Kelley (now Renault) was about fifteen years old at the time, so this incident probably occurred in 1968.

21. Wilson interview, October 16, 2005.

22. Ibid.

23. Chancel, *Marguerite Yourcenar: Radioscopie*, 24–26.

24. Yourcenar, *Fires*, 116.

25. Marguerite Yourcenar to Georges de Crayencour, May 15, 1979, MYP (868).

26. Marguerite Yourcenar to Georges de Crayencour, May 28, 1979, in Yourcenar, *Lettres à ses amis*, 602–3.

27. Marguerite Yourcenar to Georges de Crayencour, May 28, 1979, MYC (4432).

28. Yourcenar, *Sources II*, 276.

29. Ibid.

30. See Marguerite Yourcenar to Georges de Crayencour, September 17, 1979, in Yourcenar, *Lettres à ses amis*, 612.

31. Yourcenar, *Sources II*, 276.

32. Marguerite Yourcenar to Georges de Crayencour, September 17, 1979, in Yourcenar, *Lettres à ses amis*, 276.

33. Yourcenar, *Sources II*, 276–77.

34. Author's conversations over the years with Jean Lunt, Shirley McGarr, Deirdre Wilson, and others.

35. Deirdre Wilson, interview with the author, November 20, 2009.

36. Wilson interview, October 16, 2005.

37. Shirley McGarr, interview with the author, September 4, 2005.

38. Marguerite Yourcenar, conversation with the author, August 27, 1985.

39. Marguerite Yourcenar to Georges de Crayencour, October 15, 1979, MYC (4432).

40. Deirdre Wilson, interview with the author, January 15, 2009. Wilson also said that Frick did not need oxygen to breathe until a week before her death (Savigneau, *Inventing a Life*, 372). But she did use oxygen for going to doctors and climbing stairs.

41. Readers familiar with the Yourcenar biographies will note that my depiction of Grace Frick's death differs from the standard account, most prominently with regard to the music box that Yourcenar played at Frick's bedside. In 1980 Yourcenar spoke to Matthieu Galey of "the modest little Swiss music box that plays pianissimo an arietta of Haydn, which I started playing at Grace's bedside one hour before her death, when she ceased to respond to word or touch"; Yourcenar, *With Open Eyes*, 261–62. That music box still resides on a bookshelf in Frick's bedroom. The *Merry Pranks* music box, by contrast, has disappeared. But Deirdre Wilson, the only person who was present with Yourcenar that evening until Frick died, remembers the experience as if it were yesterday.

42. Indeed, Till's Flemish roots went back to the era of religious Reformation and wars that played such a significant role in the life of Yourcenar's beloved Zeno.

Though often identified with his playful antics, Till was also a fighter, like Frick, for the rights of common people.

43. Deirdre Wilson, interviews with the author, September 17, 2007, April 27, 2009, and January 21, 2010.

44. Westphal interview, September 20, 2007.

45. Wilson interview, September 23, 2007.

46. Biographical material on Grace Frick, MYP (1376).

47. Obituary of Grace Frick, *Bar Harbor Times*, November 22, 1979.

48. Ruth Westphal, interview with the author, September 24, 2007.

Epilogue

1. Deirdre Wilson, interview with the author, January 26, 2007.

2. Grace Frick funeral service, MYC (565), translated by Marguerite Yourcenar.

3. Marguerite Yourcenar, handwritten note in green Flair pen, found at Petite Plaisance. On June 25, 1985, she would reiterate her desire for a funeral service identical in every respect to Frick's. Her handwritten note identifies the readings listed above as "having served from [*sic*] Grace Frick's funeral at Union church, Northeast Harbor in Nov. 1979" and requests that they "serve unchanged and without any omissions *or* additions for the funeral service of Marguerite Yourcenar either in same church or in any other place." Yourcenar, handwritten note, Grace Frick funeral service, MYC (565).

4. In the end the stones were made of granite overlaid with slate. Yourcenar preferred slate because it was "more *natural* than the bronze, in a setting that we wish to make as natural as possible." Marguerite Yourcenar to Brooke Roberts, January 22, 1980, MYC (564).

5. Marguerite Yourcenar to Gertrude Fay, November 25, 1979, MS Fr 423 (6), Houghton Library, Harvard University.

6. "Hospes Comesque" also serves as the capstone to Yourcenar's beautiful homage "to G.F." in "Reflections on the Composition of *Memoirs of Hadrian*," which became an integral part of the novel after 1951. See chapter 15.

7. Koelb, *Legendary Figures: Ancient History in Modern Novels*, 121.

8. Yourcenar, entry dated July 25, 1973, in *Sources II*, 274.

9. Marguerite Yourcenar to Brookside Cemetery Society, December 26, 1979, MYC (564).

10. Author's personal journal entry, July 23, 1983. "This is lovely," I added.

11. Emmanuel Boudot-Lamotte to Marguerite Yourcenar, October 4, 1980, MYC (564). Yourcenar spoke of Nel's proximity to her first meeting with Grace in a letter dated October 5, 1945: "Grace is the friend I went to see in America in 1939, and I have lived with her since that time. You may remember that it was after having heard about your thwarted journey to America, aboard the *Normandie*, and our plan to travel to Persia (which events would thwart as well) that Grace decided to speak to me in the little bar of the *Wagram*. So your silhouette is in a sense magically mingled with the beginning of my present life." Yourcenar, *En 1939*, 118.

12. Katherine Gatch to Marguerite Yourcenar, March 7, 1980, MYP (309).

Bibliography

Alesch, Jeanne. *Marguerite Yourcenar: The Other/Reader*. Birmingham, Ala.: Summa, 2007.

Arnold, Matthew. *Poems*. London: Lane, 1900.

Barranger, Milly S. *Margaret Webster: A Life in the Theater*. Ann Arbor: University of Michigan Press, 2004.

Baudelaire, Charles. *The Flowers of Evil*. Translated by William Aggeler. Fresno, Calif.: Academy Library Guild, 1954.

Bekker, Scott. "Pendergast's Ghost: Fifteen Indicted in Two Years in Missouri." *Austin American Statesman*, November 29, 1996, A23.

Blanchet-Douspis, Mireille. *L'Influence de l'histoire contemporaine dans l'œuvre de Marguerite Yourcenar*. Amsterdam: Rodopi, 2008.

Bloom, Harold. *John Donne*. Broomall, Penn.: Chelsea House, 1999.

Bosseaux, Charlotte. *How Does It Feel? Point of View in Translation*. Amsterdam, New York: Rodopi, 2007.

Brissac, Elvire de. *Ballade américaine*. Paris: Stock, 1976.

Cahiers André Gide. Vol. 3, *Le Centenaire*. Paris: Gallimard, 1972.

Caïmi, Giulio. *Karaghiozi, ou la Comédie grecque dans l'âme du théâtre d'ombres*. Athens: Hellinikes Technes, 1935.

Castaneda, Carlos. *The Teachings of Don Juan: A Yaqui Way of Knowledge*. Berkeley: University of California Press, 1968.

Cather, Willa. *La Mort de l'archevêque*. Translated by M. C. Carel. Paris: Delamain et Boutelleau, 1940.

———. *Willa Cather on Writing: Critical Studies on Writing as an Art*. Lincoln: University of Nebraska Press, 1988.

Chalon, Jean. *Journal de Paris, 1963–1983*. Paris: Plon, 2000.

———. *Portrait of a Seductress: The World of Natalie Barney*. Translated by Carol Barko. New York: Crown, 1979.

Chance, Jane, ed. *Women Medievalists and the Academy*. Madison: University of Wisconsin Press, 2005.

Chancel, Jacques. *Marguerite Yourcenar: Radioscopie de Jacques Chancel*. Monaco: Rocher, 1999.

Chapman, Don. *Oxford Playhouse: High and Low Drama in a University City*. Hatfield, England: University of Hertfordshire Press, 2008.

Christensen, Lawrence O., William E. Foley, Gary R. Kremer, and Kenneth H. Winn, eds., *Dictionary of Missouri Biography*. Columbia: University of Missouri Press, 1999.

Chung, Unyoung E. *Grants for Scholarships: A Resource Guide to Scholarship Funds for Education Institutions*. Burlington, Mass.: Jones and Bartlett Learning, 1997.

Davenport, Guy. *The Guy Davenport Reader*. Translated by Guy Davenport. Edited by Erik Reece. Berkeley: Counterpoint, 2013.

DeJean, Joan. *Fictions of Sappho, 1546–1937*. Chicago: University of Chicago Press, 1989.

[Delarue-Mardrus, Lucie.] *Nos Secrètes Amours*. Paris: "Les Isles," 1951.

Delcroix, Maurice, comp. *Portrait d'une voix: Vingt-trois entretiens (1952–1987)*. Paris: Gallimard, 2002.

Deprez, Bérengère. *Marguerite Yourcenar and the USA: From Prophecy to Protest*. Brussels: Lang, 2009.

———. *Marguerite Yourcenar et les États-Unis: Du nageur à la vague*. Brussels: Racine, 2012.

Desfons, Pierre, dir. *Saturday Blues*. Paris: Société française de production, 1984. Documentary film.

Du Bos, Charles. *Approximations*. Sixième série. Paris: Corrêa, 1934.

Dudley, Louise. *The Study of Literature*. Cambridge, Mass.: Riverside, 1928.

Dudley, Louise, and Austin Faricy. *The Humanities: Applied Aesthetics*. New York: McGraw-Hill, 1940.

———. *The Humanities: Applied Aesthetics*. 4th ed. New York: McGraw-Hill, 1967.

Fergusson, Peter, James F. O'Gorman, and John Rhodes. *The Landscape and Architecture of Wellesley College*. Wellesley, Mass.: Wellesley College, 2000.

Flanner, Janet. *Paris Journal*. Vol. 2, *1965–1971*. New York: Atheneum, 1971.

Frederics, Diana. *Diana, a Strange Autobiography*. New York: Citadel, 1939.

Gaddis, Eugene R. *Magician of the Modern: Chick Austin and the Transformation of the Arts in America*. New York: Knopf, 2000.

Gaskell, Elizabeth. *The Life of Charlotte Brontë*. London: John Murray, 1900; rpt., 1926.

Gelderman, Carol. *Mary McCarthy: A Life*. New York: St. Martin's, 1988.

Gibson, Michelle, and Deborah T. Meem, eds. *Lesbian Academic Couples*. New York: Harrington Park, 2005.

Glasscock, Jean, gen. ed. *Wellesley College, 1875–1975: A Century of Women*. Wellesley, Mass.: Wellesley College, 1975.

Goslar, Michèle, ed. *Marguerite Yourcenar: Dix Ans après . . .* Brussels: CIDMY, 1997.

———, ed. *Les Voyages de Marguerite Yourcenar*. Brussels: CIDMY, 1996.

———. *Yourcenar: "Qu'il eût été fade d'être heureux."* Brussels: Racine, 1998. Rev. ed., 2014.

Halley, Achmy. *Marguerite Yourcenar en poésie: Archéologie d'un silence*. Amsterdam: Rodopi, 2005.

Hommage de la France à Thomas Mann à l'occasion de son quatre-vingtième anniversaire. Paris: Flinker, 1955.

Howard, Joan E. *From Violence to Vision: Sacrifice in the Works of Marguerite Yourcenar.* Carbondale, Ill.: Southern Illinois University Press, 1992.

Jaloux, Edmond. *Du rêve à la réalité.* Paris: Corrêa, 1932.

James, Henry. *Ce que savait Maisie.* Translated by Marguerite Yourcenar. Paris: Lafont, 1947.

Jayadeva. *Gita Govinda: Les Amours de Krishna.* Paris: Émile Paul, 1957.

Johnson, Graham, and Richard Stokes. *A French Song Companion.* New York: Oxford University Press, 2000.

Koelb, Clayton. *Legendary Figures: Ancient History in Modern Novels.* Lincoln: University of Nebraska Press, 1998.

Kolokotroni, Vassiliki, and Efterpi Mitsi, eds. *Women Writing Greece: Essays on Hellenism, Orientalism, and Travel.* Amsterdam: Rodopi, 2008.

Lalonde, Robert. *Un Jardin entouré de murailles.* Montreal: Boréal, 2002.

Latimer, Tirza True. *Women Together/Women Apart: Portraits of Lesbian Paris.* New Brunswick, NJ: Rutgers University Press, 2005.

Leopold, Ellen. *A Darker Ribbon: Breast Cancer, Women, and Their Doctors in the Twentieth Century.* Boston: Beacon, 1999.

Lonoff de Cuevas, Sue. *Marguerite Yourcenar: Croquis et griffonnis.* Paris: Gallimard, 2008.

Louÿs, Pierre. *Les Chansons de Bilitis, traduites du Grec pour la première fois.* Paris: Librairie de l'art indépendant, 1895.

Malcolm, Janet. *Two Lives: Gertrude and Alice.* New Haven, Conn.: Yale University Press, 2007.

Mann, Erika. *School for Barbarians.* New York: Modern Age, 1938.

McCarthy, Mary. *The Groves of Academe.* New York: Harcourt, Brace, 1951.

———. *On the Contrary.* New York: Farrar, Straus, and Cudahy, 1961.

McKenna, Neil. *The Secret Life of Oscar Wilde.* London: Century, 2003.

Merton, Thomas. *Seeds of Destruction.* New York: Farrar, Straus and Giroux, 1964.

Palmieri, Patricia Ann. *In Adamless Eden: The Community of Women Faculty at Wellesley.* New Haven, Conn.: Yale University Press, 1995.

Peterson, Virgilia. *A Matter of Life and Death.* New York: Atheneum, 1961.

Rimbaud, Arthur. *Complete Works, Selected Letters: A Bilingual Edition.* Rev. ed. Translated by Wallace Fowlie. Chicago: University of Chicago Press, 2010.

Rodriguez, Suzanne. *Wild Heart: Natalie Clifford Barney's Journey from Victorian America to Belle Époque Paris.* New York: HarperCollins, 2002.

Rosbo, Patrick de. *Entretiens radiophoniques avec Marguerite Yourcenar.* Paris: Mercure de France, 1972.

Rousseau, George. *Yourcenar.* London: Haus, 2004.

Sandomenico, Ciro. *Il "viaggio di nozze" di Marguerite Yourcenar a Capri.* Naples: Liguori, 2001.

Sarde, Michèle. *Vous, Marguerite Yourcenar: La Passion et ses masques.* Paris: Robert Laffont, 1995.

Sarton, May. *I Knew a Phoenix: Sketches for an Autobiography.* New York: Norton, 1959.

Savigneau, Josyane. *Marguerite Yourcenar: Inventing a Life.* Translated by Joan E. Howard. Chicago: University of Chicago Press, 1993.

———. *Marguerite Yourcenar: L'Invention d'une vie.* Paris: Gallimard, 1990.

Seymour, James William Davenport, ed. *History of the American Field Service: "Friends of France," 1914–1917, Told by Its Members.* Boston: Houghton Mifflin, 1920.

Shakespeare, William. *The Tragedy of Hamlet, Prince of Denmark by William Shakespeare.* Edited by George Lyman Kittredge. Boston: Athenaeum, 1939.

Sisson, Richard, Christian K. Zacher, and Andrew Robert Lee Cayton, eds. *The American Midwest: An Interpretive Encyclopedia.* Bloomington: Indiana University Press, 2007.

Smith, John Saumarez, ed. *The Bookshop at 10 Curzon Street: Letters between Nancy Mitford and Heywood Hill, 1952–1973.* London: Lincoln, 2004.

Sontag, Susan. *Illness as Metaphor.* New York: Farrar, Straus and Giroux, 1978.

Souhami, Diana. *Wild Girls: Paris, Sappho, and Art: The Lives and Loves of Natalie Barney and Romaine Brooks.* New York: St. Martin's, 2007.

Stein, Gertrude. *Fernhurst, Q.E.D., and Other Early Writings.* Edited by Leon Katz. New York: Liveright, 1971.

———. *Paris France.* New York: Scribner's, 1940.

———. *Things as They Are.* Pawlet, Vt.: Banyan, 1950.

Stevens, Walter Barlow. *Centennial History of Missouri (The Center State): One Hundred Years in the Union, 1820–1921.* Vol. 4. St. Louis: Clarke, 1921.

Tamagne, Florence. *The History of Homosexuality in Europe: Berlin, London, Paris, 1919–1939.* New York: Algora, 2004.

Thrale, Hester Lynch. *Thraliana: The Diary of Mrs. Hester Lynch Thrale.* Edited by Katharine C. Balderston. 2 vols. Oxford: Clarendon, 1942.

Tóibín, Colm. *New Ways to Kill Your Mother: Writers and Their Families.* New York: Scribner, 2012.

Vickery, Margaret Birney. *Smith College: An Architectural Tour.* New York: Princeton Architectural Press, 2007.

Villon, François. *Poems.* Translated by John Payne. New York: Modern Library, n.d.

Werth, Barry. *The Scarlet Professor: Newton Arvin, a Literary Life Shattered by Scandal.* New York: Anchor, 2002.

Wickes, George. *The Amazon of Letters: The Life and Loves of Natalie Barney.* New York: Putnam, 1976.

Wilson, J. Dover. *The Essential Shakespeare: A Biographical Adventure.* Cambridge: Cambridge University Press, 1932.

Woolf, Virginia. *The Diary of Virginia Woolf.* Vol. 5, *1936–1941.* Edited by Anne Olivier Bell. New York: Harcourt Brace Jovanovich, 1984.

———. *Three Guineas.* New York: Harcourt, 2006.

———. *Les Vagues.* Translated by Marguerite Yourcenar. Paris: Stock, 1937.

Wordsworth, William. *The Prelude, or Growth of a Poet's Mind.* Edited by Helen Darbishire. London: Clarendon, 1928.

———. *Wordsworth's Guide to the Lakes.* 5th ed. Edited by Ernest de Sélincourt. London: Milford, 1835.

Yourcenar, Marguerite. *The Abyss*. Translated by Grace Frick in collaboration with the author. Farrar, Straus and Giroux, 1976.

———. *Anna, soror . . .* Paris: Gallimard, 1981.

———. *Archives du Nord*. Paris: Gallimard, 1977.

———. *Blues et gospels*. Paris: Gallimard, 1984.

———. *Les Charités d'Alcippe*. Liège, Belgium: La Flûte enchantée, 1956.

———. *A Coin in Nine Hands*. Translated by Dori Katz in collaboration with the author. New York: Farrar, Straus and Giroux, 1982.

———. *Correspondance avec Joseph Massabuau*. Brussels: CIDMY, 2011.

———. *Le Coup de grâce*. Paris: Gallimard, 1939.

———. *Coup de Grâce*. Translated by Grace Frick in collaboration with the author. New York: Farrar, Straus and Cudahy, 1957.

———. *The Dark Brain of Piranesi and Other Essays*. Translated by Richard Howard in collaboration with the author. New York: Farrar, Straus and Giroux, 1984.

———. *Dear Departed*. Translated by Maria Louise Ascher. New York: Farrar, Straus and Giroux, 1991.

———. *Denier du rêve*. Paris: Gallimard, 1971.

———. *D'Hadrien à Zénon: Correspondance, 1951–1956*. Text prepared and annotated by Colette Gaudin and Rémy Poignault with the collaboration of Joseph Brami and Maurice Delcroix. Edition coordinated by Élyane Dezon-Jones and Michèle Sarde. Preface by Josyane Savigneau. Paris: Gallimard, 2004.

———. *Dreams and Destinies*. Translated by Donald Flanell. New York: St. Martin's, 1999.

———. *En 1939, l'Amérique commence à Bordeaux*. Edited by Élyane Dezon-Jones and Michèle Sarde. Paris: Gallimard, 2016.

———. *En pèlerin et en étranger*. Paris: Gallimard, 1989.

———. *Essais et mémoires*. Paris: Bibliothèque de la Pléiade, 1991.

———. *Feux*. Paris: Grasset, 1936.

———. *Fires*. Translated by Dori Katz in collaboration with the author. New York: Farrar, Straus and Giroux, 1981.

———. *Fleuve profond, sombre rivière*. Paris: Gallimard, 1964.

———. *How Many Years*. Translated by Maria Ascher. New York: Farrar, Straus and Giroux, 1995.

———. *Lettres à ses amis et quelques autres*. Edited by Michèle Sarde and Joseph Brami with the assistance of Élyane Dezon-Jones. Paris: Gallimard, 1995.

———. *Memoirs of Hadrian*. Translated by Grace Frick in collaboration with the author. New York: Farrar, Straus and Giroux, 1954.

———. *Memoirs of Hadrian and Reflections on the Composition of Memoirs of Hadrian*. Translated by Grace Frick in collaboration with the author. New York: Farrar and Straus, 1963.

———. *La Mort conduit l'attelage*. Paris: Grasset, 1934.

———. *La Nouvelle Eurydice*. Paris: Grasset, 1931.

———. *L'Œuvre au Noir*. Paris: Gallimard, 1968.

———. *Œuvres romanesques*. Paris: Bibliothèque de la Pléiade, 1982.

————. *Oriental Tales*. Translated by Alberto Manguel in collaboration with the author. New York: Farrar, Straus and Giroux, 1983.

————. *Persévérer dans l'être: Correspondance, 1961–1963*. Text prepared and annotated by Joseph Brami and Rémy Poignault with the collaboration of Maurice Delcroix, Colette Gaudin, and Michèle Sarde. Paris: Gallimard, 2011.

————. *Plays*. Translated by Dori Katz in collaboration with the author. New York: Performing Arts Journal, 1984.

————. *Présentation critique de Constantin Cavafy, 1863–1933*. Paris: Gallimard, 1958.

————. *Présentation critique d'Hortense Flexner suivie d'un choix de poèmes*. Paris: Gallimard, 1969.

————. *Quoi? L'Éternité*. Paris: Gallimard, 1988.

————. *Réception de Madame Marguerite Yourcenar à l'Académie royale de langue et de littérature françaises de Belgique*. Paris: Gallimard, 1971.

————. *Les Songes et les sorts*. Paris: Grasset, 1938.

————. *Sources II*. Paris: Gallimard, 1999.

————. *Sous bénéfice d'inventaire*. Paris: Gallimard, 1962.

————. *Souvenirs pieux*. Paris: Gallimard, 1974.

————. *That Mighty Sculptor, Time*. Translated by Walter Kaiser. New York: Farrar, Straus and Giroux, 1992.

————. *Théâtre I* and *II*. Paris: Gallimard, 1971.

————. *Le Tour de la prison*. Paris: Gallimard, 1991.

————. *Two Lives and a Dream*. Translated by Walter Kaiser in collaboration with the author. New York: Farrar, Straus and Giroux, 1987.

————. *Une Volonté sans fléchissement: Correspondance, 1957–1960*. Text prepared and annotated by Joseph Brami and Maurice Delcroix. Edition coordinated by Colette Gaudin and Rémy Poignault with the collaboration of Michèle Sarde. Paris: Gallimard, 2007.

————. *With Open Eyes: Conversations with Matthieu Galey*. Translated by Arthur Goldhammer. Boston: Beacon, 1980.

Index

About the Author

 JOAN E. HOWARD is the director of Petite Plaisance, the former home of Marguerite Yourcenar and Grace Frick, and is the author of *From Violence to Vision: Sacrifice in the Works of Marguerite Yourcenar*. She divides her time between Augusta and Northeast Harbor, Maine.